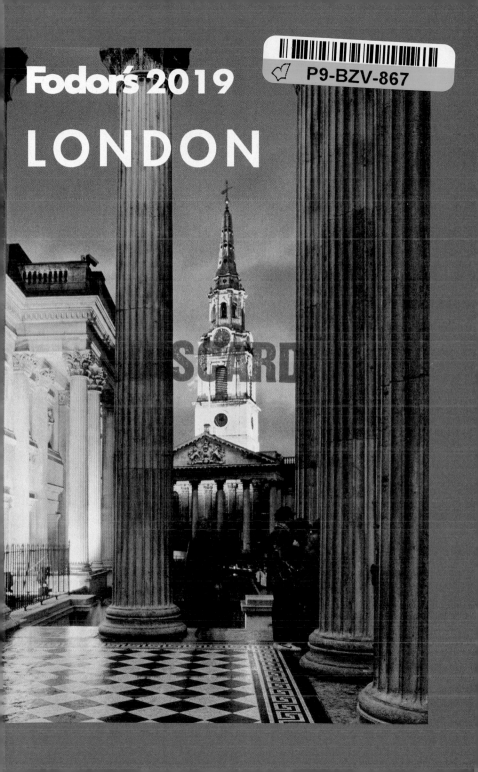

Fodor's 2019
LONDON

WELCOME TO LONDON

History and tradition greet you at every turn in London; it's also one of the coolest, most modern cities in the world. If London contained only landmarks such as Westminster Abbey and Buckingham Palace, it would still rank as one of the world's great destinations, but Britain's capital is much more. People come to glimpse the royals and stop by hot galleries; to take in theater and trendy shops; to sample tea and scones or cutting-edge cuisine. When you need a break from the action, pop into a pub, relax in a park—or take a walk and make London your own.

TOP REASONS TO GO

★ **Architectural Icons:** The Tower of London and Big Ben are quintessential London.

★ **Art Museums:** From the National Gallery to the Tate Modern, a visual feast awaits.

★ **Top Theater:** Whether it's Shakespeare or avant-garde drama, the play's the thing.

★ **City of Villages:** Unique neighborhoods from Mayfair to the East End invite discovery.

★ **Shopping:** Fun markets, famous flagship department stores, chic boutiques.

★ **Parks and Squares:** Distinctive green spaces large and small are civilized retreats.

20 ULTIMATE EXPERIENCES

London offers terrific experiences that should be on every traveler's list. Here are Fodor's top picks for a memorable trip.

1 Big Ben and Houses of Parliament

Officially known as the Palace of Westminster, the neo-Gothic Houses of Parliament contains the Houses of Commons and Lords (the legislative bodies of the United Kingdom's government) and the giant clock tower known as Big Ben (one of London's most beloved icons). *(Ch. 2)*

2 Drinking in Historic Pubs

The history of London's taverns and pubs is the history of the city itself. Grab a pint or a gin cocktail, and get to know how the locals live. *(Ch. 16)*

3 British Museum

It would take a lifetime to do justice to the extraordinary collection (spanning 8 million artifacts from over 2 million years) here at Britain's most visited tourist attraction. *(Ch. 5)*

4 Hampton Court Palace

One of Britain's grandest royal palaces, Hampton Court contains some of the finest Tudor architecture in the world and is imbued with an overwhelming sense of history. *(Ch. 13)*

5 Gallery Hopping in East London

With one of the highest concentrations of artists in Europe, East London is fertile ground for some serious contemporary art gallery hopping, from Whitechapel to Hackney. *(Ch. 7)*

6 Hyde Park & Kensington Gardens

London is famous for its awesome Royal Parks, and the contiguous Hyde Park and Kensington Gardens are perfect for escaping the hustle and bustle of the city. *(Ch. 10)*

7 The Markets

From gourmet food to antiques, you can find nearly everything at London's most famous street markets, Portobello Market in Notting Hill and Borough Market on Southbank. *(Ch. 18)*

8 London Eye

For an unrivalled bird's-eye view of the metropolis and beyond, take a ride on one of the world's tallest observation wheels. *(Ch. 8)*

9 Afternoon Tea

For a quintessential English ritual, enjoy a pot of tea served in bone china alongside finger sandwiches, fruit scones, and cakes at one of the city's fanciest hotels. *(Ch. 1)*

10 Shakespear's Globe

A replica of the original Globe Theatre just yards from where Shakespeare's Elizabethan playhouse stood, the modern-day Globe still hosts open-air performances of the Bard's plays. *(Ch. 8)*

11 Indian food in Brick Lane

Thanks to successive waves of immigrants, Whitechapel's Brick Lane is famous for London's highest concentration of curry houses and some of the best Indian food outside India. *(Ch. 14)*

12 Victoria and Albert Museum

With a vast collection of 2.3 million objects, the V&A is one of the world's greatest museums of decorative arts and design. *(Ch. 9)*

13 Tate Modern

A must-visit for global art lovers, the Tate Modern wows with its extensive collection of constantly rotating modern art. *(Ch. 8)*

14 St. Paul's Cathedral

With the second largest cathedral dome in the world, St. Paul's is a towering masterpiece of English Baroque design, both inside and out. *(Ch. 6)*

15 Covent Garden

Covent Garden is considered the very heart of London, thanks to its markets, pubs, restaurants, museums, theaters, open-air cafés , boutique shops, street entertainers, and more. *(Ch. 4)*

16 Buckingham Palace

The official residence of the British monarch is opulently filled with priceless tapestries, artwork, and marble and gilt galore. *(Ch. 2)*

17 Theater in the West End

Thanks to some of the world's best actors and directors (and the most historic theaters), London's contributions to the theater world give Broadway a run for its money. *(Ch. 17)*

18 National Gallery

With more than 2,300 of the world's masterpieces, this museum is considered Britain's greatest art collection. *(Ch. 2)*

19 Tower of London

With a gory 950-year history of beheadings, imprisonments, and torture, myths and legends shroud England's most perfect medieval fortress and home of the Crown Jewels. *(Ch. 6)*

20 Westminster Abbey

The site of all but two royal coronations since 1066, the Abbey is steeped in English history— from tombs of monarchs to monuments for great nobles, statesmen, and poets. *(Ch. 2)*

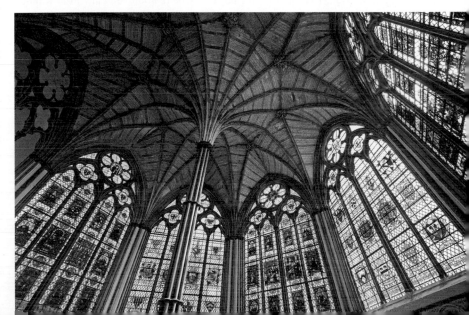

Fodor's LONDON 2019

Editorial: Douglas Stallings, *Editorial Director*; Margaret Kelly, Jacinta O'Halloran, *Senior Editors*; Kayla Becker, Alexis Kelly, Amanda Sadlowski, *Editors*; Teddy Minford, *Content Editor*; Rachael Roth, *Content Manager*

Design: Tina Malaney, *Design and Production Director*; Jessica Gonzalez, *Production Designer*

Photography: Jill Krueger, *Senior Photo Editor*

Maps: Rebecca Baer, *Senior Map Editor*; Mark Stroud (Moon Street Cartography) and David Lindroth, *Cartographers*

Production: Jennifer DePrima, *Editorial Production Manager*; Carrie Parker, *Senior Production Editor*; Elyse Rozelle, *Production Editor*

Business & Operations: Chuck Hoover, *Chief Marketing Officer*; Joy Lai, *Vice President and General Manager*; Stephen Horowitz, *Director of Business Development and Revenue Operations*; Tara McCrillis, *Director of Publishing Operations*

Public Relations and Marketing: Joe Ewaskiw, *Manager*; Esther Su, *Marketing Manager*

Writers: Jo Caird, Jack Jewers, James O'Neill, Toby Orton, Ellin Stein, Alex Wijeratna

Editors: Amanda Sadlowski (lead editor), Debbie Harmsen

Production Editor: Jennifer DePrima

ISBN 978-1-64097-114-1

ISSN 0149-631X

Library of Congress Control Number 2018954451

All details in this book are based on information supplied to us at press time. Always confirm information when it matters, especially if you're making a detour to visit a specific place. Fodor's expressly disclaims any liability, loss, or risk, personal or otherwise, that is incurred as a consequence of the use of any of the contents of this book.

SPECIAL SALES

This book is available at special discounts for bulk purchases for sales promotions or premiums. For more information, e-mail SpecialMarkets@fodors.com.

PRINTED IN THE UNITED STATES OF AMERICA

10 9 8 7 6 5 4 3 2 1

CONTENTS

Fodor's Features

CONTENTS

MAPS

ABOUT THIS GUIDE

Fodor's Ratings

Everything in this guide is worth doing—we don't cover what isn't—but exceptional sights, hotels, and restaurants are recognized with additional accolades. Fodor's Choice★ indicates our top recommendations. Care to nominate a new place? Visit Fodors.com/contact-us.

Trip Costs

We list prices wherever possible to help you budget well. Hotel and restaurant price categories from $ to $$$$ are noted alongside each recommendation. For hotels, we include the lowest cost of a standard double room in high season. For restaurants, we cite the average price of a main course at dinner or, if dinner isn't served, at lunch. For attractions, we always list adult admission fees; discounts are usually available for children, students, and senior citizens.

Hotels

Our local writers vet every hotel to recommend the best overnights in each price category, from budget to expensive. Unless otherwise specified, you can expect private bath, phone, and TV in your room. For expanded hotel reviews, visit Fodors.com.

Top Picks	Hotels &
★ Fodor's Choice	Restaurants
	⊡ Hotel
Listings	↩ Number of
⊠ Address	rooms
⊠ Branch address	�"⊙�" Meal plans
☎ Telephone	✗ Restaurant
🖷 Fax	⟅ Reservations
⊕ Website	🏛 Dress code
✉ E-mail	▭ No credit cards
💳 Admission fee	Ⓢ Price
⊙ Open/closed	
times	**Other**
Ⓜ Subway	⇨ See also
♣ Directions or	↻ Take note
Map coordinates	⅄ Golf facilities

Restaurants

Unless we state otherwise, restaurants are open for lunch and dinner daily. We mention dress code only when there's a specific requirement and reservations only when they're essential or not accepted.

Credit Cards

The hotels and restaurants in this guide typically accept credit cards. If not, we'll say so.

EUGENE FODOR

Hungarian-born Eugene Fodor (1905–91) began his travel career as an interpreter on a French cruise ship. The experience inspired him to write *On the Continent* (1936), the first guidebook to receive annual updates and discuss a country's way of life as well as its sights. Fodor later joined the U.S. Army and worked for the OSS in World War II. After the war, he kept up his intelligence work while expanding his guidebook series. During the Cold War, many guides were written by fellow agents who understood the value of insider information. Today's guides continue Fodor's legacy by providing travelers with timely coverage, insider tips, and cultural context.

EXPERIENCE LONDON

LONDON TODAY

Welcome to London—variously described by great poets and statesmen as "modern Babylon," "Unreal City," "enormous Babel," and "..the City of the free." Indeed, majestic London has always been a great city in flux, and these days it's hard to turn a corner without stumbling into some work-in-progress crater so vast you can only imagine what was there before. New neighborhoods continually bubble up and burst to the fore—for example, a visit to Shoreditch at the eastern edge of The City should provide you with your quotient of London hipness. The anything-goes creative fervor that swirls through London like a fog shows up in DIY art galleries, cutting-edge boutiques, pop-up restaurants, nighttime street-food markets, and slick hipster hotels.

Discovery can take a bit of work, however. Modern London still largely reflects its medieval layout, a difficult tangle of streets and alleys. Even Londoners get lost in their own city. But London's bewildering street pattern will be a plus for the visitor who wants to experience its indefinable historic atmosphere. London is a walker's city and will repay every moment you spend exploring on foot.

Although many images are seared on your consciousness before you arrive—the guards at Buckingham Palace, the big red double-decker buses, Big Ben, and the River Thames—time never stands still in this ancient and yet gloriously modern city. Instead, "London, the buskin'd stage. ... The heart, the centre of the living world!" is in permanent revolution, and evolves, organically, mysteriously, historically through time.

Architecture

With the exceptions of Canary Wharf, the former Swiss Re HQ ("the Gherkin"), the Lloyd's of London building, and the London Eye, London's skyline has traditionally been low-key, with little of the sky-scraping swagger of, say, Manhattan, Hong Kong, or Shanghai. But a spectacular crop of soaring new office towers with wonderful monikers—the Quill, the Shard, the Pinnacle, the Cheese Grater, and the Walkie-Talkie—is taking over the city skyline. With an astonishing 250-odd new skyscrapers being planned or built, opinions are split. Not everyone loves Renzo Piano's spire-like Shard and its 95-floor cloud-piercing "Vertical City" at London Bridge, which has stunning viewing galleries on the 68th, 69th, and 72nd floors. However, once you whiz up and enjoy the 40-mile views, your take on the vast immensity of London is transformed forever.

Immigration

There's no doubt that London was built on immigration and is now one of the most diverse cities on Earth, with 300 languages spoken on the streets and nearly every world religion practiced at its places of worship. Immigrants make up over a third of the population and "white Britons" are in the minority for the first time, representing 45% of London's population of 8.2 million. The largest first-generation immigrant communities are from India, Poland, Ireland, Nigeria, Pakistan, Bangladesh, and Jamaica. To Londoners, this is no big deal, as this has always been a city of immigrants—from invaders like the Romans, Anglo-Saxons, Vikings, and Normans to those seeking sanctuary like the French Huguenots and east European Jews, along with those seeking their postwar fortunes from Caribbean islands, the Indian subcontinent, and the rest of the British Commonwealth. Despite the populist tendencies sprouting up in other parts of the United Kingdom and Europe, London remains proud of its immigrant heritage, and welcoming to any who wish to call themselves a Londoner.

Arts and Culture

Have you scanned a free copy of the daily London *Evening Standard* newspaper lately? They're full of world-class shows, plays, jazz performances, readings, recitals, concerts, fashion follies, lectures, talks, tastings, cabarets, burlesque, and art auctions and exhibitions. Whether it's modern art and rare Old Masters paintings at Frieze London art fair in Regents Park or a Dinerama nighttime vinyl-and-food-truck feast in Hoxton, London is one of the most happening places on the planet.

Public Transportation

Despite being horribly expensive, you'll notice that the public transport in London is generally nicer and more reliable than mass transit in other major cities. The £15 billion high-speed Crossrail undergound railway—known as the Elizabeth Line, after Queen Elizabeth II—is an epic feat of engineering that has shortened the journey time for east–west trips. With 10 new stations and quick trips linking Paddington Station with Heathrow Airport and Canary Wharf in the east, even the notorious over-congestion seems to have been solved. In addition, the Night Tube now runs 24 hours a day on weekends on six key Underground lines. Don't miss London's popular bike-sharing program, Santander Cycles, which has over 11,000 bikes at some 700-odd central London docking stations, with unlimited short rides costing just £2 over a 24-hour period.

Politics

With its heady mix of modernity, migrants, and money, London is historically a pretty liberal city. It elected its first Muslim mayor in 2016, Sadiq Khan, a former London MP, human rights lawyer, and son of a London bus driver, but the city keeps adjusting to the fallout from the 2016 Brexit vote. The majority of Londoners voted to remain in the European Union, and many of the city's E.U.-origin residents, students, and workers are nervous about what leaving the E.U. means for them and their legal rights to live, work, and study in the United Kingdom. But whatever the final agreed terms of Brexit are (discussions are still in progress), London carries on as ever—vibrant, vital, diverse, and open for business.

New Upgrades and Exhibits

Some of London's top cultural attractions seem to be caught in an arts upgrade arms race and are investing heavily in new galleries, exhibits, extensions, and assorted shiny new bells and whistles. Look for the major £56 million revamp of the eminent Royal Academy of Arts in Piccadilly, which includes extended public galleries and a slick new bridge, or enjoy the recently sprung-to-life Granary Square at King's Cross, where 1,080 choreographed water jets are the buzzy area's answer to an Italian piazza. Tate Modern has added a £50 million modern brick extension, but look for the city's quirkier historic openings such as the 670-year-old Charterhouse in Smithfield, which you can now tour with residents of this Wolf Hall–like former Carthusian monastery, mansion, boys' school, and latter-day almshouse.

WHAT'S WHERE

1 Westminster and St. James's. This is the place to embrace your inner tourist. Snap pictures of the mounted Horse Guards, watch kids clambering onto the monumental bronze lions in Trafalgar Square, and visit stacks of world-class art in the fantastic national galleries. Brave the crowds to peruse historic Westminster Abbey and its ancient narrative in stone.

2 Mayfair and Marylebone. You may not have the wallet for London's most prestigious shops, but remember window-shopping in historic Mayfair is free. Meanwhile, chic boutiques in Marylebone are a refreshing change from gaudy Oxford Street a few blocks south.

3 Soho and Covent Garden. More sophisticated than seedy these days, the heart of London puts Theatreland, strip joints, Chinatown, burger boîtes, and the trendiest of film studios side by side. Hold tight through the hectic hordes in Leicester Square. Covent Garden's historic paved piazza is one of the most raffishly enjoyable parts of the city.

4 Bloomsbury and Holborn. Once the bluestocking and intellectual center of London, elegant 17th- and 18th-century Bloomsbury is now also a mixed business district. The British Museum has enough amazing objets d'art and artifacts to keep you busy for a month; the Law Courts, University of London, and quaint Lamb's Conduit Street are worth a gander. Clerkenwell, meanwhile, is a hotbed of history and culinary reinvention.

5 The City. London's Wall Street might be the oldest part of the capital, but thanks to new skyscrapers and a sleek Millennium Bridge, it also looks like the newest. History fans won't be short-changed, however: head for St. Paul's Cathedral, Tower Bridge, and the Tower of London.

6 East London. Once famed for the noxious 19th-century slums immortalized by Charles Dickens and Jack the Ripper, today the area is a fulcrum of London's contemporary art scene and a hip party zone. For spit-and-sawdust sensations of market London on the weekend, dive headfirst into the eclectic wares at Spitalfields, Brick Lane (popular for Bangladeshi curry houses and 24-hour Jewish bagel bakeries), and Columbia Road's much-loved early-morning flower market.

1

WHAT'S WHERE

7 South of the Thames. The Southbank Centre—including the National Theatre and Royal Festival Hall, the Haywood Gallery, Purcell Room, and Queen Elizabeth Hall, plus nearby Shakespeare's Globe and Tate Modern—showcases the capital's crowning artistic glories. Or put it all in aerial perspective from the 72nd floor of the Shard.

8 Kensington, Chelsea, Knightsbridge, and Belgravia. Although the many boutiques of King's Road have lost much of their heady '60s swagger, the free museums are as awe-inspiring as ever. Kensington High Street is slightly more affordable than King's Road; otherwise, flash your cash at London's snazziest department stores, Harrods and Harvey Nichols.

9 Notting Hill and Bayswater. North of Kensington, around Portobello Road, Notting Hill Gate is a trendsetting couple of square miles of multiethnic finds, photographers' galleries, indie bookshops, fashionable boutiques, and hip restaurants. Nearby, Bayswater mixes eclectic ethnic fashions, organic fresh food shops, and gaudy Middle Eastern and Chinese restaurants.

10 Regent's Park and Hampstead. Surrounded by elegant, stucco-fronted "terraces"—in truth, mansions as big as palaces—designed by 19th-century architect John Nash, Regent's Park is a Regency extravaganza. The nearby ancient hilltop villages of Hampstead and Primrose Hill attract starry residents like Kate Moss and Jude Law.

11 Greenwich. The Royal Observatory, Sir Christopher Wren's architecture, the Old Royal Naval College, British clipper ship *Cutty Sark,* and the Prime Meridian all add up to one of the best Thames-side excursions beyond the cut-and-thrust of central London.

12 The Thames Upstream. As an idyllic retreat from the city, stroll around London's historic gardens and enjoy the stately homes of Kew, Richmond, and Putney. Better yet, take a gentle river cruise and end up at the famous Hampton Court Palace.

LONDON PLANNER

When to Go

The heaviest tourist season runs April through September, with another peak around Christmas. Late spring is the time to see the Royal Parks and gardens at their freshest; fall brings autumnal beauty and fewer people. Summer gives the best chance of good weather, although the crowds are intense. Winter can be dismal—it's dark by 5—but all the theaters, concerts, and exhibitions go full speed ahead, and Christmas lights bring a major touch of festive magic. Weather-wise, winter is cold and wet with occasional light snow and spring is colorful and fair. June through August can range from a total washout to a long hot summer and anything in between. Autumn ranges from warm to cool to mild. It's impossible to forecast London weather, but you can be certain that it will not be what you expect.

When Not to Go

The October "half-term," when schools in the capital take a break for a week or two, results in most attractions being overrun by children. The start of August can be a very busy time, and hot weather makes Tube travel a sweltering and sweaty nightmare. Air-conditioning is far from the norm in London, even in hotels; although it rarely tops 90°F, it can feel much hotter. And festive shopping in central London just before Christmas borders on the insane.

Getting Around

London is, above all, a walker's city, and will repay every moment you spend exploring on foot. But if you're in a rush, there are other options. By far the easiest and most practical way to get around is on the Underground, known as the Tube. Trains run daily from early morning to past midnight during the week, with five key lines now operating 24 hours a day on weekends. Frequent cash-free, double-decker buses crisscross London and often have their own lanes, which only buses and black taxis can use. They are a great way to see London, but navigation can be more complicated than the Tube's; scan the route posted at the bus stop and check the number and destination on the front of the bus, and ask the bus conductor if in doubt.

Put a deposit on an Oyster card for £5, which will allow you to use London's transport—including bus, Tube, tram, Dockland Light Railway (DLR), London Overground, and most National Rail services in London—at a lower cost than using paper tickets. The plastic card can be topped up as often as you want, and your £5 deposit is reimbursed when you hand the card back.

Alternatively, buy a Travelcard pass (from £13 per day in the central Zones 1 and 2), which offers unlimited use of the Tube, buses, and the commuter rail. Check ⊕ *www.tfl.gov.uk* for details on ongoing Tube renovations and schedules.

Addresses

Central London and its surrounding districts are divided into 32 boroughs (33, counting The City of London). More useful for navigating, however, are the subdivisions of London into postal districts. Throughout the guide we've given the abbreviated postal code for most listings. The first one or two letters give the location: N means north, NW means northwest, and so on. Don't expect the numbering to be logical, however. (You won't, for example, find W2 next to W3.) The general rule is that the lower numbers, such as W1 or SW1, are closest to the city center.

London Hours

The usual shop hours are Monday to Saturday 9–6 and Sunday 11–5. Around Oxford Street, Kensington High Street, and Knightsbridge, hours are 9:30–6, with late-night hours (until 7:30 or 8) on Wednesday or Thursday.

Many businesses are closed on Sunday and national ("bank") holidays, except in the center, where most are open 10–4. Banks are open weekdays 9:30–4:30; offices are generally open 9–6.

The major national museums and galleries are open daily, mainly 10–6, and often they're open late one night a week.

Street Smarts

On long-term high alert against terrorist attacks, London is generally a safe and surprisingly friendly place, but like any large city it's wise to take a few precautions. Make sure your possessions are properly insured before you travel, and don't carry all your valuables around with you. Carry as much cash as you'll need that day, and leave the rest in your hotel safe. Don't use ATMs after dark, avoid isolated or poorly lighted spots, and try not to travel around on your own late at night. Keep bags zipped up and close to you in the Tube, on buses, and at pubs and other crowded places. Never leave bags unattended in any public place—they may be stolen or seen as a security threat. Finally, use black cabs and don't get into a minicab on your own.

Saving Money

There's no getting around it: London can be as expensive as—or even more expensive than—New York, Paris, or any other large global city. So it's best to accept this fact in advance and factor it into your vacation planning, tailoring outings and trips to your interests—and your budget.

Often, booking in advance, harnessing cut-price and low-season deals, and taking advantage of Internet specials for flights and hotel rooms can cut down on costs. London is also great at offering things for free (particularly the museums), and the quality of the culture, entertainment, relaxation, and general fun to be had in the city means that if you target your spending wisely, you'll go home penny-pinched but deeply satisfied.

WHAT IT COSTS		
	IN LONDON	IN NEW YORK
Pair of theater tickets	£40–£130	$75–$260
Museum admission	Usually free; sometimes £5–£17	Usually $8–$38; rarely free
Fast-food value meal	£11	$12
Tall latte	£5	$5
Pint of beer in a pub	£5 and up	$7 and up
1-mile taxi ride before tip	£10	$9
Subway ride within city center	Up to £9 without Oyster or Travelcard	$3

UNDER-THE-RADAR THINGS TO DO IN LONDON

Buckingham Palace, Big Ben, and the British Museum are famous for good reason, and of course, they should be on any London visitor's bucket list. But once you've checked off the major sights, it's time to try the more unusual, unique, and extraordinary activities that London has to offer.

Bermondsey Beer Mile

London is well known for its drinking culture, and the Bermondsey Beer Mile makes for an intense lesson in some of London's best craft beer. Nine independent craft breweries and bottle shops are housed in the old brick railway arches of Bermondsey, and their close proximity and the decision to synchronize opening times on Saturdays has led to the birth of the Bermondsey Beer Mile. Start at Fourpure Brewery in South Bermondsey with a half-pint of their thirst-quenching Juice Box before following the winding route towards Southwark Brewing Company, where it halts just short of Tower Bridge Road.

All nine stops on the microbrewery mile might leave you asleep in your hotel room by 6 pm, so hit the highlights of Fourpure, Partizan Brewing, Brew by Numbers, and buy a keepsake from the legendary Kernel Brewery's now take-away-only bottle shop.

Maltby Street Market

While Borough Market is the most famous food market in the city and Broadway Market in Hackney is undoubtedly the hippest, Maltby Street Market might just be London's most underappreciated weekend stop for exotic cuisine. Perhaps due to its compact size—a long narrow stretch of Bermondsey sidewalk sandwiched between railway arches—Maltby even flies under the radar of some Londoners. Luckily this means fewer lines for the assorted stalls and shops that contribute to the weekly Saturday and Sunday events. From gourmet grilled cheese toasties to authentic jerk chicken, there's enough variety to excite even the most jaded gourmand. Other highlights include the incredible doughnuts of St. John (fresh from the bakery on the edge of the market), a classic salt beef sandwich from Monty's Deli, and a *pav bhaji* from Devi's.

Highgate Cemetery

For a unique way to enjoy some peace and quiet within the metropolis, check out London's Victorian cemeteries. Known informally as the "Magnificent Seven," the city's seven 19th-century cemeteries were part of a societal trend of visiting cemeteries for peace and relaxation rather than as a duty to pay respects to departed loved ones. Highgate Cemetery is the most famous of the Magnificent Seven and modern Londoners have carried on the traditions of the Victorians, exploring its flora and fauna and finding an appealingly atmospheric—not to mention beautiful—place to wander. Admission to the East Cemetery, where graves of Karl Marx, Malcolm McClaren, and George Eliot can be found, costs £4, while the catacombs, monuments, and mausoleums of the West Cemetery are accessible by guided tour only (£12 for adults).

Regents Canal

London's canal network might not be quite as famous or as sprawling as some of its European counterparts, but what it lacks in notoriety and size, it makes up for in hipness. Dotted with stylish cafés, pubs, breweries, and one whimsical floating bookshop (Words on the Water), the length of the Regents Canal between Angel and Hackney Wick is an ideal way to explore the East End. For the full tour, start in Angel and make the roughly two-and-a-half hour walk to Hackney Wick where the pizza and microbrewed beer of the Crate Brewery provide a nice reward for all that walking.

Barbican Centre

Long before the Brutalist revival, the Barbican Centre was voted London's ugliest building, underappreciated thanks to its divisive blocky and gray façade, which many see as too foreboding a structure. Having recently enjoyed something of a renaissance, it's now acceptable to enjoy the bold, rigid lines of this Brutalist masterpiece, which houses Europe's largest performing arts center. With a cinema, theater, library, and exhibition spaces, the Barbican Centre is a haven of creativity and artistic expression where visitors can find anything from classical concerts and avant-garde pop performances to cult movies and the Royal Shakespeare Company.

Victoria & Albert Museum After-Hours

London's museum of decorative arts and design is the largest of its kind, with a collection that features an eclectic permanent collection to support its annual blockbuster exhibitions. Think Balenciaga's ball gowns, 16th-century marble sculptures, John Constable paintings, and a Buddha stone head that dates back to the 4th century. The V&A Museum was also one of the first museums in London to host regular after-hours events. The Friday Late series runs on the last Friday of every month, when DJs, pop-up cocktail bars, artists, and designers help create one of the best free nights out in town.

Cabaret at Wilton's Music Hall

Once one of London's best kept secrets, Wilton's Music Hall is fresh from a four-year renovation that has brought the evocative building back to its former glory. Built in 1859, a visit to Wilton's rewards on two fronts. First, there's the beautiful architecture of the vaulted ceilings, rustic brickwork, and original timber beams. But then there's also the entertainment; alongside theater, classical music performances, and piano concertos, there's the timeless fun of cabaret. Extravagant characters, Cockney sing-alongs, and comedy bring back the Blitz spirit and represent the bawdy music hall performances of old.

Sir John Soane's Museum

Ever wonder what kind of house your favorite 19th-century London architect might have lived in? Luckily for you, the former residence of the famous neoclassical architect Sir John Soane has been perfectly preserved in the state it was left at the time of his death in 1837. Reflecting his refined tastes, the John Soane's Museum is filled with furniture, architectural models, curiosities, antiquities, and paintings by artists including Hogarth, Turner, and Canaletto. Free to visitors at all times, nostalgic candlelight tours are held on the first Tuesday of every month between 6 pm and 9 pm, with the first 200 visitors granted access on a first-come, first-served basis. Closed to the public for 160 years and renovated in 2015, it is now possible to enjoy tours of Soane's private apartments on the second floor of the museum.

LONDON'S ROYAL LEGACY

The Rocky Monarchy

From medieval castles and keeps, to Royal Parks, palaces, pageants, ceremonies and processions, London has had a tumultuous and sometimes bloody royal history, which can still be encountered at practically every turn. London has been the royal capital of England since 1066, when the Norman king William the Conqueror began the tradition of royal coronations at Westminster Abbey. All but two reigning monarchs since then—from Richard I (the "Coeur de Lion") in 1189 to the current Queen Elizabeth II in 1953—have been crowned at the Abbey. Many of England's illustrious—and sometimes downright notorious—kings and queens have left a legacy or their majestic mark on the city. You'll find many of the finest places have royal associations: William I subjugated London with the imposing Tower of London; Henry VIII hunted deer at Hampton Court; Elizabeth I enjoyed bear baiting in Southwark; and Charles I was publicly executed on Whitehall. Tyrannical but weak monarchs like King John (1199–1216) granted the City of London extra power under the Magna Carta, while the first "Parliament" sat at the royal Palace of Westminster in 1265 under Henry III. The late medieval Tudors, however, rarely brooked dissent: Elizabeth I's half-sister, "Bloody" Mary I (1553–58), burned heretic Protestant bishops at the stake, and traitors were hung, drawn, and quartered, with their heads stuck on pikes on London Bridge.

A Cultural Renaissance

From 1558 to 1601, peace under Elizabeth I ("the Virgin Queen") led to a cultural renaissance and the great flowering of English theater, poetry, letters, music, and drama, centered on Shakespeare's Globe and the open-air playhouses of Southwark. Charles I was later captured by the formidable Puritan Oliver Cromwell during the English Civil War, and beheaded on a freezing day outside Banqueting House in Westminster in 1649. Although the Interregnum lasted only 16 years (outlawing simple pleasures, such as dancing and theater), the Restoration of Charles II in 1660 and subsequent monarchs saw London grow and transform into a teeming metropolis. These monarchs included the Dutch Protestant William III and Mary II—who moved into Kensington Palace, now the current home of the Duke and Duchess of Cambridge—and the House of Hanover's four Georgian kings and later Queen Victoria.

The Modern Royals

These days you might spot the Duke and Duchess of Sussex (Prince Harry and Meghan Markle) walking in Kensington Gardens, or the Duke and Duchess of Cambridge (Prince William and Kate Middleton) walking with their three young children. Besides the color, pageantry, and marching bands of the Changing of the Guard ceremony at Buckingham Palace, there's also a rich calendar of royal ceremonies. The Ceremony of the Keys to lock up the Tower of London has taken place at 9:53 pm each night for more than 700 years (bar the odd bombing during the Blitz), and you can see the Monarch take the Royal Salute from the Household Division at the annual Trooping the Colour march from Horse Guards Parade to St. James's Park. The Queen is also drawn by four horses in the dazzling Irish State Coach from Buckingham Palace to the Palace of Westminster in a huge royal procession for the State Opening of Parliament each autumn, and you can see her pay homage to the war dead at the Cenotaph on Remembrance Sunday.

SPORTS IN LONDON

Sports in the capital are probably best watched rather than participated in. If you're lucky enough to score a ticket for a Premier League football match, you'll experience a seething mass of jeering, mockery, and tribal chanting. Rugby, tennis, horse-racing, and cricket also impinge on Londoners' horizons at crucial times of the year, but you're unlikely to see grown men crying at the outcome of the Wimbledon Men's Final.

Cricket

At its best, cricket can be a slow build of smoldering tension and unexpected high-wire excitement. At its worst, it can be too slow and uneventful for the casual observer, as five-day games crawl toward a draw or as rain stops play. But try to visit Lord's—known as the home of cricket—on match days, just to hear the *thwack* of leather on willow and to see the English aristocracy and upper middle classes on full display.

Lord's. Lord's Cricket Ground, home of the venerable 1787 Marylebone Cricket Club (MCC), has been hallowed cricketing turf since 1814, and MCC rules codified the game. Tickets for major Test matches are hard to come by: obtain an application form online and enter the ballot (lottery) to purchase them. ⊠ *Marylebone Cricket Club, Lord's Cricket Ground, St. John's Wood Rd., St. John's Wood* ☎ *020/7432–1000* ⊕ *www.lords.org* Ⓜ *St. John's Wood.*

Football

London's top soccer teams—Chelsea, Tottenham Hotspur, Arsenal, and West Ham—are top-class outfits and the first three often progress in the Europe-wide Champions League. It's unlikely you'll get tickets for anything except the least popular Premier League games during the August–May season, despite the high ticket prices—£30 for a walk-up match-day seat at Chelsea, and £91 for the most expensive tickets at Arsenal.

Rowing

The Boat Race. Join more than a quarter of a million merry devotees along the banks of the River Thames between Putney and Mortlake for a glimpse of the annual Oxford and Cambridge University Boat Race, held on the last Saturday of March or the first Saturday of April. Sink a few pints and soak up the tweed-cap-and-Barbour clad atmosphere as these heavyweight eight-man university crews clash oars and tussle head-to-head for supremacy. First raced in 1829, the 4-mile route is a picturesque stretch between Putney and Chiswick bridges. The equally exciting women's eight Boat Race is also held the same day. ⊠ *Putney Bridge, Putney* ⊕ *www.theboatraces.org.*

Tennis

Wimbledon Lawn Tennis Championships. The All England Club's Wimbledon Lawn Tennis Championships are famous for Centre Court, strawberries and cream, a gentle spot of rain, and a nostalgic old-school insistence on players wearing white. Thankfully, the rain has been banished on Centre Court by the nifty retractable roof, but whether you can get tickets for Centre Court all comes down to the luck of the draw—there's a ballot system for advance purchase (see website for more details). ⊠ *The All England Lawn Tennis Club, Church Rd.* ☎ *020/8971–2473 for general inquiries* ⊕ *www.wimbledon.com.*

FREE AND CHEAP

The exchange rate may vary, but there is one conversion that will never change: £0 = $0. Here are our picks for the top free (and cheap) things to do in London.

Concerts

St. Martin-in-the-Fields, St. Stephen Walbrook, St. Olaves in The City, and St. James's Church Piccadilly all host free lunchtime concerts and recitals, as does St. George in Bloomsbury on Sunday afternoons. There are also regular organ recitals at Westminster Abbey.

Of the elite music colleges, the Royal Academy of Music, the Royal College of Music, the Guildhall, Trinity College, and the Royal Opera House offer free recitals. For contemporary ears, there's free jazz and classical music on an exquisite 1897 Bechstein on the first Sunday of the month at the Dysart Petersham restaurant (☎ 07967/481–625) in Richmond and live jazz at the Lamb & Flag (✉ 33 Rose St. ☎ 0207/497–9504) in Covent Garden, from 8 pm one Sunday a month. For free blues Sunday–Thursday or before 8:30 pm on Friday and Saturday, head to the Ain't Nothin But … honky-tonk blues bar in Soho (✉ 20 Kingly St. ☎ 020/7287–0514).

Film, Theater, and Opera

If all seats have been sold, the National Theatre sells unobstructed-view £5 standing-room tickets on the day of performances at their Olivier, Lyttleton, and Dorfman theaters. Standing-room tickets are £3–£15 at the Royal Opera House, with 49 cheap tickets available each Friday at 1 pm for sold-out performances. If you're under 30 or a student, becoming an "Access all Arias" member of the English National Opera is free and allows you to buy £10–£30 tickets. There are 500 £5 standing-room tickets available for every performance at the Shakespeare's Globe theater, as well as £10 standing-room tickets for magical candlelit plays and concerts at the adjacent indoor Sam Wanamaker Playhouse. At Sloane Square, the Royal Court Theatre has a limited number of standing-room tickets for 10 pence each at the Jerwood Theatre Downstairs, available an hour before performances.

Sightseeing

Prop yourself on the top deck of a red double-decker bus for a fantastic sightseeing tour through the most scenic parts of the city. Routes 9 and 15 also operate Heritage routes on the traditional 1950s Routemaster buses. With all buses now cashless, you can instead use your Oyster card or buy tickets from machines at bus stops for the following routes:

Bus 11: King's Road, Sloane Square, Victoria Station, Westminster Abbey, Houses of Parliament and Big Ben, Whitehall, Trafalgar Square, the Strand, Royal Courts of Justice, Fleet Street, and St. Paul's Cathedral.

Bus 19: Sloane Square, Knightsbridge, Hyde Park Corner, Green Park, Piccadilly Circus, Shaftsbury Avenue, Bloomsbury, Angel, and Islington.

Bus 88: Oxford Circus, Conduit Street, Piccadilly Circus, Haymarket, Trafalgar Square, Whitehall, Horse Guards Parade, Westminster Station, Westminster Abbey, Horseferry Road, and Tate Britain.

LONDON WITH KIDS

Activities

Ride the London Eye. Europe's largest observation wheel looks like a giant fairground ride, and you can see across what seems like half of London from the top.

Pose with a Queen's Horse Guard. There's always the Queen's mounted guards in uniform by the entrance to Horse Guards on the Trafalgar Square end of Whitehall. They don't mind posing for pictures, but they're not allowed to smile.

Ice-skating at Somerset House. Send your kids whizzing, arms whirling, across ice mid-November–January at this spotlighted open-air ice rink in a former Renaissance royal palace.

Pedalo on the Serpentine. Pack a picnic and take a blue pedalo out into the middle of Hyde Park's famed Serpentine lake; settle back and tuck in to lunch.

Lose the kids at Hampton Court Maze. The topiary might be more than 300 years old, but the quest to reach the middle of Hampton Court's world-famous trapezoid-shape yew hedge maze remains as challenging as ever.

West End musicals. Foot-stompingly good West End musicals and shows like *Les Misérables, Billy Elliot, Matilda, Mamma Mia!, The Lion King, Oliver!, Grease,* and *Harry Potter and the Cursed Child* will captivate the over-seven crowd.

Education Without Yawns

Kew Gardens. The Royal Botanic Gardens in Kew is great for young ones, with activities, the "climbers and creepers" play zone, a 60-foot high treetops Sky Walk, zip wires, scramble slides, and children's trails; it's free for kids under four.

The London Dungeon. It's guts and gore galore at this top South Bank attraction that plunges you into the blood-soaked depths of London history, with tales from a gruesome Jack the Ripper pub, Sweeney Todd barbers, and Mrs. Lovett's infamous pie shop.

London Zoo. Disappear into the animal kingdom among the enclosures, complete with sessions for kids about all kinds of bugs and spiders in this popular animal retreat in Regent's Park.

Natural History Museum. It doesn't get more awe-inspiring than bloodsucking bats, a cabinet of hummingbirds, simulated Kobe earthquakes, and a life-size blue whale. Just make sure you know your dodo from your *daspletorsaurus*.

Science Museum. Special effects, virtual space voyages, 800 interactive exhibits, puzzles, and mysteries from the world of science can keep kids effortlessly engaged all day.

Tower of London. Perfect for playing prince and princess in front of the Crown Jewels, but not so perfect for imagining what becomes of the fairy tale—watch your royal necks.

Performances

Covent Garden street performers. You can't beat the open-air gaggle of jugglers, fire-eaters, unicyclists, mime artists, and human statues tantalizing crowds at Covent Garden piazza.

Regent's Park Open-Air Theatre. Welcome to the land of fairy dust and magic. Don't miss an evening performance under the stars of *A Midsummer Night's Dream* in high summer.

GREAT ITINERARIES

The sheer diversity of what London offers, along with its constantly evolving culture, means you can easily live a lifetime here and still not see it all. But if you're like most visitors and only visiting for a short time, you can still get a taste of London life. In one day, you can get to the heart of the city's history and feel the force of its river setting. With five days, you can tick off many of the main attractions, and have a deeper sense of the seen and unseen majesty of this global metropolis.

LONDON IN 1 DAY

Do a giant best-of loop of the city by open-top boat and bus through six key districts, with a stop at the 953-year-old Tower of London and fun in Soho at the end. Start early, with the first ride of the London Eye at 10 am; you'll have the rest of the day to explore at whatever pace you wish, but be sure to get to Buckingham Palace before the sun sets or you'll miss out on some great photo opportunities.

On your morning ride on the **London Eye,** you'll be able to get an unrivaled bird's-eye view of the city. Then launch from the Eye's namesake pier for a swivel-eyed Thames River cruise past four famous bridges and Traitors' Gate before landing in front of the iconic **Tower of London.**

Once inside the Tower, take in the Crown Jewels and gory royal history on a Yeoman Warder's tour, before jumping on a double-decker bus over **Tower Bridge,** past Monument, the Embankment, Park Lane, Oxford, and Piccadilly circuses and stopping at **Trafalgar Square,** where you can glimpse **Big Ben** and the **Houses of Parliament,** before stopping for lunch at a historic Westminster pub. Then take a walk over to **Westminster Abbey,** where a self-guided tour will take you through

centuries of British history within one awe-inspiring building (note that the Abbey closes early on Saturday). Then take another short stroll through **St. James's Park** to **Buckingham Palace;** you'll have missed the daily Changing of the Guard, but that means the palace grounds will be less crowded, with more photo ops. End the day by meandering over to the hip Soho neighborhood, where foodies will find endless eclectic restaurants for dinner, and partygoers will find some of the city's best nightlife.

LONDON IN 5 DAYS

In five days you can check off most of London's cultural and sightseeing highlights, and weave in enough time for some world-class shopping and people-watching.

Day 1: Buckingham Palace, Trafalgar Square, and the National Portrait Gallery

Start day one with coffee in a Dickensian alleyway just north of **St. James's Palace,** before being first into the 19 impossibly grand State Rooms at **Buckingham Palace.** Afterward, join the crowds outside the palace to watch a sea of bearskin Foot Guards perform the **Changing of the Guard** ceremony, held 11:30 am most days. Some Palace tickets include tours of the **Queen's Gallery,** which showcases top Old Masters art from the Royal Collection. Then take a stroll through **St. James's Park** before lunch at a historic Pall Mall pub. It's a short walk to the **National Gallery** at **Trafalgar Square.** Hit its quieter Sainsbury Wing, pick up an audio guide, and hunt down a few choice early Renaissance masterpieces. Enjoy stern portraits of Tudor monarchs at the **National Portrait Gallery** next door, before browsing the antiquarian booksellers on Charring Cross Road or Cecil Court and enjoying fresh hand-made dim sum in **Chinatown.**

Day 2: Westminster Abbey, Houses of Parliament, and the East End

Devote the early morning of day two to a 90-minute verger guided tour of solemn **Westminster Abbey.** Then investigate the **Houses of Parliament.** If in session, you can attend debate in the Public Galleries or take a 75-minute tour of both houses. The stately **Members' and Strangers' Dining Rooms** in the House of Commons are occasionally open to the public for lunch; otherwise have a ploughman's lunch at a historic pub. Take pics of **Big Ben** and walk up Whitehall to the gates of **No 10. Downing Street,** the Prime Minister's residence. For a complete change of tune, take the Tube over to the gritty yet hip East End and Bangladeshi-influenced Brick Lane, where you can stroll along the art galleries and have a classic Indian curry for dinner.

Day 3: The South Bank

Day three is all about the South Bank and its unique art-infused culture. Start with a ride on the **London Eye** for eye-popping city panoramas. Take a long walk along the Thames, popping into any galleries, cinemas, or shops that catch your eye, like the excellent **Hayward Gallery.** Eventually meander along to **Tate Modern** for a modern art fix, stopping for lunch nearby. Then enjoy a Shakespeare hit with tours of the replica Elizabethan **Shakespeare's Globe.** Wiggle along for venison burgers and foodie stall heaven at **Borough Market** before backtracking over the pedestrian **Millennium Bridge** for a stunning approach to **St. Paul's Cathedral.** Hopefully you'll catch Choral Evensong there at 5 pm, then head east towards Bow Lane alleyway for a customary City pub fish-and-chips dinner.

Day 4: The British Museum and Soho

On day four, start early at the **British Museum** in Bloomsbury and leave a few hours to explore hits like the Egyptian mummies, Rosetta Stone, and 7th-century Anglo-Saxon Sutton Hoo treasures. Afterward, Tube it to restaurant-mad **Soho** where you can stop for Sri Lankan rice-and-curry at Hoppers, before browsing **Carnaby Street** and the surrounding indie fashion boutiques. Cut across Regent Street via the dapper gentlemen's tailors of **Savile Row** and head south for **Fortnum & Mason** and the old-world gentlemen's outfitters and bespoke shoe shops on Jermyn Street. Work back through the twinkly Regency red-carpet **Burlington Arcade** and pop into the **Royal Academy** gallery before taking Afternoon Tea at the cozy Brown's Hotel in Mayfair.

Day 5: Kensington's Museums, Piccadilly, and the West End

Finally on day five, start with a one-hour tour of the **V&A Museum** of decorative arts and design, whose collection ranges from rare Persian rugs to Tudor chalices. Once out, refuel with a crêpe on pedestrianized Exhibition Road near the South Kensington Tube, then choose either all things science at the **Science Museum,** or the *T. rex* dinosaur trail at the **Natural History Museum.** Then stroll up Knightsbridge to **Harrod's** famous Food Hall, where you can drool over salamis and people-watch to your heart's content. Either duck in for the ace fashion at **Harvey Nichols** or sip early cocktails at **The Ritz** at Green Park. Then enjoy the giant neon lights of **Piccadilly Circus** and **Leicester Square** before having a pretheater dinner in **Covent Garden** and then catching a West End play or musical.

BEST TOURS IN LONDON

With its crooked medieval streets, layers of history, and atmospheric buildings, London is a true walking city often best explored on a guided tour. Tours are a great way to investigate out-of-the-way, hidden, historic, and secret districts; to get an insider's eye on where locals like to eat, drink, and be merry; and to learn all the interesting and infamous aspects of London's history, architecture, and inhabitants.

Boat Tours

City Cruises. In nice weather, an open top-deck ride from Westminster, the London Eye, or Tower Piers to the ancient royal romping ground of Greenwich along the Thames River is one of the best ways to get acquainted with the city. You'll pass sights like Tower Bridge, the Tower of London, and St. Paul's Cathedral, all with a chirpy Cockney boatman running commentary. Lunch, Afternoon Tea, and nighttime cruises are also available. ⊠ *Cherry Garden Pier, Cherry Garden St.* ☎ *020/7740–0400* ⊕ *www.citycruises. com* ☒ *From £10.25.*

London Duck Tours. Hop aboard one of the garish yellow, vintage amphibious trucks (originally used during World War II), and get ready to sputter past a stack of sights including 10 Downing Street and Westminster Abbey. Once at the spy agency MI6 building, you'll take like a duck to water and gently amble up the Thames to the Houses of Parliament. Other tours focus on James Bond and the D-Day Landings. ⊠ *55 York Rd.* ☎ *020/7928–3132* ⊕ *www.londonduck-tours.co.uk* ☒ *From £27.*

Thames RIB Experience. Make like James Bond in an exhilarating special forces–style inflatable speedboat as you whiz past the MI6 building, Shakespeare's Globe, and Tower Bridge on a high-speed 50-minute round-trip to Canary Wharf. There are also 40-minute roller-coaster blasts to the O2 Arena in Greenwich and 75-minute round-trips from Tower Pier to the Thames Barrier. ⊠ *Embankment Pier* ☎ *020/3613–7838* ⊕ *www.thamesribexperience.com* ☒ *From £26.50.*

Bus Tours

Golden Tours. Various hop-on, hop-off open-top double-decker tours with this company take in the main sites on three key loops. With 60 drop-off points and 48-hour passes, they also offer discount tickets to attractions like the Tower of London and the London Dungeon, as well as nighttime tours, free walking tours, and boat rides on the Thames. ⊠ *London* ☎ *020/7630–2028* ⊕ *www.goldentours. com* ☒ *From £35.*

The Original London Sightseeing Tour. Like its double-decker competitors, the Original London Sightseeing Tour offers various hop-on, hop-off open-top tours of the city, but its most popular feature is its 48-hour pass that includes loops of the main historic sites, The City, Westminster, and the South Kensington museum districts. They also throw in free tickets for a Thames boat cruise, plus Jack the Ripper, Changing of the Guard, and Rock 'n' Roll walking tours. ⊠ *London* ☎ *020/8877–1722* ⊕ *www.theoriginaltour.com* ☒ *From £29.*

Free Tours

City Tours. The City of London City Guides offer a small program of top-quality daily walks, including an insider tour of Guildhall, Mansion House, the Bank of England, and Royal Exchange, plus others focusing on topics like The City's gardens, Charles Dickens, Dr. Samuel Johnson, and famed architect Sir

Christopher Wren's churches. ⊕ *www. cityoflondonguides.com* ▨ *from £7.*

Sandemans New Europe London. It seems almost too good to be true: Sandemans offers an excellent free, two-and-a-half-hour Royal London walking tour daily, which winds from Buckingham Palace to Big Ben. Led by wisecracking actors, poets, and esteemed art historians, other paid walks include a boozy five-stop pub crawl and spooky East End's Dark Secrets tours. ☎ *30/5105–0030* ⊕ *www.neweuropetours.eu/london* ▨ *Free.*

Specialty Tours

Brit Movie Tours. See the exterior of Grantham House and the spot where Branson first confesses his love for Lady Sybil on this insiders' central London tour of *Downton Abbey* filming locations. Other tours focusing on James Bond, *Sherlock, The Da Vinci Code,* and Harry Potter filming locations, among many others, are also available. ☎ *0844/247–1007* ⊕ *www.britmovietours.com* ▨ *From £90.*

Walking Tours

Context Travel. This company takes a high-brow approach to its intellectually curious small-group walks program, providing PhD- and MA-level scholars, authors, architects, and historians to lead walks of no more than six people. Lasting up to three hours, walks include the evolution of London theater to Charles Dickens and Victorian London. ☎ *800/691–6036* ⊕ *www.contexttravel.com/cities/london* ▨ *From £85.*

London Food Lovers. Combine walking, talking, and eating (but not at the same time) on these fabulous multistop trails, featuring interesting restaurants and London cultural history. There are four half-day Soho-focused food tours complete with 10 stops, as well as two shorter three-hour evening options that include 5 stops, like the Jack the Ripper Happy Hour tasting tour, which focuses on gin, bagels, and locally brewed craft ales. ☎ *0777/409–9306* ⊕ *www.londonfoodlovers.com* ▨ *From £60.*

London Walks. With London's oldest established walking tours, there's no need to book ahead; instead, just turn up at the meeting point at the allotted hour and pay £10 for a first-rate, guided two-hour walk with themes like Secret London, Literary London, Harry Potter film locations, Haunted London, and much more. Top crime historian and leading Ripper authority Donald Rumbelow often leads the 7:30 pm Jack the Ripper walk in Whitechapel. ☎ *020/7624–3978* ⊕ *www. walks.com* ▨ *From £10.*

Sophie Campbell. Travel journalist and former BBC *Travel Show* broadcaster Sophie Campbell specializes in superlong London walks. Full-day walks include Old Church Chelsea (by the river) to St. Michael's Highgate (high on a north London hill); or Hampton Court Palace to Richmond Palace via the noble palazzi of the nontidal Thames. Half-day hikes include a forensic examination of Fleet Street journalism and James Bond's London. ☎ *07743/566–323* ⊕ *www.sophiecampbell.london* ▨ *From £200.*

AFTERNOON TEA

An Age-Old Tradition

So what is Afternoon Tea, *exactly*? Well, it is real loose-leaf tea—Earl Grey, English Breakfast, Ceylon, Darjeeling, or Assam—brewed in a silver or porcelain pot and served with fine bone china cups and saucers, milk or lemon, and silver spoons, taken between noon and 6 pm. For the traditional full English experience, there should be elegant finger foods on a three-tier silver cake stand: finely cut crustless finger sandwiches on the bottom; scones with Cornish clotted cream and strawberry preserve in the middle; and rich English fruitcake, shortbread, patisseries, macarons, and dainty *petits gateaux* on top.

Tea goers dress smartly, and conversation by tradition should naturally avoid politics and religion.

Classic Choices

The Savoy on the Strand offers one of the most beautiful settings for Afternoon Tea. The Thames Foyer, a symphony of grays and golds centered on a winter garden wrought-iron gazebo and great glass cupola, is just the place for the house pianist to accompany you as you enjoy 72 rare house teas along with finger sandwiches, homemade scones, and pastries.

Setting the standard in its English Tea Room for some of London's best-known traditional teas, **Brown's Hotel** in Mayfair offers Afternoon Tea for £55 in an Agatha Christie–esque wood-paneled salon or, if you wish to splurge, Champagne Afternoon Tea for £65.

If you seek timeless chic, the art deco dining room at **The Delaunay** grand café at the Aldwych remains a deeply fashionable hangout. The silver service teas here—light Cream Tea is £9.50, Viennese Tea is £19.75, and Champagne Tea,

£29.75—come with wheat-free poppyseed *Gugelhupf* cakes and are among the best in town.

Something Different

Add spice to your tea time by trying a popular Moroccan-style Afternoon Tea (£25 or £35) at the souk-chic tearoom at **Momo** off Regent Street, where you'll enjoy sweet mint tea plus scones with fig jam, Maghrebian pastries, Moroccan chicken wraps, and honey-and-nut-rich Berber-style crepes.

Alternatively, you can munch Coronation chicken wraps and look out onto the immaculate lawns amid mini potted orange trees at **The Orangery** at Prince William and Kate's London pad, Kensington Palace, inside resplendent Kensington Gardens. Afternoon Tea is £19.95, and a suitably Royal Afternoon Tea (with a glass of Laurent-Perrier Brut NV) is £29.95.

Covent Garden's grand French brasserie **Balthazar** has a fabulous floral-focused English Afternoon Tea, curated by the online flower delivery company Flowerbx. From Coronation chicken and apricot sandwiches to coconut and Yuzu hydrangea cakes, everything has a flowery twist.

An Edwardian Escape

For some gilt-edged Rococo grandeur, few can compete with Afternoon Tea at **The Ritz** on Piccadilly. It's served in the stunning Palm Court, replete with linen-draped tables, Louis XIV chaise longues, sparkling chandeliers, resplendent bouquets, and discrete musical accompaniment; it's a true taste of Edwardian London in the 21st century. Afternoon Tea is £57, and Celebration Champagne Tea is £76. There are five sittings from 11:30 am to 7:30 pm; be sure to book three months ahead, and men should wear a jacket and tie.

WESTMINSTER AND ST. JAMES'S

Getting Oriented

Westminster and
St. James's

TOP REASONS TO GO

Westminster Abbey: This Gothic church was not only the site of William and Kate's marriage in 2011 but also has seen 38 coronations, starting with William the Conqueror in 1066.

Buckingham Palace: Even if you miss the palace's summer opening, keep pace with the marching soldiers as they enact the time-honored Changing the Guard.

The National Gallery: Leonardo, Raphael, Van Eyck, Rembrandt, and many other artistic greats are shown off in the gorgeous rooms at the National Gallery.

Churchill War Rooms: Listen to Churchill's radio addresses to the British people as you explore this atmospheric underground wartime hideout.

Trafalgar Square: With London's most famous photo op (the 320-foot-high clock tower Big Ben) under scaffolding until 2020, head to Trafalgar Square for a snap with the enormous bronze lions at the base of Nelson's Column.

FEELING PECKISH?

Iris & June. The area between Victoria and Westminster is something of a wasteland in terms of quick-bite eateries, but this minimalist café serves excellent coffee, salads, wraps, and more. ⊠ *1 Howick Pl.* ⊕ *www.irisandjune.com* Ⓜ *Victoria.*

Notes Music and Coffee. Next door to the London Coliseum (home of the English National Opera), this hip café serves some of the best sandwiches, salads, and coffee in the neighborhood. ⊠ *31 St. Martin's La., Westminster* ☎ *020/7240–0424* ⊕ *www.notes-uk.co.uk* Ⓜ *Charing Cross.*

St. James's Café. Come to this always bustling spot at lunch for delicious homemade soups, salads, and light mains, or for an early evening glass of wine before it closes at 7 pm. ⊠ *St. James's Park, St. James's* ☎ *020/7839–1149* ⊕ *www.benugo.com/public-spaces/st-james-s-park* Ⓜ *St. James's Park.*

2

GETTING THERE

Trafalgar Square is in the center of the action. Take the Tube to Embankment (Northern, Bakerloo, District, and Circle lines) and walk north until you cross the Strand, or exit to Northumberland Avenue at Charing Cross (Bakerloo and Northern lines). Buses are another great option, as almost all roads lead to Trafalgar Square.

Two Tube stations are right in the heart of St. James's: Piccadilly Circus (Piccadilly and Bakerloo lines) and Green Park (Piccadilly, Victoria, and Jubilee lines).

MAKING THE MOST OF YOUR TIME

For royal pageantry, begin with Buckingham Palace, Westminster Abbey, and the Guards Museum, followed by the Houses of Parliament and Big Ben. For art, the National Gallery, Tate Britain, and the Queen's Gallery top anyone's list.

NEAREST PUBLIC RESTROOMS

Paid restrooms (50 p) are across the street from Westminster Abbey at the bottom of Victoria Street. Banqueting House and the Queen's Gallery have elegant restrooms.

Sightseeing
★★★★★
Nightlife
★★
Dining
★★★
Lodging
★
Shopping
★★

This is postcard London at its best. Crammed with historic churches, grand state buildings, and some of the world's best art collections, Royal London and Westminster unite politics and high culture. (Oh, and the Queen lives here, too.) The places you'll want to explore are grouped into four distinct areas—Trafalgar Square, Whitehall, St. James's, and Buckingham Palace—each nudging a corner of triangular St. James's Park. There is as much history in these few acres as in many whole cities, so pace yourself—this is concentrated sightseeing.

WESTMINSTER

Updated by
Jo Caird

Home to London's most photogenic pigeons, **Trafalgar Square** is the official center of the district known as **Westminster,** nominally a separate city but in fact the official center of London. What will bring you here are the two magnificent museums on the northern edge of the square, the **National Gallery** and the **National Portrait Gallery.** From the square, two boulevards lead to the seats of different areas of governance. The avenue called **Whitehall** drops south to the neo-Gothic **Houses of Parliament,** where members of both (Commons and Lords) hold debates and vote on pending legislation. Just opposite, **Westminster Abbey** is a monument to the nation's history and for centuries the scene of daily worship, coronations, and royal weddings. Poets, political leaders, and 17 monarchs are buried in this world-famous, 13th-century Gothic building. Sandwiched between the two is the **Jewel Tower,** the only surviving part of the medieval Palace of Westminster (a name still given to Parliament and its environs). Halfway down Whitehall, **10 Downing Street** is both the residence and the office of the prime minister. One of the most celebrated occupants, Winston Churchill, is commemorated in the **Churchill War Rooms,** his underground wartime headquarters off

A BRIEF HISTORY OF WESTMINSTER

The Romans may have shaped The City, but England's royals created Westminster. Indeed, it's still technically a separate city—notice it reads "City of Westminster" on street signs, not "City of London"—although any formal divide between the two vanished centuries ago, along with the open countryside that once lay between them. Edward the Confessor started the first Palace of Westminster in the 11th century; in the 1040s, he also founded Westminster Abbey, where every British coronation has taken place. The district became the focus of political power in England after the construction of Whitehall Palace in the 16th century; a vast and opulent building, it was the official residence of the monarch until it burned down in 1698. It survives both as the name of Westminster's most important road, and as a term still used in Britain to refer to the seat of government in general. The first

Parliament building was part of the same complex; it, too, was nearly destroyed by the Gunpowder Plot of 1605 (still commemorated annually on November 5, Guy Fawkes Day) and eventually succumbed to fire In 1834. The Westminster we see today took shape during the Georgian and Victorian periods, as Britain reached the zenith of its imperial power. Grand architecture sprang up, and Buckingham Palace became the principal royal residence in 1837, when Victoria acceded to the throne. Trafalgar Square and Nelson's Column were built in 1843, to commemorate Britain's most famous naval victory, and the Houses of Parliament were rebuilt in the 1840s in the trendy neo-Gothic style of the time. The Illustrious Clarence House, built in 1825 for the Duke of Clarence (later William IV), is now the home of Prince Charles and Camilla, Duchess of Cornwall.

Whitehall. Just down the road is the **Cenotaph,** built for the dead of World War I and since then a focal point for the annual remembrance of those lost in war.

The Mall, a wide elegant avenue beyond the stone curtain of **Admiralty Arch,** heads southwest from Trafalgar Square toward the **Queen Victoria Memorial** and **Buckingham Palace,** the sovereign's official residence. The building is open to the public only in summer (or for tours on select dates throughout the year), but you can see much of the royal art collection in the **Queen's Gallery** and spectacular ceremonial coaches in the **Royal Mews,** both open all year. Farther south toward Pimlico, **Tate Britain** focuses on prominent British artists from 1500 to today.

The main drawback to sightseeing here is that half the world is doing it at the same time. So, for a large part of the year a lot of Royal London is floodlit at night (when there's more elbow room), adding to the theatricality of the experience.

Banqueting House. James I commissioned Inigo Jones, one of England's great architects, to undertake a grand building on the site of the original Tudor Palace of Whitehall, which was (according to one foreign visitor) "ill-built, and nothing but a heap of houses." Jones's Banqueting House, finished in 1622 and the first building in England to be completed in the neoclassical style, bears all the hallmarks of the Palladian sophistication and purity that so influenced Jones during his time in Italy. James's son, Charles I, enhanced the interior by employing the Flemish painter Peter Paul Rubens to glorify his father and himself (naturally) in a series of vibrant painted ceiling panels called *The Apotheosis of James I*. As it turned out, these allegorical paintings, depicting a wise monarch being received into heaven, were the last thing Charles saw before he stepped through the open first-floor window onto the scaffold, which had been erected directly outside for his execution by Cromwell's Parliamentarians in 1649. Twenty years later, his son, Charles II, would celebrate the restoration of the monarchy in the exact same place. ⊠ *Whitehall, Westminster* ☎ *084/4482–7777* ⊕ *www.hrp.org.uk/BanquetingHouse* ⊠ *£7.20* Ⓜ *Charing Cross, Embankment, Westminster.*

FAMILY
Fodor's Choice
★

Churchill War Rooms. It was from this small warren of underground rooms—beneath the vast government buildings of the Treasury— that Winston Churchill and his team directed troops in World War II. Designed to be bombproof, the whole complex has been preserved almost exactly as it was when the last light was turned off at the end of the war. Every clock shows almost 5 pm, and the furniture, fittings, and paraphernalia of a busy, round-the-clock war office are still in situ, down to the colored map pins.

During air raids, the leading government ministers met here, and the Cabinet Room is arranged as if a meeting were about to convene. In the Map Room, the Allied campaign is charted on wall-to-wall maps with a rash of pinholes showing the movements of convoys. In the hub of the room, a bank of differently colored phones known as the "Beauty Chorus" linked the War Rooms to control rooms around the nation. The Prime Minister's Room holds the desk from which Churchill made his morale-boosting broadcasts; the Telephone Room (a converted broom cupboard) has his hotline to FDR. You can also see the restored rooms that the PM used for dining and sleeping. Telephonists (switchboard operators) and clerks who worked 16-hour shifts slept in lesser quarters in unenviable conditions.

An excellent addition to the War Rooms is the Churchill Museum, a tribute to the great wartime leader himself. ⊠ *Clive Steps, King Charles St., Westminster* ☎ *020/7416–5000* ⊕ *www.iwm.org.uk/visits/churchill-war-rooms* ⊠ *£21* Ⓜ *Westminster.*

Downing Street. Were it not for the wrought-iron gates and armed guards that block the entrance, you'd probably miss this otherwise unassuming Georgian side street off Whitehall—but this is the location of the famous **No. 10**, London's modest equivalent of the White House. The Georgian entrance to the mid-17th-century mansion is deceptive; it's actually a huge complex of discreetly linked buildings. Since 1732 it has been the official home and office of the prime minister—the last private resident was the magnificently named Mr. Chicken (the current prime minister actually lives in the private apartments above No. 11, traditionally the residence of the Chancellor of the Exchequer, the head of the Treasury). There are no public tours, but the famous black front door to No. 10 is clearly visible from Whitehall. Keep your eyes peeled for Larry the cat, whose official title is Chief Mouser to the Cabinet

2

Office. Just south of Downing Street, in the middle of Whitehall, is the **Cenotaph,** a stark white monolith built to commemorate the 1918 armistice. On Remembrance Day (the Sunday nearest November 11), it's strewn with red poppy wreaths to honor the dead of both world wars and all British and Commonwealth soldiers killed in action since; the first wreath is always laid by the Queen. A hundred yards farther, toward Parliament, is the **Monument to the Women of World War II.** The prominent black marble sculpture uses a string of empty uniforms to symbolize the vital service of women in then-traditionally male jobs during the war, as well as in frontline roles, such as medics and auxiliary officers. ⊠ *Whitehall* Ⓜ *Westminster.*

FAMILY **Horse Guards Parade.** Once the tiltyard for jousting tournaments, Horse Guards Parade is best known for the annual Trooping the Colour ceremony, in which the Queen takes the salute on her official birthday, on the second Saturday in June. (Though it's called a birthday it's actually the anniversary of her coronation—her real birthday is April 21.) It's a must-see if you're around, with marching bands and throngs of onlookers. Throughout the rest of the year, the changing of two mounted sentries known as the **Queen's Life Guard** at the Whitehall facade of Horse Guards provides what may be London's most popular photo opportunity. The ceremony takes place daily from April to July, and on alternate days from August to March (usually odd numbered days, but check the monthly schedule at ⊕ *www.householddivision.org.uk/ changing-the-guard-calendar*). It starts at 10:30 am at St. James's Palace, where the guard begins its march to Buckingham Palace, and the new guards take up their posts in a ceremony at 11. (It's sometimes cancelled in bad weather.) At 4 pm daily is the dismounting ceremony, aka the 4 O'Clock Parade, during which sentries are posted and horses are returned to their stables. It began in 1894, when Queen Victoria discovered the guards on duty drinking and gambling. As a punishment she decreed that the regiment should be inspected every day at 4 pm for the next 100 years—by the time 1994 swung around they decided to continue the tradition indefinitely. ⊠ *Whitehall* ☎⊕ *www.household-division.org.uk/changing-the-guard* 🖾 *Free* Ⓜ *Westminster.*

FAMILY **Household Cavalry Museum.** Hang around Horse Guards for even a short time and you'll see a member of the Household Cavalry on guard, or trotting past on horseback, resplendent in a bright crimson uniform with polished brass armor. Made up of soldiers from the British Army's most senior regiments, the Life Guards and the Blues and Royals, membership is considered a great honor; they act as the Queen's official bodyguards and play a key role in state occasions (they also perform the famed Changing the Guard ceremony). Housed in the cavalry's original 17th-century stables, the museum has displays of uniforms and weapons going back to 1661 as well as interactive exhibits on the regiments' current operational roles. In the tack room you can handle saddles and bridles, and try on a trooper's uniform, including a distinctive brass helmet with horsehair plume. You can also observe the working horses being tended to in their stable block behind a glass wall. ⊠ *Horse Guards Parade, Whitehall* ☎ *020/7930–3070* ⊕ *www.householdcavalrymuseum.co.uk* 🖾 *£8.50* Ⓜ *Charing Cross, Westminster.*

Fodor's Choice   **Houses of Parliament.** The Palace of Westminster, as the complex is called,
★   was first established on this site by Edward the Confessor in the 11th
century. William II built a new palace in 1097, and this became the
seat of English power. A fire destroyed most of the palace in 1834, and
the current complex dates largely from the mid-19th century. The best
view is from the opposite (south) bank of the Thames, across Lambeth
Bridge. It is most dramatic at night when lighted green and gold.

The **Visitors' Galleries** of the House of Commons provide a view of
democracy in action when the benches are filled by opposing MPs
(members of Parliament). Debates are formal but raucous, especially
during the **Prime Minister's Questions** (PMQs), when any MP can put
a question to the nation's leader. Tickets to PMQs are free but highly
sought after, so the only way for non-U.K. citizens to gain access is by
lining up on the day and hoping for returns or no-shows. The action
starts at noon every Wednesday when Parliament is sitting, and the
whole shebang is broadcast live on television. For non-PMQ debates,
Embassies and High Commissions have a quota of tickets available to
their citizens, which can help you avoid long lines. The easiest time
to get into the Commons is during an evening session—Parliament
is still sitting if the top of the Clock Tower is illuminated. There are
also Visitors Galleries for the House of Lords. The Clock Tower—
renamed **Elizabeth Tower** in 2012, in honor of the Queen's Diamond
Jubilee—was completed in 1858, and contains the 13-ton bell known
as **Big Ben.** ⚠ Renovations of the tower and clock will be taking place
throughout 2019, with scaffolding getting in the way of photo ops during this period. At the southwest end of the main Parliament building
is the 323-foot-high Victoria Tower.

Engaging guided and audio tours of Parliament are available on Saturday and weekdays when Parliament isn't sitting, but sell out six
months in advance. Other tours, including afternoon tea on the Pavillion Terrace, overlooking the Thames, are also available. ⊠ *St. Stephen's
Entrance, St. Margaret St., Westminster* ☎ *0207/219–4114 for public
tours* ⊕ *www.parliament.uk/visiting* ⊠ *Free; tours £28, audio tours
£20.50* ☉ *Closed Sun.* Ⓜ *Westminster.*

The Jewel Tower. Overshadowed by the big-ticket attractions of Parliament to one side and Westminster Abbey to the other, this is the only
significant portion of the Palace of Westminster complex to have sur-
vived intact from medieval times. Built in the 1360s to contain treasures
belonging to Edward III, it once formed part of the palace's defensive
walls—hence the fortresslike appearance. Check out the original ribbed
stone ceiling on the ground floor; look up to see the carved stone images
of men and beasts. The Jewel Tower was later used as a records office
for the House of Lords, but hasn't served any official function since
the rest of the old palace was destroyed by fire in 1834 and the ancient
documents were moved to the greater safety of the Tower of London.
Today it contains an exhibition on the history of the building. ⊠ *Abing-
don St., Westminster* ☎ *020/7222–2219* ⊕ *www.english-heritage.org.
uk/visit/places/jewel-tower* ⊠ *£5.40* Ⓜ *Westminster.*

FAMILY
Fodor'sChoice
★
National Gallery. Anyone with even a passing interest in art will want to put this near the top of their to-do lists while visiting London, for it is truly one of the world's great art museums. More than 2,300 masterpieces are on show here, including works by Michelangelo, Leonardo, Turner, Monet, Van Gogh, Picasso, and more. Enter through the grand portico overlooking the north side of Trafalgar Square to delve headlong into the highlights of the collection, although the Sainsbury Wing (the modern building immediately to the left), which focuses mainly on medieval art, is invariably less crowded. You could easily spend all day discovering what the National Gallery has to offer, but among the best-known highlights are: in Room 4, *The Ambassadors* by Hans Holbein (1497–1543), a portrait of two wealthy visitors from France, surrounded by objects laden with enough symbolism to fill a book—including, most beguilingly, a giant skull at the base, which only takes shape when viewed from an angle; in Room 60, the *Arnolfini Portrait* by Van Eyck (1390–1441), in which a solemn couple holds hands, the fisheye mirror behind them mysteriously illuminating what can't be seen from the front view; in Room 61, *The Virgin of the Rocks* by Leonardo da Vinci (1452–1519), a magnificent sculpted altarpiece commissioned in 1480; and in Room 34, *Rain, Steam and Speed–The Great Western Railway* by J.M.W. Turner (1775–1851), which seems, in its mad whirl of rain, steam, and mist, to embody the mystical dynamism of the steam age (spot the fleeing hare). Special exhibitions, of which there are several every year, tend to be major events. Generally they're ticketed, so booking is advisable if it's a big name. The permanent collection, however, is always free. Also free are weekday lunchtime lectures and Ten Minute Talks, which illuminate the story behind a key work of art. Daily hour-long free guided tours start at the Sainsbury Wing at 11:30 and 2:30. ⊠ *Trafalgar Sq., Westminster* ☎ *020/7747–2885* ⊕ *www.nationalgallery.org.uk* ⊠ *Free; special exhibitions £7–£22; audio guide £5* Ⓜ *Charing Cross, Embankment, Leicester Sq.*

FAMILY
Fodor'sChoice
★
National Portrait Gallery. The National Portrait Gallery was founded in 1856 with a single aim: to gather together portraits of famous (and infamous) Britons throughout history. More than 150 years and 200,000 portraits later, it is an essential stop for all history and literature buffs. If you visit with kids, ask at the desk about the excellent Family Trails, which make exploring the galleries with children much more fun. Galleries are arranged clearly and chronologically, from Tudor times to contemporary Britain. A Holbein miniature of Henry VIII is among the most famous images in the Tudor Gallery, although the enormous portrait of Elizabeth I—bejeweled and literally astride the world in a powerful display of imperial intent—may be the most impressive. The huge permanent collections include portraits of Shakespeare, the Brontë sisters, and Jane Austen. Look for the four Andy Warhol *Queen Elizabeth II* silkscreens from 1985 and Maggi Hambling's surreal self-portrait. Contemporary portraits range from the iconic (*Julian with T-shirt*—an LCD screen on a continuous loop—by Julian Opie) to the extreme (Marc Quinn's *Self,* a realization of the artist's head done in frozen blood). Temporary exhibitions can be explored on the first three floors, particularly in the Wolfson and Porter galleries on the ground

floor. ■TIP➔ On the top floor, the Portrait Restaurant has one of the best views in London—a panoramic vista of Nelson's Column and the backdrop along Whitehall to the Houses of Parliament. ⊠ *St. Martin's Pl., Westminster* ☎ *020/7306–0055* ⊕ *www.npg.org.uk* 🌣 *Free; special exhibitions £6–£18; audiovisual guide £3; family audio guides £6 for 5 people* Ⓜ *Charing Cross, Leicester Sq.*

St. Margaret's Church. Dwarfed by its neighbor, Westminster Abbey, St. Margaret's was probably founded in the 11th century and rebuilt between 1482 and 1523. It's the unofficial parish church of the House of Commons—Winston Churchill tied the knot here in 1908, and since 1681, a pew off the south aisle has been set aside for the Speaker of the House (look for the carved portcullis). Samuel Pepys and John Milton also worshipped here. The stained glass in the north windows is classically Victorian, facing abstract glass from John Piper in the south, while the east windows date from the early 16th century. These were to replace the originals, which were ruined in World War II. ⊠ *St. Margaret's St., Parliament Sq., Westminster* ☎ *020/7222–5152* ⊕ *www. westminster-abbey.org/st-margarets-church* 🌣 *Free* Ⓜ *Westminster.*

FAMILY **St. Martin-in-the-Fields.** One of London's best-loved and most welcoming of churches is more than just a place of worship. Named after St. Martin of Tours, known for the help he gave to beggars, this parish has long been a welcome sight for the homeless, who have been given soup and shelter at the church since 1914. The church is also a haven for music lovers; the internationally known Academy of St. Martin-in-the-Fields Chamber Ensemble was founded here, and a popular program of concerts continues today (many of the shows are free, although some do charge an entry fee). The crypt is a hive of activity, with a popular café and shop. Here you can also make your own life-size souvenir knight, lady, or monarch from replica tomb brasses, with metallic waxes, paper, and instructions. ⊠ *Trafalgar Sq., Westminster* ☎ *020/7766–1100* ⊕ *www.smitf.org* 🌣 *Free* Ⓜ *Charing Cross, Leicester Sq.*

The Supreme Court. The highest court of appeal in the United Kingdom is a surprisingly young institution, only having heard its first cases in 2009. Visitors are welcome to drop by and look at the three courtrooms, housed in the carefully restored Middlesex Guildhall, including the impressive Court Room 1, with its magnificent carved wood ceiling. The Court's art collection, on permanent display, includes portraits by Thomas Gainsborough and Joshua Reynolds. Guided tours are available on Friday year-round and Monday through Thursday during the summer recess; book ahead. There is a café downstairs. The library is open on selected dates. ⊠ *Parliament Sq., Westminster* ☎ *020/7960–1500* ⊕ *www.supremecourt.uk* 🌣 *Free; guided tour £7* ⊘ *Closed weekends* Ⓜ *Westminster.*

FAMILY **Tate Britain.** First opened in 1897, and funded by the sugar magnate Sir
Fodor'sChoice Henry Tate, this stately neoclassical institution may not be as ambitious
★ as its Bankside sibling, Tate Modern, but its bright galleries lure only a fraction of the Modern's overwhelming crowds and are a great place to explore British art from 1500 to the present. The museum includes the Linbury Galleries on the lower floors, which stage temporary

The Tate Britain showcases British art from the last 500 years, including contemporary works.

exhibitions, and a permanent collection on the upper floors. And what a collection it is—with classic works by John Constable, Thomas Gainsborough, Rachel Whiteread, Francis Bacon, Duncan Grant, Barbara Hepworth, and Vanessa Bell, and an outstanding display from J.M.W. Turner in the Clore Gallery, including many later vaporous and light-infused works such as *Sunrise with Sea Monsters*. Sumptuous Pre-Raphaelite pieces are a major draw, while the Contemporary British Art galleries bring you face to face with Damien Hirst's *Away from the Flock* and other recent conceptions. The Tate Britain also hosts the annual Turner Prize exhibition, with its accompanying furor over the state of contemporary art, from about October to January each year. There's a good little café, and the excellent Rex Whistler Restaurant has been something of an institution since it first opened in 1927. It's open daily for lunch, and for dinner on semiregular Late at Tate Friday evening events, when the gallery is open late for talks or performances; check the website for details.

■TIP→ Craving more art? Head down the river on the Tate Boat (£8.30 one-way) to the Tate Modern; it runs between the two museums every 40 minutes. A Family River Roamer ticket (£37 for two adults and three children) permits a day's travel, with stops including the London Eye and the Tower of London. You get a discount of roughly a third if you have a Travelcard. ⊠ *Millbank, Westminster* ☎ *020/7887-8888* ⊕ *www. tate.org.uk/britain* ☜ *Free; special exhibitions £13–£22; audio guide £4.50* Ⓜ *Pimlico*

Fodor's Choice   **Trafalgar Square.** This is officially the center of London: a plaque on
★   the corner of the Strand and Charing Cross Road marks the spot from
which distances on U.K. signposts are measured. (London's *actual* geo-
graphic center is a rather dull bench on the Victoria Embankment.)
Medieval kings once kept their aviaries of hawks and falcons here;
today the humbler gray pigeons flock en masse to the open spaces
around the ornate fountains (feeding them is banned). The square was
designed in 1830 by John Nash, who envisaged a new public space
with striking views of the Thames, the Houses of Parliament, and Buckingham Palace. Of those, only Parliament is still clearly visible from
the square, but it remains an important spot for open-air concerts,
political demonstrations, and national celebrations, such as New Year's
Eve. Dominating the square is 168-foot **Nelson's Column,** erected as a
monument to the great admiral in 1843. Note that the lampposts on
the south side, heading down Whitehall, are topped with ships—they
all face Portsmouth, home of the British navy. The column is flanked on
either side by enormous bronze lions. Climbing them is a very popular
photo op, but be extremely careful, as there are no guardrails and it's
a long fall onto concrete if you slip. Four plinths border the square;
three contain militaristic statues, but one was left empty—it's now used
for contemporary art installations, often with a wry and controversial
edge. Surprisingly enough, given that this was a square built to honor
British military victories, the lawn at the north side, by the National
Gallery, contains a statue of George Washington—a gift from the state
of Virginia in 1921. At the southern point of the square is the **equestrian statue of Charles I.** After the Civil War and the king's execution,
Oliver Cromwell, the antiroyalist leader, commissioned a brazier, John
Rivett, to melt the statue down. The story goes that Rivett instead
merely buried it in his garden. He made a fortune peddling knickknacks
wrought, he claimed, from its metal, only to produce the statue miracu-
lously unscathed after the restoration of the monarchy—and then made
another fortune reselling it. In 1675 Charles II had it placed where it
stands today, near the spot where his father was executed in 1649. Each
year, on January 30, the day of the king's death, the Royal Stuart Society
lays a wreath at the foot of the statue. ✉ *Westminster* Ⓜ *Charing Cross.*

FAMILY   **Wellington Barracks and the Guards Museum.** These are the headquarters
of the Guards Division, the Queen's five regiments of elite foot guards
(Grenadier, Coldstream, Scots, Irish, and Welsh), who protect the sovereign and, dressed in tunics of gold-purled scarlet and tall bearskin
caps, patrol her palaces. Guardsmen alternate these ceremonial post-
ings with serving in current conflicts, for which they wear more practical uniforms. If you want to learn more about the guards, visit the
Guards Museum, which has displays on all aspects of a guardsman's
life in conflicts dating back to 1642; the entrance is next to the Guards
Chapel. Next door is the **Guards Toy Soldier Centre,** a great place for
a souvenir. ✉ *Birdcage Walk, Westminster* ☎ *020/7414–3428* ⊕ *www.
theguardsmuseum.com* 💷 *£8* Ⓜ *St. James's Park, Green Park.*

Fodor's Choice   **Westminster Abbey.** Steeped in hundreds of years of rich and occasion-
★   ally bloody history, Westminster Abbey is one of England's most iconic
buildings. An abbey has stood here since the 10th century, although the

One of London's most iconic sites, Westminster Abbey contains more than 600 monuments and memorials, and serves as the final resting place of some of England's most famous citizens.

current building mostly dates to the 1240s. It has hosted 38 coronations—beginning in 1066 with William the Conqueror—and no fewer than 16 royal weddings, the latest being that of Prince William and Kate Middleton in 2011. But be warned: there's only one way around the abbey, and it gets very crowded, so you'll need to be alert to catch the highlights. The **Coronation Chair**, which you'll find in St. George's Chapel by the east door, has been used for nearly every coronation since Edward II's in 1308, right up to Queen Elizabeth II's in 1953. Farther along, the exquisite confection of the Henry VII's **Lady Chapel** is topped by a magnificent fan-vaulted ceiling. The tomb of Henry VII lies behind the altar. Elizabeth I is buried above her sister "Bloody" Mary I in the tomb in a chapel on the north side, while her arch enemy, Mary Queen of Scots, rests in the tomb to the south. The **Chapel of St. Edward the Confessor** contains the shrine of the pre-Norman king, who reigned from 1042 to 1066. Because of its great age, you must join the vergers' tours to be admitted to the chapel (£5; book at the admission desk). To the left, you'll find **Poets' Corner**. Geoffrey Chaucer was the first poet to be buried here, and other statues and memorials include those to William Shakespeare, D. H. Lawrence, T. S. Eliot, and Oscar Wilde. The medieval **Chapter House** is adorned with 14th-century frescoes and a magnificent 13th-century tiled floor, one of the finest in the country. Near the entrance is Britain's oldest door, dating from the 1050s. If you walk toward the West Entrance, you'll see a plaque to Franklin D. Roosevelt—one of the abbey's very few tributes to a foreigner. The poppy-wreathed **Grave of the Unknown Warrior** commemorates soldiers who lost their lives in both world wars. Exact hours for the various parts of the abbey are frustratingly long and complicated, and can change daily, so it's important to check before setting out, particularly if you're visiting early or late in the day, or off-season. The full schedule is posted online daily (or you can call). Certain areas of the abbey are completely inaccessible to wheelchair users; however, you will get free entry for yourself and one other. ⊠ *Broad Sanctuary, Westminster* ☎ *020/7222–5152* ⊕ *www.westminster-abbey.org* ☜ *£22* ☉ *Closed Sun., except for worship* Ⓜ *Westminster, St. James's Park.*

Westminster Cathedral. Tucked away on traffic-clogged Victoria Street lies this remarkable neo-Byzantine gem, seat of the Archbishop of Westminster, head of the Roman Catholic Church in England and Wales. Faced with building a church with Westminster Abbey as a neighbor, architect John Francis Bentley looked to the east for inspiration, to the basilicas of St. Mark's in Venice and the Hagia Sofia in Istanbul. The asymmetrical redbrick edifice, dating to 1903, is banded with stripes of Portland stone and abutted by a 272-foot bell tower at the northwest corner, ascendable by elevator for sterling views. The interior remains incomplete, the unfinished overhead brickwork of the ceiling lending the church a dark brooding intensity. The side chapels, including the Chapel of the Blessed Sacrament and the Holy Souls Chapel, are beautifully finished in glittering mosaics. The Lady Chapel—dedicated to the Virgin Mary—is also sumptuously decorated. Look out for the Stations of the Cross, done here by Eric Gill, and the striking baldachin—the enormous stone canopy standing over the altar with a giant cross suspended in front of it. The nave, the widest in the country, is constructed in green marble, which also has a Byzantine connection—it was cut from the same place as the marble used in the Hagia Sofia, and was almost confiscated by warring Turks as it traveled west. All told, more than 100 different types of marble can be found within the cathedral's interior. There's a café in the crypt. ⊠ *Ashley Pl., off Victoria St., Westminster* ☎ *020/7798–9055* ⊕ *www.westminstercathedral.org.uk* ☜ *Bell Tower and viewing gallery £6, Treasures of the Cathedral exhibition £5; combination ticket £9* Ⓜ *Victoria.*

ST. JAMES'S

As a fitting coda to all of Westminster's pomp and circumstance, St. James's—packed with old-money galleries, restaurants, and gentlemen's clubs that embody the history and privilege of traditional London—is found to the south of Piccadilly and north of the Mall.

When Whitehall Palace burned down in 1698, all of London turned its attention to St. James's Palace, the new royal residence. In the 18th and 19th centuries, the area around the palace became the place to live, and many of the estates surrounding the palace disappeared in a building frenzy, as mansions were built and streets laid out. Most of the homes here are privately owned and therefore closed to visitors, but there are some treasure houses that you can explore (such as Spencer House), as well as many fancy shops that have catered to the great and good for centuries.

ROYALTY WATCHING

You've seen Big Ben, the Tower, and Westminster Abbey. But somehow you feel something is missing: a close encounter with Britain's most famous attraction—Her Royal Majesty, Elizabeth II. The Queen and the Royal Family attend hundreds of functions a year, and if you want to know what they are doing on any given date, turn to the Court Circular, printed in the major London dailies, or check out the Royal Family website (⊕ www.royal.uk) for the latest events on the Royal Diary. Trooping the Colour is usually held on the second Saturday in June, to celebrate the Queen's official birthday. This spectacular parade begins when she leaves Buckingham Palace in her carriage and rides down the Mall to arrive at Horse Guards Parade at 11 exactly. To watch, just line up along the Mall with your binoculars.

Another time you can catch the Queen in all her regalia is when she and the Duke of Edinburgh ride in state to open the Houses of Parliament. The famous black

and gilt-trimmed Irish State Coach travels from Buckingham Palace—on a clear day, it's to be hoped, for this ceremony takes place in late October or early November. The Gold State Coach, an icon of fairy-tale glamour, is used for coronations and jubilees only.

But perhaps the most relaxed, least formal time to see the Queen is during Royal Ascot, held at the racetrack near Windsor Castle—a short train ride out of London—usually during the third week of June (Tuesday–Saturday). The Queen and members of the Royal Family are driven down the track to the Royal Box in an open carriage, giving spectators a chance to see them. After several races, the famously horse-loving Queen invariably walks down to the paddock, greeting racegoers as she proceeds. If you meet her, the official etiquette is to first make a short bow or curtsy, and then to address her first as "Your Majesty," and then "Ma'am" thereafter.

Today, St. James's remains a rather masculine enclave, containing most of the capital's celebrated gentlemen's clubs (especially the classic Athenaeum), long-established men's outfitters and clothiers, and some interesting art galleries and antiques shops. In one corner is St. James's Park, framed on its western side by the biggest monument in the area: Buckingham Palace, the official London residence of the Queen. The smaller St. James's Palace is where much of the office work for the House of Windsor gets done; nearby is Clarence House, London home of Prince Charles and his wife, Camilla.

Fodor'sChoice ★ **Buckingham Palace.** If Buckingham Palace were open year-round, it would be by far the most visited tourist attraction in Britain; as it is, the Queen's main residence, home to every British monarch since Victoria in 1837, opens its doors to the public only in the summertime, with a handful of other dates throughout the year. The Queen is almost never there at the time—traditionally she heads off to Scotland for a couple of months every summer, where she takes up residence at Balmoral Castle. (Here's a quick way to tell if the Queen's at home: if she's in

A classic photo op: cavalry from the Queen's Life Guard at Buckingham Palace

residence, the Royal Standard flies above the palace; if not, it's the more famous red, white, and blue Union Jack.) The tour covers the palace's 19 State Rooms, with their fabulous gilt moldings and walls adorned with Old Masters. The **Grand Hall,** followed by the **Grand Staircase** and **Guard Room,** are visions in marble and gold leaf, filled with massive, twinkling chandeliers. Don't miss the theatrical **Throne Room,** with the original 1953 coronation throne, or the sword in the Ballroom, used by the Queen to bestow knighthoods and other honors with a touch on the recipient's shoulders. Royal portraits line the **State Dining Room,** and the **Blue Drawing Room** is dazzling in its splendor. The bow-shape **Music Room** features lapis lazuli columns between arched floor-to-ceiling windows, and the alabaster-and-gold plasterwork of the **White Drawing Room** is a dramatic statement of wealth and power. Admission is by timed-entry ticket every 15 minutes throughout the day. It's also worth adding a guided tour of the sprawling gardens to your visit. Allow up to two hours to take it all in. **Changing the Guard** remains one of London's best free shows and culminates in front of the palace. Marching to live military bands, the old guard proceed up the Mall from St. James's Palace to Buckingham Palace. Shortly afterward, the new guard approach from Wellington Barracks. Then within the forecourt, the captains of the old and new guards symbolically transfer the keys to the palace. Get there early for the best view. ⊠ *Buckingham Palace Rd., St. James's* ☎ *020/7766–7300* ⊕ *www.royalcollection.org. uk/visit* 🎫 *£24 (£33 including garden highlights tour)* ⊗ *Closed Oct.– July except on selected dates* Ⓜ *Victoria, St. James's Park, Green Park.*

The Mall. This stately, 115-foot-wide processional route sweeping towards Trafalgar Square from the Queen Victoria Memorial at Buckingham Palace is an updated 1911 version of a promenade laid out around 1660 for the game of *paille-maille* (a type of croquet crossed with golf), which also gave the parallel road Pall Mall its name. (That's why Mall is pronounced to rhyme with "pal," not "ball.") The tarmac is colored red to represent a ceremonial red carpet. During state visits, several times a year, the Mall is traditionally bedecked with the flag of the visiting nation, alongside the Union Jack. The **Duke of York Memorial** up the steps toward Carlton House Terrace is a towering column dedicated to George III's second son, who was further immortalized in the English nursery rhyme "The Grand Old Duke of York." Be sure to stroll along the Mall on Sunday when the road is closed to traffic, or catch the bands and troops of the Household Division on their way from St. James's Palace to Buckingham Palace for the Changing the Guard. At the northernmost end of the Mall is Admiralty Arch, a stately gateway named after the adjacent Royal Navy headquarters. It was designed by Sir Aston Webb and built in 1910 as a memorial to Queen Victoria. Actually comprising five arches—two for pedestrians, two for traffic, and the central arch, which is only opened for state occasions—it was a government building until 2012, and has even served as an alternative residence for the Prime Minister while Downing Street was under renovation. It is currently being transformed into a luxury hotel. Look out for the bronze nose grafted onto the inside wall of the right-hand traffic arch (when facing the Mall); it was placed there in secret by a mischievous artist in 1997 and has been allowed to remain. ⊠ *St. James's* Ⓜ *Charing Cross, Green Park.*

Piccadilly Circus. The origins of the name "Piccadilly" relate to a humble 17th-century tailor from the Strand named Robert Baker who sold piccadills—stiff ruffled collars all the rage in courtly circles—and built a house with the proceeds. Snobs dubbed his new-money mansion Piccadilly Hall, and the name stuck. Pride of place in the circus—a circular junction until the construction of Shaftesbury Avenue in 1886—belongs to the statue universally referred to as Eros, dating to 1893 (although even most Londoners don't know that it is, in reality, a representation of Eros's brother Anteros, the Greek God of requited love). The other instantly recognizable feature of Piccadilly Circus is the enormous bank of lit-up billboards on the north side; if you're passing at night, frame them behind the Tube entrance sign on the corner of Regent Street for an unforgettable photograph. ⊠ *St. James's* Ⓜ *Piccadilly Circus.*

The Queen's Gallery. Technically speaking, the sovereign doesn't "own" the rare and exquisite works of art in the Royal Collection: she merely holds them in trust for the nation—and what a collection it is. Only a selection is on view at any one time, presented in themed exhibitions. Let the excellent (and free) audio guide take you through the elegant galleries filled with some of the world's greatest artworks.

A rough timeline of the major royal collectors starts with Charles I (who also commissioned Rubens to paint the Banqueting House ceiling). An avid art enthusiast, Charles established the basis of the Royal Collection, purchasing works by Raphael, Titian, Caravaggio, and Dürer.

During the Civil War and in the aftermath of Charles's execution, many masterpieces were sold abroad and subsequently repatriated by Charles II. George III, who bought Buckingham House and converted it into a palace, scooped up a notable collection of Venetian (including Canaletto), Renaissance (Bellini and Raphael), and Dutch (Vermeer) art, and a large number of baroque drawings, in addition to patronizing English contemporary artists such as Gainsborough and Beechey. The Prince Regent, later George IV, had a particularly good eye for Rembrandt, equestrian works by Stubbs, and lavish portraits by Lawrence. Queen Victoria had a penchant for Landseer animals and landscapes, and Frith's contemporary scenes. Later, Edward VII indulged Queen Alexandra's love of Fabergé, and many royal tours around the empire produced gifts of gorgeous caliber, such as the Cullinan diamond from South Africa and an emerald-studded belt from India. Tickets are valid for one year from the date of entry. ⊠ *Buckingham Palace, Buckingham Palace Rd., St. James's* ☎ *030/3123–7334* ⊕ *www.royalcollection.org. uk* ◳ *£11; joint ticket with Royal Mews £19* Ⓜ *Victoria, St. James's Park, Green Park.*

FAMILY **Royal Mews.** Fairy-tale gold-and-glass coaches and sleek Rolls-Royce state cars emanate from the Royal Mews, next door to the Queen's Gallery. Designed by John Nash, the Mews serves as the headquarters for Her Majesty's travel department (so beware of closures for state visits), complete with the Queen's own special breed of horses, ridden by wigged postilions decked in red-and-gold regalia. Between the stables and the riding school arena are exhibits of polished saddlery and riding tack. The highlight of the Mews is the splendid Gold State Coach, a piece of art on wheels, with its sculpted tritons and sea gods. There are activities for children, and free guided tours are available April through October (daily at 10:15, then hourly 11–4). ⊠ *Buckingham Palace, Buckingham Palace Rd., St. James's* ☎ *030/3123–7302* ⊕ *www. royalcollection.org.uk* ◳ *£11; joint ticket with Queen's Gallery £19* ⊘ *Closed Dec.–Jan. and Sun. in Nov.* Ⓜ *Victoria, St. James's Park.*

Spencer House. Ancestral abode of the Spencers—Princess Diana's family—this is perhaps the finest extant example of an elegant 18th-century London town house. Reflecting his passion for the Grand Tour and classical antiquities, the first Earl Spencer commissioned architect John Vardy to adapt designs from ancient Rome for a magnificent private palace. Vardy was responsible for the exteriors, including the gorgeous west-facing Palladian facade, its pediment adorned with classical statues, and the ground-floor interiors, notably the lavish Palm Room, with its spectacular screen of columns covered in gilded carvings that resemble gold palm trees. The lavish style was meant not only to attest to Spencer's power and wealth but also to celebrate his marriage, a love match then rare in aristocratic circles (the palms are a symbol of marital fertility). Midway through construction—the house was built between 1756 and 1766—Spencer changed architects and hired James "Athenian" Stuart, whose designs were based on a classical Greek aesthetic, to decorate the gilded State Rooms on the first floor. These include the Painted Room, the first completely neoclassical room in Europe. Since the 1940s, the house has been leased by the Spencers to a succession of wealthy residents. Entry is by tours only, which occur on Sundays only. ■ TIP→ Note that children under 10 are not allowed inside. ⊠ *27 St. James's Pl., St. James's* ☏ *020/7514–1958* ⊕ *www.spencerhouse.co.uk* ☏ *£15* ⊙ *Closed Mon.–Sat.* Ⓜ *Green Park.*

St. James's Church. Bombed by the German Luftwaffe in 1940 and not restored until 1954, this was one of the last of Sir Christopher Wren's London churches—and his favorite. Completed in 1684, it contains one of the finest works by the master carver Grinling Gibbons (1648–1721): an ornate limewood *reredos* (the screen behind the altar). The church is a lively place, with all manner of lectures and concerts (some are free). A café occupies a fine location right alongside the church, while a small sedate garden is tucked away at the rear. The market out front is full of surprises; come Monday and Tuesday for food stalls, and Wednesday through Saturday for arts and crafts. ⊠ *197 Piccadilly, St. James's* ☏ *020/7734–4511* ⊕ *www.sjp.org.uk* ☏ *Free* Ⓜ *Piccadilly Circus, Green Park.*

St. James's Palace. Commissioned by Henry VIII, this Tudor brick palace was the residence of kings and queens for more than 300 years; indeed, while all monarchs have actually lived at Buckingham Palace since Queen Victoria's day, it is still one of the official residences of the Royal Family. (This is why foreign ambassadors are received by the "Court of St. James.") Today it contains various royal apartments and offices, including the working office of Prince Charles. The palace is not open to the public, but the surprisingly low-key Tudor exterior is well worth the short detour from the Mall. Friary Court out front is a splendid setting for Trooping the Colour, part of the Queen's official birthday celebrations. Everyone loves to take a snapshot of the scarlet-coated guardsman standing sentry outside the imposing Tudor gateway. Note that the Changing the Guard ceremony at St. James's Palace occurs only on days when the guard at Buckingham Palace is changed. If you're approaching from St. James Street, take a quick peek at the delightfully old-looking **Berry Bros. & Rudd** wine store at No. 3, near the back entrance to the palace; it's been trading here continuously since 1698. ⊠ *Friary Ct., St. James's* Ⓜ *Green Park.*

FAMILY
Fodor's Choice
★
St. James's Park. There is a story that, many years ago, a royal once inquired of a courtier how much it would cost to close St. James's Park to the public. "Only your crown, ma'am" came the reply. Bordered by three palaces—Buckingham, St. James', and the governmental complex of the Palace of Westminster—this is one of London's loveliest public parks. It's also the oldest; the former marshland was acquired by Henry VIII in 1532 as a nursery for his deer. Later, James I drained the land and installed an aviary, which gave Birdcage Walk its name, and a zoo (complete with crocodiles, camels, and an elephant). When Charles II returned from exile in France, where he had been hugely impressed by the splendor of the gardens at the Palace of Versailles, he transformed the park into formal gardens, with avenues, fruit orchards, and a canal. Lawns were grazed by goats, sheep, and deer, and in the 18th century the park became a different kind of hunting ground, for wealthy lotharios looking to pick up nighttime escorts. A century later, John Nash redesigned the landscape in a more naturalistic, romantic

style, and if you gaze down the lake toward Buckingham Palace, you could easily believe yourself to be on a country estate.

A large population of waterfowl—including pelicans, geese, ducks, and swans (which belong to the Queen)—breed on and around Duck Island at the east end of the lake. The pelicans are fed at 2:30 daily. From March to October, the deck chairs (charge levied) come out, crammed with office workers at midday, eating lunch while being serenaded by music from the bandstands. One of the best times to stroll the leafy walkways is after dark, with Westminster Abbey and the Houses of Parliament rising above the floodlit lake. ⊠ *The Mall or Horse Guards approach or Birdcage Walk, St. James's* ⊕ *www.royalparks.org.uk* Ⓜ *St. James's Park, Westminster.*

St. James's Square. One of London's oldest squares, St. James's was first laid out in the 1660s. It soon became the capital's most fashionable address; by 1720, it was home to 14 dukes and earls. These days you're more likely to find it populated with office workers eating their lunches under the shade of its leafy old trees on a warm summer's day, but it still has some prestigious residents. Most famous among them is the **London Library** at No. 14, one of the several 18th-century residences spared by World War II bombs. Founded by Thomas Carlyle, it contains a million or so volumes, making it the world's largest independent lending library, and is also considered the best private humanities library in the land. Nonmembers can take an evening tour of the library, although reservations must be made in advance. ⊠ *St. James's* Ⓜ *Piccadilly Circus.*

MAYFAIR AND MARYLEBONE

Getting Oriented

Mayfair and Marylebone

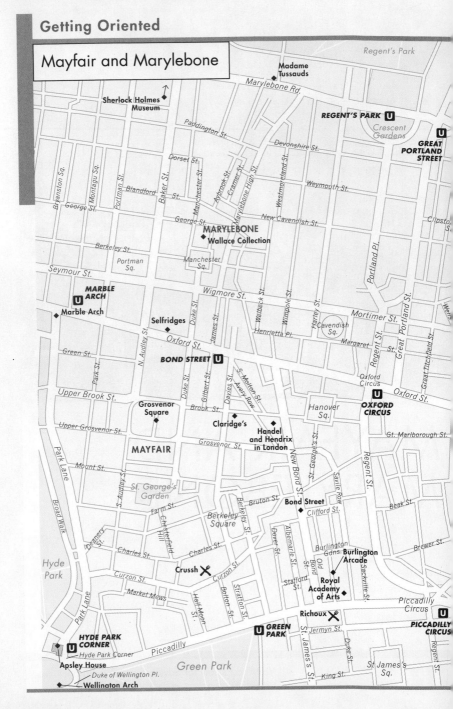

Regent's Park

Madame Tussauds
Marylebone Rd.

Sherlock Holmes Museum

Paddington St.

REGENT'S PARK U

Crescent Gardens

GREAT PORTLAND STREET U

Devonshire St.

Dorset St.

Blandford St.
Baker St.
Weymouth St.

Bryanston Sq.
Montagu Sq.
Portman St.
Clipsto.

George St.
Dorset St.
Manchester St.
Aybrook St.
Cramer St.
Marylebone High St.
Westmoreland St.

George St.
New Cavendish St.

Berkeley St.
MARYLEBONE
Wallace Collection

Portman Sq.
Manchester Sq.

Seymour St.
Portland Pl.

MARBLE ARCH U
Wigmore St.
Welbeck St.
Wimpole St.
Harley St.
Mortimer St.
Great Portland St.
Wells

Marble Arch
Henrietta Pl.
Cavendish Sq.
Margaret St.
Gt. Titchfield St.

Selfridges
Duke St.
Oxford St.
James St.

Green St.
BOND STREET U

N. Audley St.
Park St.
Duke St.
Gilbert St.
Davies St.
S. Molton St.
Avery Row
Oxford Circus
OXFORD St.

Upper Brook St.
OXFORD CIRCUS U

Grosvenor Square
Brook St.
Hanover Sq.

Upper Grosvenor St.
Claridge's
Handel and Hendrix in London
Gt. Marlborough St.

MAYFAIR
Grosvenor St.
New Bond St.
St. George's St.
Regent St.

Mount St.
St. George's Garden
Savile Row

Park Lane
S. Audley St.
Chesterfield Hill
Farm St.
Bruton St.
Bond Street
Beak St.

Broad Walk
Deanery St.
Charles St.
Berkeley Square
Clifford St.
Brewer St.

Hyde Park
Charles St.
Dover St.
Albemarle St.
Old Bond St.
Burlington Gdns.
Burlington Arcade
Sackville St.

Crussh
Curzon St.
Stafford St.
Royal Academy of Arts
Piccadilly Circus

Market Mews
Half Moon St.
Bolton St.
Stratton St.
Richoux
PICCADILLY CIRCUS

HYDE PARK CORNER U
GREEN PARK U
Jermyn St.
St. James's St.
Duke St.
Regent St.

Apsley House
Hyde Park Corner
Piccadilly
King St.
St James's Sq.

Wellinaton Arch
Duke of Wellington Pl.
Green Park

TOP REASONS TO GO

The Duke of Wellington's home: The Iron Duke's Apsley House is filled with splendid salons lined with grand Old Master paintings.

Fashion galore: There's great shopping aplenty on Bond and Mount streets, where the likes of McQueen and McCartney will keep your credit card occupied, but don't forget stylish, gigantic Selfridges.

London's most charming shopping arcade: Built for Lord Cavendish in 1819, the beautiful Burlington Arcade is right out of a Victorian daguerreotype.

The Wallace Collection: Savor room after room of magnificent furniture, porcelain, silver, and top Old Master paintings, in the former residence of the marquesses of Hertford.

Claridge's: Afternoon tea at this sumptuous art deco gem is the perfect end to a shopping spree in Mayfair.

FEELING PECKISH?

Crussh. This successful chain serves up delicious juices and smoothies, as well as sandwiches, soups, and wraps. Decamp to nearby Green Park, where—if you're lucky—you can grab one of the deck chairs. ✉ *1 Curzon St., Mayfair* ☎ *020/7629–2554* ⊕ *www.crussh.com* ⊙ *Closed weekends* Ⓜ *Green Park.*

Richoux. This has been an affordable refuge from busy Piccadilly for more than a century. Simple but well-executed French bistro food is served all day, as well as scrumptious afternoon tea. ✉ *172 Piccadilly, Mayfair* ☎ *020/7493–2204* ⊕ *www.richoux.co.uk* Ⓜ *Green Park, Piccadilly Circus.*

GETTING THERE

Three Tube stations on the Central Line are handy for reaching these neighborhoods: Marble Arch, Bond Street (also on the Jubilee Line), and Oxford Circus (also on the Victoria and Bakerloo lines).

You can also take the Piccadilly or Bakerloo Line to the Piccadilly Circus Tube Station, the Piccadilly Line to the Hyde Park Corner Station, or the Piccadilly, Victoria, or Jubilee Line to the Green Park Station.

The best buses are the 22, which takes in Green Park, Berkeley Square, and New Bond Street, and the 9—London's oldest existing bus route—which runs along Piccadilly.

MAKING THE MOST OF YOUR TIME

Set aside at least a day to experience Mayfair and Marylebone. Leave enough time for shopping and also to wander casually through the streets and squares.

The only areas to avoid are the Tube stations at rush hour, and Oxford Street if you don't like crowds. At all costs, stay away from Oxford Circus around 5 pm, when the commuter rush can, at times, resemble an East African wildebeest migration—but without the charm.

The area becomes quiet at night, so plan to party elsewhere.

3

Sightseeing
★★★★
Nightlife
★
Dining
★★★★
Lodging
★★★★
Shopping
★★★★

Mayfair forms the core of London's West End, the city's most stylish central area. This neighborhood oozes class and old-school style. The sense of being in one of the world's most wealthy and powerful cities is palpable as you wander along its grand and graceful streets. Scoot across the district's one exception to all this elegance—Oxford Street—and you'll discover the pleasant thoroughfares of Marylebone, the most central of London's many "villages."

MAYFAIR

Updated by
James O'Neill

Ultra-ritzy Mayfair, lined with beautiful 18th-century mansions (along with Edwardian apartment buildings made of deep-red brick), is the address of choice for many of London's wealthiest residents—note the number of Rolls-Royces, Bentleys, and Jaguars on the streets. Even the delivery vans all seem to bear some royal coat of arms, advertising that they've been purveyors of fine goods for as long as anyone can remember.

The district can't claim to be stuffed with must-sees, but that is part of its appeal. There is no shortage of history and gorgeous architecture; the streets here are custom-built for window-shopping, expansive strolling, and getting a peek into the lifestyles of London's rich and famous, past and present. Mayfair is primarily residential, so its homes are off-limits except for one satisfyingly grand example: **Apsley House,** the Duke of Wellington's home, built by Robert Adam in 1771, and once known as No. 1, London; the nearby **Wellington Arch** also commemorates the great hero.

Despite being bordered by four of the busiest streets in London—the busy budget-shopping mecca Oxford Street (to the north), the major traffic artery Park Lane (to the west), and the bustling Regent Street and Piccadilly (to the east and south, respectively)—Mayfair itself is remarkably traffic-free and a delight to explore. Starting at **Selfridges,**

Each June for the past 240 years, the iconic Royal Academy of Arts has put on its Summer Exhibition, a huge draw for art-loving visitors and Londoners alike.

on Oxford Street, a southward stroll will take you through quiet streets lined with Georgian town houses (the area was largely developed in the 17th and 18th centuries). From there, with a bit of artful navigating, you can reach four pleasant patches of green: **Grosvenor Square, Berkeley Square, Hanover Square,** with its splendid **St. George's Church** where Handel worshipped, and the quiet **St. George's Gardens,** bounded by a maze of streets and mews. Some of London's most exclusive shopping destinations are here, including **Mount Street, Bruton Street, Savile Row,** and the **Burlington Arcade.** The **Royal Academy of Arts** is at the southern fringe of Mayfair on Piccadilly, beyond which begins the more sedate St. James's.

Fodor's Choice
★

Apsley House. Apsley House was built by Robert Adam in the 1770s and was bought by the Duke of Wellington two years after his famous victory over Napoléon at the Battle of Waterloo in 1815. Long known simply as No. 1, London, on account of its being the first mansion at the old tollgate from Knightsbridge village, the Duke's old regency abode continues to look quite grand. Victory over the French made Wellington the greatest soldier and statesman in the land. The so-called Iron Duke lived here from 1817 until his death in 1852, and, although the 7th Duke of Wellington gave the house to the nation, the family retained some residential rights. As you'd expect, the mansion has many uniforms and weapons on display, but it also houses a celebrated art collection, the bulk of which was once owned by Joseph Bonaparte, onetime King of Spain and younger brother of Napoléon. With works by Brueghel, Van Dyck, and Rubens, as well as the Spanish masters Velázquez and Murillo (note the former's famous portrait of

Marble Arch was originally a gateway to Buckingham Palace before it was moved to the corner of Hyde Park.

Pope Innocent X), the collection also includes a Goya portrait of the duke himself on horseback. An 11-foot-tall statue of a nude (fig-leafed) Napoléon looms over you as you approach the grand central staircase. The statue was taken from the Louvre and given as a gift to Wellington from the grateful British government in 1816. ✉ *149 Piccadilly, Hyde Park Corner, Mayfair* ☎ *0370/333–1181* ⊕ *www.english-heritage.org. uk* 🎟 *£10; joint ticket with Wellington Arch £12.70* ☽ *Closed Mon. and Tues. year-round and Wed.–Fri. in Nov.–Mar.* Ⓜ *Hyde Park Corner.*

Bond Street. This world-class shopping haunt is divided into northern "New" (1710) and southern "Old" (1690) halves. You can spot the juncture by a bronzed bench on which Franklin D. Roosevelt sits companionably next to Winston Churchill. At No. 34-35, on New Bond Street, you'll find **Sotheby's,** the world-famous auction house, as well as upscale retailers like Asprey's, Burberry, Louis Vuitton, and Church's. You'll find even more opportunities to flirt with financial ruin on Old Bond Street, with flagship boutiques of top-end designers like Chanel, Gucci, and Yves Saint Laurent; an array of fine jewelers including Tiffany & Co.; and art dealers Richard Green, Spink Leger, and Trinity Fine Art. **Cork Street,** which parallels the top half of Old Bond Street, is where many top dealers in contemporary art have their galleries. ✉ *Mayfair* ⊕ *www.bondstreet.co.uk* Ⓜ *Bond St., Green Park.*

Fodor'sChoice
★   **Burlington Arcade.** With ceilings and lights now restored to how they would have looked when it was built in 1819, Burlington Arcade is the finest of Mayfair's enchanting covered shopping alleys. Originally built for Lord Cavendish, it was meant to stop commoners from flinging garbage into his garden at next-door Burlington House. Top-hatted

watchmen called beadles—the world's smallest private police force—still patrol, preserving decorum by preventing you from singing, running, or carrying an open umbrella. The arcade is also the main link between the Royal Academy of Arts and its extended galleries at 6 Burlington Gardens. ⊠ *Piccadilly, Mayfair* ☎ *020/7493–1764* ⊕ *www. burlington-arcade.co.uk* Ⓜ *Green Park, Piccadilly Circus.*

Grosvenor Square. Pronounced *"Grove*-na," this leafy square was laid out in 1725–31 and is as desirable an address today as it was then. Americans have certainly always thought so—from John Adams, the second president, who as ambassador lived at No. 38, to Dwight D. Eisenhower, whose wartime headquarters was at No. 20. The entire west side of the square was home to the U.S. Embassy for over 50 years until its relocation south of the river. In the square itself stand memorials to Franklin D. Roosevelt and those who died on September 11, 2001. Grosvenor Chapel, completed in 1730 and used by Eisenhower's men during World War II, stands a couple of blocks south of the square on South Audley Street, with the entrance to pretty **St. George's Gardens** to its left. ⊠ *Mayfair* Ⓜ *Bond St.*

Handel and Hendrix in London. This fascinating museum celebrates the lives of not one, but two, musical geniuses: classical composer George Frederick Handel and rock guitar legend Jimi Hendrix. Comprising two adjoining buildings, the bulk of the museum centers on the life and works of Handel who lived at No. 25 for more than 30 years until his death in 1759. In rooms decorated in fine Georgian style, you can linger over original manuscripts and gaze at portraits. Some of the composer's most famous pieces were created here, including the *Messiah* and *Music for the Royal Fireworks*. Fast-forward 200 years or so, and the apartment on the upper floors of No. 23 housed one of rock's great innovators, Jimi Hendrix, for a short but creative period in the late 1960s. The apartment has been lovingly restored, complete with replica furniture, fixtures, and fittings from Hendrix's heyday. ⊠ *23–25 Brook St., entrance in Lancashire Court, Mayfair* ☎ *020/7495–1685* ⊕ *www. handelhendrix.org* 🎟 *£10* 🕙 *Closed Sun.* Ⓜ *Bond St.*

Marble Arch. John Nash's 1827 arch, moved here from Buckingham Palace in 1851, stands amid the traffic whirlpool where Bayswater Road segues into Oxford Street, at the top of Park Lane. The arch actually contains three small chambers, which served as a police station until the mid-20th century. Search the sidewalk on the traffic island opposite the movie theater for the stone plaque recalling the Tyburn Tree, an elaborately designed gallows that stood here for 400 years, until 1783. The condemned would be conveyed here in their finest clothes from Newgate Prison in The City, and were expected to affect a casual indifference or face a merciless heckling from the crowds. Towering across the grass from the arch toward Tyburn Way is *Horse at Water,* a vast patina-green statue of a horse's head by sculptor Nic Fiddian. Cross over (or under) to the northeastern corner of Hyde Park for Speakers' Corner, a parcel of land long-dedicated to the principle of free speech. On Sunday, people of all views—or none at all—come to pontificate, listen, and debate about everything under the sun. ⊠ *Park La., Mayfair* Ⓜ *Marble Arch.*

Fodor's Choice   **Royal Academy of Arts.** Burlington House was built in 1664, with later
★   Palladian additions for the 3rd Earl of Burlington in 1720. The piazza
in front dates from 1873, when the Renaissance-style buildings around
the courtyard were designed by Banks and Barry to house a gaggle of
noble scientific societies, including the Royal Society of Chemistry and
the Royal Astronomical Society.

The house itself is home to the Royal Academy of Arts and an ambitious redevelopment for the academy's 250th anniversary in 2018
has meant that even more of its 46,000 treasures are now on display.
The statue of the academy's first president, Sir Joshua Reynolds, pal-
ette in hand, stands prominently in the piazza. Free tours show off
part of the collection and the excellent temporary exhibitions. Every
June through August, the RA puts on its Summer Exhibition, a huge
and eclectic collection of art by living Royal Academicians and many
other contemporary artists. ⊠ *Burlington House, Piccadilly, Mayfair*
☎ *020/7300–8000* ⊕ *www.royalacademy.org.uk* 🔳 *£12–£18* Ⓜ *Piccadilly Circus, Green Park.*

Wellington Arch. Opposite the Duke of Wellington's mansion, Apsley
House, this majestic stone arch surveys the traffic rushing around Hyde
Park Corner. Designed by Decimus Burton and completed in 1828, it
was created as a grand entrance to the west side of London and echoes
the design of that other landmark gate, Marble Arch. Both were tri-
umphal arches commemorating Britain's victory against France in the
Napoleonic Wars. Atop the building, the Angel of Peace descends on the
quadriga, or four-horse chariot of war. Inside the arch, three floors of
permanent and temporary exhibits reveal the monument's history. From
the balconies at the top of the arch you can peek into the Queen's back
garden at across-the-road Buckingham Palace. ⊠ *Hyde Park Corner,
Mayfair* ☎ *020/7930–2726* ⊕ *www.english-heritage.org.uk* 🔳 *£5; joint
ticket with Apsley House £12.70* Ⓜ *Hyde Park Corner.*

MARYLEBONE

A favorite of newspaper style sections everywhere, Marylebone High
Street forms the heart of Marylebone Village (pronounced "Marr-le-
bone"), a vibrant, upscale neighborhood that encompasses the squares
and streets around High Street and nearby Marylebone Lane. The district took its name from a church dedicated to St. Mary and the bourne
(another word for "stream") that ran through the original village.
Nowadays, it's hard to believe you're just a few blocks north of gaudy
Oxford Street as you wander in and out of Marylebone's small shops
and boutiques, the best of which include Cadenheads Whisky Shop
and Tasting Room (26 Chiltern Street); La Fromagerie (2–6 Moxon
Street), an excellent cheese shop; Daunt Books (Nos. 83–84 Marylebone High Street), a superlative travel bookshop; the "Cabbages and
Frocks" market (Saturday 11–5) on the grounds of the St. Marylebone
Parish Church, purveying specialty foods and vintage clothing; and a
large farmers' and artisanal-food market (Sunday 10–2) in a parking
lot on Cramer Street, just behind High Street. But some memorable

At 221B Baker Street, you can immerse yourself in the world of one Mr. Sherlock Holmes.

sights await, too, including the best remnant of ancien régime France in London, the fabled Wallace Collection.

FAMILY **Madame Tussauds.** One of London's busiest tourist attractions, this is nothing less than the world's most famous exhibition of lifelike wax-work models of celebrities. Madame T. learned her craft while making death masks of French Revolution victims, and in 1835 she set up her first show of the famous ones near this spot. Top billing still goes to the murderers in the Chamber of Horrors, who stare glassy-eyed at visitors—one from an electric chair, one sitting next to the tin bath where he dissolved several wives in quicklime. ■TIP→ Beat the crowds by booking timed-entry tickets in advance. You can also buy nondated, "priority access" tickets via the website (at a premium). ✉ *Marylebone Rd., Regent's Park* ☎ *0844/248–2624 for timed-entry tickets* ⊕ *www.madametussauds.com* ✉ *£29–£70* Ⓜ *Baker St.*

Sherlock Holmes Museum. Outside Baker Street Station, by the Maryle-bone Road exit, is a 9-foot-high bronze statue of Arthur Conan Doyle's celebrated detective, who "lived" around the corner at number 221B Baker Street—now a museum to all things Sherlock. Inside, Mrs. Hudson, Holmes's housekeeper, guides you into a series of Victorian rooms where the great man lived, worked, and played the violin. It's all carried off with such genuine enthusiasm and attention to detail that you could be forgiven for thinking that Mr. Holmes actually *did* exist. ✉ *221B Baker St., Regent's Park* ☎ *020/7224–3688* ⊕ *www.sherlock-holmes. co.uk* ✉ *£15* Ⓜ *Baker St.*

FAMILY   **Wallace Collection.** With its Great Gallery stunningly refurbished, there's
Fodor'sChoice   even more reason to visit this exquisite gem of an art gallery—although
★   housing one of the world's finest collections of Old Master paintings is
reason enough. This glorious collection and the 18th-century mansion
in which it's located were bequeathed to the nation by Lady Julie-Amé-
lie-Charlotte Wallace, the widow of Sir Richard Wallace (1818–90).
Wallace's father, the 4th Marquess of Hertford, took a house in Paris
after the French Revolution and set about snapping up paintings by
what were then dangerously unpopular artists. Frans Hals's *Laughing
Cavalier* is probably the most famous painting here, or perhaps Jean-
Honoré Fragonard's *The Swing*. The full list of painters in the collection
reads like a "who's who" of classical European art—from Rubens,
Rembrandt, and Van Dyck to Canaletto, Titian, and Velázquez. English
works include paintings by Gainsborough and Turner. There are also
fine collections of furniture, porcelain, Renaissance gold, and *majolica*
(15th- and 16th-century Italian tin-glazed pottery). With craft activities,
hands-on sessions, the "Little Draw" drawing workshops, as well as the
chance to try on a suit of armor in the "Arms and Armour" collection,
there's plenty to keep kids occupied, too. The conditions of the bequest
mean that no part of the collection can leave the building; this is the
only place in the world you'll ever be able to see these works. ⊠ *Hertford House, Manchester Sq., Marylebone* ☎ *020/7563–9500* ⊕ *www.
wallacecollection.org* ⊠ *Free* Ⓜ *Bond St.*

4

SOHO AND COVENT GARDEN

Getting Oriented

GETTING THERE	TOP REASONS TO GO
Almost all Tube lines cross the Covent Garden and Soho areas, so it's easy to hop off for dinner or a show in one of the hippest parts of London. For Soho, take any train to Piccadilly Circus, Leicester Square, Oxford Circus, or Tottenham Court Road. For Covent Garden, get off at Covent Garden Station on the Piccadilly Line. (It may be easier to exit the Tube at Leicester Square or Holborn and walk.) Thirty buses connect to the Covent Garden area from all over London; check out the area's website (⊕ *www.covent-garden.london*).	**Newburgh Quarter:** Head to this adorable warren of cobblestone streets for stylish boutiques, edgy stores, and young indie upstarts. **Dining:** London has fallen in love with its chefs, and Soho is home to many of the most talked-about restaurants in town. **Covent Garden Piazza:** Eliza Doolittle's former backyard has been taken over by boutiques and street performers who play to the crowds from morning to night. **Royal Opera House:** Even if you're not going to the opera or ballet, take in the beautiful architecture and sense of history. **West End Theater:** Shaftesbury Avenue is the heart of London's theater district, where more than 40 West End theaters pull in the crowds with a mix of extravagant musicals, Shakespeare, and new plays.

Soho and Covent Garden

MAKING THE MOST OF YOUR TIME

You can comfortably tour all the sights around Soho and Covent Garden in a day. Make sure to leave plenty of time to watch street entertainment or shop at the stalls around Covent Garden Piazza or in the fashion boutiques of Soho in the afternoon. Save some energy for a night on the town in Soho.

GAY LONDON

Old Compton Street in Soho is the epicenter of London's affluent, stylish gay scene. There are some fun nightclubs in the area, with crowds forming in Soho Square, south of Oxford Street. Some of the more well-known clubs and bars in the area include Friendly Society, Ku Bar, the Yard, and She.

FEELING PECKISH?

The coffee shops on Covent Garden Piazza can be overpriced and mediocre. Head north for Seven Dials or west for Soho when the munchies strike.

Canela. Bright and casual by day, intimate and atmospheric by night, this is a great spot for refueling mid–shopping trip, grabbing a bite before a show (think filling dishes like pork stew or salted cod, plus charcuterie and sandwiches), or lingering over a glass of reasonably priced Portuguese wine. ✉ 33 Earlham St., Covent Garden ☎ 020/7240–6926 ⊕ www.canelacafe.com Ⓜ Covent Garden, Leicester Sq.

Maison Bertaux. This eccentric little place has been around since the end of the 19th century. Not the finest coffee around, but a nice range of teas and glasses of wine, plus fab French cakes, tarts, and savory quiches more than make up for that. ✉ 28 Greek St., Soho ☎ 020/7437–6007 ⊕ www.maisonbertaux.com Ⓜ Leicester Sq.

Sightseeing
★★★

Nightlife
★★★★★

Dining
★★★★

Lodging
★★

Shopping
★★★

A red-light district no more, today's Soho is more stylish than seedy and offers some of London's best bars, live music venues, restaurants, and theaters. By day, this hotbed of media production reverts to the business side of its late-night scene. If Soho is all about showbiz, neighboring Covent Garden is devoted to culture. Both districts offer an abundance of narrow streets packed with one-of-a-kind shops and lots of antique character.

SOHO

Updated by
Jo Caird

Soho, which, along with Covent Garden, is loosely known as "the West End," has long been known as the entertainment and arts quarter of London's center. Bordered to the north by Oxford Street, Regent Street to the west, and Chinatown and Leicester Square to the south, the narrow streets of Soho are unabashedly devoted to pleasure. Wardour Street bisects the neighborhood, with lots of interesting boutiques and some of London's best-value restaurants to the west (especially around Foubert's Place and on Brewer and Lexington streets). Most nightlife lies to the east—including the gay clubs of Old Compton Street—and beyond that is the city's densest collection of theaters, on Shaftesbury Avenue. London's compact Chinatown is wedged between Soho and Leicester Square. A bit of erudition surfaces to the east of the square on Charing Cross Road, famous for its secondhand bookshops, and on tiny Cecil Court, a pedestrianized passage lined with small antiquarian booksellers.

Fodor's Choice
★

Newburgh Quarter. Want to see the hip style of today's London? Find it one block east of Carnaby Street—where the look of the '60s "Swinging London" was born—in an adorable warren of cobblestone streets now lined with specialty boutiques, edgy stores, and young indie upstarts. A check of the ingredients reveals one part '60s London, one part futuristic fetishism, one part steampunk, and one part British street swagger.

A BRIEF HISTORY OF SOHO

Almost as soon as a 17th-century housing development covered what had been a royal park and hunting ground, Soho earned a reputation for entertainment, bohemianism, and cosmopolitan liberality. When the authorities adopted a zero-tolerance policy towards soliciting in 1991 (the most recent of several attempts to end Soho's sex trade), they cracked down on an old neighborhood tradition that still resurfaces from time to time.

Successive waves of refugees—French Huguenots in the 1680s, followed by Germans, Russians, Poles, Greeks, Italians, and Chinese—settled and brought their national cuisines with them. So when dining out became fashionable after World War I, Soho was the natural place for restaurants to flourish (as they continue to do today).

Among the luminaries who have made their home here are landscape painter John Constable; Casanova; Canaletto, the great painter of Venice; the poet William Blake; and Karl Marx. In the 1950s and '60s, Soho was London's artists' quarter and the place to find the top jazz clubs and art galleries.

The outlines of present-day Covent Garden took shape in the 1630s, when Inigo Jones turned what had been agricultural land into Britain's first planned public square. After the Great Fire of 1666, it became the site of England's largest fruit-and-vegetable market (the flower market arrived in the 19th century). The district's many theaters and taverns gave the area a somewhat dubious reputation, and after the produce market relocated in 1973, the surviving buildings were scheduled for demolition. A local campaign saved them, and the restored market opened in 1980.

The new-bohemian look best flourishes in shops like Peckham Rye, a tiny boutique crowded with rockers and fashionistas who adore its grunge–meets- *Brideshead Revisited* vibe. Quality independent coffee shops abound—take a break at Department of Coffee and Social Affairs, where you can also browse for home coffee making equipment. ⊠ *Newburgh St., Foubert's Pl., Ganton St., and Carnaby St., Soho* ⊕ *www.carnaby.co.uk.*

COVENT GARDEN

To the east of Charing Cross Road lies Covent Garden, the famous marketplace–turned–shopping mall. Although boutiques and haute fashion shops line the surrounding streets, many Londoners come to Covent Garden for its two outposts of culture: the **Royal Opera House** and the **Donmar Warehouse,** one of London's best and most innovative theaters. The area becomes more sedate just to the east, at the end of Wellington Street, where semicircular Aldwych is lined with grand buildings, and from there the Strand leads to the huge stately piazza of **Somerset House,** a vibrant center of contemporary arts and home to the many masterpieces on view at the **Courtauld Gallery.** You'll get a sense of old-fashioned London just behind the Strand, where small lanes are little changed since the 18th century. On the way to the verdant **Embankment Gardens** bordering the Thames, you may pass the **Adam Houses,** the remnants of a grand 18th-century riverside housing development, and the **Benjamin Franklin House,** where the noted statesman lived in the years leading up to the American Revolution.

Covent Garden joins Soho as an arts-and-entertainment center in the city, popularly referred to as "the West End." The neighborhood centers on the Piazza, site of the original Covent Garden market. High Holborn to the north, Kingsway to the east, and the Strand to the south form its other boundaries.

The Adam Houses. Only a few structures remain of what was once a regal riverfront row of houses on a 3-acre site, but such is their quality that they are worth a detour from the Strand. The work of 18th-century Scottish architects and interior designers (John, Robert, James, and William Adam, known collectively as the Adam brothers), the original development was damaged in the 19th century during the building of the Embankment, and mostly demolished in 1936 to be replaced by an art deco tower. The original houses still standing are protected, and give a glimpse of their former grandeur. Numbers 1–4 Robert Street and 7 and 10 Adam Street are the best. ⊠ *Robert St. and Adam St., off The Strand, Covent Garden* Ⓜ *Charing Cross, Embankment.*

Benjamin Franklin House. This architecturally significant 1730 house is the only surviving residence of American statesman, scientist, writer, and inventor Benjamin Franklin, who lived and worked here for 16 years preceding the American Revolution. The restored Georgian town house has been left unfurnished, the better to show off the original features: 18th-century paneling, stoves, beams, bricks, and windows. Visitors are led around the house by the costumed character of Polly Hewson, the daughter of Franklin's landlady, who interacts with engaging video projections and recorded voices (Wednesday–Sunday). On Monday you can take a guided tour focusing on the architectural details of the building, and a walking tour of the surrounding area lasting up to 90 minutes sets off from the house every morning at 10:30. ⊠ *36 Craven St., Covent Garden* ☎ *020/7839–2006* ⊕ *www.benjaminfranklinhouse.org* ✉ *Historical experience £8; architectural tour £6; walking tour £5 (reservations recommended)* ⊘ *Closed Tues.* Ⓜ *Charing Cross, Embankment.*

Covent Garden Piazza. Once home to London's main flower market, where *My Fair Lady's* Eliza Doolittle peddled her blooms, the square around which Covent Garden pivots is known as the Piazza. In the center, the fine old market building now houses stalls and shops selling expensive clothing, plus several restaurants and cafés, and knickknack stores that are good for gifts. One particular gem is Benjamin Pollock's Toyshop at No. 44 in the market. Established in the 1880s, it sells delightful toy theaters. The superior **Apple Market** has good crafts stalls on most days, too. On the south side of the Piazza, the indoor **Jubilee Market,** with its stalls of clothing, army-surplus gear, and more crafts and knickknacks, feels a bit like a flea market. In summer it may seem that everyone in the huge crowds

DID YOU KNOW?

Somerset House was lapped
by the River Thames before
the Victoria Embankment
was built in the 19th century.
The neoclassical building's
grand courtyard is home to
ice-skating in winter and
dancing fountains in summer.

Leicester Square is home to many movie theaters and a half-price theater ticket booth.

around you in the Piazza is a fellow tourist, but there's still plenty of office life in the area. Londoners who shop here tend to head for Neal Street and the area to the north of Covent Garden Tube station, rather than the market itself. In the Piazza, street performers—from global musicians to jugglers and mimes—play to the crowds, as they have done since the first English Punch and Judy Show, staged here in the 17th century. ✉ *Covent Garden* ⊕ *www.coventgarden.london* Ⓜ *Covent Garden.*

Leicester Square. Looking at the neon of the major movie houses, the fast-food outlets, and the disco entrances, you'd never guess that this square (pronounced "Lester") was a model of formality and refinement when it was first laid out around 1630. By the 19th century, the square was already bustling and disreputable, and although it's not a threatening place, you should still be on your guard, especially at night—any space so full of people is bound to attract pickpockets, and Leicester Square certainly does. Although there's a bit of residual glamour (red-carpet film premieres sometimes happen here), Londoners generally tend to avoid the place, though it's worth a visit for its hustle and bustle, its mime artists, and the pleasant modern fountain at its center. Also in the middle is a statue of a sulking Shakespeare, perhaps remembering the days when the movie houses were live theaters—burlesque houses, but live all the same. On the northeast corner, in Leicester Place, stands the church of **Notre Dame de France,** with a wonderful mural by Jean Cocteau in one of its side chapels. For more in the way of atmosphere, head north and west from here, through Chinatown and the narrow streets of Soho. ✉ *Covent Garden* Ⓜ *Leicester Sq.*

FAMILY
Fodor'sChoice
★

London Transport Museum. Housed in the old flower market at the southeast corner of Covent Garden, this stimulating museum is filled with impressive vehicle, poster, and photograph collections. As you watch the crowds drive a Tube-train simulation and gawk at the steam locomotives and horse-drawn trams (and the piles of detritus that remained behind), it's unclear who's enjoying it more: children or adults. Best of all, the kid-friendly museum (under 18 admitted free, and there's a play area) has a multilevel approach to education, including information for the youngest visitor and the most advanced transit aficionado alike. Food and drink are available

ICE-SKATING

It's hard to beat the skating experience at Somerset House, where November to January a rink is set up in the grand courtyard of this central London palace. Check the website for current prices; its popularity is enormous, and if you can't get a ticket, other atmospheric venues such as Hampton Court, the Tower of London, the London Eye, and the Natural History Museum are following Somerset House's lead in having temporary winter rinks. ☎ *0844/847–1520* ⊕ *www. somersethouse.org.uk/ice-rink.*

at the Upper Deck café, and the shop has lots of good options for gift-buying. ■TIP→ **Tickets are valid for unlimited entry for 12 months.** ⊠ *Covent Garden Piazza, Covent Garden* ☎ *020/7379–6344* ⊕ *www. ltmuseum.co.uk* £17.50 Ⓜ *Covent Garden, Leicester Sq.*

FAMILY
Fodor'sChoice
★

Somerset House. This huge complex—the work of Sir William Chambers (1723–96), and built during the reign of George III to house offices of the Navy—has been transformed from dusty government offices to one of the capital's most buzzing centers of culture and the arts, often hosting several interesting exhibitions at one time. The cobblestone Italianate courtyard, where Admiral Nelson used to walk, makes a great setting for 55 playful fountains and is transformed into a romantic ice rink in winter; the grand space is the venue for music and outdoor movie screenings in summer. The **Courtauld Gallery** (currently closed for renovations) occupies most of the north building, facing the busy Strand. Across the courtyard are the Embankment Galleries, with a vibrant calendar of design, fashion, architecture, and photography exhibitions. The East Wing has another fine exhibition space, and events are sometimes also held in the atmospherically gloomy cellars below the Fountain Court. Fernandez & Wells is a great spot for an informal meal or snack. In summer eating and drinking spills out onto the large terrace next to the Thames. ⊠ *Strand, Covent Garden* ☎ *020/7845–4600* ⊕ *www. somersethouse.org.uk* Embankment Galleries price varies, other areas free Ⓜ *Charing Cross, Waterloo, Blackfriars.*

St. Paul's Church. If you want to commune with the spirits of Vivien Leigh, Noël Coward, Edith Evans, and Charlie Chaplin, this might be just the place. Memorials to them and many other theater greats are found in this 1633 work of the renowned Inigo Jones, who, as the King's Surveyor of Works, designed the whole of Covent Garden Piazza. St. Paul's Church has been known as "the actors' church" since the Restoration, thanks to the neighboring theater district and St. Paul's prominent parishioners. (Well-known actors often read the lessons at services, and the church still hosts concerts and small-scale productions.) Fittingly, the opening scene of Shaw's *Pygmalion* takes place under its Tuscan portico. The western end of the Piazza is a prime pitch for street entertainers, but if they're not to your liking, you can repair to the serenity of the garden entered from King or Bedford streets. Charming open-air theater performances of Shakespeare plays and other works are staged there in the summertime. ✉ *Bedford St., Covent Garden* ☎ *020/7836–5221* ⊕ *www.actorschurch.org* Ⓜ *Covent Garden.*

BLOOMSBURY
AND HOLBORN

Getting Oriented

Euston Station

Wellcome Collection

The Betjeman Arms ✕

KING'S CROSS

St. Pancras Station

King's Cross Station

ISLINGTON

WARREN STREET Ⓤ

EUSTON SQUARE Ⓤ

Euston Rd.

Gower Pl.

British Library ◆

London Canal Museum ◆

Ⓤ **KING'S CROSS**

Euston Rd.

York Way

Grafton Way

Petrie Museum ◆

Endsleigh Grdns.

Upper Woburn Pl.

Bidborough St.

St. Chad's St.

University St.

University College London ◆

Gordon St.

Taviton St.

Endsleigh St.

Burton St.

Cartwright Gdns.

Judd St.

Argyle St.

Argyle St.

Whitfield St.

Tottenham Court Rd.

Torrington Place

Gordon Square

Tavistock Square

Bedford Way

Woburn Pl.

Marchmont St.

Coram St.

Tavistock Pl.

Hunter St.

Regent Square

St. George's Gdns.

Chenies St.

Gower St.

Alfred Pl.

GOODGE STREET Ⓤ

The Hare and Tortoise Dumpling & Noodle Bar ✕

Brunswick Square

Mecklenburgh Square

Store St.

Malet St.

University of London

Russell Square

Bernard St.

Coram's Fields

RUSSELL SQUARE Ⓤ

Guilford St.

Bayley St.

Bedford Square

Montague Pl.

Queen Square

Gt. Ormond St.

Milman St.

Doughty St.

Charles Dickens Museum ◆

Brownlow Mews

Bedford Ave.

Bloomsbury St.

British Museum ◆

Montague St.

Bedford Pl.

Southampton Row

BLOOMSBURY

Roger St.

Northington St.

Gt. James St.

Great Russell St.

Truckles of Pied Bull Yard ✕

Bloomsbury Square

Lamb's Conduit Street ◆

TOTTENHAM COURT ROAD Ⓤ

Bury

Bloomsbury Way

Theobald's Rd.

Bedford Row

CLERKENWELL →

FITZROVIA

New Orford St.

Red Lion Square

Gray's Inn Gdns.

Gray's Inn Rd.

High Holborn

Shaftesbury Ave.

HOLBORN Ⓤ

Proctor St.

Red Lion St.

Whetstone Park

Sir John Soane's Museum ◆

Gray's Inn ◆

Ⓤ **CHANCERY LANE**

Shorts Gdns.

Neal St.

Endell St.

Great Queen St.

Kingsway

Wild St.

Lincoln's Inn Fields

Monmouth St.

Long Acre

Floral St.

Ⓤ **COVENT GARDEN**

Drury La.

Portsmouth St.

Lincoln's Inn Fields

Portugal St.

Lincoln's Inn ◆

Cursitor St.

Furnival St.

New Fetter La.

High Holborn

Covent Garden

New Square

Bream's Bldgs.

Letter La.

Aldwych

Carey St.

Royal Courts of Justice

Chancery La.

HOLBORN

½ mi

½ km

Strand

Strand

Devereux Ct.

Inner Temple La.

Temple Church ◆

Victoria

Waterloo Bridge

Arundel St.

Surrey St.

Temple Pl.

Essex St.

TEMPLE Ⓤ

Middle Temple

Middle Temple La.

Inner Temple

King's Bench Wk.

Whitefriars St.

Fleet St.

Tudor St.

Golden Jubilee Bridges

Embankment

River Thames

Blackfriars Bridge

Ⓤ **BLACKFRIARS**

Bloomsbury and Holborn

TOP REASONS TO GO

The British Museum: From the Rosetta Stone to the Elgin Marbles, the British Museum is the golden hoard of treasure amassed over centuries by the British Empire.

The Inns of Court: The quiet courts, leafy gardens, and magnificent halls that make up the heart of Holborn are the closest thing to the spirit of Oxford in London.

Sir John Soane's Museum: Quirky and fascinating, the former home of the celebrated 19th-century architect is a treasure trove of antiquities and oddities.

The British Library: In keeping with Bloomsbury's literary traditions, this repository holds the Magna Carta, a Gutenberg Bible, and Shakespeare's First Folio.

Charles Dickens: The former residence of the *Oliver Twist* author is now a fascinating museum.

FEELING PECKISH?

The Betjeman Arms. Inside St. Pancras International's renovated Victorian station, this pub is the perfect place to grab a pint and some pub fare. ⊠ *Pancras Rd., Unit 53, King's Cross* ☎ *020/7923–5440* ⊕ *www.thebetjemanarms. co.uk* Ⓜ *King's Cross St. Pancras.*

The Hare and Tortoise Dumpling & Noodle Bar. This informal eatery serves scrumptious Asian fast food in huge portions at reasonable prices. ⊠ *11–13 Brunswick Shopping Centre, Brunswick Sq., Bloomsbury* ☎ *020/7278–9799* ⊕ *www.hareandtortoise.co.uk/bloomsbury* Ⓜ *Russell Sq.*

Truckles of Pied Bull Yard. The main attraction of this wine bar and café is the Georgian courtyard, where you can relax within a stone's throw of the British Museum. ⊠ *Off Bury Pl., Bloomsbury* ☎ *020/7404–5338* ⊕ *www.davy.co.uk/truckles* ⊘ *Closed Thurs. and Sun.*

GETTING THERE

The Russell Square Tube stop on the Piccadilly Line leaves you right at the corner of Russell Square.

The best Tube stops for the Inns of Court are Holborn on the Central and Piccadilly lines or Chancery Lane on the Central Line.

Tottenham Court Road on the Northern and Central lines is best for the British Museum.

Once you're in Bloomsbury, you can easily get around on foot.

MAKING THE MOST OF YOUR TIME

If you plan to visit the Inns of Court as well as the British Museum, and you'd like to get a feel for the neighborhood, devote an entire day to this literary and legal enclave.

An alternative scenario is to set aside a separate day for a visit to the British Museum, which can easily consume as many hours as you have to spare.

It's a pleasure to wander through the leafy squares at your leisure, examining historic Blue Plaques or relaxing at a street-side café. The students in the neighborhood add a bit of street life.

5

With the British Library, the British Museum, and countless colleges of the University of London among its residents, Bloomsbury might appear all bookish and cerebral—but fear not, it's much more than that. There's a youthfulness about its buzzing thoroughfares, and this vitality extends from down-by-the-Thames Holborn—once Dickens territory, now the heartbeat of legal London—way up to revamped King's Cross and classy Islington to the north, and cool Clerkenwell out east.

BLOOMSBURY

Updated by
James O'Neill

Fundamental to the region's spirit of open expression and scholarly debate is the legacy of the Bloomsbury Group, an elite corps of artists and writers who lived in this neighborhood during the first part of the 20th century. **Gordon Square** was at one point home to Virginia Woolf, John Maynard Keynes (both at No. 46), and Lytton Strachey (at No. 51). But perhaps the best-known square in Bloomsbury is the large, centrally located **Russell Square,** with its handsome gardens. Scattered around the **University of London** campus are Woburn Square, Torrington Square, and Tavistock Square. The **British Library,** with its vast treasures, is a few blocks north, across busy Euston Road.

Bloomsbury is bordered by Tottenham Court Road on the west, Euston Road on the north, Woburn Place (which becomes Southampton Row) on the east, and New Oxford Street on the south.

The area from Somerset House on the Strand, all the way up Kingsway to the Euston Road, is known as London's **Museum Mile** for the myriad historic houses and museums that dot the area. The **Charles Dickens Museum,** in the house where the author wrote *Oliver Twist,* pays homage to the master, and artists' studios and design shops share space near the majestic **British Museum.** And guaranteed to raise a smile from the most blasé and footsore tourist is **Sir John Soane's Museum**, where the colorful collection reflects the eclectic interests of the namesake founder.

Bloomsbury's liveliness extends north to the exciting redevelopment of King's Cross, now fast becoming a cultural and culinary destination in its own right. Newly polished King's Cross merges seamlessly into upscale Islington, with its bustling streets and elegant squares. Due south of Islington, and east of Bloomsbury, don't miss out on the charms of easygoing, fashionable Clerkenwell.

FAMILY **British Library.** With a collection totaling more than 150 million items, plus 3 million new additions every year, the British Library is a world-class repository of knowledge. Its greatest treasures are on view to the general public: the Magna Carta, the Codex Sinaiticus (an ancient bible containing the oldest complete copy of the New Testament), Jane Austen's writings, and Shakespeare's First Folio. Musical manuscripts by G.F. Handel as well as the Beatles are on display in the Sir John Ritblat Gallery. ✉ *96 Euston Rd., Bloomsbury* ☎ *0330/333–1144* ⊕ *www. bl.uk* 🎫 *Free, donations appreciated; charge for special exhibitions* Ⓜ *Euston, Euston Sq., King's Cross St. Pancras.*

FAMILY
Fodor's Choice
★

British Museum. One of the world's great repositories of human civilization, the scale and importance of the British Museum's treasures are impossible to overstate. Established in 1753 and initially based on the library and "cabinet of curiosities" of the Royal Physician Sir Hans Sloane, the collection grew exponentially over the following decades, partly due to bequests and acquisitions, but also as a result of plundering by the burgeoning British Empire.

The neoclassical grandeur of the museum's Great Russell Street entrance befits what lies in wait inside. Here you'll find the **Rosetta Stone,** whose inscriptions were key to deciphering hieroglyphics (Room 4); the controversial but exquisite **Elgin Marbles** (aka the Parthenon Sculptures) that once stood on the Acropolis in Athens (Room 18); and stunning fragments and friezes from the **Mausoleum of Halikarnassos** (aka one of the Seven Wonders of the Ancient World; Room 21).

Other perennial favorites include the **Egyptian mummies** (Rooms 62–63); the colossal **Statue of Ramesses II,** dating to circa 1270 BC and weighing in at just over 7 tons (Room 4); and the glittering 4th-century **Mildenhall Treasure** and the equally splendid 8th-century Anglo-Saxon **Sutton Hoo Treasure** with magnificent helmets and jewelry aplenty (Room 41).

KING'S CROSS STATION

Sick of living in the shadow of its sumptuously renovated next-door neighbor, St. Pancras Station, King's Cross—and the area behind it—has undergone a major makeover of its own, with bars, restaurants, shops, cultural venues, and a stunning fountain display for all to enjoy. It's also a place dear to Harry Potter fans everywhere, because it was from the imaginary platform 9¾ that our hero boarded the *Hogwarts Express* (the station has helpfully put up a sign for platform 9¾ if you want to take a picture there).

5

Leave time for exploring the glass-covered **Great Court** designed by celebrated architect Norman Foster at the turn of the present millennium—it has become a focal point of the museum. Likewise, don't miss the revered circular **Reading Room** where Karl Marx wrote *Das Kapital* under the room's beautiful blue-and-gold papier-mâché dome. If pushed for time, consider one of the excellent museum tours. Eye-opener Tours (free; 30–40 minutes) focus on 15 individual galleries each day, while the 90-minute Highlights Tour covers all the major exhibits plus a few lesser-known ones, and begins at 11:30 am and 2 pm on Friday and weekends (£14; book online or at the information desk in the Great Court). Alternatively, Audio Guides can be rented from the information desk for £7. ⊠ *Great Russell St., Bloomsbury* ☎ *020/7323–8000* ⊕ *www.britishmuseum.org* ⊠ *Free; donations encouraged* Ⓜ *Russell Sq., Holborn, Tottenham Court Rd.*

Charles Dickens Museum. This is one of the few London houses Charles Dickens (1812–70) inhabited that is still standing, and it's the place where the master wrote *Oliver Twist* and *Nicholas Nickleby* and finished *The Pickwick Papers*. The house looks exactly as it would have in Dickens's day, complete with first editions, letters, and a tall clerk's desk (Dickens wrote standing up). The museum also houses a shop and a garden café. ⊠ *48 Doughty St., Bloomsbury* ☎ *020/7405–2127* ⊕ *www.dickensmuseum.com* ⊠ *£9.50* ⊙ *Closed Mon.* Ⓜ *Chancery La., Russell Sq.*

Lamb's Conduit Street. If you think Bloomsbury is about all things intellectual, then think again. Lamb's Conduit Street, a pedestrian-only street of gorgeous Georgian town houses nestled to the east of Russell Square, is building a reputation as one of the capital's most charming—and fashionable—shopping thoroughfares. Avail yourself of what the boutiques have to offer, from fashion to ceramics, books to jewelry, fine art to flowers; there's even an excellent run-by-locals food cooperative called the People's Supermarket. Alternatively, you could just window-shop your way down to **The Lamb,** a Victorian-era pub whose patrons have included Ted Hughes, Sylvia Plath, and Mr. Dickens himself. ⊠ *Bloomsbury* Ⓜ *Russell Sq.*

OFF THE BEATEN PATH

London Canal Museum. This quirky museum, dedicated to the rise and fall of London's once-extensive canal network, is based in the former warehouse of ice-cream maker Carlo Gatti (hence it also partly features the ice-cream trade as well as London's canals). Children enjoy the activity zone and learning about Henrietta, the museum's horse. Outside, on the Battlebridge Basin, you'll find the painted narrowboats of modern canal dwellers—a stone's throw from the hustle and bustle of the King's Cross redevelopment. You can walk to the museum along the towpath from Camden Lock; download a free audio tour from the museum's website to accompany the route. ⊠ *12–13 New Wharf Rd., King's Cross* ☎ *020/7713–0836* ⊕ *www.canalmuseum.org.uk* ⊠ *£5* ⊙ *Closed Mon.* Ⓜ *King's Cross.*

Petrie Museum. If you don't get your fill of Egyptian artifacts at the British Museum, you can see more in the neighboring Petrie Museum, located on the first floor of the DMS Watson library. The museum houses an outstanding collection of Egyptian and Sudanese archaeological objects, including jewelry, toys, and some of the world's oldest garments. ⊠ *Malet Pl., Bloomsbury* ☎ *020/7679-2884* ⊕ *www.ucl.ac.uk/ museums/petrie* ✉ *Free, donations appreciated* ⊘ *Closed Sun. and Mon.* Ⓜ *Euston Sq., Goodge St.*

Fodor's Choice **Sir John Soane's Museum.** Sir John (1753–1837), architect of the Bank of
★ England, bequeathed his eccentric house to the nation on one condition: that nothing be changed. It's a house full of surprises. In the Picture Room, two of Hogarth's famous *Rake's Progress* paintings swing away to reveal secret gallery recesses where you can find works by Canaletto and Turner. Everywhere, mirrors play tricks with light and space, and split-level floors worthy of a fairground fun house disorient you. Restoration work has opened up Soane's private apartments to the public, but they can be viewed only as part of a first-come, first-served tour at 1:15 pm and 2 pm, daily. ⊠ *13 Lincoln's Inn Fields, Bloomsbury* ☎ *020/7405-2107* ⊕ *www.soane.org* ✉ *Free; guided tours £12.50* ⊘ *Closed Mon. and Tues.* Ⓜ *Holborn.*

University College London. Founded in 1826 the college is set in a classical edifice designed by the architect of the National Gallery, William Wilkins. Committed to providing higher education without religious exclusion, in 1878 it also became the first British University to accept women on an equal footing with men. The college has within its portals the **Slade School of Fine Art,** which did for many of Britain's artists what the nearby Royal Academy of Dramatic Art (on Gower Street) did for actors. The South Cloisters contain one of London's weirder treasures: the skeleton of one of the university's founders, Jeremy Bentham, who bequeathed himself to the college. ⊠ *Malet Pl., Bloomsbury* ⊕ *www. ucl.ac.uk* Ⓜ *Euston Sq., Goodge St.*

Wellcome Collection. If you fancy something quirky, sample this collection by U.S. pharmaceutical millionaire and philanthropist Henry Wellcome (1853–1936). Styled as "the free destination for the incurably curious," this museum explores the connections between medicine, life, and art (some exhibits may not be suitable for younger children). Comprising an estimated 1 million items, the collection includes Napoléon's toothbrush, Horatio Nelson's razor, and Charles Darwin's walking stick. There are also anatomical models, Peruvian mummies, and Japanese sex toys as well as two permanent exhibitions to inspire debate, Medicine Man and Medicine Now. Watch out for original artworks in the lobby by Picasso (just above the entrance when you come in) and Anthony Gormley. ⊠ *183 Euston Rd., Bloomsbury* ☎ *020/7611-2222* ⊕ *www. wellcomecollection.org* ✉ *Free* ⊘ *Closed Mon.* Ⓜ *Euston Sq., Euston.*

HOLBORN

Southeast of Bloomsbury and west of The City, Holborn may appear to be little more than a buffer zone between the two—but although it may lack the panache of its neighbors, don't underestimate this varied slice of the capital. Home to legal London and the impressive Inns of Court, this is also Charles Dickens territory, with the Old Curiosity Shop snug within its borders and the Dickens museum close by. Add to that its fair

Continued on page 94

THE BRITISH MUSEUM

Anybody writing about the British Museum had better have a large stack of superlatives close at hand: most, biggest, earliest, finest. This is the golden hoard of nearly three centuries of the Empire, the booty brought from Britain's far-flung colonies.

The first major pieces, among them the Rosetta Stone and the Parthenon Sculptures (Elgin Marbles), were "acquired" from the French, who "found" them in Egypt and Greece. The museum has since collected countless goodies of worldwide historical significance: the Black Obelisk, some of the Dead Sea Scrolls, the Lindow Man. And that only begins the list.

The British Museum is a vast space split into 94 galleries, generally divided by continent or period of history, with some areas spanning more than one level. There are marvels wherever you go, and—while we don't like to be pessimistic—it is, yes, impossible to fully appreciate everything in a day. So make the most of the tours, activity trails, and visitors guides that are available.

The following is a highly edited overview of the museum's greatest hits, organized by area. Pick one or two that

whet your appetite, then branch out from there, or spend two straight hours indulging in the company of a single favorite sculpture. There's no wrong way to experience the British Museum, just make sure you do!

✉ Great Russell St., Bloomsbury WC1

☎ 020/7323-8299

🌐 www.britishmuseum.org

💷 Free; donations encouraged. Tickets for special exhibits vary in price.

🕐 Galleries (and Reading Room exhibition space): Sat.–Thurs. 10–5:30, Fri. 10–8:30. Great Court: Sat.–Thurs. 9–6, Fri. 9–8:30.

Ⓤ Russell Square, Holborn, Tottenham Court Rd.

(left) The Great Court
(top) *Cradle to Grave* by Pharmacopoeia

MUSEUM HIGHLIGHTS

Ancient Civilizations

The Rosetta Stone. Found in 1799 and carved in 196 BC by decree of Ptolemy V in Egyptian hieroglyphics, demotic, and Greek, it was this multilingual inscription that provided French Egyptologist Jean-François Champollion with the key to deciphering hieroglyphics. *Room 4.*

Colossal statue of Ramesses II. A member of the 19th dynasty (ca. 1270 BC), Ramesses II commissioned innumerable statues of himself—more than any other preceding or succeeding king. This one, a 7-ton likeness of his perfectly posed upper half, comes from his mortuary temple, the Ramesseum, in western Thebes. *Room 4.*

(top) Portland vase
(bottom) Colossal statue of Ramesses II

The Parthenon Sculptures. Perhaps these marvelous treasures of Greece shouldn't be here—but while the debate rages on, you can steal your own moment with the Elgin Marbles. Carved in about 440 BC, these graceful decorations are displayed along with an in-depth, high-tech exhibit of the Acropolis; the **handless, footless Dionysus** who used to recline along its east pediment is especially well known. *Room 18.*

Mausoleum of Halikarnassos. All that remains of this, one of the Seven Wonders of the Ancient World, is a fragmented form of the original "mausoleum," the 4th-century tomb of Maussollos, King of Karia. The highlight of this gallery is the marble forepart of the **colossal chariot horse from the** *quadriga.* *Room 21.*

The Egyptian mummies. Another short flight of stairs takes you to the museum's most popular galleries, especially beloved by children: the Roxie Walker Galleries of Egyptian Funerary Archaeology have a fascinating collection of relics from the Egyptian realm of the dead. In addition to real corpses, wrapped mummies, and mummy cases, there's a menagerie of animal companions and curious items that were buried alongside them. *Rooms 62–63.*

Portland Vase. Made in Italy from cameo glass at the turn of the first century, it is named after the Dukes of Portland, who owned it from 1785 to 1945. It is considered a technical masterpiece—opaque white mythological figures cut by a gem-cutter are set on cobalt-blue background. *Room 70.*

The **Enlightenment Gallery** should be visited purely for the fact that its antiquarian cases hold the contents of the British Museum's first collections—Sir Hans Sloane's natural-history loot, as well as that of Sir Joseph Banks, who acquired specimens of everything from giant shells to fossils to rare plants to exotic beasts during his voyage to the Pacific aboard Captain Cook's *Endeavour.* *Room 1.*

Asia Galleries

Egypt Galleries
60–66

Egyptian Mummies

TO GALLERIES
90–94

North Korean
Socialist Realism Art

Asia Galleries
91–94

UPPER FLOOR

Roman Britain
Gallery

Mildenhall
Treasure

Sutton Hoo
Treasure

Europe
Galleries
41–48

Greece & Rome
Galleries
69–73

Portland Vase

Lindow Man

Prehistory
Galleries

Cradle to Grave

World Cultures
Galleries

Americas
Galleries
26–27

Native
American
Skin Map

Mausoleum
of Halikarnassos

Rosetta
Stone

Reading
Room

Enlightenment
Gallery

Greece
Galleries
11–23

Egypt
Galleries

Elgin
Marbles

The
Great Court

Colossal Statue
of Ramesses II

GROUND FLOOR

Paul Hamlyn
Library

Great Russell St.
Entrance

Asia

The Korea Foundation Gallery. Delve into striking examples of **North Korean Socialist Realism art** from the 1950s to the present and a reconstruction of a **sarangbang**, a traditional scholar's study, complete with hanji paper walls and tea-making equipment. *Room 67.*

The Percival David Collection. More than 1400 pieces of Chinese ceramics (the most comprehensive collection outside China) are on display. *Room 95.*

World Cultures

The North American Gallery. This is one of the largest collections of native culture outside North America, going back to the earliest hunters 10,000 years ago. Here a 1775 **native American skin map** serves as an example of the importance of such documents in the exploration and cartography of North America. Look for the beautifully displayed **native American costumes.** *Room 26.*

The Mexican Gallery. The most alluring pieces sit in this collection side by side: a 15th-century **turquoise mask of Xiuhtecuhtli**, the Mexican Fire God and Turquoise Lord, and a **double-headed serpent** from the same period. *Room 27.*

Britain and Europe

The Mildenhall Treasure. This glittering haul of 4th-century Roman silver tableware was found beneath the sod of a Suffolk field in 1942. *Room 49.*

The Sutton Hoo Treasure. Next door to the loot from Mildenhall—and equally splendid, including brooches, swords, and jewel-encrusted helmets—the treasure was buried at sea with (it is thought) Redwald, one of the first English kings, in the 7th century, and excavated from a Suffolk field in 1938–39. *Room 41.*

Lindow Man. "Pete Marsh"—so named by the archaeologists who unearthed the body from a Cheshire peat marsh—was ritually slain, probably as a human sacrifice, in the 1st century and lay perfectly pickled in his bog until 1984. *Room 50.*

Theme Galleries

Living & Dying. The "Cradle to Grave" installation pays homage to the British nation's wellbeing—or ill-being, as it were. More than 14,000 drugs (the number estimated to be prescribed to every person in the U.K. in his lifetime) are displayed in a colorful tapestry of pills and tablets. *Room 24.*

Colossal chariot horse from the *quadriga* of the Mausoleum at Halikarnassos

LOWER GALLERY

The three rooms that comprise the **Sainsbury African Galleries** are of the main interest here: together they present a staggering 200,000 objects, featuring intricate pieces of old ivory, gold, and wooden masks and carvings—highlighting such ancient kingdoms as the Benin and Asante. The displays include a collection of **55 throwing knives**; ceremonial garments including a dazzling pink and green **woman's coif** (*qufiya*) from Tunisia made of silk, metal, and cotton; and the *Oxford Man*, a 1992 woodcarving by Owen Ndou, depicting a man of ambiguous race clutching his Book of Knowledge.

DID YOU KNOW?

Galleries help divide this sprawling space into manage-able sizes for visitors. The Sainsbury African Galleries are just some of the 94 galleries; the British Museum's collection totals more than 7 million objects.

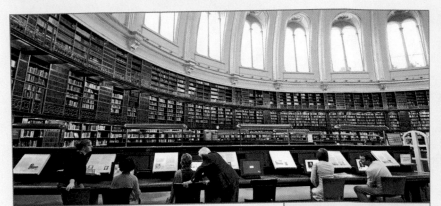

THE NATION'S ATTIC: A HISTORY OF THE MUSEUM

The collection began when Sir Hans Sloane, physician to Queen Anne and George II, bequeathed his personal collection of curiosities and antiquities to the nation. The collection quickly grew, thanks to enthusiastic kleptomaniacs after the Napoleonic Wars—most notoriously the seventh Earl of Elgin, who obtained the marbles from the Parthenon and Erechtheion on the Acropolis in Athens during his term as British ambassador in Constantinople.

Soon thereafter, it seemed everyone had something to donate—George II gave the old Royal Library, Sir William Hamilton gave antique vases, Charles Townley gave sculptures, the Bank of England gave coins. When the first exhibition galleries opened to visitors in 1759, the trustees agreed to admit only small groups guided by curators. The British Museum quickly became one of the most fashionable places to be seen in the capital, and tickets, which had to be booked in advance, were treated like gold dust.

The museum's holdings quickly outgrew their original space in Montague House. After the addition of such major pieces as the Rosetta Stone and other Egyptian antiquities (spoils of the Napoleonic War) and the Parthenon sculptures, Robert Smirke was commissioned to build an appropriately large and monumental building on the same site. It's still a hot ticket: the British Museum now receives more than 6 million visitors every year.

THE GREAT COURT & THE READING ROOM

The museum's classical Greek-style facade features figures representing the progress of civilization, and the focal point is the awesome Great Court, a massive glass-roofed space. Here is the museum's inner courtyard (now the largest covered square in Europe) that, for more than 150 years, had been used for storage.

The 19th-century Reading Room, an impressive 106-foot-high blue-and-gold-domed library, forms the centerpiece of the Great Court. H.G. Wells, Thomas Hardy, Lord Tennyson, Oscar Wilde, George Orwell, T.S. Elliot, and Beatrix Potter are just a few writers who have used this space as a literary and academic sanctuary over the past 150 years or so.

(above) Reading Room

PLANNING YOUR VISIT

Tours

The **30–40 minute eyeOpener tour (free)** by Museum Guides does just what it says; ask for details at the information desk. After this tour, you can then dip back into the collections that most captured your imagination at your leisure.

An excellent **multimedia guide** is a good way to explore the galleries at your own pace, via a series of differently-themed tours.

Alternatively, the **Visitor's Guide** gives a brief but informative overview of the museum's history and is, again, divided into self-guided themed tours.

Before you go, take a look at the online **COMPASS tour** using the museum's navigation tool (www.thebritishmuseum.org/compass), which allows users to browse past and present exhibits as well as search for specific objects. A children's version can also be found here. Computer stations in the Reading Room offer onsite access to COMPASS.

■ TIP→ The closest underground station to the British Museum is Russell Square on the Piccadilly line. However, since you will be entering via the back entrance on Montague Place, you will not experience the full impact of the museum's grand facade. To do so, alight at Holborn on the Central and Piccadilly lines or Tottenham Court Road on the Central and Northern lines. The walk from these stations is about 10 minutes.

WITH KIDS

■ Take a look at the "Family Visits" page online for the top 12 objects to see with children.

■ The Families Desk in the Great Court has trails for kids ages 3 to 5 and 6 to 11. The Ford Centre for Young Visitors has free activity backpacks.

■ Art materials are available for free from information points, where you can also find out about workshops, performances, storytelling sessions, and other free events.

■ Around the museum, there are Hands On desks open daily 11–4, which let visitors handle objects from the collections.

WHERE TO REFUEL

The British Museum's self-service **Gallery Café** gets very crowded but serves an acceptable menu beneath a plaster cast of a part of the Parthenon frieze that Lord Elgin didn't remove. It's open daily, but isn't particularly family friendly.

The **café in the Great Court** keeps longer hours and is a great place to people-watch and admire the spectacular glass roof while you eat your salad and sandwich.

If the weather is nice, exit the museum via the back entrance on Montague Place and amble over to **Russell Square,** which has grassy lawns, water fountains, and a glass-fronted café for post-sandwich coffee and ice cream.

5

IN FOCUS THE BRITISH MUSEUM

share of churches and quirky places of interest, and you'll soon discover that Holborn can be a rewarding place to while away an hour or three. Holborn's massive Gothic-style **Royal Courts of Justice** ramble all the way to the Strand, and the **Inns of Court**—Gray's Inn, Lincoln's Inn, Middle Temple, and Inner Temple—are where most British trial lawyers have offices to this day. Geographically, Holborn's borders are probably best defined as: west, Kingsway; north, Theobald's Road; east, Gray's Inn Road; south, where the Strand becomes Fleet Street.

Gray's Inn. Although the least architecturally interesting of the four Inns of Court and the one most heavily damaged by German bombs in the 1940s, Gray's still has romantic associations. In 1594 Shakespeare's *Comedy of Errors* was performed for the first time in the hall, which was restored after World War II and has a fine Elizabethan screen of carved oak. You must make advance arrangements to view the hall, but the secluded and spacious gardens, first planted by Francis Bacon in 1597, are open to the public. The four Inns of the Court—Gray's Inn, Lincoln's Inn, Middle Temple, and Inner Temple—are where most British trial lawyers have offices to this day. In the 14th century, the inns were lodging houses where barristers lived so that people would know how to easily find them (hence, the label "inn"). ⊠ *Gray's Inn Rd., Holborn* ☎ *020/7458–7800* ⊕ *www.graysinn.org.uk* ▨ *Free* ⊘ *Closed weekends* Ⓜ *Holborn, Chancery La.*

Lincoln's Inn. There's plenty to see at one of the oldest, best preserved, and most attractive of the Inns of Court—from the Chancery Lane Tudor brick gatehouse to the wide-open, tree-lined, atmospheric Lincoln's Inn Fields and the 15th-century chapel remodeled by Inigo Jones in 1620. The chapel and the gardens are open to the public, but to see more you must reserve a place on one of the official tours. But be warned: they tend to prefer group bookings of 15 or more, so it's best to check the website or call for details. ⊠ *Chancery La., Holborn* ☎ *020/7405–1393* ⊕ *www.lincolnsinn.org.uk* ▨ *Free* ⊘ *Closed weekends* Ⓜ *Chancery La.*

Royal Courts of Justice. Here is the vast Victorian Gothic pile of 35 million bricks containing the nation's principal law courts, with 1,000-odd rooms running off 3½ miles of corridors. This is where the most important civil law cases—that's everything from divorce to fraud, with libel in between—are heard. You can sit in the viewing gallery to watch any trial you like, for a live version of Court TV; the more dramatic criminal cases are heard at the Old Bailey. Other sights are the 238-foot-long main hall and the compact exhibition of judges' robes. Guided tours must be booked in advance. ⊠ *The Strand, Holborn* ☎ *020/7947–6000* ⊕ *www.theroyalcourtsofjustice.com* ▨ *Free, tours £13* ⊘ *Closed weekends* Ⓜ *Temple, Holborn, Chancery La.*

Temple Church. As featured in *The Da Vinci Code*, this church was built by the Knights Templar in the late 12th century. The Red Knights held their secret initiation rites in the crypt here. Having started poor, holy, and dedicated to the protection of pilgrims, they grew rich from showers of royal gifts until, in the 14th century, they were stripped of their wealth, charged with blasphemy and sodomy, and thrown into the Tower. ⊠ *King's Bench Walk, The Temple, Holborn* ☎ *020/7353–3470* ⊕ *www.templechurch.com* ▨ *£5* ⊘ *Closed weekends* Ⓜ *Temple.*

ISLINGTON

Islington is one of the most fashionable of London's villagelike neighborhoods. Upper Street, with its high-street stores, independent boutiques, and myriad restaurants and bars, is where most of the action takes place. But wander off the main drag and you'll discover elegant residential streets and squares, as well as bustling charming markets. You'll also find a handful of top-flight Off West End theaters and music venues in the area, including the Almeida, the hugely atmospheric Union Chapel, and—down on Islington's border with Clerkenwell—the renowned contemporary dance venue, Sadler's Wells.

Camden Passage. A pretty pedestrian thoroughfare just off Upper Street, Camden Passage is famous for its many antiques shops selling everything from vintage furniture to period jewelry to timeless timepieces. In recent years, a sprinkling of independent boutiques, delis, and cafés has given the passage an eclectic vibrant feel. Check out the antiques market held on Wednesday and Saturday. ⊠ *Islington* ⊕ *www.camdenpassageislington.co.uk* Ⓜ *The Angel.*

Chapel Market. Chapel Market is what Islington used to be: an unpretentious, working-class enclave. There's a lively food market that runs for half the length of the street every day except Monday—just listening to the stallholders advertising their wares can be entertainment enough. Although trendy eateries are beginning to pop up here and there, it is still home to London's oldest eel, pie, and mash shop, Manze's, with its marble tables and tiled interior largely untouched since it was established in 1902. ⊠ *Chapel Market, Islington* Ⓜ *The Angel.*

KING'S CROSS

What a difference a decade makes; until recently, King's Cross was a byword for sleaze and street crime, but after a multibillion-pound redevelopment—actually, make that transformation—it's become a lively urban quarter. On what was once postindustrial wasteland and railroad yards, the 67-acre site is now home to bars, restaurants, street-food vendors, and shops. What's more, with the capital's premier art college, the University of the Arts in London, having relocated to Granary Square, alongside a raft of cultural venues, this spot now has a certain air of artistic credibility about it, too. If all that weren't enough, by courtesy of the Regent's Canal, this bustling quarter even has the occasional peaceful oasis of calm as well.

Granary Square. The heart of the new King's Cross, Granary Square is one of London's liveliest open spaces. Pride of place is given to the ever-changing 1,000-strong fountain display, which is even more spectacular by night when lights accompany the choreography. The immense, six-story granary building—designed in 1852 to store wheat for London's bakers—has been renovated to house the University of the Arts in London, as well as a selection of excellent eateries. The square's south-facing steps double as an amphitheater for site-specific arts events; at times, the steps themselves become the installation—such as when they're covered with carved pumpkins at Halloween or a blanket of flowers in spring. ⊠ *King's Cross* Ⓜ *King's Cross St. Pancras.*

5

CLERKENWELL

Once home to medieval religious orders such as the Knights of the Hospitallers of St. John of Jerusalem, Clerkenwell later became an epicenter of the industrial revolution in the capital and, subsequently, of political radicalism (a young Joseph Stalin is said to have met a young Vladimir Lenin at the Crown Tavern pub in Clerkenwell Green). The monks are long gone—so, too, the communists—and the neighborhood's warehouses and factory floors are now home to cutting-edge design agencies, new media start-ups, and ubertrendy apartments. With its fashionable boutiques, bars, and restaurants, Clerkenwell can be a pleasant place to spend a few hours. Like its neighbor immediately to the east, The City, this area can be quite deserted on weekends.

Museum of the Order of St. John. This fascinating museum tells the story of the Knights Hospitallers of St. John, from the Order's 11th-century Crusader origins in Jerusalem to its present-day incarnation as the St. John Ambulance service. The museum is spread across two adjacent sites: the arched St. John's Gatehouse, which dates back to 1504, and the Priory Church with its atmospheric Norman crypt. An excellent interactive display explores the Order's past, both as a military force and a religious institution that cared for sick pilgrims, and the eclectic variety of objects on display reflects that colorful history: from antique medicinal jars and medical equipment to pieces of armor worn by the Knights when they defended Malta from the Ottomans in the 16th century, as well as a bronze cannon given by Henry VIII before he dissolved the Order altogether a few years later. ⊠ *St. John's Gate, St. John's La., Clerkenwell* ☎ *020/7324–4005* ⊕ *www.museumstjohn. org.uk* ✍ *Free, guided tours £5 (suggested donation)* ⊙ *Closed Sun. Oct.–June* Ⓜ *Farringdon.*

FITZROVIA

To the north of Soho, on the other side of Oxford Street, is Fitzrovia, famed for its dining and drinking. It is known affectionately by some as "Noho." Like its brasher southern sibling, it has some excellent bars and restaurants (especially on Charlotte Street) but more breathing space and fewer crowds. Its name most likely derives from nearby Fitzroy Square. Originally designed by the Adam brothers, the square and its environs quickly became fashionable for haute bohemia; George Bernard Shaw and James McNeil Whistler lived here. To the west, Great Portland Street separates it from Marylebone, while Tottenham Court Road marks its eastern border, beyond which is Bloomsbury. Busy Euston Road (and the Circle Line beneath it) is its northern extent.

6

THE CITY

Getting Oriented

The City

GETTING THERE	TOP REASONS TO GO

GETTING THERE

The City is well served by a concentration of Tube stations—St. Paul's and Bank on the Central Line, and Mansion House, Cannon Street, and Monument on the District and Circle lines. Liverpool Street and Aldgate border The City's eastern edge, while Chancery Lane and Farringdon lie to the west. Barbican and Moorgate provide easy access to the theaters and galleries of the Barbican, and Blackfriars, to the south, leads to Ludgate Circus and Fleet Street.

TOP REASONS TO GO

St. Paul's Cathedral: Although the cathedral is increasingly surrounded by skyscrapers, the beauty of Sir Christopher Wren's 17th-century masterpiece nevertheless remains undiminished.

The Millennium Bridge: Travel from past to present on this promenade between St. Paul's and Tate Modern—and get a great river view, too.

The Tower of London: This medieval complex is home to atmospheric towers, the dazzling Crown Jewels, and hundreds of years of history.

The Museum of London: From skimpy leather briefs dating to Roman times and Queen Victoria's crinolines to Selfridges's art deco elevators and a diorama of the Great Fire (including sound effects and flickering flames), this gem of a museum has got it all.

FEELING PECKISH?

City Càphê. This unpretentious but charming family-run Vietnamese street-food café offers delicious quick bites and take-out dishes for lunch. Try the pho, banh mi, or spring rolls. ⊠ *17 Ironmonger La., City of London* ⊕ *www.citycaphe.com* ⊗ *Closed weekends* Ⓜ *Mansion House, Bank.*

Sweetings. At this site for more than 100 years, this City institution is pricey, takes no reservations, is only open weekdays, and closes at 3 pm—but serves excellent fish and crustaceans in an atmospheric setting. ⊠ *39 Queen Victoria St., City of London* ☎ *020/7248–3062* ⊕ *www.sweetingsrestaurant.co.uk* ⊗ *Closed weekends* Ⓜ *Mansion House.*

White Mulberries. This friendly coffee shop at St. Katharine Docks serves outstanding breakfast (with fresh juices and baked goods) plus homemade soups, cakes, and light bites for lunch. ⊠ *D3 Ivory House, St. Katharine Docks, City of London* ☎ *07507/572600* ⊕ *www.whitemulberries.com* Ⓜ *Tower Hill, Tower Gateway (DLR).*

MAKING THE MOST OF YOUR TIME

The City is also known as the "Square Mile," which hints at how compact it is with little distance between points of interest. This means you can pack a lot of sightseeing into one afternoon. For full immersion in the Tower of London, however, set aside half a day, especially if seeing the Crown Jewels is a priority. Allow an hour minimum each for the Museum of London, St. Paul's Cathedral, and Tower Bridge. On weekends, without the workers who make up 90% of the daytime population, The City is nearly deserted and many affordable lunch places are closed—and yet this is when the major attractions are at their busiest.

A GOOD WALK

Crossing the Millennium Bridge from Tate Modern to St. Paul's is one of the finest walks in London—with the river to either side and Christopher Wren's iconic dome gleaming at one end.

Sightseeing	The capital's fast-beating financial heart, The City is associ-
★★★★★	ated with power and pomp, embodied in the three institutions
Nightlife	
★	at its epicenter: the Bank of England, the Royal Exchange,
Dining	
★★★	and Mansion House. The site of the original Roman settle-
Lodging	
★	ment from which all of London grew, the "Square Mile" has
Shopping	
★★★	statement skyscrapers cheek-by-jowl with some of London's

most iconic historic buildings, from Wren's uplifting St. Paul's Cathedral to the Tower of London, a royal fortress, prison, and jewel house surrounded by a moat.

Updated by
Ellin Stein

Home to both the latest financial high-tech and the descendants of medieval guilds, The City is where the historic past and fast-moving present collide. Begin your explorations on **Fleet Street,** the site of England's first printing press and the undisputed seat of British journalism until the 1980s. Nestled behind Fleet Street is **Dr. Johnson's House,** where the noted lexicographer, famous for asserting "when a man is tired of London, he is tired of life," compiled the original *Dictionary of the English Language.* Nearby **St. Bride's,** a Wren gem recognizable by its tiered-wedding-cake steeple, is still known as "the journalists' church" while to the east is Wren's masterpiece of the English baroque, **St. Paul's Cathedral.** Legacies of London's past are everywhere: at the **Central Criminal Court,** better known as The Old Bailey (and, in its various incarnations, the venue for many of London's most notorious criminal trials); the soaring Victorian **Smithfield Market,** built on a site where livestock has been sold since the 14th century and where a dusk-to-dawn wholesale meat market—the largest in Britain—still operates; the Romanesque church **St. Bartholomew the Great** and next to it **St. Bartholomew's Hospital,** both begun in 1123 at the eastern end of Smithfield; the **Guildhall,** from whose Gothic Great Hall The City was governed and where you can see recently excavated remains of the only Roman amphitheater in London; the church of **St. Mary-le-Bow,** home of the "Bow Bells," of which true Cockneys are supposedly born within earshot; and the maze of charmingly old-fashioned, narrow streets around **Bow Lane.**

To the south is another Wren edifice, the **Monument,** begun in 1671 to commemorate the Great Fire of London five years earlier, while farther east is the historically rich **Tower of London,** which has dominated the riverbank for over a thousand years. Looking towards the river, you'll immediately spot the Victorian Gothic **Tower Bridge,** one of London's most recognizable landmarks. You can put all this history into context at the **Museum of London,** where the archaeological displays include a segment of the **Roman Wall** that ringed The City when it was known to Romans as "Londinium."

The City is also home to some of London's most distinctive contemporary architecture. To the north of Smithfield is the **Barbican Centre,** a Brutalist concrete complex of arts venues and apartments that was controversial when it was built between 1965 and 1976, but has since become an indispensable part of the London streetscape. A plethora of distinctive new structures now tower over The City, not all of which are popular; bold designs such as **20 Fenchurch Street** (aka The Walkie Talkie) and the **Swiss Re Tower** (The Gherkin) are almost as contentious today as the Barbican was 40 years ago (but several have top-floor restaurants, where you can take in superb views). They all add to the mix in this constantly evolving area, and whenever you return—whether in months or years—The City is guaranteed not to be the same as when you saw it last.

Bank of England. Since its establishment in 1694 as England's central bank, the role of the "Old Lady of Threadneedle Street" (a political cartoon caption that stuck) has grown to include managing foreign exchanges, issuing currency, storing the nation's gold reserves, and regulating the United Kingdom's banking system. Since 1997, it has had operational responsibility for Britain's monetary policy, most visibly setting interest rates (similar to the Federal Reserve in the United States). The 3-acre site is enclosed in a massive, neoclassical curtain wall designed by Sir John Soane. This 1828 windowless outer wall is all that survives of Soane's original Bank building, which was demolished in 1925. You can discover more about the bank's history in the surprisingly varied Bank of England Museum (the entrance is around the corner on Bartholomew Lane). In addition to the bank's original Royal Charter, there's a lively program of special exhibitions, plus interactive displays (you can even try your hand at controlling inflation). The most popular exhibit remains the solid-gold bar in the central trading hall that you can actually hold—but before you get any ideas, there's security everywhere. ✉ *Threadneedle St., City of London* ☎ *020/3461–4878* ⊕ *www.bankofengland.co.uk* ▣ *Free* ⊙ *Closed weekends and bank holidays* Ⓜ *Bank, Monument.*

Dr. Johnson's House. Built in 1700, this elegant Georgian residence, with its restored interiors, paneled rooms, and period furniture, is where Samuel Johnson lived between 1748 and 1759, compiling his landmark *A Dictionary of the English Language* in the garret as his health deteriorated. There's a research library with two early editions on view,

A BRIEF HISTORY

Although there is evidence of scattered Celtic rural settlements on the north bank of the Thames, London truly begins with the Romans, who established an outpost of the empire called Londinium (which was about the size of Hyde Park) in 47 AD. In 60 AD, the warrior queen Boudicca led an uprising of the native Iceni, burning the city to the ground, but the Romans soon regained control, adding a defensive wall. Not much is known of what happened to the city after the Romans left in the 5th century (while England as a whole suffered successive invasions by the Angles, Saxons, Jutes, and Vikings), beyond the establishment of a 7th-century cathedral dedicated to Saint Paul (the famous one now stands on the same site). After the Norman invasion of 1066 and William the Conqueror's building of the fortress-cum-castle that became known as the Tower of London, the city started to prosper again within those old Roman walls. By the early 13th century, King John acknowledged the city's importance by granting it the right to elect a Lord Mayor. During the Middle Ages, powerful guilds took root that helped nurture commerce, and in the Tudor era, London became the center of both government and trade, reaching a population of some 200,000 people.

Dockyards were built to service the British ships that plied lucrative new trade routes, both to the New World and India, laying the foundations for London's role as the world's premier city for the next three centuries.

After the Restoration of 1660, London immediately faced two disasters: the Great Plague of 1665, which killed almost a quarter of the city's population, and then, in 1666, the Great Fire, which destroyed most of its old medieval wood structures. However, the reconstruction gave rise to buildings created by one of Britain's greatest architects, Sir Christopher Wren. He, along with John Nash in the 18th century, gave shape to much of the city we see today. Subsequent Regency and Victorian expansion created the characteristic look of new neighborhoods to the west and north like Kensington, Notting Hill, Camden, and Hampstead. Another disaster befell London, particularly in the East End and The City, when Luftwaffe bombs rained down relentlessly during World War II (a destruction equalled by, some argue, the unimaginative urban planners of the 1960s and 1970s). However, as the plethora of shiny new skyscrapers attest, the capacity for reinvention that has enabled this city to thrive for 2,000 years remains undimmed.

along with other mementos of Johnson and his friend and biographer, James Boswell, one of literature's greatest diarists. After your visit, enjoy more 17th-century atmosphere around the corner in Wine Office Court at the venerable pub **Ye Olde Cheshire Cheese,** once Johnson and Boswell's favorite watering hole. ⊠ *17 Gough Sq., City of London* ☎ *020/7353–3745* ⊕ *www.drjohnsonshouse.org* ✆ *£7* ⊗ *Closed Sun. and bank holidays* ☞ *Admission is cash-only* Ⓜ *Holborn, Chancery La., Temple.*

Walking over the Millennium Bridge takes you to St. Paul's Cathedral, the Sir Christopher Wren–designed masterpiece that is one of the most beautiful cathedrals in England.

Guildhall. For centuries, this building has been the administrative and ceremonial base of the Corporation of London, the world's oldest continuously elected municipal governing authority (the Corporation still oversees The City's civic administration but now in a more modern building). Built between 1411 and 1440, it is The City's only surviving secular medieval building, and although it lost roofs to both the Great Fire of 1666 and the Blitz of 1940, its Gothic Great Hall has remained intact. Adding to the Hall's period atmosphere are the colorful coats of arms and banners of the 110 City Livery Companies, descendants of medieval trade guilds, which still officially elect the Lord Mayor of London. These range from older Companies originally formed by trades of yesteryear to new ones representing modern activities like information technology, along with several that remain eternally relevant (e.g., carpenters, upholsterers, and fishmongers).

The Hall has been the site of several historic trials, including that of "the Nine Day Queen" Lady Jane Grey in 1553 and the landmark *Zong* case (1783), which helped end Britain's involvement in the slave trade. Even more ancient are the 11th Century East and West Crypts, survivors of the original Saxon Hall and the largest remaining medieval crypts in London. To the right of Guildhall Yard is the Guildhall Art Gallery, which includes portraits of notables, cityscapes, and a slightly cloying pre-Raphaelite section. The construction of the gallery in the 1980s led to the exciting discovery of London's only Roman Amphitheater, which had lain undisturbed for more than 1,800 years. Visitors can walk through the excavation, although most of the artifacts are now at the Museum of London. There are 75-minute guided tours on select Thursdays when the city council meets at 10:45 am (advance booking required); check the website for dates. ⊠ *Off Guildhall Yard, Gresham St., City of London* ☎ *020/7332–1313* ⊕ *www.cityoflondon.gov.uk* ⊠ *Guildhall tours £8* ⊗ *Closed Aug.* Ⓜ *St. Paul's, Moorgate, Bank, Mansion House.*

The Monument. Designed by Sir Christopher Wren and Dr. Robert Hooke to commemorate 1666's "dreadful visitation" of the Great Fire of London (note the gilded orb of flame at the column's pinnacle), the world's tallest isolated stone column offers spectacular views of the city from the viewing platform 160 feet up. The two architects were asked to erect the monument as close as possible to where the fire began, and so it's located exactly 202 feet from the alleged point of origin, Farrier's baking house on Pudding Lane. Built between 1671 and 1677, the fluted Doric column also stands 202 feet tall, so if climbing the 311 steps of the beautiful spiral staircase to the public balcony seems too arduous, you can watch a live view from the platform played on a screen at the entrance. ⊠ *Monument St., City of London* ☎ *020/7403–3761* ⊕ *www.themonument.info* ⊠ *£4.50, combined ticket with Tower Bridge £11* ☞ *Admission is cash only* Ⓜ *Monument.*

FAMILY
Fodor's Choice
★
Museum of London. This fascinating museum reveals London in its many incarnations, from its first days as a Roman settlement around AD 50 (and even before, with finds going back to 450,000 BC) up to the present. The more than 7,000 objects encompass everything from Queen Victoria's crinolines and Selfridges's original art deco elevators to grim Georgian iron doors from the city's infamous Newgate Prison and Thomas Heatherwick's cauldron from the 2012 London Olympics. Permanent galleries are devoted to nearly every era of English history, including the current globalized megalopolis period. The Roman London collection contains some extraordinary gems, including an astonishingly well-preserved floor mosaic uncovered just a few streets away; don't miss the extraordinary Bronze Age and Roman artifacts unearthed during construction of the new Crossrail underground railway. There are also themed temporary exhibitions, themed walking tours (such as "Hogarth's London"), and an offshoot branch near Canary Wharf devoted to the history of the area and the River Thames. ⊠ *150 London Wall, City of London* ☎ *020/7001–9844* ⊕ *www.museumoflondon.org.uk* ⊠ *Free* Ⓜ *Barbican, St. Paul's.*

The Old Bailey. Visitors are allowed into the public galleries of the 16 courtrooms at London's **Central Criminal Court** (universally known as "the Old Bailey," a reference to the street where it's located, which follows the line of the original fortified city wall, or "bailey" in Middle English). Historically it has been the venue for many of Britain's most famous criminal trials. It was here that Oscar Wilde was condemned for "gross indecency" in 1895, where notorious murderers like the Kray twins in the 1960s and the Yorkshire Ripper in the 1980s were convicted, and, more recently, where high-profile terrorism cases have been tried. Originally the site of a medieval courthouse destroyed in the Great Fire, a courthouse was built here next to the grim Newgate Prison, the poor man's version of the Tower, in 1673. The building went through two more incarnations before the present Edwardian baroque building opened in 1907 (it was rebuilt again after the Blitz). Until 1868, executions were held on the street outside (a great public attraction) and you can still see the "Dead Man's Walk" along which condemned prisoners were taken from their cells to the gallows under a series of ever-narrowing arches. Note the 12-foot gold leaf statue of Lady Justice at the top of the dome, not wearing a blindfold as she is usually portrayed.

Visitors are only allowed access to the public galleries to view trials; there is no visitor access to the rest of the building. Trials take place from 10 am to 1 pm and 2 pm to 4:30 pm. There are security restrictions, and children under 14 and overly casual dress are not allowed. ⊠ *The Old Bailey, City of London* ☎ *020/7248-3277* ⊕ *www.cityoflondon.gov.uk* 🖾 *Free* ⊙ *Closed weekends, bank holidays, and when court not in session.* Ⓜ *St. Paul's.*

Fodor'sChoice
★ **St. Bartholomew the Great.** Originally founded in 1123 as part of an Augustinian monastery, this is one of the oldest churches in London and one of the city's few surviving Norman buildings. Although much of the church has been destroyed or demolished over the centuries, with restoration only beginning in the mid-19th century (it even saw use as a stable and a factory in the interim), it nevertheless remains perhaps the best preserved example of Romanesque architecture in London. Most notable are the 13th-century arch with a half-timbered gatehouse at the entrance and the fine Romanesque chancel, apse, and triforium at the east end of the interior. The artist William Hogarth was baptized in the font, which dates back to 1404. The redolent atmosphere has made it a favorite filming location, and you can see it in *The Other Boleyn Girl*, *Four Weddings and a Funeral*, and *Shakespeare in Love*, to name just a few. ⊠ *Cloth Fair, West Smithfield, City of London* ☎ *020/7600-0440* ⊕ *www.greatstbarts.com* 🖾 *£5 (free for prayer in the chapel), photography £1.50* Ⓜ *Barbican, Farringdon.*

St. Bride's. Located just off Fleet Street in the city's former epicenter of English print and newspaper, St. Bride's is known as "the journalists' church," and indeed a small altar in the north aisle marks a memorial dedicated to the sadly ever-growing list of reporters, photographers, and crew who have lost their lives covering 21st-century conflicts. St. Bride's is another of Sir Christopher Wren's English baroque gems, built nine years after the Great Fire of 1666. The distinctively tiered steeple, Wren's highest, for which Benjamin Franklin designed a lightning rod, allegedly inspired a baker parishioner to make a similarly shaped tiered cake for his own wedding, thus creating the modern wedding cake design. This is thought to be the eighth church on the site (there's still a medieval chapel in the northeast corner), with the first one built during the 7th century. Evidence for this, along with a section of a Roman mosaic sidewalk, was discovered in the crypt, where you can now see the many archaeological finds unearthed from the thousands of coffins there. Ninety-minute guided tours are held on Tuesday afternoon. ⊠ *Fleet St., City of London* ☎ *020/7427-0133* ⊕ *www.stbrides.com* 🖾 *Free; guided tours £6* Ⓜ *St. Paul's, Blackfriars.*

St. Mary-le-Bow. Founded around 1080 as the Archbishop of Canterbury's London seat, this church is a survivor; it collapsed and was rebuilt three times before being completely destroyed in the Great Fire of 1666. Once again, Sir Christopher Wren was called in, creating a new building that was completed in 1673, but sadly this, too, was destroyed during the Blitz. The version you see today is a re-creation of Wren's design that was reconsecrated in 1965. According to tradition, only Londoners born within earshot of the church's famous "Bow Bells" (which used to echo more widely than they do now) can be considered true Cockneys, a concept that may date back to the 9 pm curfew bells rung during the 14th century. The Norman crypt is the oldest parochial building in London still in use, and you can see the bow-shape arches from which the church takes its name. The garden contains a statue of former parishioner Captain John Smith, the founder of the Virginia Colony. Opening times on weekends and holidays are irregular, so calling ahead is advised. Guided tours available by arrangement. Classical music concerts are held here regularly; check the website for listings. ⊠ *Cheapside, City of London* ☎ *020/7248–5139* ⊕ *www.stmarylebow. co.uk* ▢ *Free* ⊙ *Closed most weekends* Ⓜ *Mansion House, St. Paul's.*

Fodor's Choice
★ **St. Paul's Cathedral.** For centuries, this iconic building has represented London's spirit of survival and renewal, and it remains a breathtaking structure, inside and out. Sir Christopher Wren started planning the current cathedral in 1666, immediately after the previous medieval building, founded in 1087, was destroyed in the Great Fire, hence the word "resurgam" ("I shall rise again") inscribed on the pediment of the south door. St. Paul's again became a symbol of the city's resilience during the Blitz, when local volunteers risked death to put out a blaze on the dome (despite these efforts, much of the cathedral's east end and its high altar were destroyed). It has often been the scene of great state occasions, such as Winston Churchill's funeral and the wedding of Prince Charles and Princess Diana.

Construction started in 1675 and took 35 years to finish. It was actually Wren's third design: the first was rejected for being too modern; the second for being too modern *and* too Italian, that is, Catholic (you can see the 20-foot "Great Model" of this design in the crypt). Despite mollifying the Anglican clergy with the promise of a traditional English spire, Wren installed a neoclassical triple-layered dome, the second-largest cathedral dome in the world after St. Peter's in Rome.

The interior is a superb example of the English baroque. Climb 257 steps up the Geometric Staircase, a perfectly engineered stone spiral, to the Whispering Gallery, so named because a whisper against one wall can be heard on the wall 112 feet opposite. Another 119 steps up is the Stone Gallery, which encircles the exterior of the dome and provides panoramic views over London. If you have a head for heights, tackle another 152 steps to the small Golden Gallery, an observation platform at the dome's highest point. At 278 feet above the cathedral floor, it offers even more spectacular vistas. Back on the ground, in the south choir aisle, you'll find the grave of John Donne, the poet who was dean of St. Paul's from 1621 until his death in 1631. His marble effigy is the oldest memorial in the cathedral and one of the few to survive the Great

Continued on page 114

THE TOWER OF LONDON

The Tower is a microcosm of the city itself—a sprawling, organic hodgepodge of buildings that inspires reverence and terror in equal measure. See the block on which Anne Boleyn was beheaded, marvel at the Crown Jewels, and pay homage to the ravens who keep the monarchy safe.

An architectural patchwork of time, the oldest building of the complex is the fairytale White Tower, conceived by William the Conqueror in 1078 as both a royal residence and a show of power to the troublesome Anglo-Saxons he had subdued at the Battle of Hastings. Today's Tower has seen everything, as a palace, barracks, a mint for producing coins, an armoury, and the Royal menagerie (home of the country's first elephant). The big draw is the stunning opulence of the Crown Jewels, kept on-site in the heavily fortified Jewel House. Most of all, though, the Tower is known for death: it's been a place of imprisonment, torture, and execution for the realm's most notorious traitors as well as its martyrs. These days, unless you count the killer admission fees, there are far less morbid activities taking place in the Tower, but it still breathes London's history and pageantry from its every brick and offers hours of exploration.

TOURING THE TOWER

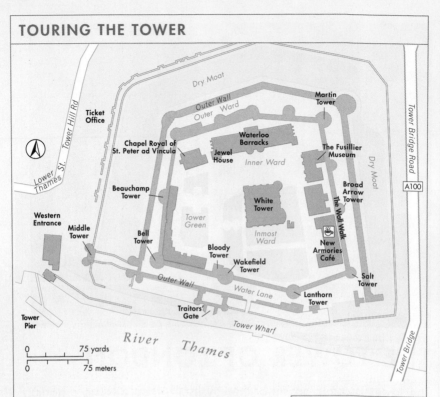

Entry to the Tower is via the **Western Entrance** and the **Middle Tower,** which feed into the outermost ring of the Tower's defenses.

Water Lane leads past the dread-inducing **Traitors' Gate,** the final point of entry for many Tower prisoners.

Toward the end of Water Lane, the **Lanthorn Tower** houses by night the ravens rumored to keep the kingdom safe, and by day a timely high-tech reconstruction of the Catholic Guy Fawkes's plot to blow up the Houses of Parliament in 1605.

The **Bloody Tower** earned its name as the apocryphal site

of the murder of two young princes, Edward and Richard, who disappeared from the Tower after being put there in 1483 by their uncle, Richard III. Two little skeletons (now in Westminster Abbey) were found buried close to the White Tower in 1674 and are thought to be theirs.

The **Beauchamp Tower** housed upper-class miscreants: Latin graffiti about Lady Jane Grey can be glimpsed today on its walls.

Like a prize gem set at the head of a royal crown, the **White Tower** is the centerpiece of the complex. Its four towers dominate the Inner

GOLD DIGGER?

Keep your eyes peeled as you tour the Tower: according to one story, Sir John Barkstead, goldsmith and Lieutenant of the Tower under Cromwell, hid £20,000 in gold coins here before his arrest and execution at the Restoration of Charles II.

Ward, a fitting and forbidding reminder of Norman strength at the time of the conquest of England.

Once inside the White Tower, head upstairs for the **Armouries,** where the biggest attraction, quite literally,

Jewel House, Waterloo Barracks

ROYAL BLING

The Crown of Queen Elizabeth, the Queen Mother, from 1937, contains the exotic 105-carat Koh-i-Noor (mountain of light) diamond.

TIME KILLERS

Some prisoners managed to keep themselves plenty amused: Sir Walter Raleigh grew tobacco on Tower Green, and in 1561 suspected sorcerer Hugh Draper carved an intricate astronomical clock on the walls of his Salt Tower cell.

is the suit of armor worn by a well endowed Henry VIII. There is a matching outfit for his horse.

Other fascinating exhibits include the set of Samurai armor presented to James I in 1613 by the emperor of Japan, and the tiny set of armor worn by Henry VIII's young son Edward.

The **Jewel House** in **Waterloo Block** is the Tower's biggest draw, perfect for playing pick-your-favorite-crown from the wrong side of bul-

letproof glass. Not only are these crowns, staffs, and orbs encrusted with heavy-duty gems, they are invested with the authority of monarchical power in England, dating back to the 1300s.

Outside, pause at **Tower Green,** permanent departure point for those of noble birth. The hoi polloi were dispatched at nearby Tower Hill. The Tower's most famous female victims—Anne Boleyn, Margaret Countess of Salisbury, Catherine Howard, and Lady Jane Grey—all went this "priviledged" way.

Behind a well-kept square of grass stands the **Chapel Royal of St. Peter ad Vincula,** a delightful Tudor church and final resting place of six beheaded Tudor bodies. ■TIP→ **Visitors are welcome for services and can also enter after 4:30 pm daily.**

The **Salt Tower,** reputedly the most haunted corner of the complex, marks the start of the **Wall Walk,** a bracing promenade along the stone spiral steps and battlements of the Tower that looks down on the trucks, taxis, and shimmering high-rises of modern London.

The Wall Walk ends at the **Martin Tower,** former home of the Crown Jewels and now host to the crowns and diamonds exhibition that explains the art of fashioning royal headwear and tells the story of some of the most famous stones.

On leaving the Tower, browse the **gift shop,** and wander the wharf that overlooks the Thames, leading to a picture-postcard view of Tower Bridge.

WHO ARE THE BEEFEATERS?

First of all, they're Yeoman Warders, but probably got the nickname "beefeater" from their position as Royal Bodyguards which entitled them to eat as much beef as they liked. Part of the "Yeoman of the Guard," started in the reign of Edmund IV, the warders have formed the Royal Bodyguard as far back as 1509 when Henry VIII left a dozen of the Yeoman of the Guard at the Tower to protect it.

Originally, the Yeoman Warders also served as jailers of the Tower, doubling as torturers when necessary. (So it would have been a Beefeater tightening the thumb screws, or ratchetting the rack another notch on some unfortunate prisoner. Smile nicely.) Today 36 Yeoman Warders (men and women since 2007), along with the Chief Yeoman Warder and the Yeoman Gaoler, live within the walls of the Tower with their families, in accommodations in the Outer Ward. They stand guard over the Tower, conduct tours, and lock up at 9:53 pm every night with the Ceremony of the Keys.

■ TIP→ Free tickets to the Ceremony of the Keys are available by writing several months in advance; check the Tower Web site for details.

HARK THE RAVENS!

Legend has it that should the hulking black ravens ever leave, the White Tower will crumble and the kingdom fall. Charles II, no doubt jumpy after his father's execution and the monarchy's short-term fall from grace, made a royal decree in 1662 that there should be at least six of the carrion-eating nasties present at all times. There have been some close calls. During World War II, numbers dropped to one, echoing the precarious fate of the war-wracked country. In 2005, two (of eight) died over Christmas when Thor—the most intelligent but also the largest bully of the bunch—killed new recruit Gundolf, named after the Tower's 1070 designer. Pneumonia put an end to Bran, leaving lifelong partner Branwen without her mate.

of blood-soaked biscuits, rabbit, and scraps from the mess kitchen that keeps them coming back. Their lifting feathers on one wing are trimmed, meaning they can manage the equivalent of a lop-sided air-bound hobble but not much more. For the first half of 2006 the ravens were moved indoors full-time as a preventive measure against avian flu but have since been allowed out and about again. In situ they are a territorial lot, sticking to Tower Green and the White Tower, and lodging nightly by Wakefield Tower. They've had free front-row seats at all the most grisly moments in Tower history— Anne Boleyn's execution included.

■ DID YOU KNOW? In 1981 a raven named Grog, perhaps seduced by his alcoholic moniker, escaped after 21 years at the Tower. Others have been banished for "conduct unbecoming."

The six that remain, each one identified by a colored band around a claw, are much loved for their fidelity (they mate for life) and their cheek (capable of 440 noises, they are witty and scolding mimics). It's not only the diet

■ TIP→ Don't get too close to the ravens: they are prone to pecking and not particularly fond of humans, unless you are the Tower's Raven Master.

And *WHAT* are they wearing?

A **pike** (or halberd), also known as a partisan, is the Yeoman Warder's weapon of choice. The Chief Warder carries a staff topped with a miniature silver model of the White Tower.

Anyone who refers to this as a costume will be lucky to leave the Tower with head still attached to body: this is the ceremonial uniform of the Yeoman Warders, and it comes at a cool £13,000 a throw.

The black Tudor **bonnet** is made of velvet; the blue undress consists of a felt top hat, with a single Tudor rose in the middle.

This **Tudor-style ruff** helps date the ceremonial uniform, which was first worn in 1552.

Insignia on a Yeoman Warder's upper right arm denote the rank he carried in the military.

The **medals** on a Yeoman Warder's chest are more than mere show: all of the men and women have served for at least 22 years in the armed forces.

This version of the **royal livery** bears the insignia of the current Queen ("E" for Elizabeth) but originally dates from Tudor times. The first letter changes according to the reigning monarch's Christian name; the second letter is always an "R" for *rex* (king) or *regina* (queen).

Slits in the **tunic** date from the times when Beefeaters were expected to ride a horse.

Red socks and **black patent shoes** are worn on special occasions. Visitors are more likely to see the regular blue undress, introduced in 1858 as the regular working dress of the Yeoman Warders.

The **red lines down the trousers** are a sign of the blood from the swords of the Yeoman Warders in their defense of the realm.

(IN)FAMOUS PRISONERS OF THE TOWER

Anne Boleyn   Lady Jane Grey   Sir Walter Raleigh

Sir Thomas More. A Catholic and Henry VIII's friend and chancellor, Sir Thomas refused to attend the coronation of Anne Boleyn (Henry VIII's second wife) or to recognize the multi-marrying king as head of the Church. Sent to the Tower for treason, in 1535 More was beheaded.

Anne Boleyn. The first of Henry VIII's wives to be beheaded, Anne, who failed to provide the king with a son, was accused of sleeping with five men, including her own brother. All six got the chop in 1536. Her severed head was held up to the crowd, and her lips were said to be mouthing prayer.

Margaret, Countess of Salisbury. Not the best-known prisoner in her lifetime, she has a reputation today for haunting the Tower. And no wonder: the elderly 70-year-old was condemned by Henry VIII in 1541 for a potentially treacherous bloodline (she was the last Plantagenet princess) and hacked to death by the executioner after she refused to put her head on the block like a common traitor and attempted to run away.

Queen Catherine Howard. Henry VIII's fifth wife was locked up for high treason and infidelity and beheaded in 1542 at age 20. Ever eager to please, she spent her final night practicing how to lay her head on the block.

Lady Jane Grey. The nine-days-queen lost her head in 1554 at age 16. Her death was the result of sibling rivalry gone seriously wrong, when Protestant Edward VI slighted his Catholic sister Mary in favor of Lady Jane as heir, and Mary decided to have none of it.

Guy Fawkes. The Roman Catholic soldier who tried to blow up the Houses of Parliament and kill the king in the 1605 Gunpowder plot was first incarcerated in the chambers of the Tower, where King James I requested he be tortured in ever-worsening ways. Perhaps unsurprisingly, he confessed. He met his seriously grisly end in the Old Palace Yard at Westminster, where he was hung, drawn, and quartered in 1607.

Sir Walter Raleigh. Once a favorite of Elizabeth I, he offended her by secretly marrying her Maid of Honor and was chucked in the Tower. Later, as a conspirator against James I, he paid with his life. A frequent visitor to the Tower (he spent 13 years there in three stints), he managed to get the Bloody Tower enlarged on account of his wife and growing family. He was finally executed in 1618 in Old Palace Yard, Westminster.

Josef Jakobs. The last man to be executed in the Tower was caught as a spy when parachuting in from Germany and executed by firing squad in 1941. The chair he sat in when he was shot is preserved in the Royal Armouries' artifacts store.

FOR FURTHER EVIDENCE . . .

A trio of buildings in the Inner Ward, the **Bloody Tower, Beauchamp Tower,** and **Queen's House,** all with excellent views of the execution scaffold in Tower Green, are the heart of the Tower's prison accommodations and home to a permanent exhibition about notable inmates.

TACKLING THE TOWER (without losing your head)

MAKING THE MOST OF YOUR TIME:
Without doubt, the Tower is worth two to three hours. A full hour of that would be well spent by joining one of the Yeoman Warders' tours (included in admission). It's hard to better their insight, vitality, and humor—they are knights of the realm living their very own fairytale castle existence.

The Crown Jewels are worth the wait, the White Tower is essential, and the Medieval Palace and Bloody Tower should at least be breezed through.

■ TIP➜ **It's best to visit on weekdays, when the crowds are smaller.**

WITH KIDS: The Tower's centuries-old cobblestones are not exactly stroller-friendly, but strollers are permitted inside most of the buildings. If you do bring one, be prepared to leave it temporarily unsupervised (the stroller, that is—not your child) outside the White Tower, which has no access. There are baby-changing facilities in the Brick Tower restrooms behind the Jewel House. Look for regular free children's events such as the Knight's school where children can have a go at jousting, sword-fighting, and archery.

■ TIP➜ Tell your child to find one of the Yeoman Warders if he or she should get lost; they will in turn lead him or her to the Byward Tower, which is where you should meet.

IN A HURRY? If you have less than an hour, head down Wall Walk, through a succession of towers, which eventually spit you out at the Martin Tower. The view over modern London is quite a contrast.

TOURS: Tours given by a Yeoman Warder leave from the main entrance near Middle Tower every half-hour from 10–4, and last about an hour. Beefeaters give occasional 30-minute talks in the Lanthorn Tower about their daily lives. Both tours are free. Check website for talks and workshops

Fire. The intricate lively figures on the choir-stall nearby are the work of master carver Grinling Gibbons, who also embellished the Wren-designed great organ. Behind the high altar is the American Memorial Chapel, dedicated to the 28,000 American GIs stationed in the United Kingdom during World War II. Among the notables buried in the crypt are the Duke of Wellington, Admiral Lord Nelson, Sir Joshua Reynolds, Henry Moore, and Wren himself. The Latin epitaph above his tomb fittingly reads, "Reader, if you seek his monument, look around you."

Free, introductory 20-minute talks are offered regularly throughout the day. Free 90-minute guided tours take place Monday through Saturday at 10, 11, 1, and 2; reserve a place at the welcome desk when you arrive. ■ TIP➔ Save £2 per ticket and get fast-track entry by booking online. ⊠ *St. Paul's Churchyard, City of London* ☎ *020/7246–8350* ⊕ *www. stpauls.co.uk* ✉ *£18* ☉ *Closed Sun. except for services* Ⓜ *St. Paul's.*

Tower Bridge. Despite its medieval appearance, London's most iconic bridge was actually built at the tail end of the Victorian era in the then-popular neo-Gothic style, first opening to traffic in 1894. With a latticed steel construction clad in Portland stone, the bridge is famous for its enormous bascules—the 1,000-ton "arms" that open to allow ships taller than its normal 28-foot clearance to glide beneath. The steam-powered bascules were a marvel of Victorian engineering when they were created (you can still visit the Engine Room, now with explanatory films and interactive displays), and required 80 people to raise and lower. Initially, heavy river traffic meant this happened 20 to 30 times a day, but it's now reduced to just a few times per month (see the bridge's website for a schedule).

The family-friendly **Tower Bridge Exhibition** includes the ground-level Engine Room, displays in the North Tower documenting the bridge's history, access to the east and west walkways that run alongside the road between the turrets and provide views over the river and city, and for those untroubled by vertigo, a transparent walkway 138 feet up between the towers that lets you look down on the traffic or, if the bascules are raised, the ships below. ⊠ *Tower Bridge Rd., City of London* ☎ *020/7403–3761* ⊕ *www.towerbridge.org.uk* ✉ *£9.80; joint admission with Monument £11* Ⓜ *Tower Hill.*

FAMILY

Fodor's Choice

★

Tower of London. Nowhere else does history seem so vividly alive as in this minicity begun by the Normans more than 1,000 years ago. In its time, the Tower has been a fortress, a mint, a palace, an archive, and the Royal Menagerie (which formed the kernel of the London Zoo). Most of all, however, it has been known as a place of imprisonment and death. Thousands of unfortunate souls, including numerous aristocrats and even a few sovereigns (some notorious traitors, some complete innocents), spent their last days here, several etching their final recorded thoughts onto their cell walls, and pints of royal blood have been spilled on its stones. Executions at the Tower were reserved for the nobility, with the most privileged beheaded in the privacy of **Tower Green** instead of before the mob at Tower Hill. In fact, only seven people received this dubious "honor," among them Anne Boleyn and Catherine Howard, two of Henry VIII's six wives. The **White Tower,**

the oldest building in the complex (which is actually made up of 20 towers, not just one) is also its most conspicuous. Begun by William the Conqueror in 1078 and whitewashed (hence the name) by Henry III (1207–72), it contains the **Armouries,** a splendid collection of arms and armor. Across the moat to the right is the riverside **Traitors' Gate,** to which the most famous prisoners were rowed to bring them to their impending doom.

Opposite is the **Bloody Tower,** where the "little princes in the Tower"— the uncrowned boy king Edward V and his brother—were consigned by their wicked uncle, who then took the crown for himself, thus becoming Richard III. The boys were never seen again, widely assumed to have been murdered in their tower prison. Also not-to-be-missed are the gorgeous **Crown Jewels** in the Jewel House. The original crown, orb, and scepter, symbols of monarchial power, were destroyed during the English Civil War; the ones you see here date back to after the Restoration in 1661. The most impressive gems were added only in the 20th century, when their countries of origin were part of the British Empire. Free 60-minute tours of the Tower depart every half hour or so (until mid-afternoon) from the main entrance. They are conducted by the Yeoman Warders, more popularly known as Beefeaters, who have guarded the Tower since Henry VII appointed them in 1485. Veterans of Britain's armed forces, they're easy to spot in their resplendent navy-and-red Tudor uniforms (scarlet-and-gold on special occasions). Keep an eye out for the ravens upon whose residency of the Tower, legend has it, the safety of the kingdom depends. ■ TIP➔ Avoid lines by buying a ticket in advance online, by phone, or from the automatic kiosks on Tower Hill. For free tickets to the 700-year-old Ceremony of the Keys (the locking of the main gates, nightly between 9:30 and 10), write several months in advance; check the Tower website for details. ⊠ *Tower Hill, City of London* 🕾 *020/3166–6000* ⊕ *www.hrp.org.uk* ⊠ *£26.80 (£22.70 online)* Ⓜ *Tower Hill.*

6

EAST LONDON

Getting Oriented

Dunston Rd.
Pownall Rd.
Broadway Market
Bush Rd.
e5 Bakehouse
Northiam St.
Regents Row
Grand Union Canal
Laburnum St.
Whiston Rd.
Andrew's Rd.
Sutton House
Nuttall St.
Kingsland Rd.
Hows St.
Appleby St.
Ormsby St.
Gettrye St.
Haggerston Park
Pritchards Rd.
Cambridge Heath Rd.
Bishop's Way
The ArcellorMittal Orbit
Regent's Canal
HOXTON
Coate St.
Cambridge Heath Station
Queen Elizabeth Olympic Park
Hoxton St.
Falkirk St.
Dunloe St.
Temple St.
Hoxton Station
Cremer St.
Hackney Rd.
Warner Pl.
Victoria Pk. S.
SHOREDITCH
Columbia Road Flower Market
Old Bethnal Green Rd.
V & A Museum of Childhood
Barnet Grove
Gosset St.
BETHNAL GREEN
Old St.
Curtain Rd.
Shoreditch High St.
Swanfield St.
Brick La.
Turin St.
Vallance Rd.
Bethnal Green Rd.
BETHNAL GREEN
Weavers Fields
Maureen Paley Gallery
Great Eastern St.
Redchurch St.
Bethnal Green Station
Cambridge Heath Rd.
Cleveland Way
Bethnal Green Rd.
Cheshire St.
Dunbridge St.
Cottingwood St.
SHOREDITCH HIGH STREET
Spitalfields City Farm
Brady St.
Quaker St.
Buxton St.
Burial Ground
Mile End Rd.
Commercial
Old Truman Brewery
SPITALFIELDS
Vallance Rd.
Appold St.
Folgate St.
Hanbury St.
WHITECHAPEL
Raven Row
Dennis Severs' House
Lamb St.
Old Spitalfields Market
Poppie's of Spitalfields
Brushfield St.
Fournier St.
Hanbury St.
Greatorex St.
Whitechapel Rd.
Stepney Way
Liverpool St. Station
Christ Church, Spitalfields
Fashion St.
Old Montague St.
LIVERPOOL STREET
White's Row
Settles St.
Greenfield Rd.
Myrtle St.
New Rd.
Royal London Hospital Museum
Cavell St.
Sidney St.
Bishopsgate
Middlesex St.
Whitechapel Art Gallery
Castle St.
Adler St.
Varden St.
Houndsditch St.
Bevis Marks
Whitechapel High St.
ALDGATE EAST
Nelson St.
Commercial Rd.
Bevis Marks Synagogue
ALDGATE
Braham St.
Alie St.
Gowers Wk.
Cannon St.
Bigland St.

0   1/4 mi

East London

0   1/4 km

TOP REASONS TO GO

Dennis Severs' House: The atmospheric set-pieces in this Georgian town house use visuals, sounds, and aromas to evoke the lives of its fictional previous inhabitants.

Broadway Market: Check out more than 100 food stalls here on Saturday, offering everything from cheeses to oysters.

London's hottest art scene: Edgy galleries mix with large collections.

Jack the Ripper: Track Britain's most infamous serial killer through streets that were part of a major slum area in Victorian times.

The ArcelorMittal Orbit: This enormous sculpture offers great views over London and a rush of adrenaline if you take the quick route back down to earth via the slide.

SAFETY

Around Shoreditch, Spitalfields, and Brick Lane, streets are largely safe during daylight hours. Be cautious on the rougher streets of Whitechapel, Bethnal Green, and Hackney at night.

FEELING PECKISH?

E5 Bakehouse. This bakery, which supplies bread to many of East London's top eateries, has a friendly café on-site, where you can sample some of the tastiest toasted sandwiches in the city, plus pizzas on Sunday. ⊠ *Mentmore Terr., Arch 395, Dalston* ☎ *020/8986–9600* ⊕ *www.e5bakehouse.com* ☾ *No dinner* Ⓜ *Overground: London Fields.*

Poppies of Spitalfields. Poppies of Spitalfields strikes a balance between trendy and traditional with retro-diner style and efficient service. The specialty is fish-and-chips, but if fish isn't your thing, try the free-range grilled chicken. ⊠ *6–8 Hanbury St., Spitalfields* ☎ *0207/247–0892* ⊕ *www.poppies-fishandchips.co.uk* Ⓜ *Shoreditch High Street.*

GETTING THERE

The London Overground, with stops at Shoreditch High Street, Hoxton, Whitechapel, Dalston Junction, Dalston Kingsland, London Fields, Hackney Central, and Hackney Wick is the easiest way to reach East London. Alternatively, the best Tube stations to use are Old Street on the Northern Line, Bethnal Green on the Central Line, and Liverpool Street on the Metropolitan and Circle lines.

MAKING THE MOST OF YOUR TIME

To experience East London at its most lively, visit on the weekend. Spitalfields Market bustles all weekend, while Brick Lane and Columbia Road are best on a Sunday morning and Broadway Market on Saturday. If you're planning to explore East London's art galleries, pick up a free map at the Whitechapel Art Gallery. As for the area's booming nightlife scene, there's no time limit: you'll find people partying Wednesday through Sunday.

GUIDED TOURS

The two-hour **Jack the Ripper Walk** (⊕ *www.walks. com*) departs from Tower Hill Tube station daily at 7:30 pm, plus Saturday at 3. **Street Art London** (⊕ *www.streetartlondon.co.uk*) offers two- and four-hour walking tours of East London's street art on Tuesday and Thursday at 10 am and weekends at 11 am.

7

Sightseeing
★★★
Nightlife
★★★★★
Dining
★★★★
Lodging
★★★
Shopping
★★★★

Made famous by Dickens and infamous by Jack the Ripper, East London is one of London's most enduringly evocative neighborhoods, rich in popular history, architectural gems, and artists' studios. Since the early 1990s, hip gallerists, designers, and new-media entrepreneurs have colonized its handsome Georgian buildings and converted industrial lofts. Today, this collection of neighborhoods lays claim to being the city's hippest area.

Updated by
Jo Caird

The British equivalent of parts of Brooklyn, East London is a patchwork of districts encompassing struggling artists, multicultural enclaves, and upscale professionals occasionally teetering, like its New York equivalent, on the edge of self-parody. The vast area ranges from gentrified districts like Spitalfields, where bankers and successful artists live in desirable renovated town houses, to parts of Hackney, where seemingly derelict, graffiti-covered industrial buildings are hives of exciting creative activity. It remains a little rough around the edges, so stick to busier streets at night.

At the start of the new millennium, Hoxton, an enclave of Shoreditch, became the glossy hub of London's buzzing contemporary art scene, which accelerated the gentrification process. Some artists, such as Tracey Emin and Gilbert & George, long-term residents of Spitalfields' handsome Georgian terraces—and successful enough to still afford the area—have remained.

One such residence, **Dennis Severs' House,** was transformed two decades ago by the eponymous American artist into a unique "living house museum" that evokes how past generations of a fictional Huguenot family might have lived there. Not far away, **Spitalfields Market** offers an ever-changing selection of crafts and funky clothes stalls under a glass roof in what was once a Victorian produce market. Across from the market, **Christ Church, Spitalfields,** Nicholas Hawkmoor's masterpiece, soars above Fournier Street.

DID YOU KNOW?

The Columbia Road Flower Market opens at 8 am on Sunday. Arrive early to see the photogenic market at its best and to find the freshest selection. The road is lined with funky shops selling antiques, vintage clothing, horticultural accessories, and more.

GUIDE TO THE STREETS IN LONDON'S EAST END

Brick Lane and the narrow streets running off it offer a paradigm of East London's development. Its population has moved in waves: communities seeking refuge, others moving out in an upwardly mobile direction.

Brick Lane has seen the manufacture of bricks (during the 16th century), beer, and bagels, but nowadays it's primarily known as the heart of Banglatown—Bangladeshis make up one-third of the population in this London borough, and you'll see that the names of the surrounding streets are written in Bengali—where you find many kebab and curry houses along with shops selling DVDs, colorful saris, and stacks of sticky sweets. On Sunday morning, cars aren't allowed on the upper section of the street. Shops and cafés are open, and several stalls are set up, creating a companion market to the one on nearby **Petticoat Lane.**

Fournier Street contains fine examples of the neighborhood's characteristic Georgian terraced houses, many of them built by the richest of the early-18th-century Huguenot silk weavers (note the enlarged windows on the upper floors to maximize light for the intricate work). Most of those along the north side of Fournier Street have since been restored.

Wilkes Street, with more 1720s Huguenot houses, is north of Christ Church, Spitalfields; and neighboring **Princelet Street** was once important to East London's Jewish community. Where No. 6 stands now, the first of several thriving Yiddish theaters opened in 1886. **Elder Street,** just off Folgate, is another gem of original 18th-century houses. On the south and east side of Spitalfields Market are yet more time-warp streets that are worth a wander, such as **Gun Street,** where artist Mark Gertler (1891–1939) was born, at No. 16.

In the last decade, streets around the Old Street roundabout (as well as converted warehouses in Hackney and Dalston) have flourished with start-ups, with attendant stylish boutiques (especially on Redchurch Street), destination restaurants, and hipster bars as part of a government initiative to attract IT-oriented businesses to the neighborhood. Old and new Shoreditch meet on **Brick Lane,** the heart of the Bangladeshi community, lined with innumerable curry houses and glittering sari shops, plus vintage-clothing emporia. Here you'll also find the **Old Truman Brewery,** an East London landmark converted into a warren of street fashion and pop-up galleries. On Sunday, the Columbia Road Flower Market to the north of Brick Lane becomes a colorful, fragrant oasis of greenery.

As property prices have climbed, up-and-coming artists have sought more affordable studio spaces in former industrial buildings eastward toward Whitechapel and Bethnal Green, where there are also some notable galleries. Here you'll find the **V&A Museum of Childhood,** a delight for children of all ages, and—a design connoisseur's favorite—the **Geffrye Museum,** a collection of domestic interiors through the ages that

The East End Art Scene

Banksy, the Bristol-based artist and provocateur who has maintained his anonymity despite works that now command six figures, is widely credited with making Londoners see street art as more than mere vandalism. He first came to public attention in the East End in the late '80s, and the area continues to attract new talent from around the globe today. Unfortunately, much of Banksy's early work has been lost, either from being covered over by local councils and building owners, defaced by other graffiti artists, or removed by profiteers. Currently murals remain at Rivington Street near Old Street (in the garden of Cargo bar and nightclub), and Stoke Newington Church Street. **Street Art London** (🌐 www.streetartlondon.co.uk) offers a knowledgeable, insider view on the ever-changing scene, taking you through the history of street art and graffiti in this area and highlighting the best of Banksy's successors. Take the Saturday tour to avoid the noise of weekday traffic.

Today, East London is a global hotbed of contemporary art, but its avant-garde roots go way back. **Shoreditch's** cheap industrial units

and Georgian–Victorian terraced streets have attracted artists since the 1960s, when op-art pioneer Bridget Riley established a service to find affordable studio space for her contemporaries. In the early '90s it gained new notoriety when Young British Artists Sarah Lucas and Tracey Emin began selling their own and their friends' work in The Shop, joining Maureen Paley's influential Bethnal Green gallery, and the long-established Whitechapel Art Gallery, where many leading abstract expressionists and pop artists had their first U.K. shows. **Hoxton** truly became a destination for well-heeled collectors when Jay Jopling, the most important modern-art dealer in town, set up his White Cube gallery in 2000 (it's now in Bermondsey, with a second location at Mason's Yard in Westminster), followed by Kate MacGarry's gallery in 2002.

Priced out by the area's fashionability, the emerging artists themselves have relocated farther off the beaten path to edgier neighborhoods such as **Hackney,** with several trendsetting galleries found clustered around **Cambridge Heath Road** and **Vyner Street.**

7

occupies a row of early-18th-century almshouses (although the museum will be closed for renovations the entirety of 2019).

Probably the best start to an East London tour is via the London Overground, getting off at Shoreditch High Street Station. Immediately northwest of the station, on the west side of Shoreditch High Street, is the heart of the neighborhood that aspires to be the U.K. equivalent to Silicon Valley. To the northeast is Shoreditch's boutique, gallery, and restaurant zone. The subneighborhood of Hoxton is located just above Shoreditch, north of the Old Street roundabout. To the southeast of the station are the handsome Georgian streets of Spitalfields. Bethnal Green is due east, past busy Brick Lane. Whitechapel, formerly Jack the Ripper's patch, is to the south of Spitalfields. All of these neighborhoods

On Sunday, additional clothing and craft stalls surround Spitalfields covered market.

are within what is traditionally referred to as the "East End," although East London extends farther to the north and east.

Bevis Marks Synagogue. This is Britain's oldest synagogue still in use and is certainly its most splendid. It was built in 1701, after the Jews, having been expelled from England in 1290, were allowed to return under Cromwell in 1656. Inspired by the Spanish and Portuguese Great Synagogue of Amsterdam, the interior is embellished with rich woodwork, seven hanging brass candelabra (representing the seven days of the week), and 12 trompe-l'oeil wood columns painted to look like marble. The magnificent Ark, which contains the sacred scrolls of the five books of Moses, is modeled on contemporary Wren neoclassical altarpieces, with oak doors and Corinthian columns. In 1992 and 1993 the synagogue was seriously damaged by IRA bombs, but was subsequently completely restored. ⊠ *Bevis Marks, Whitechapel* ☎ *020/7621–1188* ⊕ *www.sephardi.org.uk/bevis-marks* ⊠ *£5* ⊙ *Closed Sat.* Ⓜ *Aldgate, Liverpool St.*

Fodor'sChoice **Christ Church, Spitalfields.** This is the 1729 masterpiece of Sir Christopher
★ Wren's associate Nicholas Hawksmoor, one of his six London churches and an example of English baroque at its finest. It was commissioned as part of Parliament's 1711 "Fifty New Churches" Act, passed in response to the influx of immigrants with the idea of providing for the religious needs of the "godless thousands"—and to help ensure they joined the Church of England, as opposed to such nonconformist denominations as the Protestant Huguenots. (It must have worked; you can still see gravestones with epitaphs in French in the crypt.) As the local silk industry declined, the church fell into disrepair, and by 1958

the structure was crumbling, with the looming prospect of demolition. But after 25 years—longer than it took to build the church—and a huge local fund-raising effort, the structure was meticulously restored and is a joy to behold, from the colonnaded Doric portico and tall spire to its soaring, heavily ornamented plaster ceiling. Its excellent acoustics make it a superb concert venue. Tours that take you "backstage" to the many hidden rooms and passages, from the tower to the vaults, are offered by appointment. There's also a café in the crypt. ⊠ *Commercial St., Spitalfields* ☎ *020/7377–2440* ⊕ *www.ccspitalfields.org* ✎ *Free, tours £6* ⊘ *Closed Sat.* Ⓜ *Overground: Shoreditch High St.*

Columbia Road Flower Market. On Sunday morning this largely built-up area is transformed into a riot of color and scent with the arrival of the flower sellers. There's everything from bedding plants to banana trees, including herbs, cut flowers, and bouquets at very reasonable prices. The vendors' patter is part of the fun. Columbia Road itself is lined with some 60 independent shops, so you can pick up some art, antiques, handcrafted jewelry, or, of course, garden accessories to go with your greenery. To avoid the crowds, get here the earlier the better. ⊠ *Columbia Rd., Hackney* ⊕ *www.columbiaroad.info* Ⓜ *Old St., Northern Line.*

Fodor's Choice
★

Dennis Severs' House. The remarkable interiors of this extraordinary time machine of a house are the creation of Dennis Severs (1948–99), a performer-designer-scholar from Escondido, California, who dedicated his life to restoring this Georgian terraced house. More than that, he created "still-life dramas" using sight, sound, and smell to evoke the world of a fictitious family of Huguenot silk weavers, the Jervises, who might have inhabited the house between 1728 and 1914. Each of the 10 rooms has a distinctive compelling atmosphere that encourages visitors to become lost in another time, deploying evocative design details like rose-laden Victorian wallpaper, Jacobean paneling, Georgian wing-back chairs, baroque carved ornaments, rich "Catholic" wall colors downstairs, and more sedate "Protestant" shades upstairs. The Silent Night candlelight tour offered Monday, Wednesday, and Friday evenings, a stroll through the rooms with no talking allowed, is the most theatrical and memorable way to experience the house. The Exclusive Silent Night visits, which conclude with champagne or mulled wine by the fire and a chat with the curators, are available one night per month (more frequently near the Christmas holiday), and private group visits can also be arranged. ⊠ *18 Folgate St., Shoreditch* ☎ *020/7247–4013* ⊕ *www.dennissevershouse.co.uk* ✎ *£10 Sun. and Mon., £15 Mon., Wed., and Fri. evenings* ⊘ *Closed Tues., Thurs., and Sat.* Ⓜ *Overground: Shoreditch High St.*

Maureen Paley Gallery. Inspired by the DIY punk aesthetic and the funky galleries of New York's Lower East Side, Maureen Paley started putting on exhibitions in her East End home back in 1984, when it was virtually the only gallery in the area. Since then, this American artist and gallerist has shown such respected contemporary artists as Gillian Wearing, Helen Chadwick, Jenny Holzer, Peter Fischli, and Wolfgang Tillmans and, today, is considered the doyenne of East End gallerists. The gallery has been in its current home, a converted warehouse in Bethnal Green, since 1999. ✉ *21 Herald St., Bethnal Green* ☎ *020/7729–4112* ⊕ *www.maureenpaley.com* ✉ *Free* ⊘ *Closed Mon. and Tues.* Ⓜ *Bethnal Green.*

FAMILY **Old Truman Brewery.** The last East End brewery still standing—a handsome example of Georgian and 19th-century industrial architecture, and in late Victorian times the largest brewery in the world—has been transformed into a cavernous hipster mall housing galleries, record shops, fashion-forward boutiques, bars, clubs, and restaurants, along with an array of international street-food vendors. The retailers are at street level with offices and studios on the upper floors. Events include fashion shows for both new and established designers, excellent sample sales, art installations, and, on weekends, a food hall and a vintage clothes fair. The brewery itself shut down in 1989. ✉ *91 Brick La., Spitalfields* ☎ *0207/770–6000* ⊕ *www.trumanbrewery.com* Ⓜ *Overground: Shoreditch High St.*

FAMILY **Queen Elizabeth Olympic Park.** Built for the London 2012 Olympic and
Fodor's Choice Paralympic games, this 560-acre parkland still boasts some of the city's
★ best sporting arenas. The Stadium, site of the London 2012 athletics competitions, is now home to local soccer team Westham United; it also hosts major athletic events. In addition, it's open for behind-the-scenes tours; check the website for dates. You can try four types of cycling (track, road-racing, BMX, and mountain-biking) at the Lee Valley VeloPark or go for a swim in the magnificent pool within the London Aquatics Centre. The ArcelorMittal Orbit, an enormous sculpture, is well worth a visit—the views across London from the top are terrific. Thrill-seekers have a couple of options when it comes to getting back down: a gasp-inducing slide that twists its way around the outside of the structure (art buffs might recognize it as the work of Belgian artist Carsten Höller) or via vertical rappelling (available on selected dates, advance booking essential). ✉ *East End* ☎ *020/3288–1800* ⊕ *www.queenelizabetholympicpark.co.uk* ✉ *Orbit £11.20, Orbit and slide £16.50, rappelling £85, stadium tours £19, cycling sessions (including bike and helmet hire) £15–£45* Ⓜ *Stratford, Hackney Wick, Pudding Mill Lane, Leyton.*

Fodor's Choice **Regent's Canal.** The 19th-century waterway known as Regent's Canal
★ officially starts in Little Venice in West London, but you'll find this quirky section east of City Road Basin. Join the towpath, where horses once walked as they pulled barges carrying all manner of cargo, at Wharf Road in Islington (N1) then head east on foot or by bike to experience the East End from an unusual perspective. What was once a no-go area is now a route lined with trendy cafés, floating bookshops, and a distinct community of water-dwelling Londoners. The Regent's Canal runs through Hackney, before heading south through Bethnal Green and Mile End, ending up at Limehouse Basin and the River Thames. Or you can continue eastwards by turning off along the Hertford Union Canal at Victoria Park, a route that eventually leads to the Queen Elizabeth Olympic Park. ✉ *East End.*

Royal London Hospital Museum. Located in the crypt of a Victorian church, the Royal London Hospital Museum uses exhibits of historic medical equipment, surgical instruments, and archives to document the history of this East London institution from its foundation in 1740 to the present day. Highlights include a forensic medicine section with documentation and original materials connected to the Jack the Ripper murders and the RLH surgeon who helped investigate them. There are also artifacts and documents relating to Joseph Merrick (aka the Elephant Man) who spent his final years in the hospital, and a set of dentures worn by George Washington. Opening hours are subject to change on short notice, so call ahead. ✉ *St. Augustine with St. Philip's Church, Newark St., Whitechapel* ☎ *020/7377–7608* ⊕ *www.bartshealth.nhs. uk/the-royal-london-hospital-museum-and-archives* ⌨ *Free* ⊘ *Closed Sat.–Mon.* Ⓜ *Whitechapel.*

FAMILY **Spitalfields City Farm.** An oasis of rural calm in an urban landscape, this little community farm raises a variety of animals, including some rare breeds, to help educate city kids about life in the country. A tiny farm shop sells freshly laid eggs, along with organic seasonal produce. ✉ *Buxton St., Spitalfields* ☎ *020/7247–8762* ⊕ *www.spitalfieldscity-farm.org* ⌨ *Free* ⊘ *Closed Mon.* Ⓜ *Overground: Shoreditch High St.*

FAMILY **Sutton House.** Built by a courtier to King Henry VIII, this Tudor mansion has since been home to merchants, Huguenot silk weavers, and, in the 1980s, a group of arty squatters. The house dates back to 1535, when Hackney was a village on the outskirts of London surrounded by fields. Later, in 1751, it was split into two self-contained houses. Its oak-paneled rooms, tranquil courtyard, and adorable café are an unexpected treat in an area that's yet to entirely shake off its grit. Guided tours are available by appointment. ✉ *2–4 Homerton High St., Hackney* ☎ *020/8986–2264* ⊕ *www.nationaltrust.org.uk/sutton-house* ⌨ *£6.30, tours £20* ⊘ *Closed Mon. and Tues., except Aug.* Ⓜ *Overground: Hackney Central.*

FAMILY
Fodor's Choice
★ **V&A Museum of Childhood.** A treat for children of all ages, this East London outpost of the Victoria & Albert Museum—in an iron, glass, and brown-brick building transported here from South Kensington in 1868—houses one of the world's biggest toy collections. One highlight (among many) is the large Dolls' Houses collection, with interiors from 1673 up to the present. You'll find everything from board games and puzzles to teddy bears and train sets. The collection is organized into galleries: Moving Toys, which includes everything from rocking horses to Xboxes; Creativity, which encompasses dolls, puppets, chemistry sets, play kitchens, construction toys, and musical instruments; and Childhood, with areas devoted to babies, an exhibit of children's clothes from the mid-1600s to the present, and toys inspired by adult pursuits, such as toy soldiers, toy guns, and toy hospitals. Don't miss the magnificent 18th-century commedia dell'arte puppet theater, thought to have been made in Venice. There are special activities for the under-fives. The shop has replica toys that make great presents. ✉ *Cambridge Heath Rd., Bethnal Green* ☎ *020/8983–5200* ⊕ *www.museumofchildhood.org.uk* ⌨ *Free* Ⓜ *Bethnal Green.*

7

Fodor's Choice   **Whitechapel Art Gallery.** Founded in 1901, this internationally renowned
★   gallery mounts exhibitions that rediscover overlooked masters and
showcase tomorrow's legends. Painter and leading exponent of abstract
expressionism Jackson Pollock was exhibited here in the 1950s as was
pop artist Robert Rauschenberg in the 1960s; the 1970s saw a young
David Hockney's first solo show. The exhibitions continue to be on
the cutting edge of contemporary art. The gallery also hosts talks, film
screenings, workshops, and other events; tours of local galleries take
place on the first Thursday of every month. Pick up a free East London
art map to help you plan your visit to the area. ✉ *77–82 Whitechapel
High St., Whitechapel* ☎ *020/7522-7888* ⊕ *www.whitechapelgallery.
org* ⌖ *Free–£15* ⊘ *Closed Mon.* Ⓜ *Aldgate East.*

SOUTH OF
THE THAMES

Getting Oriented

South of the Thames

GETTING THERE	TOP REASONS TO GO
For the South Bank, use Embankment on the District, Circle, Northern, and Bakerloo lines and walk across the Golden Jubilee Bridges; or Waterloo on the Northern, Jubilee, and Bakerloo lines, from where it's a 10-minute walk.	**Shakespeare's Globe:** See one of Shakespeare's plays in this historically accurate replica of the Elizabethan theater where they were first performed.
	The Tate Modern: One of the world's great collections of post-1900 modern art, the centerpiece of this Tate branch is the huge renovated electric turbine hall, now an exhibition space used for large installations.
London Bridge on the Northern and Jubilee lines is five minutes from Borough Market and Southwark Cathedral. The station also serves Bermondsey Street, although, confusingly, the next stop on the Jubilee Line is called Bermondsey. Brixton has its own stop on the Victoria Line.	**Sunset on Waterloo Bridge:** This is one of London's most romantic views, with St. Paul's to the east and the Houses of Parliament to the west.
	The London Eye: One of the city's tallest structures, this observation wheel gives you a bird's-eye view of some of the city's most iconic sights.

MAKING THE MOST OF YOUR TIME

Don't attempt to visit the area south of the Thames in one go. Tate Modern alone deserves a whole afternoon, especially if you want to do justice to both the temporary exhibitions and the permanent collection. The Globe requires about two hours for the exhibition theater tour and two to three hours for a performance. Finish with drinks at the Oxo Tower or one of the Shard's restaurants, with their spectacular views. You can return across the river to central London via Southwark on the Jubilee Line from Tate Modern, although it's a good walk to the station. Crossing the Millennium Bridge for St. Paul's on the Central Line or the Golden Jubilee Bridge to Embankment Station offers longer but more scenic alternatives.

8

FEELING PECKISH?

Pieminister. In the shopping enclave of Gabriel's Wharf, you'll find this branch of Pieminister, which began life in Borough Market. Have a meat pie made with ingredients like free-range chicken with bacon and tarragon. ✉ *Gabriel's Wharf, 56 Upper Ground, South Bank* ☎ *020/7928–5755* ⊕ *www.pieminister.co.uk* ☽ *No dinner* Ⓜ *Waterloo.*

Wahaca. This canteen-style outpost of the eco-conscious chain serves mildly spiced Mexican food like marinated grilled chicken or tostadas with Devon crab, plus the usual burritos, quesadillas, tacos, and salads. ✉ *119 Waterloo Rd., South Bank* ☎ *020/3697–4140* ⊕ *www.wahaca.co.uk* Ⓜ *Waterloo.*

Sightseeing
★★★★★
Nightlife
★★★★
Dining
★★★
Lodging
★
Shopping
★★

This area is one of London's leading destinations, with attractions including the IWM London, the Southbank Centre (Europe's largest arts center), and the heavenly Borough Market. Most are clustered around the South Bank and in Bankside and Southwark, but the surrounding neighborhoods of Bermondsey and Lambeth are rising rapidly, with galleries, shops, and restaurants proliferating. And the formerly drab Nine Elms area (near Vauxhall) is in the process of being totally transformed, with luxury high-rises and shops proliferating in the wake of the huge, fairly new U.S. embassy in the area.

Updated by
Ellin Stein

A borough of the City of London since 1327, Southwark first became well known for its inns (the pilgrims in Chaucer's *A Canterbury Tale* set off from one), theaters, prisons, tanneries, and brothels, as well as entertainments such as cockfighting. For four centuries, this was a sort of border town outside the city walls (and jurisdiction) where Londoners went to let their hair down and behave badly. Originally, you were just as likely to see a few bouts of bearbaiting at the Globe as you were Shakespeare's most recent work. But now that south London encompasses a world-class museum, high-caliber art, music, film, and theater venues, as well as an aquarium, a historic warship, two popular food markets, and greatly improved transportation links, this neighborhood has become one of London's leading destinations.

Today, you can walk the **Thames Path** along the river from the London Eye all the way to Greenwich. The segment beside the South Bank is alive with skateboarders, secondhand-book stalls, and street entertainers. At one end the **London Eye,** a 21st-century landmark that became an instant favorite with both Londoners and out-of-towners, rises next to the **London Aquarium** and the **Southbank Centre,** home to the **Royal Festival Hall,** the **Hayward Gallery,** the **BFI Southbank,** and the **National Theatre.**

The restaurant at Tate Modern has some of the best views in London. Here you can see St. Paul's Cathedral in the distance.

Farther east you'll come to a reconstruction of Sir Francis Drake's 16th-century ship the *Golden Hinde*; **Butler's Wharf,** where some notable restaurants occupy what were once shadowy Dickensian docklands; **the Shard,** the tallest building in the EU, which offers spectacular views over the city; and, next to **Tower Bridge,** the massive headlight-shape **City Hall.** Nearby Bermondsey Street (from "Beormund's Eye," as it was known in Saxon times) is home to the bright yellow Fashion Museum, the White Cube Gallery, and lots of trendy shops, restaurants, and cafés. Meanwhile, younger visitors will enjoy the **London Dungeon** and **HMS** *Belfast,* a decommissioned Royal Navy cruiser, while food lovers should make a straight line to London's oldest food market, **Borough Market,** where the independent stallholders sell farm-fresh produce, artisanal bread and cheese, and specialty fish and meat.

Even from the Shard's lofty viewing platform 1,016 feet up, the area south of the Thames still isn't one of London's most beautiful, but you'll be able to see how this patchwork of neighborhoods fits together. The heart is the South Bank, which extends east from the London Eye to Blackfriars Bridge, with the river to the north and Waterloo Station to the south. From Blackfriars Bridge east to London Bridge is Bankside, where you'll find the Globe and Tate Modern. Moving east from London Bridge is Borough, with its cobbled streets and former factories now turned into expensive lofts. Next, southeast of Borough, is buzzy, urban Bermondsey, while leafy Dulwich, with its renowned gallery and charming period streets, is quite a distance to the south. Returning up the river to the west of the South Bank is Lambeth and then Vauxhall, with the imposing IWM London (formerly the Imperial

War Museum), a thriving gay scene, and scary through-traffic routes. It's a rapidly changing district, thanks to a regeneration spearheaded by the opening of the U.S. Embassy in adjacent Nine Elms and a slew of upscale riverside residential developments. South of here is Brixton, long the heartland of London's Afro-Caribbean community—with a lively club scene—and now attracting young families priced out of nearby Clapham.

Bankside Gallery. Two artistic societies—the Royal Society of Painter–Printmakers and the Royal Watercolour Society—have their head-quarters in this gallery next to Tate Modern. Together they mount exhibitions of current members' work, which is usually for sale, along with art books, making this a great place for finding that unique, not too expensive gift. There are also regular themed exhibitions. ⊠ *48 Hopton St., Southwark* ☎ *020/7928–7521* ⊕ *www.banksidegallery.com* 🖾 *Free* ☉ *Call ahead for hrs* Ⓜ *Mansion House, Southwark, St. Paul's.*

FAMILY **The Clink Prison Museum.** This attraction devoted to re-creating life in a medieval prison is built on the site of the original "Clink," the oldest of Southwark's five prisons and the reason why the "clink" is now slang for jail. Owned by the Bishops of Winchester from 1144 to 1780, it was the first prison to detain women, many for prostitution. Because of the bishops' relaxed attitude toward the endemic trade—they decided to license prostitution rather than ban it—the area within their jurisdiction was known as "the Liberty of the Clink." Inside, you'll discover how grisly a Tudor prison could be, operating on a code of cruelty, deprivation, and corruption. The prison was only a small part of Winchester Palace, a huge complex that was the bishops' London residence. You can still see the remains of the early 13th-century Great Hall, with its famous rose window, next to Southwark Cathedral. ⊠ *1 Clink St., Borough* ☎ *020/7403–0900* ⊕ *www.clink. co.uk* 🖾 *£7.50* Ⓜ *London Bridge.*

FAMILY **Dulwich Picture Gallery.** Famed for its regal Old Master painting collec-
Fodor'sChoice tion, the Dulwich (pronounced "Dull-ich") Picture Gallery, designed by
★ Sir John Soane, was the world's first purpose-built art museum when it opened in 1811 (the recent extension was designed by Rick Mather). The permanent collection includes landmark works by Rembrandt, Van Dyck, Rubens, Poussin, and Gainsborough, and the museum also hosts three or so major temporary exhibitions each year. Check the website for its schedule of family activities; there's a lovely café here, too. While you're in the area, take a short wander and you'll find a handful of cute clothing and crafts stores and the well-manicured Dulwich Park, which has lakeside walks and a fine display of rhododendrons in late May. Development in Dulwich Village is tightly controlled, so it feels a bit like a time capsule, with old-fashioned street signs and hand-some 18th-century houses on the main street. ⊠ *Gallery Rd., Dulwich* ☎ *020/8693–5254* ⊕ *www.dulwichpicturegallery.org.uk* 🖾 *£8 (tempo-rary exhibitions may be extra)* ☉ *Closed Mon.* Ⓜ *Brixton Station, then Bus P4. National Rail: West Dulwich from Victoria or North Dulwich from London Bridge.*

Fashion and Textile Museum. The bright yellow-and-pink museum (it's hard to miss) designed by Mexican architect Ricardo Legorreta features changing exhibitions devoted to developments in fashion design, textiles, and jewelry from the end of World War II to the present. Founded by designer Zandra Rhodes, and now owned by Newham College, the FTM is a favorite with fans of style and costumes. There are weekday fashion-based workshops and lectures on design and aspects of fashion history; the excellent gift shop sells books on fashion and one-of-a-kind pieces by local designers. After your visit, check out the many restaurants, cafés, and boutiques that have bloomed on Bermondsey Street. ✉ *83 Bermondsey St., Bermondsey* ☎ *020/7407–8664* ⊕ *www. ftmlondon.org* 🖆 *£9.90* ⊙ *Closed Mon.* Ⓜ *London Bridge.*

Florence Nightingale Museum. Compact, highly visual, and engaging, this museum on the grounds of St. Thomas's Hospital is dedicated to Florence Nightingale, who founded the first school of nursing and played a major role in establishing modern standards of health care. Exhibits are divided into three areas: one is devoted to Nightingale's Victorian childhood, the others to her work tending soldiers during the Crimean War (1854–56) and her subsequent health-care reforms, including a display on how she developed a program for training nurses. The museum incorporates Nightingale's own books and famous lamp as well as interactive displays of medical instruments and medicinal herbs. There are free 15-minute tours on Tuesdays at 3:30, evening lectures, temporary exhibitions, and a shop with unexpectedly amusing gifts like syringe-shaped highlighters. ✉ *2 Lambeth Palace Rd., Lambeth* ☎ *020/7620– 0374* ⊕ *www.florence-nightingale.co.uk* 🖆 *£7.50* Ⓜ *Waterloo.*

The Garden Museum. This celebration of one of England's favorite hobbies was created in the mid-1970s after two gardening enthusiasts came upon a medieval church, which, they were horrified to discover, was about to be bulldozed. The churchyard contained the tombs of two adventurous 17th-century plant collectors, a father and son both called John Tradescant, who introduced many new species to England, as well as the tombs of William Bligh, captain of the *Bounty,* several members of the Boleyn family, and quite a few archbishops of Canterbury. Inspired to action, the gardeners rescued the church, and created the museum now inside it. Here you'll find one of the largest collections of historic garden tools, artifacts, and curiosities in Britain, plus photographs, paintings, and films—virtually all donated by individuals. An extension houses temporary exhibitions on subjects ranging from noted garden designers like Charles Jencks to the contemporary Guerilla Gardening movement (cultivating neglected land that doesn't belong to you). There's also a green-thumb gift shop, a glass-fronted café, and, of course, the museum's own four beautiful gardens that are maintained year-round by dedicated volunteers. ✉ *5 Lambeth Palace Rd., Lambeth* ☎ *020/7401–8865* ⊕ *www.gardenmuseum.org.uk* 🖆 *£10* ⊙ *Closed 1st Mon. of month and for occasional events; check website* Ⓜ *Lambeth North, Vauxhall.*

FAMILY **Golden Hinde II.** This is a full-size reconstruction of the little galleon in which the famed Elizabethan explorer Sir Francis Drake circumnavigated the globe in 1577–80. Launched in 1973, the exact replica made one full and one partial round-the-world voyage, calling

8

in at ports—many along the Pacific and Atlantic coasts of the United States—to do duty as a maritime museum. Now berthed at the St. Mary Overie Dock, the ship continues its educational purpose, complete with a "crew" in period costumes and three decks of artifacts. The puppet show and pirate training sessions are especially popular with younger visitors. Call for information on guided tours. ⊠ *St. Mary Overie Dock, Cathedral St., Bankside* ☎ *020/7403–0123* ⊕ *www.goldenhinde.co.uk* 🔁 *£5* Ⓜ *London Bridge.*

FAMILY   **HMS *Belfast*.** At 613½ feet, this large light cruiser is one of the last remaining big-gun armored warships from World War II, in which it played an important role in protecting the Arctic convoys and supporting the D-Day landings in Normandy; the ship later saw action during the Korean War. This floating museum has been moored in the Thames as a maritime branch of **IWM London** since 1971. A tour of all nine decks—including an engine room 15 feet below sea level, the admiral's quarters, mess decks, bakery, punishment cells, operations room, and more—gives a vivid picture of life on board the ship, while the riveting interactive gun-turret experience puts you in the middle of a World War II naval battle. ⊠ *The Queen's Walk, Borough* ☎ *020/7940–6300* ⊕ *www.iwm.org.uk* 🔁 *£17* Ⓜ *London Bridge.*

▌OFF THE
BEATEN
PATH

Horniman Museum. Set amid 16 acres of gardens, this eclectic museum is considered something of a well-kept secret by the residents of south London—perhaps because of its out-of-the-way location. You can explore world cultures, natural history, and a fine collection of some 1,300 musical instruments (including a giant tuba) here. The emphasis is on fun and a wide range of activities, including London's oldest nature trail that features domesticated creatures such as sheep, chickens, and alpacas, and an aquarium stocked with endangered species. There's also a café and shop. It's a 15-minute bus ride from here to the Dulwich Picture Gallery; Bus P4, heading toward Brixton, takes you from door to door. ⊠ *100 London Rd., Forest Hill, London* ☎ *020/8699–1872* ⊕ *www.horniman.ac.uk* 🔁 *Free (small charge for temporary exhibitions and aquarium)* Ⓜ *Overground: Forest Hill.*

FAMILY
Fodor's Choice
★

IWM London. Despite its name, the cultural venue formerly known as the Imperial War Museum (one of five IWM branches around the country) does not glorify either Empire or bloodshed but emphasizes understanding through conveying the impact of 20th- and 21st-century warfare on citizens and soldiers alike. A dramatic six-story atrium at the main entrance encloses an impressive amount of hardware—including a Battle of Britain Spitfire, a German V2 rocket, the remains of a car blown up in post-invasion Iraq, tanks, guns, and submarines—along with accompanying interactive material and a café. The First World War galleries explore the wartime experience on both the home and fighting fronts, with the most comprehensive collection on the subject in the world—some 1,300 objects ranging from uniforms, equipment, and weapons to letters and diaries. Three permanent exhibitions in the Second World War galleries shed light on that conflict: an extensive and haunting Holocaust exhibition; *A Family In Wartime,* which documents the story of one London family living through the Blitz; and *Turning Points 1934–1945,* which relates key moments in the conflict to objects

Built at the site of the original theater where Shakespeare's plays were performed, the modern-day Globe is a painstaking reconstruction of an open-air theater.

on display. *Peace and Security 1945–2015* looks at more contemporary hostilities, including the Cold War, Iraq, Afghanistan, and Kosovo. Other galleries are devoted to works relating to conflicts from World War I to the present day by painters, poets, documentary filmmakers, and photographers. James Bond fans won't want to miss the intriguing Secret War Gallery, which charts the work of secret agents. ⊠ *Lambeth Rd., South Bank* ☎ *020/7416–5000* ⊕ *www.iwm.org.uk* ✉ *Free (charge for special exhibitions)* Ⓜ *Lambeth North.*

FAMILY **London Dungeon.** Saved by a keen sense of its own borderline ridiculousness, this gory attraction is full of over-the-top tableaux depicting the bloody demise of famous figures alongside the torture, murder, and ritual slaughter of lesser-known victims, all to a sound track of screaming, wailing, and agonized moaning. There are lively dramatizations about the Great Plague, Henry VIII, (the fictional) Sweeney Todd, and (the real) Jack the Ripper, to name a few, with costumed characters leaping out of the gloom to bring the information to life and add to the fear and fun. Perhaps most shocking are the crowds of children baying to get in: most kids absolutely love this place, although those with more a sensitive disposition may find it too frightening (that goes for adults as well). Expect long lines on weekends and during school holidays. There are also adults-only evening tours that include drinks. ■TIP→ Tickets bought online and in advance can be up to 30% less than walk-up prices. ⊠ *Riverside Bldg., County Hall, Westminster Bridge Rd., South Bank* ☎ *0207/654–0809* ⊕ *www.thedungeons.com/london* ✉ *From £21* Ⓜ *Waterloo.*

Designed by renowned architect Renzo Piano, the Shard punctures the London skyline with its record-breaking height and spectacular modernity.

FAMILY
Fodor's Choice
★

London Eye. To mark the start of the new millennium, architects David Marks and Julia Barfield devised this instant icon that allows Londoners and visitors alike to see the city from a completely new perspective. The giant Ferris wheel was the largest cantilevered observation wheel ever built at the time, and remains one of the city's tallest structures. The 25-minute slow-motion ride inside one of the enclosed passenger capsules is so smooth you'd hardly know you were suspended over the Thames. On a clear day you can see up to 25 miles, with a bird's-eye view of London's most famous landmarks as you circle 360 degrees. If you're looking for a special place to celebrate, champagne and canapés can be arranged ahead of time. ■TIP➔ Buy your ticket online to avoid the long lines and get a 15% discount. For an extra £9, you can save even more time with a Fast Track flight (check in 15 minutes before your "departure"). You can also buy a combination ticket for the Eye and other London attractions (check online for details) or combine with a river cruise for a 40-minute sightseeing voyage on the Thames. In December, there's a scenic ice rink just below the wheel. ✉ *Jubilee Gardens, South Bank* ☎ *0871/781–3000* ⊕ *www.londoneye.com* ✉ *From £24.30; cruise package from £31 (bookable online only)* Ⓜ *Waterloo.*

Newport Street Gallery. Putting the seal on Vauxhall's status as an up-and-coming neighborhood, business-savvy artist Damien Hirst opened this gallery in a cavernous space that was a former Victorian scenery-painting workshop. It currently houses a rotating selection from his large private collection of contemporary art that includes works by Francis Bacon, Banksy, Picasso, Jeff Koons, Richard Hamilton, and Tracey Emin, to name just a few, along with six-month-long solo shows for emerging artists. There's also a shop selling artists' books, limited-edition prints, and sculptures, as well as a restaurant, Pharmacy 2, a reincarnation of Hirst's fashionable millennium-era Notting Hill watering hole. ⊠ *Newport St., London* ☎ *020/3141–9320* ⊕ *www.newport-streetgallery.com* ⌨ *Free* ☉ *Closed Mon.* Ⓜ *Vauxhall, Lambeth North.*

The Old Operating Theatre Museum and Herb Garret. This rare example of a 19th-century operating theater, the oldest in Europe, dates back to 1822, when part of the large herb garret in the roof of the 17th-century St. Thomas's Church was converted for surgical use. The English baroque church was part of St. Thomas's Hospital, which was founded in the 12th century as a monastery that looked after the sick. In 1862, the hospital moved to its present Lambeth location and the operating theater was closed. It remained abandoned until 1956, when it was restored and turned into a medical museum. Today you can see the artifacts of early 19th century medical practice: the wooden operating table under a skylight; the box of sawdust underneath used for absorbing blood; and the surrounding banks of seats where students crowded in to observe operations. Every Saturday at 2 and Sunday at noon, there are demonstrations of pre-anesthetic surgical practices incorporating the knives, pliers, and handsaws that were the surgeons' tools back in the day (not for the fainthearted or small children). Next door is a re-creation of the 17th century **Herb Garret**, with displays of the medicinal herbs St. Thomas's apothecary would have used, along with Sunday-afternoon "gore tours," a hands-on survey of Victorian surgical instruments, at 2. △ **Access is by a 52-step spiral staircase, although disabled access by elevator is available by prior arrangement.** ⊠ *9A St. Thomas St., Lambeth* ☎ *020/7188–2679* ⊕ *www.oldoperatingtheatre. com* ⌨ *£6.50* ☉ *Closed Mon. except bank holidays* Ⓜ *London Bridge.*

FAMILY **Sea Life London Aquarium.** The curved, colonnaded, neoclassical former County Hall that once housed London's municipal government is now home to a superb three-level aquarium where you can walk above sharks and stingrays and view more than 600 other aquatic species, both common and rare. There are also hands-on displays. It's not the biggest aquarium you've ever seen, but the educational exhibits are particularly well arranged, with 17 themed zones for different oceans, water environments, and climates, ranging from a stunning coral reef to a seahorse colony to a rain forest. Regular feeding times and free talks are offered throughout the day. There are also special experiences that include behind-the-scenes tours and feeding (or, for the brave, snorkeling with) sharks at an extra charge. ■ TIP→ **Admission at peak periods is by 15-minute timed entry slot, but for an additional £10 you can purchase flexible priority-entry tickets that also avoid the long lines.** ⊠ *County Hall, Westminster Bridge Rd., South Bank* ☎ *0871/663–1678* ⊕ *www.visitsealife.com* ⌨ *From £26 (£20.40 online)* Ⓜ *Westminster, Waterloo.*

FAMILY
Fodor's Choice
★
Shakespeare's Globe. This spectacular theater is a replica of Shakespeare's open-roof, wood-and-thatch Globe Playhouse (built in 1599 and burned down in 1613), where most of the Bard's greatest works premiered. American actor and director Sam Wanamaker worked ceaselessly for several decades to raise funds for the theater's reconstruction 200

yards from its original site, using authentic materials and techniques, a dream that was finally realized in 1997. "Groundlings" (patrons with £5 standing-only tickets) are not allowed to sit during the performance, but you get the best view of the stage and the most authentic viewing experience. Fortunately, you can reserve an actual seat on any one of the theater's three levels, but you will want to rent a cushion for £2 (or bring your own) to soften the backless wooden benches (cushions must be booked when you book your tickets). The show must go on, rain or shine, warm or chilly, so come prepared for anything. Umbrellas are banned, but you can bring a raincoat or buy a cheap Globe rain poncho, which doubles as a great souvenir. In the winter months, the Sam Wanamaker Playhouse, a 350-seat re-creation of an indoor Jacobean theater lighted by candles, offers plays and concerts in a less exposed though still atmospheric setting. Some Wanamaker benches are backless, and there are fixed standing positions in the theater's upper gallery.

Shakespeare's Globe Exhibition, a museum under the theater (the entry is adjacent), provides background material on Shakespeare's life, the London in which he lived, the original Elizabethan Globe, and the construction of the modern version. Admission to the museum also includes a 30-minute tour of the theater (tours leave every half hour 9:30–5 in fall/winter and spring/summer Mondays, Tuesday to Saturday mornings only in spring/summer, but may be unavailable due to performances, rehearsals, or events). You can also book a tour of the surrounding Bankside area, emphasizing places Shakespeare would have frequented, including the archaeological remains of the nearby Rose Theatre, the oldest theater in Bankside. Or take a tour of the Wanamaker, offered every half hour between 1:30 and 5 on limited dates due to the performance schedule. On days when no tours are available, the Exhibition has reduced-price admission (check the website). ⊠ *21 New Globe Walk, Bankside* ☎ *020/7902–1500 general info, 020/7401–9919 box office* ⊕ *www.shakespearesglobe.com* ⊠ *Exhibition and Globe Theatre tour £17; Bankside tour £12.50; Wanamaker Playhouse tour £13.50 (all £2 off with valid performance ticket); Globe performances £5 (standing), £22–£47 (seated); Wanamaker performances £10 (standing), £15–£62 (seated)* ⊗ *No Globe performances mid-Oct.–mid-Apr.; no Wanamaker Playhouse performances mid-Apr.–mid.-Oct.* Ⓜ *London Bridge; Mansion House, then cross Southwark Bridge.*

Southbank Centre. *Please see listing in the Performing Arts chapter.*

Southwark Cathedral. Pronounced "Suth-uck," this is the oldest Gothic church in London, parts of it dating back to the 12th century. It remains off-the-beaten track, despite being the site of some remarkable memorials and a concert program that offers free half-hour organ recitals at 1:10 pm every Monday (except in August and December) and classical music at 3:15 pm every Tuesday (except in December). Originally the priory church of St. Mary Overie (as in "over the water," on the South Bank), it became a palace church under Henry VIII (when it became known as St Saviour's) until some merchant parishioners bought it from James I in 1611. It was only promoted to cathedral status in 1905. Look for the vivid 15th-century roof bosses (small ornamental wood carvings); the gaudily renovated 1408 tomb of John Gower, Richard II's poet laureate and a friend of Chaucer's; and the Harvard Chapel, where John Harvard, a local butcher's son who went on to found the American university, was baptized. Another notable buried here (between the choir stalls) is Edmond Shakespeare, brother of William. Forty-five-minute tours are offered on Wednesday at 2 pm, Friday at 11 am, and Sunday at 1 pm (£4.50). ⊠ *London Bridge, Bankside* ☎ *020/7367–6700* ⊕ *cathedral.southwark.anglican.org* ⊡ *Free (suggested donation £4)* Ⓜ *London Bridge.*

FodorśChoice
★

Tate Modern. This spectacular renovation of a mid-20th-century power station is one of the most-visited museums of modern art in the world. Its great permanent collection, which starts in 1900 and ranges from modernist masters like Matisse to the most cutting-edge contemporary artists, is arranged in eight areas by theme (for example, "Media Networks," about artists' responses to mass media) rather than by chronology. Its blockbuster temporary exhibitions have showcased the work of individual artists like Gaugin, Rauschenberg, Modigliani, Picasso, and O'Keefe, among others. Other major temporary exhibitions have a conceptual focus, like works created in response to the American Black Power movement or by Soviet and Russian artists between the Revolution and the death of Stalin.

The vast **Turbine Hall** is a dramatic entrance point used to showcase big audacious installations that tend to generate a lot of publicity. Past highlights include Olafur Eliasson's massive glowing sun, Ai Weiwei's porcelain "sunflower seeds," and Carsten Holler's huge metal slides.

On the ground floor of a 10-story addition, you'll find The Tanks, galleries devoted to various types of new art, including moving image, performance, soundscapes, and interactive works, while at the top is a roof terrace offering spectacular views of the London skyline. In between are three exhibition floors offering more room for large-scale installations, for art from outside Europe and North America, and for digital and interactive projects. The Start display provides an introduction to the collection, highlighting art from various countries, cultures, and periods, all linked by color. Not to be missed in the original building is the collection of Rothko murals, originally created for the Four Seasons restaurant in New York, and displays devoted to Gerhard Richter (both on Level 2) and works by the video pioneer Nam June Paik (Level 4).

Head to the café on Level 1 or the Espresso Bar on Level 3 for stunning vistas of the Thames. The view of St. Paul's from the Espresso Bar's balcony is one of the best in London. Near the café you'll find the Drawing Bar, which lets you create work on one of several digital sketch pads and then project your result on the gallery wall.

You can join free 45-minute guided tours, each covering a different gallery: The Artist and Society at 11, In the Studio at noon, Materials and Objects at 2, and Media Networks at 3. If you plan to visit Tate Britain, too, take advantage of the Tate Boat, which takes visitors back and forth between the two Tates every 40 minutes. ⊠ *Bankside* ☎ *020/7887–8888* ⊕ *www.tate.org.uk/modern* ⊡ *Free (charge for special exhibitions)* Ⓜ *Southwark, Blackfriars, St. Paul's.*

8

The View from the Shard. At 800 feet, this addition to the London skyline currently offers the highest vantage point in Western Europe. Designed by the noted architect Renzo Piano, it has attracted both admiration and disdain. While the building itself is generally highly regarded, many felt it would have been better sited in Canary Wharf (or perhaps Dubai), as it spoils views of St. Paul's Cathedral from traditional vantage points such as Hampstead's Parliament Hill. No matter how you feel about the building, there's no denying that it offers a spectacular 360-degree view over London (extending 40 miles on a clear day) from viewing platforms on level 69, and the open-air skydeck on level 72—almost twice as high as any other viewpoint in the city. Digital telescopes provide information about 200 points of interest. There's a weather guarantee that lets you return on a more clement day if visibility is seriously impeded, and various themed events like silent discos or early morning yoga classes are offered at an extra charge. Admission is by timed ticket only. If you find the price as eye-wateringly high as the viewing platforms, there's a less dramatic but still very impressive (and free) view from the lobby of the Shangri-La hotel on the 35th floor, or, in the evenings, the hotel's chic Gong bar on the 52nd floor (over-18s only). ⊠ *Railway Approach, Borough* ☎ *0344/499–7222* ⊕ *www.theviewfromtheshard.com* ✉ *From £30.95* Ⓜ *London Bridge.*

White Cube Bermondsey. When the United Kingdom's highest-profile commercial gallery moved to this huge converted 1970s-era warehouse on Bermondsey Street, it sealed the area's reputation as a rising art-scene hot spot. This is the home gallery of some of today's top contemporary artists, including Jake and Dinos Chapman, Gilbert and George, Gary Hume, Anthony Gormley, Sam Taylor-Wood, Chuck Close, Anselm Kiefer, and several other artists with international reputations. An antiseptic central cuboid gallery, the "white cube"—also called 9 x 9 x 9 (meters, that is)—rests between two other spaces that host smaller exhibitions. There is also a bookshop and auditorium. ⊠ *144–152 Bermondsey St., Bermondsey* ☎ *0207/930–5373* ⊕ *whitecube.com* ⊘ *Closed Mon.* Ⓜ *London Bridge.*

KENSINGTON, CHELSEA, KNIGHTSBRIDGE, AND BELGRAVIA

Getting Oriented

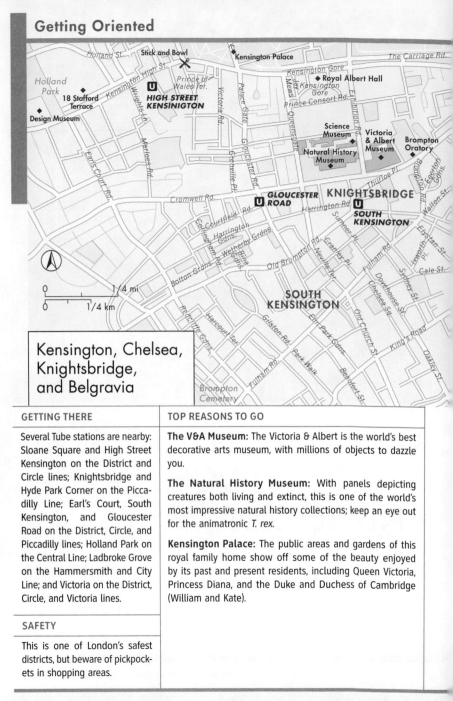

Kensington, Chelsea, Knightsbridge, and Belgravia

GETTING THERE

Several Tube stations are nearby: Sloane Square and High Street Kensington on the District and Circle lines; Knightsbridge and Hyde Park Corner on the Piccadilly Line; Earl's Court, South Kensington, and Gloucester Road on the District, Circle, and Piccadilly lines; Holland Park on the Central Line; Ladbroke Grove on the Hammersmith and City Line; and Victoria on the District, Circle, and Victoria lines.

SAFETY

This is one of London's safest districts, but beware of pickpockets in shopping areas.

TOP REASONS TO GO

The V&A Museum: The Victoria & Albert is the world's best decorative arts museum, with millions of objects to dazzle you.

The Natural History Museum: With panels depicting creatures both living and extinct, this is one of the world's most impressive natural history collections; keep an eye out for the animatronic *T. rex.*

Kensington Palace: The public areas and gardens of this royal family home show off some of the beauty enjoyed by its past and present residents, including Queen Victoria, Princess Diana, and the Duke and Duchess of Cambridge (William and Kate).

MAKING THE MOST OF YOUR TIME

You could fill three or four days in this borough, especially if you enjoy museums. Give yourself at least a half day for the Victoria & Albert Museum, a half day for Kensington Palace, and a half day for either the Natural History Museum or the Science Museum.

A GRAZER'S PARADISE

Duke of York Square Farmers' Market. West London's answer to Borough Market, this Saturday open-air market is in a pedestrian-only plaza off Duke of York Square, a chic shopping precinct. It hosts 40 stalls purveying artisanal and locally produced products from more than 150 small producers. Like Borough Market, this is a grazer's paradise, giving you the chance to sample fresh oysters and cooked sausages as well as yummy hot snacks from countries ranging from Brazil to Thailand. ✉ *Duke of York Sq., Chelsea* ☎ *020/7823–5577* ⊕ *www.dukeofyorksquare. com* ⊙ *Closed Sun.–Fri.* Ⓜ *Sloane Sq.*

FEELING PECKISH?

Stick and Bowl. This hole-in-the-wall restaurant, a neighborhood favorite for more than 20 years, is an amazing bargain for this pricey part of town, serving good basic Chinese food at reasonable prices. Standouts on the extensive menu include roast duck, BBQ pork, and seafood ho-fun. ✉ *31 Kensington High St., Kensington* ☎ *020/7937–2778* ⊟ *No credit cards* Ⓜ *High St. Kensington.*

THE CHELSEA FLOWER SHOWER

Run by the Royal Horticultural Society, the Chelsea Flower Show, the year's highlight for thousands of garden-obsessed Brits, is held every May (usually the third week). The huge showcase for garden design and horticultural innovation takes up all of the Royal Hospital's large grounds. You can buy all manner of gardening supplies and accessories from the many exhibitors, and the end of the last day sees a scrimmage for discount plants from the displays. ⊕ *www.rhs.org.uk*

9

Sightseeing
★★★★
Nightlife
★★
Dining
★★★★
Lodging
★★★★
Shopping
★★★★★

The Royal Borough of Kensington & Chelsea (or K&C, as the locals call it) is where you'll find London at its richest, and not just in the moneyed sense. South Kensington offers a concentration of great museums near Cromwell Road, with historic Kensington Palace nearby in Kensington Gardens. Once-raffish Chelsea, where the Pre-Raphaelites painted and Mick Jagger partied, is now a thoroughly respectable home for the discreetly wealthy, while flashier Knightsbridge has become a haven for international plutocrats, with shopping to match their tastes.

KENSINGTON

Updated by
Ellin Stein

Kensington comprises the area along the southern edge of Hyde Park from Exhibition Road (where the big museum complex is) and the area to the west of the park bordered by leafy Holland Park Avenue on the north and traffic-heavy Cromwell Road on the south. This more westerly zone includes the satellite neighborhood of Holland Park, with its serenely grand villas and charming park, as well as local shopping mecca Kensington High Street and the antiques shops on Kensington Church Street.

Kensington's first royal connection was created when King William III became fed up with the dampness arising from the Thames, so he bought a country place there in 1689 and converted it into **Kensington Palace.** The profits from the Great Exhibition of 1851, organized by Queen Victoria's consort Prince Albert, were used, at Albert's urging, to buy the land which became the site of a complex of colleges and museums that would eventually include the **Victoria & Albert Museum (V&A),** the **Science Museum,** and the **Natural History Museum.** Posthumous tributes to the prince in the area include the **Royal Albert Hall,** with bas-reliefs that make it resemble a giant, redbrick Wedgwood teapot, and the small but lavish **Albert Memorial.**

Turn into Derry Street or Young Street and enter **Kensington Square,** one of the most complete 17th-century residential squares in London. **18 Stafford Terrace,** the perfectly preserved family home of a well-to-do, aesthetically inclined Victorian household, is nearby.

Design Museum. Located in the former Commonwealth Institute, this museum was the first in the United Kingdom to place everyday contemporary objects in a social and cultural context and to consider their role in the history of design. A free, permanent exhibition displays some 1,000 examples of 20th- and 21st-century design—from furniture, fashion, and domestic products to digital technology, architecture, and engineering. The temporary exhibitions may be focused on leading individual designers, such as Charles and Ray Eames, Isamu Noguchi, Terence Conran, or Azzedine Alaïa, or on themes such as the global influence of Californian design. There's also a design library and archive, two shops, a café, and a restaurant. ■TIP➔ **Young designers ages 5–11 may enjoy the free, drop-in "Create and Make" workshops held the last Sunday of every month.** ✉ *224–238 Kensington High St., Kensington* ☎ *020/3862–5900* ⊕ *www.designmuseum.org* ✉ *Free (charge for temporary exhibitions)* ☉ *Closed Dec. 25 and 26* Ⓜ *High St. Kensington.*

18 Stafford Terrace. The home of *Punch* cartoonist Edward Linley Sambourne in the 1870s, this charming house is a rare example of the "Aesthetic interior" style; it displays delightful Victorian and Edwardian antiques, fabrics, and paintings, as well as several samples of Linley Sambourne's work for *Punch.* The Italianate house was the scene for society parties when Anne Messel was in residence in the 1940s. This being Kensington, there's inevitably a royal connection: Messel's son, Antony Armstrong-Jones, was married to the late Princess Margaret, and their son has preserved the connection by taking the title Viscount Linley. On Wednesday and weekends, 75-minute guided tours are given in the morning (reservations required)—with Saturday tours given by costumed actors—but in the afternoons, you are free to wander at will. There's also a costumed evening tour the third Wednesday of every month. ✉ *18 Stafford Terr., Kensington* ☎ *0207/602–3316* ⊕ *www. rbkc.gov.uk/linleysambournehouse* ✉ *£7, morning tour £10, evening tour £12* ☉ *Closed Mon., Tues., Thurs., and Fri.* Ⓜ *High St. Kensington.*

FAMILY **Kensington Palace.** This is a rare chance to get a glimpse into the more domestic and personal side of royal life. Neither as imposing as Buckingham Palace nor as charming as Hampton Court, Kensington Palace is something of a Royal Family commune, with various close relatives of the Queen occupying large apartments in the private part of the palace. Bought in 1689 by Queen Mary and King William III, it was converted into a palace by Sir Christopher Wren and Nicholas Hawksmoor, and royals have been in residence ever since. Princess Diana lived here with her sons after her divorce, and this is where Prince William now lives with his wife, Catherine, Duchess of Cambridge, and their three children. Prince Harry also shared his cottage on the grounds with Meghan Markle before their marriage.

Ice-skaters outside the Natural History Museum in South Kensington

The State Apartments are open to the public. The Queen's State Apartments are the private quarters of Queen Mary II, who ruled jointly with her husband, William II. By contrast, the lavish King's State Apartments, originally built for George I, are a stage set, a circuit of sumptuous rooms where Georgian monarchs received and entertained courtiers, politicians, and foreign dignitaries. Look for the King's Staircase, with its panoramic trompe-l'oeil painting, and the King's Gallery, with royal artworks surrounded by rich red damask walls, intricate gilding, and a beautiful painted ceiling. One permanent exhibition, *Victoria Revealed*, is devoted to the private life of Queen Victoria, who was born and grew up here.

Outside, the grounds are almost as lovely as the palace itself. There are free, history-oriented tours of the gardens on Tuesday, Thursday, and Saturday at noon and 2 pm from May through September. They also make a fine location for a picnic on one of the benches—or head for the delightful café (busy during peak hours) in the Orangery, near the Sunken Garden. An extension adjoining the Orangery is planned to house the Royal Ceremonial Dress Collection. Also at the Orangery you can indulge in a formal afternoon tea.

✉ *The Broad Walk, Kensington Gardens, Kensington* ☎ *0207/482–7799 for advance booking in U.K., 0203/166–6000* ⊕ *www.hrp.org. uk* ▨ *£23* Ⓜ *Queensway, High St. Kensington.*

FAMILY **Natural History Museum.** Originally built to house the British Museum's
Fodor's Choice natural history collection and bolstered by samples provided by Brit-
★ ain's great 19th-century explorers and scientists—notably Charles Darwin—this enormous Victorian cathedral of science is one of the world's

preeminent museums of natural history and earth sciences. As might be expected given its Darwin connection, the emphasis is on evolution and conservation. The terra-cotta facade is embellished with relief panels depicting living creatures to the left of the entrance and extinct ones to the right (although some species have subsequently changed categories). Most are represented inside the museum, which contains more than 70 million different specimens. Only a small percentage is on public display, but you could still spend a day here and not come close to seeing everything.

The skeleton of a giant blue whale dominates the vaulted, cathedral-like entrance hall. Meanwhile, similarly huge dino bones can be found in the Dinosaur Gallery (Blue Zone), along with fossils and some extremely long iguanodon teeth. You'll also come face-to-face with a virtual Jurassic sea dragon and a giant animatronic *T. rex* that's programmed to sense when human prey is near and "respond" in character. When he does, you can hear the shrieks of fear and delight all the way across the room.

An escalator takes you into a giant globe in the Earth Galleries, where there's a choice of levels to explore. Don't leave without checking out the earthquake simulation in the Volcanoes and Earthquake Gallery. The Darwin Centre houses some 80 million items the museum itself doesn't have room to display, including "Archie," a 28-foot giant squid. If you want to see Archie and some of the other millions of animal specimens preserved in spirit (including some acquired on Darwin's *Beagle* voyage), you'll need to book one of the low-cost behind-the-scenes Spirit Collection tours (around £10). These 45-minute tours take place at 11:30, 12:30, and 1:30, plus 3:30 on weekends, and can be booked on the same day (space is limited, so come early). The center's interactive Cocoon Experience is a free 45-minute tour that reveals how the museum stores, preserves, and uses specimens from its plant and insect collections. In the David Attenborough Studio, there are free, half-hour drop-in talks (usually on Friday and Saturday afternoon) given by scientists and curators, covering a wildly eclectic range of subjects. Night owls might prefer one of the evening talks or spending an entire night in the museum at one of the "Dino Snores" events.

The museum also has an outdoor ice-skating rink October through January, and a popular Christmas fair. ✉ *Cromwell Rd., South Kensington* ☎ *0207/942–5000* ⊕ *www.nhm.ac.uk* ✉ *Free (some fees for special exhibitions)* Ⓜ *S. Kensington.*

FAMILY

Fodor's Choice

★

Science Museum. With attractions ranging from entertainingly educational exhibits—like the Wonderlab interactive gallery, where kids can perform their own scientific experiments, to an exhibition on the fight against superbugs—the Science Museum brings the subject alive for visitors of all ages. Highlights include *Puffing Billy*, the oldest steam locomotive in the world; Watson and Crick's original DNA model; and the Apollo 10 capsule. The six floors are devoted to subjects as diverse as space exploration, jet fighter flight simulators, and objects on the cutting edge of innovative technology. The Information Age gallery, devoted to communication networks from the telegraph to the Internet, was opened in 2014 by Queen Elizabeth, who marked the occasion by sending her first tweet. The Winton Gallery, all about mathematics and its applications, has more than 100 math-related objects, such as a 17th-century Islamic astrolabe and an early version of Alan Turing's Enigma machine. Overshadowed by a three-story blue-glass wall, the Wellcome Wing is an annex to the rear of the museum, devoted to contemporary science and technology. It contains a 450-seat IMAX theater and the Legend of Apollo—an advanced 3-D motion simulator that combines seat vibration with other technical gizmos to re-create the experience of a moon landing. Another popular space-related immersive experience is the 360-degree VR recreation of traveling back to Earth from the International Space Station in a Soyuz capsule. If you're a group of at least five, you might be able to get a place on one of the popular monthly Science Night sleepovers by booking well in advance. ⊠ *Exhibition Rd., South Kensington* ☎ *0870/870–4868* ⊕ *www.sciencemuseum.org.uk* 🔤 *Free (charge for special exhibitions, IMAX, Wonderlab, and simulator rides)* Ⓜ *South Kensington.*

Fodor'sChoice   **Victoria & Albert Museum.** Known to all as the V&A, this huge museum
★   with more than 2 million items on display in 145 galleries is devoted to the applied arts of all disciplines, all periods, and all nationalities. First opened as the South Kensington Museum in 1857, it was renamed in 1899 in honor of Queen Victoria's late husband and has since grown to become one of the country's best-loved cultural institutions, with high-profile temporary exhibitions alongside an impressive permanent collection. Many collections at the V&A are presented not by period but by category—textiles, sculpture, jewelry, and so on. ■ TIP➔ It's a tricky building to navigate, so use the free map.

Nowhere is the benefit of the categorization more apparent than in the Fashion Gallery (Room 40), where formal 18th-century court dresses are displayed alongside the haute couture styles of contemporary designers. The museum has become known for high-profile temporary exhibitions exploring fashion icons such as Alexander McQueen and Balenciaga and pop legends including David Bowie and Pink Floyd.

The British Galleries (Rooms 52–58 and 118–125) survey British art and design from 1500 to 1900 and are full of rare and beautiful artifacts such as the Tudor Great Bed of Ware (immortalized in Shakespeare's *Twelfth Night*) and silks woven by Huguenot refugees in Spitalfields. Among the series of actual rooms that have been painstakingly reconstructed piece by piece are the glamorous rococo Norfolk House Music Room and the serenely elegant Henrietta St. Drawing Room, originally designed in 1722.

The Asian Galleries (Rooms 44–47) are full of treasures, but among the most striking items on display is a remarkable collection of ornate samurai armor in the **Japanese Gallery** (Room 44). Works from China, Korea, and the Islamic Middle East have their own displays. Also of note is a gallery thematically grouped around Buddhist sculpture from different regions and periods. The Europe Gallery (Rooms 1–7) brings together more than 1,100 objects created between 1600 and 1815, while the Medieval and Renaissance galleries, which document

European art and culture from 300 to 1600, have the largest collection of works from the period outside of Italy. An entrance off Exhibition Road offers access through the U.K.'s first porcelain-tiled public courtyard that also serves as a venue for contemporary installations and a glass-fronted café. A photography center houses books, photo equipment, and more than 270,000 prints formerly held by the Royal Photographic Society, joining the more than 500,000 photos already in the museum's collection.

As a whirlwind introduction, you could take a free one-hour Introductory tour. Occasional public lectures during the week are delivered by bigwigs from the art and fashion worlds in addition to free lectures throughout the week given by museum staff. ■TIP➔ Whatever time you visit, the spectacular sculpture hall will be filled with artists, both amateur and professional, sketching the myriad artworks on display there. Don't be shy; bring a pad and join in. ✉ *Cromwell Rd., South Kensington* ☎ *020/7942–2000* ⊕ *www.vam.ac.uk* ✆ *Free (charge for some special exhibitions, from £5)* Ⓜ *South Kensington.*

CHELSEA

Chelsea was settled before the Domesday Book was compiled and already fashionable when two of Henry VIII's wives lived there. On the banks of the Thames are the vast grounds of the **Royal Hospital,** designed by Christopher Wren. A walk along the riverside embankment will take you to **Cheyne Walk,** a lovely street dating back to the 18th century. Several of its more notable residents—from J. M. W. Turner and Henry James to Laurence Olivier and Keith Richards—are commemorated by blue plaques on their former houses.

The **Albert Bridge,** a sherbet-color Victorian confection of a suspension bridge, provides one of London's great romantic views, especially at night. Leave time to explore the tiny Georgian lanes of pastel-color houses that veer off King's Road to the north—especially **Jubilee Place** and **Burnsall Street,** leading to the hidden "village square" of **Chelsea Green.** On Saturday there's an excellent farmers' market up from the Saatchi Gallery in Duke of York's Square selling artisanal cheese and chocolates, local oysters, and organic meats, plus stalls serving international food.

Residential Chelsea extends along the river from the Chelsea Bridge west to the Battersea Bridge and north as far as the Old Brompton Road.

Royal Hospital Chelsea. Charles II founded this residence for elderly and infirm soldiers in 1682 to reward the troops who had fought for him in the civil wars of 1642–46 and 1648. No sick people are treated here today; it's more of a history-packed retirement home. A creation of three of England's greatest architects—Wren, Vanbrugh, and Hawksmoor—this small enclave of brick and Portland stone set in expansive manicured grounds (which you can visit) surrounds the Figure Court (the figure being a 1682 gilded bronze statue of Charles II dressed as a Roman general). The beautiful Wren-designed chapel

9

World-famous Harrods has been luring shoppers with its classic wares since 1834.

(a working church) and the Great Hall (the Hospital's dining room) are open to the public at certain times during the day. There is a small museum devoted to the history of the resident "Chelsea Pensioners," but the real attraction, along with the building, is the approximately 300 pensioners themselves. Recognizable by their traditional scarlet frock coats with gold buttons, medals, and tricorne hats, they are all actual veterans, who wear the uniform, and the history it represents, with a great deal of pride. On Sundays mornings (10:45) in April through November, you can see groups of pensioners in full uniform on parade in the Figure Court. Individuals can visit the grounds, chapel, Great Hall, and museum for free, or you can go on a 90-minute guided tour for groups of 10 or more (from £180 per group; must be booked a month in advance) led by one of the pensioners. ⊠ *Royal Hospital Rd., Chelsea* ☎ *020/7881–5298* ⊕ *www.chelsea-pensioners. co.uk* ✆ *Free* ⊘ *Closed Sun. and bank holidays. Museum closed weekends* Ⓜ *Sloane Sq.*

Saatchi Gallery. Charles Saatchi, who made his fortune in advertising, is one of Britain's canniest collectors of contemporary art, credited with discovering the likes of Damien Hirst and Tracey Emin. His current gallery, still largely devoted to contemporary art by emerging artists, is in the former Duke of York's HQ, just off King's Road. Built in 1803, its grand period exterior belies an imaginatively restored modern interior transformed into 15 exhibition spaces of varying size and shape. There is no permanent collection other than a few ongoing site-specific installations; at any one time, there are between one and three concurrent, imaginatively curated exhibitions that normally run for up to six months. There's also an excellent café, which is open late. ✉ *Duke of York's HQ Bldg., King's Rd., Chelsea* ☎ *020/7811–3070* ⊕ *www. saatchigallery.com* ✉ Free Ⓜ *Sloane Sq.*

KNIGHTSBRIDGE

There's no getting away from it. With two world-famous department stores, **Harrods** and **Harvey Nichols**, a few hundred yards apart; numerous boutiques selling the biggest names in international luxury and expensive jewelry; and people-watching including viewing street racers in Maseratis—London's wealthiest enclave will appeal most to those who enjoy conspicuous consumption.

Posh Sloane Street is lined with top-end designer boutiques such as Prada, Dior, and Tods. If it all starts to become a bit generic (expensive generic), **Beauchamp Place** (pronounced "Beecham") is lined with equally luxe one-off boutiques, which tend to be more distinctive and less global.

Knightsbridge is located to the east of Kensington, bordered by Hyde Park on the north and Pont Street just past Harrods on the south.

Brompton Oratory (*London Oratory*). This is a late product of the mid-19th-century English Roman Catholic revival led by John Henry Cardinal Newman (1801–90), who established the oratory in the 1840s and whose statue you see outside. Architect Herbert Gribble was an unknown 29-year-old when he won a competition to design the church, bringing a baroque exuberance to his concept for the vast, incredibly ornate interior. It's punctuated by treasures far older than the church itself, like the giant Carrara marble *Twelve Apostles* in the nave, sculpted by Giuseppe Mazzuoli in the 1680s for Siena's cathedral. The Oratory is known for the quality of its organs and choir, with exceptional music being an integral part of services here. ✉ *Brompton Rd., Knightsbridge* ☎ *0207/808–0900* ⊕ *www.bromptonoratory.com* ✉ Free Ⓜ *South Kensington.*

BELGRAVIA

Steps away from the roaring traffic of Hyde Park Corner, lying just to the east of Kensington and Chelsea, is quiet, fashionable Belgravia, one of the most impressive set pieces of 19th-century urban planning. Street after street is lined with grand, cream-color stucco terraces, once aristocrats' town houses and most still part of the Grosvenor estate owned by the Duke of Westminster. Many buildings are leased to embassies or organizations, but a remarkable number around **Lowndes Square, Eaton Place,** and **Eaton Square** remain in the hands of private owners, whether old money or new oligarchs who put their security guards in the attached mews houses. Some people consider the area near **Elizabeth Street** to be southern Belgravia; others call it Pimlico-Victoria. Whatever its name, here small, unique stores specialize in baked goods, wine, gifts, and stationery.

Belgrave Square. This is the heart of Belgravia, once the preferred address for the gentry's London town houses, although it's now mostly occupied by organizations, embassies, and the international rich. The Square and the streets leading off it share a remarkably consistent elegant architectural style thanks to all being part of a Regency redevelopment scheme commissioned by the Duke of Westminster and designed by Thomas Cubitt with George Basevi. The grand, cream-color stucco terraced houses were snapped up by aristocrats and politicians due to their proximity to Buckingham Palace just around the corner, and still command record prices on the rare occasions when they come onto the market. The private garden in the center is open to the public once a year. Walk down Belgrave Place toward Eaton Place and you pass two of Belgravia's most beautiful mews: Eaton Mews North and Eccleston Mews, both fronted by grand rusticated entrances right out of a 19th-century engraving. ■TIP→ Traffic can really whip around Belgrave Square, so be careful. ✉ *Belgravia* Ⓜ *Hyde Park Corner.*

NOTTING HILL
AND BAYSWATER

Getting Oriented

GETTING THERE

For Portobello Market and environs, the best Tube stops are Ladbroke Grove and Westbourne Park (Hammersmith and City Line); ask for directions when you emerge. The Notting Hill Gate stop on the District, Circle, and Central lines enables you to walk the length of Portobello Road while going slightly downhill.

A GOOD WALK

To spot Notting Hill's grandest houses, stroll over to Lansdowne Road, Lansdowne Crescent, and Lansdowne Square—two blocks west of Kensington Park Road.

TOP REASONS TO GO

Portobello Road: The early bird can catch considerably more than the worm; go before 10 am on Saturday to hook the good stuff at London's world-famous antiques market, or come during the week for a leisurely browse.

Hyde Park: Explore one of London's largest green spaces by walking, cycling ("Boris bikes" are available at several sites), skating with the Friday Night Skate, or rowing on the Serpentine, the tranquil lake that snakes through the park.

The Serpentine Galleries: Expand your cultural horizons at one of London's foremost showcases for modern art, or just have a bite at the café in the extension to the Serpentine Sackler Gallery, designed by famed architect Zaha Hadid and a work of art in itself.

Notting Hill and Bayswater

MAKING THE MOST OF YOUR TIME

Saturday is the most exciting day for shopping, eating, and drinking here.

The market gets crowded by noon in summer, so come early if you are serious about shopping.

Head south from the north end of Portobello Road, using the parks to take a break on the way.

On Sunday, the Hyde Park and Kensington Gardens railings along Bayswater Road are lined with artists displaying their work, which may slow your progress.

10

Well-heeled locals are often out on Sunday with friends in the pubs or with kids in the parks.

SAFETY

At night, avoid straying from the main streets north of Westbourne Park Road toward Ladbroke Grove's high-rise estates (projects) and the surrounding areas.

FEELING PECKISH?

The Prince Bonaparte. It's had an art deco makeover, but one thing hasn't changed: the high standard of its Modern British food and a fine selection of artisanal ales and carefully chosen wines. A stone's throw from Portobello Market, it's the perfect place for a drink or a bite to eat. ✉ *80 Chepstow Rd., Bayswater* ☎ *020/7313–9491* ⊕ *www. theprincebonapartew2.co.uk* Ⓜ *Notting Hill Gate, Royal Oak.*

The Tabernacle. The Victorian Gothic interior of this bar, café, and arts center combo hosts intimate music gigs, literary events with the likes of Tales of The City's Armistead Maupin, and 15-minute talks with speakers such as historian Niall Ferguson. The food is Caribbean-influenced, and the atmosphere, especially in the outdoor courtyard, is relaxed. ✉ *34–35 Powis Sq., Notting Hill* ☎ *020/7221–9700* ⊕ *www. tabernaclew11.com* ⏱ *Closed Sun.* Ⓜ *Notting Hill Gate.*

Sightseeing
★★
Nightlife
★★★
Dining
★★★
Lodging
★★★
Shopping
★★★★

The center of London's West Indian community from the 1950s through the '70s, Notting Hill these days is the address of choice for the well-heeled, be they bankers, rock stars, media and advertising types, or rich hippies. Teeming with trendy restaurants, cool bars, and buzzing street markets, the area is also studded with some of London's most handsome historic residences, crescents, and terraces. Every weekend, the hordes descend on Portobello Road to go bargain-hunting at one of the world's great antiques markets. Holland Park, to the west, has even grander villas, while Bayswater (to the east) has excellent world-cuisine restaurants.

NOTTING HILL

Updated by
James O'Neill

Notting Hill as we know it emerged in the 1840s when the wealthy Ladbroke family developed a small suburb to the west of London. Before then, the area had the far less glamorous name of "the Potteries and the Piggeries," after the two industries it was best known for: ceramics and pig farming.

During the 1980s, Notting Hill transformed from a lively but down-at-heel and sometimes dangerous West Indian enclave to a supertrendy fashionable neighborhood. The area's Caribbean legacy persists, however, not least in the form of the annual Notting Hill Carnival in late August. The new millennium saw Notting Hill's fame go global thanks to the hit rom-com of the same name, though the movie itself was criticized by locals for downplaying the area's cultural diversity. For the Notting Hill of the silver screen, head for fashionable **Westbourne Grove** and **Ledbury Road,** lined with eclectic independent boutiques offering

The Wellington Arch Monument proudly welcomes visitors to Hyde Park, one of London's largest royal parks.

highly desirable designer goods for the home and family, as well as contemporary art—prices and taste levels are high.

For less rarefied shopping, try **Portobello Road**; the famous Saturday antiques market and shops are at the southern end. A little farther southwest lies the elegant splendor of **Holland Park,** at the end of which you'll find the exotic delights of the **Leighton House Museum.**

Graffik. Not everyone thinks graffiti can be a bonus to the urban landscape, but those who do should head for this leading gallery of contemporary street art. The big name here is Banksy, but there are works for sale by several other artists in the same vein such as Trust. iCON and CODE FC, who are more concerned with social commentary than tagging. This is one gallery experience that really appeals to young people, especially if the visit coincides with one of Graffik's two-hour weekend workshops. ✉ *284 Portobello Rd., Notting Hill* ☎ *020/8354–3592* ⊕ *www.graffikgallery.com* ✉ *Free* Ⓜ *Notting Hill Gate, Ladbroke Grove.*

FAMILY **Holland Park.** Formerly the grounds of an aristocrat's house and open to the public only since 1952, Holland Park is an often-overlooked gem and possibly London's most romantic park. The northern "Wilderness" end offers woodland walks among native and exotic trees first planted in the early 18th century. Foxes, rabbits, and hedgehogs are among the residents. The central part of the park is given over to the manicured lawns—still stalked by raucous peacocks—one would expect at a stately home, although Holland House itself, originally built by James I's chancellor and later the site of a 19th-century salon frequented by Byron, Dickens, and Disraeli, was largely destroyed by

10

German incendiary bombs in 1940. The east wing was reconstructed and has been incorporated into a youth hostel, while the remains of the front terrace provide an atmospheric backdrop for the open-air performances of the April–September Holland Park Opera Festival (⊕ *www. operahollandpark.com*). The glass-walled Garden Ballroom is now the Orangery, which hosts art exhibitions and other public events, as does the Ice House, while an adjoining former granary has become the upscale Belvedere restaurant. In spring and summer the air is fragrant with aromas from a rose garden, great banks of rhododendrons, and an azalea walk. Garden enthusiasts will also not want to miss the tranquil, traditional Kyoto Garden, a legacy of London's 1991 Japan Festival. The southern part of the park is given over to sport and play: cricket and football (soccer) pitches; a golf practice area; tennis courts; a well-supervised children's Adventure Playground; and a giant outdoor chess set. ⊠ *Ilchester Pl., West Holland Park* ⊕ *www.rbkc.gov.uk/leisure-and-culture/parks/holland-park* Ⓜ *Holland Park, High Street Kensington.*

FAMILY

Fodor's Choice

★

Hyde Park. Along with the smaller St. James's and Green parks to the east, the 350-acre Hyde Park started as Henry VIII's hunting grounds. Along its south side runs Rotten Row, once Henry's royal path to the hunt—the name is a corruption of *Route du Roi* (Route of the King). It's still used by the Household Cavalry, who live at the Hyde Park Barracks—a high-rise and a low, ugly red block, now up for sale—to the left. You can see the Guardsmen in full regalia leaving on horseback for guard duty at Buckingham Palace at about 10:30 (or come at noon when they return). Hyde Park is wonderful for strolling, cycling, or just relaxing by the Serpentine, the long body of water near its southern border. On the south side, by the 1930s Serpentine Lido, is the site of the Diana Princess of Wales Memorial Fountain, which is a good spot to refuel at the café. On Sunday, close to Marble Arch you'll find the uniquely British tribute to free speech, Speakers' Corner. Though not what it was in the days before people could use the Internet to vent their spleen, it still offers a unique assortment of passionate, if occasionally irrational, advocates literally getting up on soapboxes. ⊠ *Hyde Park* 🕾 *030/0061–2114* ⊕ *www.royalparks.org.uk* 🗺 *Free* Ⓜ *Hyde Park Corner, Knightsbridge, Lancaster Gate, Marble Arch.*

FAMILY

Fodor's Choice

★

Kensington Gardens. Laid out in 1689 by William III, who commissioned Sir Christopher Wren to build Kensington Palace, the gardens are a formal counterpart to neighboring Hyde Park. Just to the north of the palace itself is the Dutch-style **Sunken Garden**. Nearby, the 1912 bronze statue *Peter Pan* commemorates the boy in J. M. Barrie's story who lived on an island in the Serpentine and who never grew up. Kids will enjoy the magical **Diana Princess of Wales Memorial Playground**, whose design was also inspired by Barrie's book. The **Elfin Oak** is a 900-year-old tree trunk that was carved with scores of tiny elves, fairies, and other fanciful creations in the 1920s. The **Italian Gardens** (1860) comprise several ornamental ponds and fountains, while the **Round Pond** attracts model-boat enthusiasts. ⊠ *Kensington* 🕾 *030/0061–2000* ⊕ *www.royalparks.org.uk* 🗺 *Free* Ⓜ *High Street Kensington, Lancaster Gate, Queensway, South Kensington.*

Fodor's Choice **Leighton House Museum.** Leading Victorian artist Frederic (Lord) Leigh-
★ ton lived and worked in this building on the edge of Holland Park,
spending 30 years (and quite a bit of money) transforming it into an
opulent "private palace of art" infused with an orientalist aesthetic
sensibility. The interior is a sumptuous Arabian Nights fantasy, with
walls lined in peacock-blue tiles designed by Leighton's friend, the
ceramic artist William de Morgan, and beautiful mosaic wall panels
and floors, marble pillars, and gilded ceilings. The centerpiece is
the Arab Hall, its marble walls adorned with even more intricate
murals made from 16th- and 17th-century ceramic tiles imported
from Syria, Turkey, and Iran, surmounted by a domed ceiling covered
in gold leaf with a gold mosaic frieze running underneath. You can
also visit Leighton's studio, with its huge north window and dome;
the house is filled with paintings, several of his own along with
works by other Pre-Raphaelites. ⊠ *12 Holland Park Rd., West Holland Park* ☎ *020/7602–3316 weekdays, 020/7471–9160 weekends*
⊕ *www.leightonhouse.co.uk* ⊠ *£9* ⊘ *Closed Tues.* Ⓜ *Holland Park,
South Kensington.*

Museum of Brands, Packaging and Advertising. This quirky museum specializes in branded toys, clothes, games, and domestic goods, and explores
how advertising has come to infiltrate our lives. Curios from the 1800s
to the present day include World War II–era toilet paper (brand name:
Nasti toilet roll) that has Adolf Hitler's face on every sheet. ⊠ *111–117
Lancaster Rd., Notting Hill* ☎ *020/7243–9611* ⊕ *www.museumof-
brands.com* ⊠ *£9* ⊘ *Closed Mon.* Ⓜ *Ladbroke Grove.*

Portobello Road. Looking for a 19th-century snuff spoon? Perhaps a
Georgian salt cellar? What about a 1960s-era minidress? Then head
to Portobello Road's famous Saturday market—and arrive at about
9 am to avoid the giant crowds. Stretching almost 2 miles from Notting Hill, the market is made up of four sections, each with a different
emphasis: antiques, fresh produce, household goods, and a flea market. The antiques stalls are packed in between Chepstow Villas and
Westbourne Grove, where you'll also find almost 100 antiques shops
plus indoor markets, which are open on weekdays, when shopping is
much less hectic. Where the road levels off, around Elgin Crescent,
youth culture and a vibrant neighborhood life kicks in, with a variety
of interesting small stores and food stalls interspersed with a fruit-and-
vegetable market. On Friday and Saturday the section between Talbot
Road and the Westway elevated highway becomes one of London's best
flea markets, specializing in discounted new household goods, while
north of the Westway you'll find secondhand household goods and
bric-a-brac. Scattered throughout, but especially under the Westway, are
vendors selling a mishmash of designer, vintage, and secondhand clothing, together with jewelry, custom T-shirts, and assorted junk. There's a
Trinidad-style Carnival centered on Portobello Road on the late August
bank-holiday weekend, a tribute to the area's past as a center of the
West Indian community. ⊠ *Notting Hill* ⊕ *www.portobelloroad.co.uk*
Ⓜ *Notting Hill Gate, Ladbroke Grove.*

10

Serpentine Galleries. Taking its name from the lake that curves its way through Hyde Park, the Serpentine Gallery, housed in a modest red-brick building in Kensington Gardens, is one of London's foremost showcases for contemporary art. Just about everyone who's anyone has exhibited here: Louise Bourgeois, Jeff Koons, Marina Abramovic, and Gerhard Richter, to name a few. A permanent work on the gallery's grounds, consisting of eight benches and a carved stone circle, commemorates its former patron, Princess Diana. The Serpentine Sackler Gallery, a second exhibition space that's in a small Georgian gunpowder storeroom just over the water, has a dramatic extension designed by Zaha Hadid as well as a stylish restaurant. If you're in town between May and September, check out the annual Serpentine Pavilion, where each year a leading architect is given free rein to create a temporary pavilion of their choosing—always with imaginative results. Past designers have included Frank Gehry, Daniel Liebeskind, and Jean Nouvel. ⊠ *Kensington Gardens, Kensington* ☎ *020/7402-6075* ⊕ *www.serpentinegalleries.org* ⬚ *Free* ⊗ *Closed Mon.* Ⓜ *Lancaster Gate, Knightsbridge, South Kensington.*

BAYSWATER

East of Notting Hill Gate Tube station, Notting Hill turns into Bayswater, characterized by wide streets lined with imposing white stucco terraced houses. Traditionally given over to cheap bed-and-breakfasts, many are being converted back to private homes as the area continues to gentrify. The eastern end of Westbourne Grove and the streets around it are known for their excellent restaurants, particularly Chinese, Lebanese, and Greek. On **Queensway**, Bayswater's main street, **Whiteleys**, originally a huge department store built in 1912, has been converted into a shopping center containing a luxury movie theater, restaurants (try Le Café Anglais for a swanky evening out), a bowling alley, and, of course, shops.

Nearby **Paddington Station** is as well known for its association with the world's most famous marmalade fan, Paddington Bear, as it is for being one of London's most handsome rail terminals.

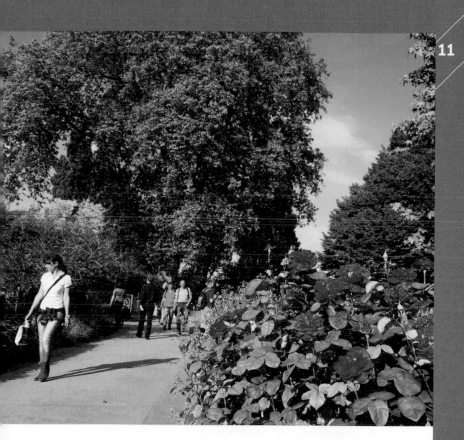

11

REGENT'S PARK
AND HAMPSTEAD

Visit Fodors.com for advice, updates, and bookings

Getting Oriented

Regent's Park and
Hampstead

◆ Kenwood House

Waterlow

◆ Highgate
Cemetery

Park

Hampstead
Heath

*Ladies
Bathing
Pond*

*Mixed
Bathing
Pond*

Parliament
Hill

2 Willow
Rd.

Burgh House and
Hampstead Museum

Fenton House ◆

HAMPSTEAD Ⓤ

HAMPSTEAD

Hampstead
Heath
Overground

Gospel Oak
Overground

● Ginger
and White

The Parish
Church of St. John's-
at-Hampstead

Keats
House

Finchley Road
& Frognal
Overground

Kentish
Town
Rail

Freud
Museum
London

✕ Marine
Ices

**CHALK
FARM** Ⓤ

PRIMROSE
HILL

CHALK
FARM

**SWISS
COTTAGE** Ⓤ

**CAMDEN
TOWN** Ⓤ

Primrose Hill ◆

CAMDEN
TOWN

Cecil Sharp House ◆

Jewish
Museum

ZSL London Zoo ◆

**ST. JOHNS
WOOD** Ⓤ

ST. JOHN'S
WOOD

Regent's Park ◆

Broad Walk

Lord's
Cricket Ground
& Museum ◆

Chester Rd.

Inner

Circle

York
Bridge

0   1/4 mi

0   1/4 km

MARYLEBONE Ⓤ

**BAKER
STREET** Ⓤ

**REGENT'S
PARK** Ⓤ

**GREAT
PORTLAND
STREET** Ⓤ

TOP REASONS TO GO

Hampstead Heath: Londoners adore the Heath for providing an escape to the countryside while still in the city.

Keats House: Visit the rooms where one of England's greatest poets wrote some of his major works, inspired by his love for the girl-next-door, Fanny Brawne.

Regent's Park: Cycle past Nash's grand neoclassical stucco terraces or walk up Primrose Hill for a great view over the city.

Kenwood House: See one of Britain's best art collections at this 18th-century gentleman's estate largely designed by Robert Adam.

The London Zoo: A VIP ticket will let you get up close and personal with the penguins at the city's zoo.

SAFETY

Avoid Hampstead Heath, Primrose Hill, and Regent's Park at night unless there's an event; all are perfectly safe during the day. Also to be avoided after dark: the canal towpath in Primrose Hill and Camden.

FEELING PECKISH?

Ginger and White. Family-friendly and thoroughly modern, Ginger and White is a delightful fusion of continental-style café and traditional British "caff"—all bound up with a sophisticated Hampstead vibe. ✉ *4A–5A Perrins Ct., Hampstead* ☎ *020/7431–9098* ⊕ *www.gingerandwhite.com* ☽ *No dinner* Ⓜ *Hampstead.*

Marine Ices. Near the Camden Lock market, this family-owned gelato and sorbet parlor is one of London's best. ✉ *Old Dairy Mews, 61 Chalk Farm Rd., Camden Town* ☎ *020/7428–9990* ⊕ *www.marineices.co.uk* Ⓜ *Chalk Farm.*

GETTING THERE

To get to Hampstead by Tube, take the Northern Line (the Edgware branch) to Hampstead or Golders Green Station, or take the London Overground to Hampstead Heath Station. The south side of Hampstead Heath can also be reached by the London Overground Gospel Oak Station. To get to Regent's Park, take the Bakerloo Line to Regent's Park Tube station or, for Primrose Hill, the Chalk Farm stop on the Northern Line. Little Venice is reachable by the Warwick Avenue stop on the Bakerloo Line and St. John's Wood has its own stop on the Jubilee Line.

MAKING THE MOST OF YOUR TIME

Regent's Park, Primrose Hill, and Hampstead can be covered in a day. Spend the morning in Hampstead, with a brief foray onto the Heath, then head south to Regent's Park in the afternoon so that you're closer to central London come nightfall, if that is where your hotel is located. (You'll also be heading downhill instead of up.) You can always return to Hampstead another day for a long walk across the Heath or to head west to Little Venice's canals.

Regent's Park, Primrose Hill, Belsize Park, and Hampstead are four of London's prettiest and most genteel neighborhoods. The city becomes noticeably calmer and greener as you head uphill from Marylebone Road through Regent's Park to the refreshing greenery of Primrose Hill and the handsome Georgian houses and Regency villas of Hampstead. To the west, the less bucolic but equally elegant St. John's Wood and Little Venice also provide a taste of moneyed London.

Updated by
Ellin Stein

Leaving the park at the London Zoo, walk up adjoining **Primrose Hill** for one of the most picturesque views of London. Long a magnet for the creative (though these days within reach of only the most well-heeled creatives), this is the kind of neighborhood where the local library's screening of *The Madness of King George* is introduced by its writer, longtime resident Alan Bennett. Peel off from the Hill to explore Regent's Park Road and its attractive independent shops and cafés, as well as the surrounding streets with their pastel Victorian villas.

Alternatively, continue hugging the Hill heading north along Primrose Hill Road. This will take you to Belsize Park, itself a celebrity hot spot (Tim Burton and Hugh Laurie have houses here) with a mixture of Victorian, Arts and Crafts, and art deco buildings. Turn right onto England's Lane, another street full of independent shops and nice cafés, then left onto Haverstock Hill and head farther uphill. At the corner of Pond Street you will see two enormous Victorian Gothic buildings: one, St. Stephen's Church, is now a community arts center. The other, AIR Studios, founded by the Beatles' producer, Sir George Martin, is where scores for movies, including *Iron Man 3, Paddington 2,* and *Darkest Hour,* have been recorded.

Turn right onto Pond Street and go downhill past the unlovely Royal Free Hospital to South End Green and the entrance to **Hampstead Heath.** Or go straight to stay on Rosslyn Hill and then Hampstead High Street, the neighborhood's main drag. Turn left onto Church Row, with its unspoiled early Georgian terraced houses leading to **St. John's-at-Hampstead**, where the painter John Constable is buried. To the northeast of Hampstead Heath is Highgate, another upscale north London "village" with a large concentration of Georgian and early Victorian buildings, particularly around The Grove (home to Kate Moss [who lives in Samuel Taylor Coleridge's former residence] and Jude Law).

To reach **Little Venice,** go to the west entrance of Regent's Park by the gold-domed London Central Mosque and then north past **Lord's Cricket Ground** to the St. John's Wood Tube stop. Turn left onto Grove End Road, which will bring you to the famous Abbey Road crosswalk featured on the Beatles' album of the same name. Head southwest for Little Venice, known as the Belgravia of north London due to its stucco terraces (found on streets such as Randolph Avenue, Clifton Avenue, and Randolph Road) that are very similar to the other neighborhoods. The "Venice" comes from its proximity to a picturesque stretch of the Grand Union Canal along Blomfield Road, where highly decorative houseboats are moored. If you happen to be here on the second Sunday in May, you'll be able to see houseboats from all over London's canals gather here in Paddington Basin for the Blessing of the Boats.

REGENT'S PARK

Commissioned by his patron the Prince Regent (later George IV) to create a master plan for this part of London, formerly a royal hunting ground, London's great urban planner and architect John Nash laid out the plans for the 410-acre Regent's Park in 1812. Bordered by grand neoclassical terraces, the park holds many attractions, including the London Zoo and the summer display of more than 400 varieties of rose in Queen Mary's Gardens.

Cecil Sharp House. The home of the English Folk Dance and Song Society, this soaring building from 1930 hosts concerts by artists ranging from Mumford & Sons and Laura Marling to the Ukulele Orchestra of Great Britain, as well as family barn dances and *céilidhs* (Irish barn dances). Meet the locals at one of the drop-in dance classes offering everything from 19th-century quadrilles and English clog dancing to zydeco and tango. There are also temporary exhibitions on British folk art, a café and bar, and an outstanding specialist library with an extensive collection of recordings, manuscripts, sheet music, and images relating to British folk song, dances, and regional cultures in general. ⊠ *2 Regent's Park Rd., Primrose Hill* ☎ *020/7485–2206* ⊕ *www.cecilsharphouse.org* ☒ *Free, classes from £4* ☉ *Library closed Aug., Mon., and 2nd and 4th Sat. of each month* Ⓜ *Chalk Farm, Camden Town.*

Jewish Museum. This fascinating museum tells the story of the Jewish people in Britain from 1066 to today, including the period between the 13th and 17th century when Judaism was outlawed in England. Using a combination of art, religious artifacts, photographs, manuscripts, and interactive displays, its permanent galleries include one on the Holocaust told through the story of a Britain-based survivor. There's also

one that explores Jewish history in Britain, which features a re-creation of a Jewish East End street from the Victorian era and displays relating to refugees from Nazism, including the 10,000 Jewish Kindertransport children who came to Britain as World War II loomed. There's also a free overview of the collection on the ground floor that includes a medieval *mikveh* (ritual bath) excavated a few miles from here in 2001. ⊠ *Raymond Burton House, 129–131 Albert St., Camden Town* ☏ *020/7284–7384* ⊕ *www.jewishmuseum.org.uk* £7.50 ⊘ *Closed on major Jewish holidays* Ⓜ *Camden Town.*

Lord's Cricket Ground & Museum. The spiritual home of this most English of games—and the headquarters of the MCC (Marylebone Cricket Club)—opens its "behind the scenes" areas to visitors during a 100-minute tour. Highlights include the beautiful Long Room, a VIP viewing area where portraits of cricketing greats are on display (you can also book a traditional Afternoon Tea here); the players' dressing rooms; and the world's oldest sporting museum, where cricket's 400-year progress from gentlemanly village-green game to worldwide sport is charted via memorabilia, equipment, trophies, and footage of memorable performances. Don't miss the prize exhibit: the urn known as the Ashes—allegedly the remains of a cricket bail (part of the wicket assembly) presented to the English captain in 1883 by a group of Australian women, a jokey allusion to a newspaper's satirical obituary for the death of English cricket published after a resounding defeat. It's been a symbol of the two nations' long-running rivalry ever since. They still play for possession of the Ashes—an official (as opposed to joke) trophy only since 1998—every two years. A Waterford crystal version changes hands these days, although the winners still hold a replica of the original urn aloft. There is no separate nontour admittance to the museum, except for match ticket holders. All tours must be booked in advance, and are not available during matches. ⊠ *St. John's Wood Rd., St. John's Wood* ☏ *020/7616–8595* ⊕ *www.lords.org* Tour £24; museum £3 with county match ticket, free with major match ticket ⊘ *Closed late Dec.; no tours Apr.–Sept. on match days, preparation days, and event days* Ⓜ *St. John's Wood.*

FAMILY
Fodor'sChoice
★
Primrose Hill. More conventionally parklike than Hampstead Heath, the rolling lawns of Primrose Hill, the northerly extension of Regent's Park, rises to 213 feet and provides outstanding views over the city to the southeast, encompassing Canary Wharf and the London Eye. Formerly the site of boxing matches and duels but now filled with families and picnickers in nice weather, it has been featured in several books—it was here that Pongo engaged in "twilight barking" in *The Hundred and One Dalmatians* and the Martians set up an encampment in H.G. Wells's *The War of The Worlds.* It's also been mentioned in songs by Blur, Madness, and Paul McCartney, among others, and served as a location for films including *Bridget Jones: The Edge of Reason,* and *Paddington.* ⊠ *Regent's Park Rd., Regent's Park* ☏ *0300/061–2300* ⊕ *www.royalparks.org.uk* Free Ⓜ *Chalk Farm.*

FAMILY **Regent's Park.** One of London's principal charms is to find the formal
Fodor's Choice cultivated serenity of Regent's Park—more country-house grounds than
★ municipal amenity—just on the edge of the intensely urban West End, a
world away from the traffic-clogged surrounding roads. The 395-acre
park, with the largest grass area for sports in central London, draws
the athletically inclined from around the city.

At the center of the park, **Queen Mary's Gardens,** created in the 1930s,
are a fragrant 17-acre circle containing some 30,000 individual specimens and more than 400 varieties of roses. Unsurprisingly, it's a favorite spot for weddings. Just to the east of the Gardens is the **Regent's
Park Open-Air Theatre** and the **Boating Lake,** the latter best explored
by renting a pedalo (paddleboat) or rowboat. Heading east from the
rose gardens along Chester Road past the **Broad Walk** brings you to
Nash's iconic white stucco **Cumberland Terrace,** with its central Ionic
columns surmounted by a triangular Wedgwood-blue pediment (home
to artist Damien Hirst). At the north end of the Broad Walk you'll find
the **London Zoo,** while to the northwest of the central circle is **The
Hub,** London's largest outdoor sports facility that has changing rooms,
exercise classes, and a café with 360-degree views of the surrounding
sports fields, used for soccer, rugby, cricket, field hockey, and softball.
There are also tennis courts toward the park's southeast (Baker Street)
entrance, and the park is a favorite north–south route for cyclists.
■TIP➔ Regent's Park also hosts two annual events: the prestigious
Frieze Art Fair, and the Taste of London, a foodie-oriented extravaganza.

✉ *Chester Rd., Regent's Park* ☎ *0300/061–2300* ⊕ *www.royalparks.
org.uk* ✉ *Free* Ⓜ *Baker St., Regent's Park, Great Portland St.*

FAMILY **ZSL London Zoo.** With an emphasis on education, wildlife conservation,
Fodor's Choice and the breeding of endangered species, London Zoo offers visitors
★ the chance to see tigers, gorillas, meerkats, and more in something
resembling a natural environment rather than a cage. Operated by
the nonprofit Zoological Society of London, the zoo was begun with
the royal animals collection, moved here from the Tower of London
in 1828; the zoo itself did not open to the public until 1847. Big
attractions include Land of the Lions, a walk-through re-creation
of an Indian forest where you can see three resident Asiatic lions
relaxing at close range; Gorilla Kingdom, which provides a similar
re-created habitat (in this case an African rain forest) for its colony
of six Western Lowland Gorillas; and the Attenborough Komodo
Dragon House, renamed to honor the renowned naturalist. The zoo
also offers the chance to get up close and personal with 15 ring-tailed
lemurs. The huge B.U.G.S. pavilion (Biodiversity Underpinning Global
Survival) is a self-sustaining, contained ecosystem for 140 less-cuddly
species, including invertebrates such as spiders and millipedes, plus
some reptiles and fish. Rainforest Life is an indoor tropical rain forest (complete with humidity) inhabited by the likes of armadillos,
monkeys, and sloths. A special nighttime section offers glimpses of
nocturnal creatures like slow lorises and bats. The Animal Adventures
Children's Zoo allows kids to closely observe coatis, as well as to
interact with llamas, donkeys, small pigs, sheep, and goats. Two of
the most popular attractions are Penguin Beach, especially at feeding

time (1:30 and 4:30), and meerkat snack time (11:15), where you can see the sociable animals keeping watch over their own sandy territory. If you're feeling flush, try to nab one of the six daily "Meet the Penguins" VIP tickets (1:45 pm) that offer a 20-minute guided close encounter with the locals (£54); there are similar VIP encounters with giraffes, meerkats, and rain forest monkeys. Other zoo highlights include Butterfly Paradise and Tiger Territory, an enclosure for four beautiful endangered Sumatran tigers (including two cubs born at the zoo). Adults-only Zoo Nights held Friday nights in June offer street food, alcoholic drinks, and entertainment. You can also experience the zoo after-hours by booking an overnight stay in one of the cozy cabins near (not *in*) the lion enclosure. Check the website or the information board out front for free events, including creature close encounters and "ask the keeper" sessions. ⊠ *Outer Circle, Regent's Park* ☎ *0844/225–1826* ⊕ *www.zsl.org* ⊠ *From £27.04* Ⓜ *Camden Town, then Bus 274.*

HAMPSTEAD

Back in 1818, even impoverished Romantic poet John Keats could afford to live in **Hampstead.** His former residence, now known as **Keats House,** is a pretty Regency villa where he spent two years and wrote several of his most famous works. These days Hampstead's bohemian past is long gone, although several distinguished writers, actors, and musicians still live here. Artisanal food shops and boutiques cluster along Hampstead High Street, where upscale high-street chains proliferate the closer you get to Hampstead Tube station. Be sure to leave the beaten path to explore the numerous narrow charming roads, like Flask Walk, Well Walk, and New End Road. Also hidden among Hampstead's winding streets are **Fenton House,** a Georgian town house with a lovely walled garden, and Burgh House, the oldest (1704) house in the village and a repository of local history.

Hampstead's biggest claim to fame, however, is **Hampstead Heath** (known locally as "The Heath"), 791 acres of verdant open space, woods, spring-fed swimming ponds, and some of Europe's oldest oaks. It's also home to one of London's highest vantage points (321 feet), Parliament Hill. On the Highgate end of Hampstead Heath, you'll find **Kenwood House,** an 18th-century mansion that was designed by Robert Adam and is noted for its remarkable art collection and grounds.

Burgh House and Hampstead Museum. One of Hampstead's oldest buildings, Burgh House was built in 1704 to take advantage of the natural spa waters of the then-fashionable Hampstead Wells. A private house until World War II, it was saved from dereliction in the 1970s by local residents, who have maintained it ever since. The building is a fine example of the genteel elegance common to the Queen Anne period, with brick frontage, oak-paneled rooms, and a terraced garden that was originally designed by Gertrude Jekyll. Today the house contains a small but diverting museum on the history of the area, and also hosts regular talks, concerts, and recitals. The secluded garden courtyard of the café is a lovely spot for lunch, tea, or a glass of wine on a summer's afternoon. ✉ *New End Sq., Hampstead* ☎ *020/7431–0144* ⊕ *www.burghhouse. org.uk* 🎫 *Free* 🕙 *Closed Mon., Tues., and Sat.* Ⓜ *Hampstead.*

Fenton House. This handsome 17th-century merchant's home, Hampstead's oldest surviving house, has fine collections of porcelain, Georgian furniture, and 17th-century needlework. The 2-acre walled garden, with its rose plantings and apple orchard, has remained virtually unchanged for 300 years; there are free garden tours led by the head gardener on Thursdays at 2 pm, from May through September. International musicians give recitals on the important collection of early keyboard instruments throughout the week; check the website for details. ✉ *Hampstead Grove, Hampstead* ☎ *020/7435–3471* ⊕ *www.nationaltrust.org.uk* 🎫 *£8; £13 combination ticket, includes 2 Willow Rd.* 🕙 *Closed Mon. and Tues.* Ⓜ *Hampstead.*

Freud Museum London. The father of psychoanalysis lived here with his family for a year, between his escape from Nazi persecution in his native Vienna in 1938 and his death in 1939. His daughter Anna (herself a pioneer of child psychoanalysis) remained in the house until her own death in 1982, bequeathing it as a museum to honor her father. The centerpiece is Freud's unchanged study, containing his remarkable collection of antiquities and his library. Also on display is the family's Biedermeier furniture—and, of course, the couch. As well, there are lectures, study groups, and themed exhibitions, in addition to a psychoanalysis-related archive and research library. Looking for a unique souvenir for the person who has everything? The gift shop here sells "Freudian Slippers." ✉ *20 Maresfield Gardens, Swiss Cottage* ☎ *020/7435–2002* ⊕ *www.freud.org.uk* 🎫 *£9* 🕙 *Closed Mon. and Tues.* Ⓜ *Swiss Cottage, Finchley Rd.*

FAMILY
Fodor's Choice
★

Hampstead Heath. For generations, Londoners have headed to Hampstead Heath to escape the dirt and noise of the city, and this unique 791-acre expanse of *rus in urbe* ("country in the city") is home to a variety of wildlife and habitat: grassy meadows, woodland, scrub, wetlands, and some of Europe's most venerable oaks. Be aware that, aside from the Parliament Hill area to the south and Golders Hill Park in the west, it is more like countryside than a park, with signs and amenities in short supply. Pick up a map at Kenwood House or at the "Enquiries" window of the Staff Yard near the tennis courts off Highgate Road, where you can also find details about the history of the Heath and its flora and fauna. An excellent café near the Edwardian bandstand serves Italian food.

Coming onto the Heath from the Savernake Road entrance on the southern side, walk past the **Playground** and **Paddling Pool** and head uphill to the top of **Parliament Hill.** At 321 feet above sea level, it's one of the highest points in London, providing a stunning panorama over the city. On clear days you can see all the way to the Surrey Hills beyond the city's southern limits. Keep heading north from Parliament Hill to find the more rural parts of the Heath.

If you keep heading east from the playground instead, turn right past the Athletics Track and you'll come to the **Lido,** an Olympic-size outdoor unheated swimming pool that gets packed on all-too-rare hot summer days. More swimming options are available at the Hampstead ponds, which have been refreshing Londoners for generations. You'll find the "Mens" and "Ladies" ponds to the northeast of Parliament Hill, with a "Mixed" pond closer to South End Green. A £2 donation is requested.

■TIP➜ Golders Hill Park, on the Heath Extension to the northwest, offers a good café, tennis courts, a duck pond, a croquet lawn, and a walled flower garden, plus a Butterfly House (May–September) and a small zoo with native species including muntjac deer, rare red squirrels, and a Scottish wildcat. ⊠ *Hampstead* ☎ *020/7332–3322* ⊕ *www.cityoflondon.gov.uk/hampstead* ⊠ *Free* Ⓜ *Overground: Hampstead Heath for west of Heath or Gospel Oak for south and east of Heath and Lido; Northern Line: Golders Green, then Bus 210 or 268 to Whitestone Pond for north and west of Heath and Golders Hill Park.*

Highgate Cemetery. Highgate is not the oldest cemetery in London, but it is probably the best known, both for its roster of famous "inhabitants" and the quality of its funerary architecture. After it was consecrated in 1839, Victorians came from miles around to appreciate the ornate headstones, the impressive tombs, and the view. Such was its popularity that 19 acres on the other side of the road were acquired in 1850, and this additional East Cemetery is the final resting place of numerous notables, including the most visited, Karl Marx (1818–83), as well as George Eliot and, a more recent internment, George Michael. At the summit is the **Circle of Lebanon,** a ring of vaults built around an ancient cypress tree, a legacy of the 17th-century gardens that formerly occupied the site. Leading from the circle is the **Egyptian Avenue,** a subterranean stone tunnel lined with catacombs, itself approached by a dramatic colonnade that screens the main cemetery from the road. Both sides are impressive, with a grand (locked) iron gate leading to a sweeping courtyard built for the approach of horses and carriages. By the 1970s the cemetery had become unkempt and neglected until a group of volunteers, the Friends of Highgate Cemetery, undertook the huge upkeep. Tours are conducted by the Friends, who will show you the most interesting graves among the numerous statues and memorials once hidden by overgrowth. The West side can only be seen during a one-hour tour. Booking is essential for weekdays but not permitted for weekends; tours of the East side on Saturday are first-come, first-served. You're expected to dress respectfully, so skip the shorts and the baseball cap; children under eight are not admitted and neither are dogs, tripods, or video cameras. ⊠ *Swains La., Highgate* ☎ *020/8340–1834* ⊕ *www.highgatecemetery.org* ⊠ *East Cemetery £4, tours £8; West Cemetery tours £12, includes admission to East Cemetery. No credit cards* Ⓜ *Archway, then Bus 210, 271, or 143 to Waterlow Park; Belsize Park, then Bus C11 to Brookfield Park.*

Keats House. It was while living in this house between 1818 and 1820 that the leading Romantic poet John Keats (1795–1821) fell in love with girl next door Fanny Brawne and wrote some of his best-loved poems. (Soon after, ill health forced him to move to Rome, where he died the following year.) After a major refurbishment to make the rooms more

The fabled cover of the Beatles' album *Abbey Road*, with the world's most famous traffic crossing

consistent with their original Regency style, the house now displays all sorts of Keats-related material, including portraits, letters, many of the poet's original manuscripts and books, the engagement ring he gave to Fanny, and items of her clothing. A pretty garden contains the plum tree under which Keats supposedly composed *Ode to a Nightingale*. There are free, half-hour guided tours daily at 3 pm, plus evening poetry readings, concerts, and special events featuring local literary luminaries. The ticket gives you entry for a full year, so you can come back as often as you like. Picnics can be taken onto the grounds during the summer. ✉ *10 Keats Grove, Hampstead* ☎ *020/7332–3868* ⊕ *www. cityoflondon.gov.uk/things-to-do/keats-house* 🎫 *£6.50* ⊙ *Closed Mon. and Tues. in Mar.–Oct. and Mon.–Thurs. in Nov.–Feb.* Ⓜ *Overground: Hampstead Heath.*

Fodor's Choice ★ **Kenwood House.** This largely Palladian villa offers an escape to a gracious country house with a magnificent collection of Old Masters and beautiful grounds, all within a short Tube ride from central London. Originally built in 1616, Kenwood was expanded by Robert Adam starting in 1767 and later by George Saunders in 1795. Adam refaced most of the exterior and added the splendid library, which, with its vaulted ceiling and Corinthian columns, is the highlight of the house's design. A major renovation restored four rooms to reflect Adam's intentions as closely as possible, incorporating the furniture he designed for them and his original color schemes. Kenwood is also home to the **Iveagh Bequest,** a world-class collection of some 60 paintings that includes masterworks like Rembrandt's *Portrait*

A TRIP TO ABBEY ROAD

The black-and-white crosswalk (known as a "zebra crossing") near the Abbey Road Studios at No. 3, where the Beatles recorded their entire output from "Love Me Do" onward, is a place of pilgrimage for Beatles' fans from around the world, many of them teenagers born long after the band split up. They converge here to re-create the cover of the Beatles' 1969 *Abbey Road* album, posing on the crossing despite the onrushing traffic. ■TIP→ Be careful if you're going to attempt this; traffic on Abbey Road is busy. One of the best ways to explore landmarks in the Beatles' story is to take one of the excellent walking tours offered by **Original London Walks** (☎ *020/7624–3978* ⊕ *www.walks.com*). Try **The Beatles In-My-Life Walk** (Saturday and Tuesday at 11 am outside Marylebone Underground) or **The Beatles Magical Mystery Tour** (Wednesday at 2 pm and Thursday except for December and January and Sunday at 11 am, at Underground Exit 1, Tottenham Court Road).

of the Artist and Vermeer's *The Guitar Player,* along with major works by Reynolds, Van Dyck, Hals, Gainsborough, Turner, and more. The grounds, designed by Humphrey Repton and bordered by Hampstead Heath, are equally elegant and serene, with lawns sloping down to a little lake crossed by a trompe-l'oeil bridge. All in all, it's the perfect home for an 18th-century gentleman. In summer, the grounds host a series of popular and classical concerts, culminating in fireworks on the last night. The Brew House café, occupying part of the old coach house, has outdoor tables in the courtyard and a terraced garden. ✉ *Hampstead La., Highgate* ☎ *0870/333–1181* ⊕ *www.english-heritage.org.uk/visit/places/kenwood* ✎ *Free, house and estate tour £16.30* Ⓜ *Golders Green or Archway, then Bus 210. Overground: Gospel Oak.*

The Parish Church of St. John-at-Hampstead. There has been a church here since 1312, but the current building—consecrated in 1747 and later extended in 1877—is a fine example of neoclassical serenity, enhanced by Ionic columns and vaulting arches. Also known as the Hampstead Parish Church, it stands at the end of Church Row, a narrow street lined with flat-fronted brick Georgian houses that gives you a sense of what Hampstead was like when it truly was a rural village as opposed to a traffic-clogged north London neighborhood. Many local notables are buried in the picturesque churchyard, including painter John Constable (some of whose most famous works depict the Heath), John Harrison (the inventor of the marine chronometer at the heart of the book *Longitude*), members of the artistic Du Maurier family, Jane Austen's aunt, and comedy god Peter Cook. ✉ *Church Row, Hampstead* ☎ *020/7794–5808* ⊕ *www.hampsteadparishchurch.org.uk* ✎ *Free* Ⓜ *Hampstead.*

2 Willow Road. Among the many artists and intellectuals fleeing Nazi persecution who settled in the area was noted architect Erno Goldfinger, who built this outstanding and influential modernist home opposite Hampstead Heath in 1939 as his family residence. (His plans drew the ire of several local residents, including novelist Ian Fleming, who supposedly got his revenge by naming a Bond villain after his neighbor.) As well as design touches and building techniques that were groundbreaking at the time, the unique house, a place of pilgrimage for 20th-century architecture enthusiasts, also contains Goldfinger's impressive collection of modern art and self-designed innovative furniture. Between 11 am and 2 pm, admission is by first-come, first-served hourly tour only, but you can visit independently after 3. ✉ *2 Willow Rd., Hampstead* 📷 *020/7435–6166* ⊕ *www.nationaltrust.org.uk* ✉ *£7; £13 combination ticket with Fenton House* ☉ *Closed Mon. and Tues.* Ⓜ *Overground: Hampstead Heath.*

GREENWICH

Getting Oriented

- Ragged School Museum
- Museum of London Docklands
- Emirates Air Line– Royal Docks
- Up at the O2
- Emirates Air Line– Greenwich Peninsula
- Thames Barrier Visitor Centre
- Eltham Palace

River Thames

Trafalgar Tavern

Crane St.

Eastner St.

Old Woolwich Rd.

Greenwich Pier

Park Row

Trafalgar Rd.

Trinity College

Old Royal Naval College

Feathers Pl.

TO WOOLWICH

The Old Brewery

Cutty Sark

Painted Hall

Park Row

Park Vista

DLR: Cutty Sark

Discover Greenwich

College App.

Greenwich Church St.

Seamen's Hospital

Romney Rd.

Queen's House

Greenwich Market

Nelson Rd.

National Maritime Museum

King William Walk

Stockwell St.

Greenwich Park

Greenwich Meridian Line

Greenwich High Rd.

Clock Tower Antiques Market

Fan Museum

Burney St.

The Pavillion Café

Gloucester Circus

Royal Observatory

Royal Hill

The Avenue

King George St.

Croom's Hill

Greenwich

0   1/8 mile
0   1/8 kilometer

Ranger's House and the Wernher Collection

TOP REASONS TO GO

The Greenwich Meridian Line: At the Royal Observatory—where the world's time is set—you can be in the eastern and western hemispheres simultaneously.

The Queen's House: Sir Inigo Jones's 17th-century building was the first in England to embrace the styles of the Italian Renaissance.

The National Maritime Museum: Discover Britain's seafaring past, and see how Britannia ruled the waves and helped shape the modern world.

Cutty Sark: Take a stroll along the deck of the last surviving 19th-century tea clipper, now shipshape after years of renovation.

FEELING PECKISH?

The Pavilion Café. Healthy snacks and lunches are served at this excellent café next to the Royal Observatory. Homemade soups and sandwiches are good for a quick refuel, or try one of the delicious stone-baked pizzas for something more substantial. ⊠ *Charlton Way, Greenwich* ☎ *020/8853–4777* ⊕ *www.royalparks.org.uk.*

The Old Brewery. Right next to Discover Greenwich, the Old Brewery is a relaxed café by day and a sophisticated restaurant at night. The artful, high-ceiling dining room merits a visit, but the Modern British cuisine is also among the best in this part of London—and reasonably priced, too. ⊠ *Pepys Bldg., Old Royal Naval College, King William Walk, Greenwich* ☎ *020/3437–2222* ⊕ *www.oldbrewerygreenwich.com.*

Trafalgar Tavern. With its excellent vista of the Thames, there is no more handsomely situated pub in Greenwich than the Trafalgar Tavern. It's still as grand a place as it ever was to have a pint and a quick tasty meal. ⊠ *Park Row, Greenwich* ☎ *020/3887–9886* ⊕ *www.trafalgartavern.co.uk.*

GETTING THERE

The Docklands Light Railway (DLR) is a zippy way to get to Cutty Sark Station from Canary Wharf or Bank Tube station in The City. Or take the DLR to Island Gardens and walk the old Victorian Foot Tunnel under the river. (Sitting at the front of a train can be disconcerting, as you watch the controls in the fully automated driver's cab move about as if a ghost were at the helm.) The best way to arrive, however—time and weather permitting—is like a sea captain of old: by water (it takes an hour from central London).

MAKING THE MOST OF YOUR TIME

Set apart from the rest of London, Greenwich is worth a day to itself—those who love maritime history will want to spend two in order to make the most of walks in the rolling parkland and to immerse yourself in the richness of Greenwich's history, science, and architecture. The boat trip takes about an hour from Westminster Pier (next to Big Ben) or 25 minutes from the Tower of London, so factor in enough time for the round-trip.

NEAREST PUBLIC RESTROOMS

Duck into Discover Greenwich, where the loo is free.

12

Sightseeing
★★★★
Nightlife
★
Dining
★★
Lodging
★
Shopping
★★★

About 8 miles downstream (meaning seaward, to the east) from central London, Greenwich is a small borough that looms large across the world. Once the seat of British naval power, it is not only home to the Old Royal Observatory, which measures time for our entire planet, but also the Greenwich Meridian, which divides the world into two—you can stand astride it with one foot in either hemisphere.

Updated by
Jo Caird

Bear in mind that the journey to Greenwich is an event in itself. In a rush, you can take the driverless DLR train, but many opt for arriving by boat along the Thames. This way, you glide past famous sights on the London skyline—there's a guaranteed spine chill on passing the Tower—and ever-changing docklands, and there's usually a chirpy Cock-er-ney navigator enlivening the journey with fun commentary.

A visit to Greenwich feels like a trip to a rather elegant seaside town—albeit one with more than its fair share of historic sites. The grandiose **Old Royal Naval Hospital,** designed by Sir Christopher Wren, was originally a home for veteran sailors. Today it's a popular visitor attraction, with a more glamorous second life as one of the most widely used movie locations in Britain.

Greenwich was originally home to one of England's finest Tudor palaces, and the birthplace of Henry VIII, Elizabeth I, and Mary I. Inigo Jones began what is considered the first "classical" building in England in 1616: the **Queen's House,** which now houses a collection of fine art. Britain was the world's preeminent naval power for more than 500 years, and the excellent **National Maritime Museum** details that history in an engaging way. Its prize exhibits include the coat worn by Admiral Lord Nelson (1758–1805) in his final battle—bullet hole and all. The 19th-century tea clipper **Cutty Sark** was nearly destroyed by fire in 2007 but reopened in 2012 after a painstaking restoration. Now it's more pristine than ever and has an impressive visitor center.

12

Greenwich Park, London's oldest royal park, is still home to fallow red deer, just as it has been since they were first introduced here for hunting by Henry VIII. The **Ranger's House** now houses a private art collection, next door to a beautifully manicured rose garden. Above it all is the **Royal Observatory,** where you can be in two hemispheres at once by standing along the **Greenwich Meridian Line,** before seeing a high-tech planetarium show.

Toward north Greenwich, the hopelessly ambitious Millennium Dome has been successfully reborn as The O2 and now hosts major concerts and stand-up comedy gigs. More adventurous visitors can also go **Up at The O2** on a climbing expedition across the massive domed surface. Meanwhile, those who prefer excursions of a gentler kind may prefer to journey a couple of miles south of the borough, farther out into London's southern suburbs, to the shamefully underappreciated **Eltham Palace,** once a favorite of Henry VIII. Parts of the mansion were transformed into an art deco masterpiece in the 1930s.

Clock Tower Antiques Market. The weekend Clock Tower Antiques Market on Greenwich High Road has vintage shopping, and browsing among the "small collectibles" makes for a good half-hour diversion. ⊠ *166 Greenwich High Rd., Greenwich* ☎ *020/7237–2001* ⊕ *www.clocktowermarket.co.uk* ☉ *Closed weekdays* Ⓜ *Greenwich Rail.*

Fodor's Choice ★ **Cutty Sark.** This sleek, romantic clipper was built in 1869, one among a vast fleet of tall-masted wooden ships that plied the oceanic highways of the 19th century, trading in exotic commodities—in this case, tea. *Cutty Sark* (named after a racy witch in a Robert Burns poem) was the fastest in the fleet, sailing the London–China route in 1871 in only 107 days. The clipper has been preserved in dry dock as a museum ship since the 1950s, but was severely damaged in a devastating fire in 2007. Yet up from the ashes, as the song goes, grow the roses of success: after a major restoration project, the visitor facilities are now better than ever. Not only can you tour the ship in its entirety, but the glittering visitor center (which the ship now rests directly above) allows you to view the hull from below. There's plenty to see here, and the cramped quarters form a fantastic time capsule to walk around in—this boat was never too comfortable for the 28-strong crew (as you'll see). Don't forget to take in the amusing collection of figureheads. The ship also hosts monthly stand-up comedy gigs. ⊠ *King William Walk, Greenwich* ☎ *020/8858–4422* ⊕ *www.rmg.co.uk/cuttysark* 💷 *£13.50; £20 combination ticket, includes Royal Observatory attractions* Ⓜ *DLR: Cutty Sark.*

Discover Greenwich. Intended as a kind of anchor point for Greenwich's big three attractions—the Old Royal Naval College, *Cutty Sark,* and the National Maritime Museum—this excellent, state-of-the-art visitor center includes interactive exhibitions on the history of Greenwich, plus an assortment of local treasures and artifacts. Most intriguing among them is a 17th-century "witch bottle," once used to ward off evil spirits. High-tech scans have revealed it to contain a mixture of human hair, fingernails, and urine. ⊠ *Pepys Bldg., King William Walk, Greenwich* ☎ *020/8269–4799* ⊕ *www.ornc.org/visitor-centre* 💷 *Free* Ⓜ *DLR: Greenwich.*

Museum of London Docklands. This wonderful old warehouse building, on a quaint cobbled quayside near the tower of Canary Wharf, is worth a visit in its own right. With uneven wood floors, beams, and pillars, the museum used to be a storehouse for coffee, tea, sugar, and rum from the West Indies, hence the name: West India Quay. The fascinating story of the old port and the river is told using films, together with interactive displays and reconstructions. Excellent permanent exhibitions include *City and River,* which chronicles the explosion of trade and industry that, by the mid-19th century, had transformed this district into the world's most important port. *Sailortown* is an effective reconstruction of the Wapping district in Victorian times, complete with period shops, a pub, spooky alleys, and costumed guides. Young kids can hunt for treasure and let off some steam in the soft play area in the Mudlarks Gallery. Special events happen year-round; check the museum's website for details. ⊠ *No. 1 Warehouse, West India Quay, Canary Wharf* ☎ *020/7001–9844* ⊕ *www.museumoflondon.org.uk/docklands* ⛴ *Free, special exhibitions sometimes extra* Ⓜ *Canary Wharf. DLR: West India Quay.*

FAMILY
Fodor's Choice
★

National Maritime Museum. From the time of Henry VIII until the 1940s, Britain was the world's preeminent naval power, and the collections here trace half a millennia of that seafaring history. The story is as much about trade as it is warfare: *Atlantic: Slavery, Trade, Empire* gallery explores how trade in goods (and people) irrevocably changed the world, while *Traders: The East India Company and Asia* focuses on how the epoch-defining company shaped trade with Asia for 250 years. One gallery is devoted to Admiral Lord Nelson, Britain's most famous naval commander, and among the exhibits is the uniform he was wearing, complete with bloodstains, when he died at the Battle of Trafalgar in 1805. Temporary exhibitions here are usually fascinating—those in recent years have included personal accounts of the First World War at sea. Borrow a tablet computer from the front desk and take it to the giant map of the world in the courtyard at the center of the museum; here, a high-tech, interactive app opens up hidden stories and games as you walk between continents. The Ahoy! gallery is filled with interactive fun for kids, where they can learn about polar exploration, pirates, and more. The adjacent **Queen's House** is home to the museum's art collection, the largest collection of maritime art in the world, including works by William Hogarth, Canaletto, and Joshua Reynolds. Permission for its construction was granted by Queen Anne only on condition that the river vista from the house be preserved, and there are few more majestic views in London than Inigo Jones's awe-inspiring symmetry. ⊠ *Romney Rd., Greenwich* ☎ *020/8312–6608* ⊕ *www.rmg.co.uk/national-maritime-museum* ⛴ *Free; tours £10; fee for special exhibitions* Ⓜ *DLR: Greenwich.*

Fodor's Choice
★

Old Royal Naval College. Begun by Sir Christopher Wren in 1694 as a rest home for ancient mariners, the college became a school in 1873. It's still used for classes by the University of Greenwich and the Trinity College of Music (the warbling of opera singers can be heard around the grounds), although you're more likely to recognize it as a film location—blockbusters to have made use of its elegant interiors include

DID YOU KNOW?

The Docklands Light Railway (DLR) connects former warehouses that have been converted to museums and malls, such as Hay's and Butler's wharves, and the gleaming office buildings of Canary Wharf shown here.

Skyfall, Les Misérables, and *The King's Speech.* Architecturally, you'll notice how the structures part to reveal the **Queen's House** across the central lawns. The **Painted Hall,** the college's dining hall, derives its name from the baroque murals of William and Mary (reigned jointly 1689–94; William alone 1695–1702) and assorted allegorical figures. James Thornhill's frescoes, depicting scenes of naval grandeur with a suitably pro-British note, were painstakingly completed 1707–12 and 1718–26, and were good enough to earn him a knighthood. In the opposite building stands the **College Chapel,** which was rebuilt after a fire in 1779 in an altogether more restrained, neo-Grecian style. Guided tours of the grounds and Painted Hall take place regularly (check the website for details). ⊠ *King William Walk, Greenwich* ☎ *020/8269–4747* ⊕ *www.ornc.org* ⊠ *Grounds and College Chapel free; Painted Hall tours, £10* Ⓜ *DLR: Greenwich.*

> ## GREENWICH FOOT TUNNEL
>
> In a brilliant piece of foresight in 1849, Greenwich Hospital bought Island Gardens, on the other side of the Thames, to guard against industrial sprawl and to preserve one of the most beautiful views in London. Take the stone spiral steps down into Greenwich Foot Tunnel and head under the Thames (enjoying the magnificently creepy echo) to Island Gardens, at the southern tip of the Isle of Dogs. Then look back over the river for a magnificent vista: the Old Royal Naval College and Queen's House in all their glory, framed by the verdant green borders of the park.

FAMILY **Ragged School Museum.** In its time, the Ragged School Museum was the largest school in London and a place where impoverished children could get free education and a good meal. The museum re-creates a classroom dating from the 1880s. It's an eye-opener for adults, and fun for kids, who get the chance to learn just like Victorian children did in one of the many organized workshops. If you really want to get into the spirit, visitors of all ages can attend an authentic, 45-minute Victorian school lesson (first Sunday of every month, 2:15 and 3:30), complete with a fully costumed schoolmistress who tests your slate-writing technique—and might give you a dunce hat if you misbehave. ⊠ *46–50 Copperfield Rd., Mile End* ☎ *020/8980–6405* ⊕ *www.raggedschoolmuseum.org.uk* ⊠ *Free; £2 donation requested for Victorian lessons* ⊗ *Closed Mon., Tues., Fri., and weekends, except 1st Sun. of month* Ⓜ *Mile End; DLR: Limehouse.*

Ranger's House and the Wernher Collection. This handsome, early-18th-century villa, which was the Greenwich Park ranger's official residence during the 19th century, is hung with Stuart and Jacobean portraits, but the most interesting diversion is the Wernher Collection, which contains nearly 700 artworks that were amassed by the diamond millionaire Sir Julius Wernher (1850–1912) and were once housed in his fabulous stately house, Luton Hoo, in Bedfordshire. The collection ranges from Old Master paintings to Renaissance jewelry and assorted pieces of decorative art and curios from the medieval period onward. The Ranger's House is just under a mile's walk from the DLR station at

Without a central support, the Tulip Stairs spiral up to the Great Hall of Queen's House.

Greenwich, or you can catch a bus there from Greenwich or Deptford DLR. ⊠ *Blackheath, Chesterfield Walk, Greenwich Park, Greenwich* ☎ *020/8294–2848* ⊕ *www.english-heritage.org.uk* ✉ *TBC* ☉ *Closed Nov.–Mar. and Thurs.–Sat.* Ⓜ *DLR: Deptford Bridge, then Bus 53; or Greenwich, then Bus 386.*

FAMILY
Fodor's Choice
★

Royal Observatory. Greenwich is on the prime meridian at 0° longitude, and the ultimate standard for time around the world has been set here at the Royal Observatory since 1884, when Britain was the world's maritime superpower. The observatory is actually split into two sites, a short walk apart: one devoted to astronomy, the other to the study of time. The enchanting **Peter Harrison Planetarium** is London's only planetarium, its bronze-clad turret glinting in the sun. Shows on black holes and how to interpret the night sky are enthralling and enlightening. Even better for kids are the high-technology rooms of the **Astronomy Center,** where space exploration is brought to life through cutting-edge interactive programs and fascinating exhibits—including the chance to touch a 4½-billion-year-old meteorite.

Across the way is **Flamsteed House,** designed by Sir Christopher Wren in 1675 for John Flamsteed, the first Royal Astronomer. The Time Ball atop Flamsteed House is one of the world's earliest public time signals. Each day at 12:55, it rises halfway up its mast. At 12:58 it rises all the way to the top, and at 1 exactly, the ball falls. A climb to the top of the house also reveals a **28-inch telescope,** built in 1893 and now housed inside an onion-shape fiberglass dome. It doesn't compare with the range of modern optical telescopes, but it's still the largest in the United Kingdom. Regular viewing evenings reveal startlingly detailed views of the lunar surface. In the **Time Galleries,** linger over the superb workmanship of John Harrison (1693–1776), whose famous **maritime clocks** won him the Longitude Prize for solving the problem of accurate timekeeping at sea, paving the way for modern navigation. Outside, a brass line laid among the cobblestones marks the meridian. As darkness falls, a green laser shoots out, following exactly the path of the meridian line. The hill that is home to the observatory gives fantastic views across London, topped off with £1-a-slot telescopes to scour the skyline. ✉ *Romney Rd., Greenwich* ☏ *020/8858–4422* ⊕ *www.rmg.co.uk/royal-observatory* ✉ *Astronomy Centre free, Flamsteed House and Meridian Line courtyard £10, planetarium shows £8; combined "Astro Ticket" £15.50; combined ticket with Cutty Sark £20* Ⓜ *DLR: Greenwich.*

OFF THE BEATEN PATH

Thames Barrier Visitors' Centre. Built in the early 1980s, the Thames Barrier is the one of the largest and most high-tech flood defense systems in the world. The barrier, which is raised to protect the city during exceptionally high tides, has a starkly futuristic design—sometimes compared to a row of crashed UFOs, bobbing out of the river. Multimedia presentations, a film about the Thames's history, working models, and views of the barrier itself put the importance of the relationship between London and its river in perspective. It's a treat for science and engineering geeks, but probably too far out of the way if your interest is only casual. ✉ *1 Unity Way, Eastmoor St., Woolwich* ☏ *020/8305–4188* ⊕ *www.visitlondon.com/things-to-do/place/26941-thames-barrier-information-centre* ✉ *£4.15* ⏱ *Closed Mon.–Wed.* Ⓜ *North Greenwich, then Bus 161 or 472; National Rail: Charlton (from London Bridge), then Bus 177 or 180.*

Fodor's Choice ★ Up at The O2. Certainly one of the most original ways to see London, this thrilling urban expedition takes you on a 90-minute journey across the giant dome of the O2 arena. After a short briefing, you're dressed in safety gear and taken in small groups across a steep walkway, running all the way to the summit and down the other side. The high point (literally) is a viewing platform, 171 feet above ground, with magnificent views of the city. On a clear day you can see for 15 miles (that's as far as Waltham Abbey to the north and Sevenoaks to the south). Climbs at sunset and twilight are also available, but the best trips are on nights when London is lit up by fireworks, such as New Year's Eve, Fireworks Night, and Diwali. It's quite an experience, but unsurprisingly there are restrictions: you have to be at least 10 years old, taller than 4 feet, have a waist measurement that's less than 49 inches, weigh less than 286 pounds, and pregnant women can't make the climb at all. Wheelchairs can be accommodated on a few tours. Advance booking is essential. ✉ *Peninsula Sq., London* ☏ *020/8463–2680* ⊕ *www.theo2.co.uk/do-more-at-the-o2/up-at-the-o2* ✉ *From £30* Ⓜ *North Greenwich.*

THE THAMES UPSTREAM

Getting Oriented

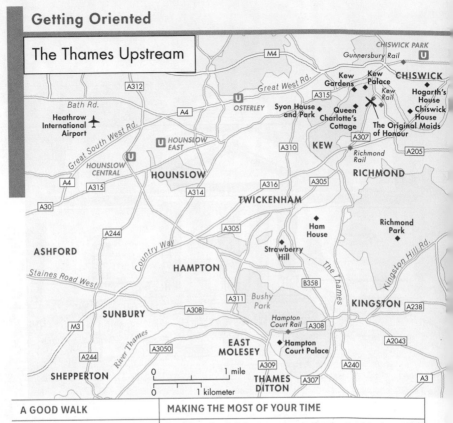

The Thames Upstream

The Thames Upstream

A GOOD WALK

From Chiswick House, follow Burlington Lane and take a left onto Hogarth Lane—which, in reality, is anything but a lane—to reach Hogarth's House. Chiswick's Church Street (reached by a rather unappealing underpass from Hogarth's House) is the nearest thing to a sleepy country village street you're likely to find in London. Follow it down to the Thames and turn left at the bottom to reach the 18th-century riverfront houses of Chiswick Mall, referred to by locals as "Millionaire's Row." There are several pretty riverside pubs near Hammersmith Bridge.

MAKING THE MOST OF YOUR TIME

Hampton Court Palace requires half a day to experience its magic, although you could make do with a few hours for the other attractions. Because of the distance between sights, it's best to focus on one sight, add in some others within the area, then a riverside walk and a pint at a pub.

FEELING PECKISH?

The Original Maids of Honour. This most traditional of old English tearooms is named for a kind of cheese tart invented near here in Tudor times. Legend has it that Henry VIII loved them so much he had the recipe kept under armed guard. ✉ 288 Kew Rd., Kew ☎ 020/8940–2752 ⊕ www.theoriginal-maidsofhonour.co.uk.

13

GETTING THERE

The District Line is your best Tube option, stopping at Turnham Green (in the heart of Chiswick but a walk from the houses), Gunnersbury (for Syon Park), Kew Gardens, and Richmond. For Hampton Court, overland train is quickest: South West trains run from Waterloo four times an hour, with roughly half requiring a change at Surbiton. There are also regular direct trains from Waterloo to Chiswick Station (best for Chiswick House), Kew Bridge, and Richmond (for Ham House). London Overground trains also stop at Gunnersbury, Kew Gardens, and Richmond.

A pleasant way to go is by river. Boats depart from Westminster Pier, by Big Ben, for Kew (1½ hours), Richmond (2 hours), and Hampton Court (3 hours). The trip is worth taking if you make it an integral part of your day, and know that it gets breezy. Round-trip tickets run £20–£25. For more details contact **Thames River Boats** (☎ 020/7930–2062 ⊕ www. wpsa.co.uk).

TOP REASONS TO GO

Hampton Court Palace: Go ghost hunting or just admire the beautiful Tudor architecture at Henry VIII's beloved home, then lose yourself in the maze as night begins to fall.

Strawberry Hill: The 19th-century birthplace of connoisseur Horace Walpole's Gothic style, this mock-castle is a joyous riot of color and invention.

Kew Gardens: See the earth from above by visiting Kew's treetop walkway at the famous Royal Botanic Gardens.

The River Thames: Enjoy a pint from the creaking balcony of a centuries-old riverside pub as you watch the boats row by on the loveliest stretch of England's greatest river.

NEAREST PUBLIC RESTROOMS

Richmond Park, Kew Gardens, and all the stately homes have public restrooms.

Sightseeing
★★★★
Nightlife
★★
Dining
★★★
Lodging
★★
Shopping
★★

The upper stretch of the Thames links a string of upmarket districts—Chiswick, Kew, Richmond, and Putney—with winding old streets, horticultural delights, cozy riverside pubs, and Henry VIII's Hampton Court Palace. The neighborhoods along the way are as proud of their villagey feel as of their stately history, witnessed by such handsome estates as Strawberry Hill and Syon House. After the sensory overload of the West End, it's easy to forget you're in a capital city.

CHISWICK

Updated by
Jo Caird

On the banks of the Thames just west of central London, far enough out to escape the crush and crowds you're just getting used to, Chiswick is a low-key, upscale district, content with its run of restaurants, stylish shops, and film-star residents. No doubt its most famous son wouldn't approve of all the conspicuous wealth, though; Chiswick was home to one of Britain's best-loved painters, William Hogarth, who tore the fabric of the 18th-century nation to shreds with his slew of satirical engravings. **Hogarth's House** has been restored to its former glory. Incongruously stranded among Chiswick's row houses are a number of fine 18th-century buildings, which are now some of the most desirable suburban houses in London. By far the grandest of all is **Chiswick House,** a unique Palladian-style mansion born from the 3rd Earl of Burlington's love of classical and Renaissance architecture—a radical style at the time.

Fodor's Choice **Chiswick House.** Completed in 1729 by the 3rd Earl of Burlington (also
★ known for Burlington House—home of the Royal Academy—and Burlington Arcade on Piccadilly), this extraordinary Palladian mansion was envisaged as a kind of temple to the arts. Burlington was fascinated by the architecture he saw in Italy while on the Grand Tour as a young man and loosely modeled this building on the Villa Capra near Vicenza and the Pantheon in Rome (note the colonnaded frontage and the domed roof, which is visible from the inside in the Upper Tribunal).

The sumptuous interiors were the work of William Kent (1685–1748), and it's easy to see how they made such a profound impact at the time; the astonishing Blue Velvet Room, with its gilded decoration and intricate painted ceiling, is an extraordinary achievement, as are the gilded domed apses that punctuate the Gallery (an homage to the Temple of Venus and Roma from the Fora Romana in Rome). Such ideas were so radical in England at the time that wealthy patrons clamored to have Kent design everything from gardens to party frocks.

The rambling grounds are one of the hidden gems of West London. Italianate in style (of course), they are filled with classical temples, statues, and obelisks. Also on the grounds are a café and a children's play area. ⊠ *Burlington La., Chiswick* ☎ *020/3141–3350* ⊕ *www.chgt. org.uk* ⊠ *£7.50, grounds free* ☉ *House closed Nov.–Mar. and Tues. in summer* Ⓜ *Turnham Green, Chiswick. National Rail: Chiswick.*

Hogarth's House. The satirist and painter William Hogarth (1697–1764), little-known in the rest of the world, is hugely famous in Britain. His witty, acerbic engravings, which railed against the harsh injustices of the time, may be called the visual equivalent of the satires of Jonathan Swift and were no less influential in their time. Unfortunately his beloved house has had an appalling streak of bad luck; as if the decision, in the 1960s, to route one of the nation's busiest highways outside the front gates wasn't ignoble enough, the house was closed after a fire in 2009. Now fully restored, the rooms contain absorbing exhibitions, featuring many of Hogarth's 18th-century prints, together with replica furniture of the period. Look out for the 300-year-old mulberry tree outside; Hogarth and his wife used its fruit to bake pies for destitute children. The original copies of some of Hogarth's most famous works can be seen elsewhere in the city: *A Rake's Progress* at Sir John Soane's Museum; *Marriage A-la-Mode* at the National Gallery; and *Gin Lane* at the British Museum. His tomb is in the cemetery of St. Nicholas's Church on nearby Chiswick Mall. ⊠ *Hogarth La., Great West Rd. (A4), Chiswick* ☎ *020/8994–6757* ⊕ *www.hounslow.info/arts/hogarthshouse* ⊠ *Free* ☉ *Closed Mon.* Ⓜ *Turnham Green. National Rail: Chiswick.*

KEW

A mile or so beyond Chiswick is Kew, a leafy suburb with little to see other than its two big attractions: the lovely **Kew Palace** and the **Royal Botanic Gardens**—anchored in the landscape for several miles around by a towering, mock-Chinese pagoda.

FAMILY   **Kew Gardens.** Enter the Royal Botanic Gardens, as Kew Gardens are
Fodor's Choice   officially known, and you are enveloped by blazes of color, extraordi-
★   nary blooms, hidden trails, and lovely old follies. Beautiful though it all is, Kew's charms are secondary to its true purpose as a major center for serious research; over 200 academics are consistently hard at work here on projects spanning 110 countries. First opened to the public in 1840, this 326-acre site has been supported by royalty and nurtured by landscapers, botanists, and architects since the 1720s. Today the

gardens, now a UNESCO World Heritage Site, hold more than 30,000 species of plants, from every corner of the globe.

Architect Sir William Chambers built a series of temples and follies, of which the crazy 10-story **Pagoda,** visible for miles around, is the star. The Princess of Wales conservatory houses 10 climate zones, and the Xstrata Treetop Walkway takes you 59 feet up into the air. Two great 19th-century greenhouses—the **Palm House** and the **Temperate House**—are filled with exotic blooms, and many of the plants have been there since the final glass panel was fixed into place, including the largest greenhouse plant in the world, a Chilean wine palm planted in 1846 (it's so big you have to climb the spiral staircase to the roof to get a proper view of it).

To get around the gardens, the Kew Explorer bus runs on a 40-minute, hop-on, hop-off route, starting at the Victoria Gate, every 30 minutes 11–4:30. Free guided tours, run by volunteers, are given daily at 11 and 1:30, plus special seasonally themed tours at other times. Discovery Tours, fully accessible for visitors in wheelchairs, are also available daily with advance booking. ✉ *Kew Rd. at Lichfield Rd., for Victoria Gate entrance, Kew* ☎ *020/8332–5000* ⊕ *www.kew.org* 🖾 *£17, Explorer bus £5, Discovery tour £5* Ⓜ *Kew Gardens. National Rail: Kew Gardens, Kew Bridge.*

FodorsChoice
★
Kew Palace and Queen Charlotte's Cottage. The elegant redbrick exterior of the smallest of Britain's royal palaces seems almost humble when compared with the grandeur of, say, Buckingham or Kensington palace. Yet inside is a fascinating glimpse into life at the uppermost end of society from the 17th to 19th century. This is actually the third of several palaces that stood here; once known as Dutch House, it was one of the havens to which George III retired when insanity forced him to withdraw from public life. Queen Charlotte had an *orné* (a rustic-style cottage retreat) added in the late 18th century. In a marvelously regal flight of fancy, she kept kangaroos in the paddock outside. The main house and gardens are maintained in the 18th-century style. Entry to the palace itself is free, but it lies within the grounds of Kew Gardens, and you must buy a ticket to that to get here. ✉ *Kew Gardens, Kew Rd. at Lichfield Rd., Kew* ☎ *020/3166–6000* ⊕ *www.hrp.org.uk* 🖾 *Free with entry to Kew Gardens* ☉ *Closed Oct.–Apr.* Ⓜ *Kew Gardens.*

RICHMOND

Named after the (long-vanished) palace Henry VII started here in 1500, Richmond is still a welcoming suburb with a small-town feel, marred only by choking levels of traffic. Duck away from the main streets to find many handsome Georgian and Victorian houses, antiques shops, a Victorian theater, a grand stately home—and, best of all, the largest of London's royal parks.

Ham House. To the west of Richmond Park, overlooking the Thames and nearly opposite the memorably named Eel Pie Island, Ham House was built in 1610 and remodeled 60 years later. It's one of the most complete examples in Europe of a lavish 17th-century house, and as such you can get a clear sense of how the English aristocracy really lived during that period (in short: comfortably). The beautiful formal gardens, with their distinctive spherical and conical topiary, have become an influential source for other palaces and grand villas seeking to restore their gardens to how they were in their heyday. The original decorations in the Great Hall, Round Gallery, and Great Staircase have been replicated, and most of the furniture and fittings are on permanent loan from the Victoria & Albert Museum. Note that from January to March, visits are by guided tour only, lasting around 30 minutes (no need to book). A tranquil and scenic way to reach the house is on foot, which takes about 30 minutes, along the eastern riverbank south from Richmond Bridge. ⊠ *Ham St., Richmond* ☎ *020/8940–1950* ⊕ *www.nationaltrust. org.uk/hamhouse* 🖾 *£11.05* Ⓜ *Richmond, then Bus 65 or 371.*

FAMILY
Fodor'sChoice
★

Hampton Court Palace. The beloved seat of Henry VIII's court, sprawled elegantly beside the languid waters of the Thames, Hampton Court is steeped in more history than virtually any other royal building in England. The Tudor mansion, begun in 1515 by Cardinal Wolsey to curry favor with the young Henry, actually conceals a larger 17th-century baroque building, which was partly designed by Sir Christopher Wren. The earliest dwellings on this site belonged to a religious order founded in the 11th century and were expanded over the years by its many subsequent residents, until George II moved the royal household closer to London in the early 18th century. After entering through the magnificent Tudor courtyard, start with a look through the **State Apartments,** decorated in the Tudor style, and on to the wood-beamed magnificence of Henry's Great Hall, before taking in the strikingly azure ceiling of the **Chapel Royal.** Watch out for the ghost of Henry VIII's doomed fifth wife, Catherine Howard, who lost her head yet is said to scream her way along the **Haunted Gallery.** (Believe it or not, what is certainly true is that the corridor is prone to sudden drops in temperature—and no one quite knows why.) Latter-day masters of the palace, the joint rulers William and Mary (reigned 1689–1702), were responsible for the beautiful **King's and Queen's Apartments** and the elaborate baroque of the **Georgian Rooms.**

Well-handled reconstructions of Tudor life take place all year, from live appearances by "Henry VIII" to cook-historians preparing authentic feasts in the **Tudor Kitchens.** (Dishes on offer in the adjacent café include a few of these traditional recipes.) The highlight of the formal grounds is undoubtedly the famous maze (the oldest hedge maze in the world), its half mile of pathways among clipped hedgerows still fiendish to negotiate. There's a trick, but we won't give it away here; it's much more fun just to go and lose yourself. Meanwhile, the **Lower Orangery Garden** shows off thousands of exotic species that William and Mary, avid plant collectors, gathered from around the globe. Family ghost tours are given on evenings from October to February. Not only are they entertainingly spooky, but they're a great opportunity to see the older parts of the palace without the crowds. Scarier, adults-only versions last two hours. Note that tours can sell out several weeks in advance. ⊠ *Hampton Court Rd., East Molesey* ☎ *020/3166–6000* ⊕ *www.hrp.org.uk/hamptoncourtpalace* 🖾 *£22.70 palace, maze, and*

Hampton Court Palace, the seat of Henry VIII's court, is a prime example of a Tudor mansion, and features the oldest hedge maze in the world.

gardens; £4.40 maze only; £7 maze and gardens Ⓜ *Richmond, then Bus R68. National Rail: Hampton Court, 35 mins from Waterloo (most trains require change at Surbiton).*

FAMILY **Richmond Park.** This enormous park was enclosed in 1637 for use as a royal hunting ground—like practically all other London parks. Unlike the others, however, Richmond Park still has wild red and fallow deer roaming its 2,500 acres (three times the size of New York's Central Park) of grassland and heath. Its ancient oaks are among the last remnants of the vast, wild forests that once encroached on London in medieval times. The Isabella Plantation (near the Ham Gate entrance) is an enchanting and colorful woodland garden, first laid out in 1831. There's a splendid protected view of St. Paul's Cathedral from King Henry VIII's Mound, the highest point in the park; find it, and you have a piece of magic in your sights. The park is also home to White Lodge, a 1727 hunting lodge that now houses the Royal Ballet School. ⊠ *Richmond* ☎ *030/0061–2200* ⊕ *www.royalparks.org.uk* ✉ *Free* Ⓜ *Richmond, then Bus 371 or 65.*

Fodor's Choice **Strawberry Hill.** From the outside, this rococo mishmash of towers, crenellations, and white stucco is dazzling in its faux-medieval splendor. Its architect and owner, Sir Horace Walpole (1717–97), knew a thing or two about imaginative flights of fancy; the flamboyant son of the first British prime minister, Robert Walpole, he all but single-handedly invented the Gothic novel with *The Castle of Otranto* (1764). Once you pass through Strawberry Hill's forbidding exterior, you'll experience an explosion of color and light, for Walpole boldly decided to take elements from the exteriors of Gothic cathedrals and move them inside. The detail is extraordinary, from the cavernous entrance hall with its vast Gothic trompe-l'oeil decorations, to the Great Parlour with its Renaissance stained glass, to the Gallery, where extraordinary fan vaulting is a replica of the vaults found in Henry VII's chapel at Westminster Abbey. The gardens have been meticulously returned to their original 18th-century design, right down to a white marble loveseat sculpted into the shape of a shell. Opening days can vary, so call ahead to check times. ✉ *268 Waldegrave Rd., Twickenham* ☎ *020/8744–1241* ⊕ *www.strawberryhillhouse.org.uk* 🖭 *£12.50* ☯ *House closed Thurs.–Sat. Mar.–Oct. and Tues.–Sat. Nov.–Feb.* Ⓜ *Richmond, then Bus 33 or R68. National Rail: Strawberry Hill.*

FAMILY

Fodor's Choice

★

Syon House and Park. The residence of the Duke and Duchess of Northumberland, this is one of England's most lavish stately homes. Set in a 200-acre park landscaped by the great gardener "Capability" Brown (1716–83), the core of the house is Tudor—it was one of the last stopping places for Henry VIII's fifth wife, Catherine Howard, and the extremely short-lived monarch Lady Jane Grey before they were sent to the Tower. It was remodeled in the Georgian style in 1762 by famed decorator Robert Adam. He had just returned from studying the sights of classical antiquity in Italy and created two rooms sumptuous enough to wow any Grand Tourist: the entryway is an amazing study in black and white, pairing neoclassical marbles with antique bronzes, and the Ante Room contains 12 enormous verd-antique columns surmounted by statues of gold—and this was just a waiting room for the duke's servants and retainers. The Red Drawing Room is covered with crimson Spitalfields silk, and the Long Gallery is one of Adam's noblest creations. ✉ *Syon Park, Brentford* ☎ *020/8560–0882* ⊕ *www.syonpark. co.uk* 🖭 *£13, £8 gardens and conservatory only* ☯ *Property closed Nov.–mid-Mar.; house closed Mon., Tues., Fri., and Sat. mid-Mar.–Oct.* Ⓜ *Gunnersbury, then Bus 237 or 267 to Brentlea.*

Thames River. The twists and turns of the Thames through the heart of the capital make it London's best thoroughfare and most compelling viewing point. Every palace, church, theater, wharf, museum, and pub along the bank has a tale to tell, and traveling on or alongside the river is one of the best ways to soak up views of the city. Frequent daily tourist-boat services are at their height April through October. In most cases you can turn up at a pier, and the next departure won't be far away; however, it never hurts to book ahead if you can. The trip between Westminster Pier and the Tower of London takes about 40 minutes, while that between the Tower and Greenwich takes around half an hour. A full round-trip can take several hours. Ask about flexible fares and hop-on, hop-off options at the various piers. ✉ *London.*

WHERE TO EAT

EAT LIKE A LOCAL

A handful of foods are forever associated with London: think fish-and-chips, full English breakfasts, and Indian curry. All these and other innovations are permanently on locals' lips, not to mention their Instagram accounts.

CHINESE

Endless waves of Londoners and tourists alike throng the lantern-strewn grid of Georgian streets centered on Chinatown's Gerrard Street. Breaking out from Hong Kong Cantonese to embrace a wider spread of Sichuan, Hunan, Jiangsu, Taiwanese, and Malaysian offerings, Londoners tend to hit old favorites like the Wardour Street Four Seasons for roast Peking duck, the Lanzhou Noodle Bar for hand-pulled shaved noodles, Beijing Dumpling for handmade dim sum, and Rasa Sayang for spicy Malay chicken curries.

CURRY

As a onetime global port and seat of the British Empire, London has enjoyed Indian cuisine for over four hundred years and opened its first dedicated Indian curry house for colonial returnees (the Hindostanee Coffee House in Marylebone) in 1809. Originally linked to Sylheti Bengali "lascar" seamen and ship boiler stokers, and later famous as an exotic cuisine championed by Queen Victoria, London's love affair with spicy Indian curry has only gotten stronger since the Edwardian era. Nowadays, the capital's curry hounds can be found along the Bengali-focused Brick Lane in the East End, but look to the newbies of Indian Accent, Brigadiers, Gunpowder, and Bombay Bustle for the best of the new-wave Indian menus.

ENGLISH BREAKFAST

A full English breakfast at one of the city's many workmen's cafés is every true Londoner's favorite guilty pleasure. While there are endless varieties, a typical English breakfast consists of fried, poached, or scrambled eggs, streaky bacon, sausages, baked beans, white toast, fried mushrooms, grilled tomatoes, black pudding, chips, fried bread, brown sauce, and scorching mugs of tea.

FISH-AND-CHIPS

With a focus on crisp batter, juicy cod or haddock, and thick crispy chips, locals seek out low-key traditional fish-and-chip shops and old-school "chippies" for their insatiable fix of that classic English meal. Old stagers like The Golden Hind in Marylebone, The Fryer's Delight in Holborn, and Rock & Sole Plaice in Covent Garden have their nostalgic charms, while a fresh batch of newcomers like The Golden Union in Soho, Poppies Fish & Chips in Spitalfields, and Fishers in Fulham tweak around with beer batters, double-cooked chips, homemade tartar sauce, and sustainably sourced fish.

GASTRO-PUBS

Londoners still love heading to their local gastro-pub for a rowdy combo of unpretentious Brit-focused dishes

and draught beer, cask ales, and cheap wines served in soaring Victorian pubs or ornate Georgian gin palaces. Ever since exotic food started being served from an open kitchen in The Eagle pub in Farringdon in 1991, the home-grown, foodie-led gastro-pub revolution has swept London asunder. From still-going-remarkably-strong The Eagle in Farringdon to game-centric The Harwood Arms in Fulham to the seafood-heavy menu at The Marksman in Hackney, ducking into a bristling gastro-pub is a surefire way of dining out like a Londoner.

NIGHT MARKETS

A welcome development to the London food scene, Street Feast's night street-food markets and "food arenas" have begun popping up in hipster zones like Shoreditch and Canada Water. Housed in edgy DIY indoor/outdoor venues, thousands of London's young foodie fanatics blitz their way through the mini–food festivals to try some of the best experimental food trucks, stalls, and stands around. With vinyl tunes, ample brews, and communal raw bench seating, it's impossible not to have a blast flipping from cheap Korean burritos to Folkestone crab buns to a hand-pressed Devil Burger with green chili sauce and double jalapeños.

Updated
by Alex
Wijeratna

British food hasn't always had the best reputation, but nowhere in the country is that reputation being completely upturned more than in London. The city has zoomed up the global gastro charts, and can now seriously compete with the world's top culinary heavyweights. The truth is that no other city—barring New York—has the immense range of global cuisines that London has to offer. Standards have rocketed at all price points, and every year it seems like the London restaurant scene is better than ever.

Feel like eating the most-tender Kagoshima Wagyu beef on planet Earth? It can be yours for £150 at CUT at 45 Park Lane. Want to try old English gastronomy from the time of Henry VIII with an ultramodern twist? Ashley Palmer-Watts is your man at Dinner by Heston Blumenthal. Do you only eat Sri Lankan *hoppers*? No worries, we've got just the thing: Hoppers in Soho will give you a taste of the Sri Lankan pancake, for £4.50 a pop. Can't stand any more snobby culinary nonsense? The low-key British wild game is so good at The Harwood Arms in Fulham that they've earned London's first gastro-pub-based Michelin star.

To appreciate how far London has risen in the food game, just look back to the days of Somerset Maugham, who was once justified in warning, "To eat well in England you should have breakfast three times a day." Change was slow after World War II, when it was understood that the British ate to live, while the French lived to eat. When people thought of British cuisine, fish-and-chips—a greasy grab-and-gulp dish that tasted best wrapped in yesterday's newspaper—first came to mind. Then there was always shepherd's pie, ubiquitously found in smoke-filled pubs, though not made, according to *Sweeney Todd*, "with real shepherd in it."

These days, standards are miles higher and shepherd's pie has been largely replaced by the city's unofficial dish, Indian curry. London's restaurant revolution is built on its extraordinary ethnic diversity, and you'll find the quality of other global cuisines has grown immeasurably in recent years, with London becoming known for its Chinese, Japanese, Indian, Thai, Spanish, Italian, French, Peruvian, and west African restaurants. Thankfully, pride in the best of British food—local, seasonal, wild, and foraged—is enjoying quite the renaissance, too.

PLANNING

EATING OUT STRATEGY

Where should you eat? With thousands of London eateries competing for your attention, it may seem like a daunting question. But fret not: our expert writers and editors have done most of the legwork. The selections here represent the best this city has to offer—from haute cuisine to humble pub food.

RESERVATIONS

Plan ahead if you're determined to snag a sought-after reservation. Many renowned restaurants like BRAT, Gymkhana or Core by Clare Smyth are booked weeks in advance. It's always a good idea to book as far ahead as you can and reconfirm when you arrive in London. Note that some top restaurants also now take credit card details when making a reservation and charge a penalty fee if you're a no-show.

DINING TOURS

FAMILY

Fodor's Choice

★

London Food Lovers Food Tours. London's a top global foodie city now, and the London Food Lovers walking tour of Soho is a fascinating way to explore the capital's gastro delights. The four-hour walk kicks off with Hawaiian blueberry pancakes at burger bar Kua'Aina and takes in off-beat stops for truffle pumpkin ravioli at Soho's retro Italian delicatessen Lina Stores, a hot chocolate tasting at SAID artisanal Roman chocolatiers, and a sit-down lunch of fish-and-chips and Indian pale ale in quaint Soho pub the Dog and Duck. Well led and synchronized throughout, you'll also stop in Chinatown to sample steamed prawn dim sum at Beijing Dumpling, and spot celebrities amid the Afternoon Tea crowds at the Maison Bertaux French patisserie and tearoom. The tour ends with a dessert and wine pairing in the Dickensian underground cellar vaults of the 1890s Gordon's Wine Bar. ⊠ *Islington* ☏ *0777/4099–306* ⊕ *www.londonfoodlovers.com* ⌑ *£60.*

WHAT TO WEAR

When in England's style capital, do as the natives do: dress up to eat out. Whatever your style, dial it up a notch and have some fun while you're at it. Pull out the clothes you've been saving for a special occasion and get a little glamorous. As unfair as it seems, the way you look can influence how you're treated—and where you're seated—in many restaurants. Generally speaking, jeans and a button-down shirt will suffice at most table-service restaurants in the budget to moderate range. Moving up from there, many pricier restaurants require jackets, and some (like The Ritz) insist on ties. Shorts, sweatpants, baseball caps, and sports jerseys are rarely appropriate.

TIPPING AND TAXES

Do not tip bar staff in pubs and bars, although you can always offer to buy them a drink. In restaurants, tip 12.5% of the check for full meals if service is not already included; tip a small token if you're just having coffee or tea. If paying by credit card, double-check that a tip has not already been included in the bill.

CHILDREN

Unless your children behave impeccably, it's best to avoid the haute-cuisine establishments, although increasingly many top places like The Wolseley and Fischer's are surprisingly child-friendly. London's many burger and rib joints, pizzerias, and Italian restaurants are popular with kids. Other family-friendly establishments include chains like Côte, Byron, and Wagamama.

HOURS

In London you can find breakfast all day, but it's generally served 7 am–noon. Lunch is noon–3, and brunch 11–4. Afternoon tea, often a meal in itself, is taken 1–6, and dinner is typically eaten 6–11, although it can be taken earlier. Many ethnic restaurants, especially Indian, serve food until midnight. Sunday is a proper lunch day, and some restaurants are open for lunch only. Over the Christmas period, London has a reputation for shutting down, but a growing number of hotels and other brave bastions are prepared to feed all visitors.

PRICES

London is a very pricey city by global standards. A modest meal for two can easily cost £45, and the £100-a-head meal is commonplace. Damage-control strategies include making lunch your main meal (the top places have bargain midday menus), going for early- or late-evening deals, or sharing an à la carte entrée and ordering a second appetizer instead. Seek out fixed-price menus, and watch for hidden extras on the check, that is, bread, vegetables, or a cover charged separately.

WHAT IT COSTS				
	$	$$	$$$	$$$$
Restaurants	Under £16	£16–£23	£24–£31	Over £31

Prices in the reviews are the average cost of a main course at dinner or, if dinner is not served, at lunch. Note: If a restaurant offers only prix-fixe (set-price) meals, it has been given the price category that reflects the full prix-fixe price.

RESTAURANT REVIEWS

Listed alphabetically within neighborhoods. Use the coordinate (✤ 1:B2) at the end of each listing to locate a property on the Where to Eat and Stay in London atlas at the end of this chapter. Restaurant reviews have been shortened. For full information, visit Fodors.com.

WESTMINSTER AND ST. JAMES'S

ST. JAMES'S

St. James's—home to Buckingham Palace and Clarence House, where Prince Charles and Camilla live—has a magnificent old-world, royal feel. Appropriately, most of the restaurants here are fit for a future king. This is where you'll find London's top-end restaurants—dining experiences that are geared toward a well-heeled, deep-pocketed clientele. You should make reservations well in advance to dine at any of these restaurants for dinner (or reserve a table for the earlier or later parts of the evening, when demand is lower). Keep in mind that no-shows mean last-minute tables often crop up, and having lunch here can be a great money-saving strategy.

14

$$$$ ✕ **The Dining Room at The Goring.** *Downton Abbey* meets *The Crown* at
BRITISH this quintessentially English, old-school dining salon located within an
Fodor's Choice Edwardian-era hotel down the road from Buckingham Palace. A favor-
★ ite with royalty and courtiers, here you can enjoy daily specials like traditional beef Wellington or antediluvian quirks such as Eggs Drumkilbo
(a hard-boiled egg/lobster seafood cocktail with caviar)—a onetime
favorite of the late Queen Mother. **Known for:** plush salon designed
by Viscount Linley; glazed lobster omelet with duck fat chips; royal
history and pedigree. $ *Average main: £34* ⊠ *The Goring, Beeston Pl.,
Victoria* ☎ *020/7396–9000* ⊕ *www.thegoring.com* Ⓜ *Victoria* ✛ *5:A3.*

$$$ ✕ **45 Jermyn St.** A sophisticated crowd enjoys the clubhouse vibe at
BRASSERIE this classic brasserie at the back of the Queen's grocer Fortnum &
FAMILY Mason. An old-school trolley trundles up table-side to serve Siberian
Sturgeon caviar with scrambled eggs, baked new potatoes, and blinis,
while creamy beef Stroganoff and whole duck with elderberry sauce gets
the full table-side *flambé* treatment. **Known for:** unique caviar trolley;
glamorous decor; collection of boozy ice cream floats. $ *Average main:
£27* ⊠ *45 Jermyn St., St. James's* ☎ *020/7205–4545* ⊕ *www.45jermynst.
com* Ⓜ *Green Park* ✛ *5:A1.*

$$$ ✕ **Hide.** A spectacular spiral oak staircase wraps its way around the
MODERN BRITISH three stories of this antique beauty overlooking Green Park. Look out
for art-like dishes strewn with wildflowers on the seasonal eight-course
tasting menus served in a fairy tale–like setting. **Known for:** signature
coddled hens' eggs served in shell with mushrooms and smoked butter;
London's best wine list; bespoke interiors. $ *Average main: £31* ⊠ *85
Piccadilly, St. James's* ☎ *020/3146–8666* ⊕ *www.hide.co.uk* Ⓜ *Green
Park* ✛ *5:A1.*

$$$ ✕ **Le Caprice.** Celebrity hot spot Le Caprice commands the deepest loy-
MODERN alty of any restaurant in London. It must be the 38-odd-year history
EUROPEAN of famous diners (think Liz Taylor, Joan Collins, Lady Di, and Victoria
FAMILY Beckham), the pitch-perfect service, and the long-standing menu that
sits somewhere between Euro peasant and trendy fashion plate. **Known
for:** celebrity sightings galore; classic fish-and-chips with minted pea
puree; live jazz on Sunday night. $ *Average main: £26* ⊠ *Arlington
House, 20 Arlington St., St. James's* ☎ *020/7629–2239* ⊕ *www.le-
caprice.co.uk* Ⓜ *Green Park* ✛ *5:A1.*

$$$$ ╳ **The Ritz Restaurant.** London's most opulent dining salon here at the
BRITISH   Ritz would impress even Marie Antoinette with its sumptuous Gilded
FAMILY   Age Rocco Revival trompe-l'oeil frescoes, tasseled silk drapery, and
towering marble columns. Sit at the late Baroness Thatcher's favorite
seat overlooking Green Park (Table 1) and luxuriate in unreconstructed
British haute cuisine such as Bresse chicken with black Périgord truffles
or beef Wellington carved table-side. **Known for:** luxurious dining made
for the British elite; possibly London's best beef Wellington; legendary
traditional Afternoon Tea. $ *Average main: £42* ✉ *The Ritz, 150 Pic-
cadilly, St. James's* ☎ *020/7300–2370 for reservations only* ⊕ *www.
theritzlondon.com* 🛈 *Jacket and tie* Ⓜ *Green Park* ✛ *5:A1.*

$$ ╳ **Rochelle Canteen at the Institute of Contemporary Arts.** Foodies, fashioni-
BRITISH   stas, and art scene insiders flock to the hearty, low-key Modern British
fare at the Institute of Contemporary Arts, one of the city's biggest art
and cultural centers. In the uncluttered, all-white space, opt for the
slab of braised ox tongue with a single broomstick carrot, or the rustic
slow-poached chicken with grilled leeks and a punchy green sauce.
Known for: pared-back Modern British dishes; relaxed arty environ-
ment; suet-rich rabbit and smoked bacon pie. $ *Average main: £17*
✉ *The Institute of Contemporary Arts, 12 Carlton House Terr., St.
James's* ☎ *020/7766–1424* ⊕ *www.ica.art/rochelle-canteen* Ⓜ *Piccadilly
Circus, Charring Cross* ✛ *5:B1.*

$$$$ ╳ **Wiltons.** Lords, Ladies, and aristocrats blow the family bank at this
BRITISH   Edwardian bastion of traditional English fine dining on Jermyn Street
(the place first opened on the Haymarket as a shellfish stall in 1742).
Posh patrons tend to order half a dozen Beau Brummell oysters, fol-
lowed by grilled Dover sole, Blythburgh pork from the carving trolley,
or fabulous native game, such as roast partridge, grouse, or teal. **Known
for:** traditional English dining focused on shellfish and game; waiter
service that would put Jeeves to shame; Bordeaux-heavy wine menu.
$ *Average main: £37* ✉ *55 Jermyn St., St. James's* ☎ *020/7629–9955*
⊕ *www.wiltons.co.uk* ⊘ *Closed Sun. and bank holidays. No lunch Sat.*
🛈 *Jacket required* Ⓜ *Green Park* ✛ *5:A1.*

$$ ╳ **The Wolseley.** A glitzy procession of famous faces, media moguls,
AUSTRIAN   and hedge-funders comes for the spectacle, swish service, and soar-
FAMILY   ing elegance at this bustling Viennese-style grand café on Piccadilly.
Located in a former Wolseley Motors luxury-car showroom, this brasserie begins its long decadent days with breakfast at 7 am and serves Dual
Monarchy delights until midnight. **Known for:** old-country Austrian
and Hungarian delights; Afternoon Tea with a Viennese twist; classic
grand café ambience. $ *Average main: £22* ✉ *160 Piccadilly, St. James's*
☎ *020/7499–6996* ⊕ *www.thewolseley.com* Ⓜ *Green Park* ✛ *5:A1.*

MAYFAIR AND MARYLEBONE

If you're looking for something more wallet-friendly, head north to
Marylebone, formerly dowdy but now prized for its überchic, villagelike feel. Here you'll find an array of low-key little cafés, boîtes, and
tapas bars, champagne-and-hot-dog joints, and the odd world-class
sizzler, offering everything from Moroccan and Spanish to Thai and
Japanese. Mayfair, on the other hand, is for the high-rollers all the way.

MAYFAIR

$$$$ ✕ **Alain Ducasse at the Dorchester.** One of only two three-Michelin-starred
FRENCH restaurants in the city, Alain Ducasse at the Dorchester achieves the
FAMILY pinnacle of classical French haute cuisine in a surprisingly fun, lively,
Fodor'sChoice and unstuffy salon. Diners feast on a blizzard of beautifully choreo-
★ graphed dishes including classic rum baba with Chantilly cream, sliced
open and served in a silver domed tureen. **Known for:** impeccable five-
star service; surprisingly unstarchy vibe; signature sauté lobster with
chicken quenelles. ⑤ *Average main: £45* ✉ *The Dorchester, Park La.,
Mayfair* ☎ *020/7629–8866 for reservations only* ⊕ *www.alainducasse-
dorchester.com* ⊘ *Closed Sun. and Mon. No lunch Sat.* Ⓜ *Marble Arch,
Green Park* ✛ *1:H6.*

$$$ ✕ **Cecconi's.** Revel with the A-listers in the glamorous buzz at this
MODERN ITALIAN upscale Italian brasserie wedged between Cork Street, Savile Row, and
the Royal Academy of Arts. Perfect for a pit stop during a West End
shopping spree or after browsing the nearby Mayfair galleries and auc-
tion houses, diners spill out onto pavement tables for breakfast, brunch,
and *cicchetti* (Italian tapas), and return later in the day for something
more substantial. **Known for:** favorite of nearby Vogue House staff and
Sotheby's clientele; popular veal Milanese; all-day jet-setter hangout.
⑤ *Average main: £29* ✉ *5A Burlington Gardens, Mayfair* ☎ *020/7434–
1500* ⊕ *www.cecconis.co.uk* Ⓜ *Green Park, Piccadilly Circus* ✛ *3:A6.*

$$$ ✕ **The Colony Grill Room.** Glide past the parked royal blue Armstrong Sid-
AMERICAN deley, through the foyer of the five-star Beaumont hotel, and into the swank
FAMILY art deco–inspired dining salon of the Colony Grill Room. Fans of 1920s
New York will admire the throwback decor, before digging into throw-
backs like the mock turtle soup, clam chowder, and the flambé bananas
Foster. **Known for:** evocative American 1920s panache and glamour;
bespoke sundae menu; classic buttermilk fried chicken. ⑤ *Average main:
£26* ✉ *The Beaumont, 8 Balderton St., Brown Hart Gardens, Mayfair*
☎ *020/7499–9499* ⊕ *www.colonygrillroom.com* Ⓜ *Marble Arch* ✛ *1:G4.*

$$$$ ✕ **CUT at 45 Park Lane.** Austrian-born star chef Wolfgang Puck amps up
STEAKHOUSE the stakes at this ultraexpensive steak house on Park Lane. Set against a
FAMILY luxe backdrop of Damien Hirst artwork and globe lights, carnivores go
crazy for the pricey prime cuts from England, Australia, Japan, and the
United States. **Known for:** rare Kagoshima Wagyu beef steaks; celebrity
chef hot spot; art gallerylike interior. ⑤ *Average main: £48* ✉ *45 Park
La., Mayfair* ☎ *020/7493–4545 for reservations only* ⊕ *www.dorches-
tercollection.com* Ⓜ *Marble Arch, Hyde Park Corner* ✛ *1:H6.*

$$$$ ✕ **Goodman.** This Manhattan-themed, Russian-owned swanky steak
STEAKHOUSE house, named after Chicago jazz legend Benny Goodman, has everyone
FAMILY in agreement: these truly are some of the best steaks in town. USDA-
certified, 150 day corn-fed, and on-site dry-aged Black Angus T-bones,
rib eye, porterhouse, and New York bone-in sirloins compete for taste
and tenderness with heavily marbled grass-fed prime cuts from Scotland
and the Lake District. **Known for:** truly impressive steaks; whole king
crab available on request; long list of classy Cornovan-extracted red
wines by the glass. ⑤ *Average main: £35* ✉ *24–26 Maddox St., Mayfair*
☎ *020/7499–3776* ⊕ *www.goodmanrestaurants.com/location/mayfair*
⊘ *Closed Sun.* Ⓜ *Oxford Circus, Piccadilly Circus* ✛ *3:A5.*

14

$$$
MODERN INDIAN
FAMILY
Fodor's Choice
★

✗ **Gymkhana.** The last days of the Raj are invoked here at one of London's finest Indian curry emporiums, where top choices include dosas with fennel-rich Chettinad duck or the famed suckling pig vindaloo. Diners admire the whirring ceiling fans, rattan chairs, and other decor inspired by the colonial-era gymkhana sporting clubs of yesteryear. **Known for:** unusual game curries; Indian punches in the basement private dining booths; signature kid goat methi keema. ⑤ *Average main: £28* ✉ *42 Albemarle St., Mayfair* ☎ *020/3011–5900* ⊕ *www.gymkhana-london.com* ☾ *Closed Sun.* Ⓜ *Green Park* ✛ *1:H5.*

$$$$
FRENCH
FAMILY

✗ **Hélène Darroze at the Connaught.** The city's wealthy flock to French virtuoso Hélène Darroze's restaurant at the Connaught for her dazzling regional French haute cuisine, served up in a stylish Edwardian wood-paneled dining salon. Taking inspiration from Les Landes in southwestern France, Darroze sallies forth with a procession of magnificent dishes, like Robert Dupérier foie gras with fig and port or Limousin sweetbreads with Jerusalem artichokes. **Known for:** sumptuous dining salon; classy French haute dishes; relatively affordable three-course set lunch. ⑤ *Average main: £38* ✉ *The Connaught, Carlos Pl., Mayfair* ☎ *020/3147–7200 for reservations only* ⊕ *www.the-connaught.co.uk* ⋔ *Jacket required* Ⓜ *Green Park* ✛ *1:H5.*

$$$
MODERN INDIAN

✗ **Indian Accent.** The bar for high-end Indian food in London has been raised at this praised New Delhi import. Unusual but homey Indian cuisine is presented in a modern, decidedly non-Indian fashion, from mini-naan stuffed with black pudding to spiced ghee roast lamb served Peking-duck style. **Known for:** mid-century Rajput palace setting; playful dishes like Bombay minced soya keema with quail eggs; top amuse bouche of spiced pumpkin and coconut shorba soup. ⑤ *Average main: £26* ✉ *16 Albemarle St., Mayfair* ☎ *020/7629–9802* ⊕ *www.indianaccent.com/london* Ⓜ *Green Park* ✛ *1:H5.*

$$
INDIAN
FAMILY

✗ **Jamavar.** There is no finer fish dish in town than the Malai stone bass *tikka* at this upmarket Indian restaurant. The food and spices here are so authentic that it regularly buzzes with Bollywood stars, wealthy Mayfair moguls, and the entire well-heeled Indian diaspora. **Known for:** stunning interior of dark wood, marble, and Indian artwork; unmissable Malai stone bass tikka; glossy, luxurious Indian crowd. ⑤ *Average main: £22* ✉ *8 Mount St., Mayfair* ☎ *020/7499–1800* ⊕ *www.jamavarrestaurants.com* Ⓜ *Bond St., Green Park* ✛ *1:H5.*

$$$
MODERN BRITISH

✗ **Kitty Fisher's.** Named after an infamous 18th-century courtesan, Kitty Fisher's is situated in a tiny, creaky Georgian town house in Mayfair's Shepherd Market. Crammed with antique prints, portraits, and silver candelabras, here you can sample some of the finest wood-grill and smokehouse fare around. **Known for:** cozy and candlelit townhouse setting; signature wood-grilled old Galician beef with scorched onions; high-end showbiz and politico diners. ⑤ *Average main: £24* ✉ *10 Shepherd Market, Mayfair* ☎ *020/3302–1661* ⊕ *www.kittyfishers.com* ☾ *Closed Sun.* Ⓜ *Green Park* ✛ *1:H6.*

$$$$
FRENCH
FAMILY

✗ **La Petite Maison.** With the legend *"Tous Célèbres Ici"* ("All Famous Here") boldly etched on the front doors, the delightful Petite Maison boasts an impressively well-sourced and balanced French Mediterranean, Ligurian, and Provençal menu. Based on the relaxed Riviera style of the original La Petite Maison in Nice, try the soft burrata cheese with sweet Datterini-tomato-and-basil spread, or aromatic baked turbot with artichokes, chorizo, five spices, and white wine sauce. **Known for:** light French Riviera-i-nspired dining; excellent selection of rosé wines; whole roast black leg chicken. $ *Average main: £35* ✉ *53–54 Brook's Mews, Mayfair* ☎ *020/7495–4774* ⊕ *www.lpmlondon.co.uk* Ⓜ *Bond St., Oxford Circus* ✣ *1:H4.*

$$$$
FRENCH
FAMILY

✕ **Le Gavroche.** Masterchef Michel Roux Jr. works the floor in the old-fashioned proprietorial way at this old-school Mayfair basement institution—established by his father and uncle in 1967—which many still rate as the best formal dining in London. Roux's mastery of classical French haute cuisine hypnotizes with signature dishes like foie gras with cinnamon-scented crispy duck pancake or saddle of rabbit with Parmesan cheese. **Known for:** swanky Mayfair basement setting; relatively affordable three-course set lunch menus; tasty souffle Suissesse. $ *Average main: £44* ✉ *43 Upper Brook St., Mayfair* ☎ *020/7408–0881* ⊕ *www.le-gavroche.co.uk* ⊗ *Closed Sun. and Mon. No lunch Sat.* 🏛 *Jacket required* Ⓜ *Bond St., Marble Arch* ✣ *1:G5.*

$$$
MODERN FRENCH

✕ **Little Social.** There's always a warm glow and convivial hubbub here at this below-the-radar French bistro hidden away in a cute alley in Mayfair. Within the narrow dining salon, you can dive into the Cornish crab salad appetizer on a round of tomato with miso dressing or the braised Irish ox cheeks with roast bone marrow and horseradish mash. **Known for:** refined classic-with-a-twist French dishes; fabulous set lunches; roast Cornish cod with Alsace bacon. $ *Average main: £27* ✉ *5 Pollen St., Mayfair* ☎ *020/7870–3730* ⊕ *www.littlesocial.co.uk* ⊗ *Closed Sun.* Ⓜ *Oxford Circus, Piccadilly Circus* ✣ *3:A4.*

$$$$
BRITISH
FAMILY

✕ **Ormer Mayfair.** Hidden away in the depths of a Mayfair hotel is famed chef Shaun Rankin's triumphant ode to all things Jersey (in the Channel Islands, that is). In the art deco–inspired basement haven, indulge on world-class dishes all caught, reared, and foraged from the Jersey seashore. **Known for:** standout Jersey crab and lobster ravioli; top English wine selection; famous treacle tart with Jersey clotted cream for dessert. $ *Average main: £32* ✉ *Flemings Hotel, 7–12 Half Moon St., Mayfair* ☎ *020/7016–5601 for reservations only* ⊕ *www.flemings-mayfair.co.uk/fine-dining-london/ormer-mayfair-restaurant* ⊗ *Closed Sun.* Ⓜ *Green Park* ✣ *5:A1.*

$$$$
MODERN
EUROPEAN

✕ **Pollen Street Social.** Gastro god Jason Atherton may not man the stoves here anymore, but his flagship in a cute Dickensian alleyway off Regent Street still knocks the London dining scene for a loop. Fans can enjoy refined small and large dishes ranging from a full English breakfast appetizer to sublime Scottish ox cheek with 50-day Black Angus rib eye. **Known for:** Michelin-star riffs on classic British dishes; dedicated dessert bar; Lake District roast lamb with shallots and mint sauce. $ *Average main: £35* ✉ *8–10 Pollen St., Mayfair* ☎ *020/7290–7600* ⊕ *www.pollenstreetsocial.com* ⊗ *Closed Sun.* Ⓜ *Oxford Circus, Piccadilly Circus* ✣ *3:A5.*

14

$$$$
MODERN ITALIAN
FAMILY

✕ **Sartoria.** Italian maestro Francesco Mazzei bestrides this plush and patterned Savile Row salon and warmly welcomes diners like the proud chef-patron that he is. Inhale a whiff of Alba truffle as it's delicately sliced table-side over an extravagantly egg yolk–rich spaghetti carbonara. **Known for:** Mayfair hedge fund clientele; the chef-patron's big smile and warm welcome; wonderfully silky handmade pastas. ⑤ *Average main: £32* ✉ *20 Savile Row, Mayfair* ☎ *020/7534–7000* ⊕ *www. sartoria-restaurant.co.uk* ☾ *No dinner Sun.* Ⓜ *Oxford Circus* ✛ *3:A5.*

$$$$
SEAFOOD
FAMILY

✕ **Scott's.** Imposing doormen in bowler hats greet visitors with a wee nod at this ever-fashionable seafood haven on Mount Street in Mayfair. Originally founded in 1851 in the Haymarket, and a former haunt of James Bond author Ian Fleming (he apparently enjoyed the potted shrimps), Scott's draws the wealthiest of London, who enjoy the fresh Lindisfarne oysters, Dover sole, and tasty shrimp burgers. **Known for:** possibly London's most magnificent crustacean bar; huge platters of fresh fruits de mer; extravagant prices. ⑤ *Average main: £37* ✉ *20 Mount St., Mayfair* ☎ *020/7495–7309 for reservations only* ⊕ *www. scotts-restaurant.com* Ⓜ *Green Park, Bond St.* ✛ *1:H5.*

$$$
INTERNATIONAL
FAMILY

✕ **34.** A-listers head straight for 34, off Grosvenor Square in Mayfair, simply because all the other celebrities seem to hang out here, too. It must be the plush Edwardian- and art deco dining salon, the neat fish, game, and steak-focused menu, and the smooth Upper Manhattan–style service. **Known for:** an endless procession of Hollywood stars; impressive global meats off an Argentine-inspired grill; nightly live jazz. ⑤ *Average main: £28* ✉ *34 Grosvenor Sq., entrance on S. Audley St., Mayfair* ☎ *020/3350–3434* ⊕ *www.34-restaurant.co.uk* Ⓜ *Marble Arch* ✛ *1:G5.*

MARYLEBONE

$$
AUSTRIAN
FAMILY

✕ **Fischer's.** It almost feels like Sigmund Freud or Gustav Klimt might doff their Homburg hats and shuffle into a dark leather banquette at this evocative, early-20th- century–style Viennese neighborhood café on Marylebone High Street. Savor the antique light fittings and distressed wallpaper before diving into brötchen chopped chicken livers with dill on rye bread. **Known for:** evocative turn-of-the-20th-century Old Vienna café decor; some of London's best breaded Wiener schnitzel; decadent strudels and ice cream coupes. ⑤ *Average main: £21* ✉ *50 Marylebone High St., Marylebone* ☎ *020/7466–5501* ⊕ *www.fischers. co.uk* Ⓜ *Baker St., Bond St.* ✛ *1:H3.*

$
SEAFOOD
FAMILY

✕ **The Golden Hind.** You'll land some of the best fish-and-chips in town at this British chippy in a retro 1914 art deco café. Marylebone locals and satisfied tourists alike hunker down for the neatly prepared and decidedly nongreasy deep-fried or steamed battered cod, haddock, and plaice, the classic hand-cut Maris Piper chips, and the traditional mushy peas and homemade tartare sauce. **Known for:** some of the city's best deep-fried battered cod and chips; hard-to-find traditional mushy peas; huge portions. ⑤ *Average main: £10* ✉ *71A-73 Marylebone La., Marylebone* ☎ *020/7486–3644* ⊕ *www.goldenhindrestaurant.com* ☾ *Closed Sun. No lunch Sat.* Ⓜ *Bond St.* ✛ *1:H3.*

$$$
FRENCH

✕ **Les 110 de Taillevent.** Dazzling classical French dishes mark out Les 110 de Taillevent as the city's top French *brasserie de luxe.* Housed in a chic former Coutts bank on Cavendish Square, diners and oenophiles delight in the exquisite cuisine and accompanying master list of 110 fine wines by the glass. **Known for:** soaring classic dining salon; brilliant list of paired fine wines by the glass; haunt for wine experts and merchants. $ *Average main: £24* ⊠ *16 Cavendish Sq., Marylebone* ☎ *020/3141– 6016* ⊕ *www.les-110-taillevent-london.com* ⊙ *Closed Sun.* Ⓜ *Bond St., Oxford Circus* ⚓ *1:H3.*

$$$$ ✗ **Roganic.** Field-to-fork, New Nordic chef Simon Rogan takes diners
MODERN BRITISH on a madcap journey with his bonkers 4- to 17-course tasting menu
Fodor's Choice here at Roganic. Hold on tight for a cyclone of mini-bites and highly
★ technical dishes, ranging from salt-baked celeriac with enoki mushroom and whey cream to burnt hispi cabbage, crab, and crispy chicken skins. **Known for:** extravagant tasting menus; fresh, local-based produce; smoked juniper fudge for dessert. $ *Average main: £32* ⊠ *5-7 Bland- ford St., Marylebone* ☎ *020/3370–6260* ⊕ *www.roganic.uk* ⊙ *Closed Sun.* Ⓜ *Bond St.* ⚓ *1:G3.*

14

SOHO AND COVENT GARDEN

Soho and Covent Garden are the city's historic playground and pleasure zone, an all-day, all-night jostling neon wonderland of glitz, glamour, grime, and greasepaint. This area is London's cultural heart, with old and new media companies, late-night dive bars, cabaret, street performers, West End musicals, and world-class theater, ballet, and opera houses. Rising rents have recently forced out many of Soho's seedier red-light businesses and ushered in more edgy, top-notch restaurants. Just follow your nose in Covent Garden and Theatreland to find copious options for pretheater dining.

SOHO

$$ ✗ **Andrew Edmunds.** Candlelit at night, with a haunting vibe, Andrew
MEDITERRANEAN Edmunds is a permanently packed, old-school dining institution. Tucked away behind Carnaby Street in an 18th-century Soho town house, it's a cozy favorite whose unpretentious and keenly priced dishes draw on the tastes of Ireland, the Mediterranean, and Middle East. **Known for:** deeply romantic, Georgian-era town-house setting; unpretentious daily changing handwritten menus; bargains galore on the acclaimed wine list. $ *Average main: £19* ⊠ *46 Lexington St., Soho* ☎ *020/7437–5708* ⊕ *www.andrewedmunds.com* Ⓜ *Oxford Circus, Piccadilly Circus* ⚓ *3:C5.*

$$$ ✗ **Aquavit.** There's a *hygge*-style glow at this ritzy New Nordic empo-
SCANDINAVIAN rium off Piccadilly Circus. Swedish designer Martin Brudnizki pulls out
FAMILY all the best Scandinavian design stops, while a hip, upscale crowd dish over the pickled Matjes herrings from the small-jars *smörgåsbord* and pair Swedish meatballs with mash and lingonberries. **Known for:** nifty Nordic smorgasbord starters; soaring Scandinavian design showcase; sea bass with creamy Sandefjord sauce. $ *Average main: £27* ⊠ *St. James's Market, 1 Carlton St., Piccadilly Circus* ☎ *020/7024–9848* ⊕ *www.aquavitrestaurants.com/london* Ⓜ *Piccadilly Circus* ⚓ *3:C6.*

$ ✗ **BAO.** Lines form daily to secure a prized seat, perch, or stool at this
TAIWANESE no-reservations 32-seater from a crack team of Taiwanese steamed bao bun specialists. The gloriously soft and plump milk-based, rice-flour

bao buns—skillfully stuffed with organic Cornish braised pork, peanut powder, and fermented greens—are the undisputed stars of the show. **Known for:** long lines for the steamed stuffed bao buns; highly Instagramable pig blood cake; bao bun Horlicks ice cream for dessert. Ⓢ *Average main: £6* ✉ *53 Lexington St., Soho* ⊕ *www.baolondon.com* ☾ *No dinner Sun.* Ⓜ *Oxford Circus, Tottenham Court Rd.* ✛ *3:B5.*

$
CAFÉ

✗ **Bar Italia.** This legendary Italian coffee bar on Frith Street is Soho's unofficial beating heart and a 22-hours-a-day classic institution. Established in 1949 during the postwar Italian coffee bar craze and still run by the founding Polledri family, today most regulars grab an espresso or frothy cappuccino made from the vintage Gaggia coffee machine, and wolf down a snack at one of the mirrored bar counters. **Known for:** tiny hole-in-the-wall setting; old-school Italian espresso; sturdy sausage or bacon sandwiches. Ⓢ *Average main: £6* ✉ *22 Frith St., Soho* ☎ *020/7437–4520* ⊕ *www.baritaliasoho.co.uk* Ⓜ *Leicester Sq.* ✛ *3:D5.*

$
STEAKHOUSE
FAMILY
Fodor's Choice
★

✗ **Blacklock.** Set in a former basement brothel, this Soho meatopia cranks out £20 platters of delectable char-grilled grass-fed lamb, beef, and pork skinny chops and juice-soaked flat bread, all served on retro antique pearlware. Supplied by organic farm butchers Philip Warren from Cornwall, Blacklock's killer chops are beautifully seared on an open charcoal grill under heavy antique Blacklock irons from Tennessee. **Known for:** young and bubbly service with top '80s tunes; huge platters of skinny chops and flat bread; £18 Sunday roasts with all the trimmings. Ⓢ *Average main: £11* ✉ *The Basement, 24 Great Windmill St., Soho* ☎ *020/3441–6996* ⊕ *www.theblacklock.com* Ⓜ *Piccadilly Circus, Oxford Circus* ✛ *3:C5.*

$$
FRENCH

✗ **Blanchette.** French tapas may sound sacrilegious, but Blanchette hits the nail on the head at this rustic hipster headquarters where a dreamy French sound track complements the charming candlelit interior. Visually feast on the Paris flea market bric-a-brac and order a few small plates to share, like the crispy frogs' legs and truffle saucisson or baked scallops with Café de Paris sauce. **Known for:** unusual French tapas-style dishes and shared plates; cool Soho crowd with jazzy sound track; crunchy French frogs' legs. Ⓢ *Average main: £18* ✉ *9 D'Arblay St., Soho* ☎ *020/7439–8100* ⊕ *www.blanchettesoho.co.uk* Ⓜ *Tottenham Court Rd.* ✛ *3:C4.*

$$
ITALIAN
FAMILY
Fodor's Choice
★

✗ **Bocca di Lupo.** This upscale Italian restaurant is always crammed and the tables are jammed too close together, but everyone still comes for the unrivalled spread of regional Italian small plates. Located off Theatreland's Shaftesbury Avenue, the family-run trattoria offers a magnificent menu featuring peasant-based pastas, stews, roasts, and crudités from Piedmont to Bologna. **Known for:** open kitchen counter serving a medley of rustic small plates; enticing all-Italian wine list; crowd-pleasing lobster spaghettini. Ⓢ *Average main: £22* ✉ *12 Archer St., Soho* ☎ *020/7734–2223* ⊕ *www.boccadilupo.com* Ⓜ *Piccadilly Circus* ✛ *3:C5.*

$
FRENCH
FAMILY
Fodor's Choice
★

✗ **Brasserie Zédal.** Enjoy great value, prix-fixe menus of classic French dishes at Piccadilly's subterranean Parisian grand brasserie. Dripping with beaux arts gilt mirrors and monumental marble pillars, you can enjoy French standards like steak haché, choucroute, and crème brûleé. **Known for:** London's largest and most spectacular beaux arts basement brasserie; fantastically cheap set meal deals; nightly live music.

14

$ *Average main: £14* ✉ *20 Sherwood St., Piccadilly Circus* ☎ *020/7734–4888* ⊕ *www.brasseriezedel.com* Ⓜ *Piccadilly Circus* ✛ *3:C6.*

$$
BURGER
FAMILY
✕**Burger & Lobster.** Don plastic bibs at this mobbed, limited-choice burger and lobster shack, where there are no reservations (apart from larger groups), no starters, and no printed menu—the blackboard says it all: "Burger or lobster or lobster roll. All with chips & salad. £22." Of the three choices available, the Nova Scotia lobster is the best value; it comes in a butter-soaked brioche bun, with truffle and tarragon mayo and a sturdy pot of fries. **Known for:** wonderfully simple menu of lobster, burgers and chips; one-and-a-half pound jumbo Canadian lobster with salad; lively, fun-loving crowd. $ *Average main: £22* ✉ *29 Clarges St., Mayfair* ☎ *020/7409–1699* ⊕ *www.burgerandlobster.com* Ⓜ *Green Park* ✛ *3:D5.*

$$$
BRITISH
FAMILY
✕**Dean Street Townhouse.** Everyone feels 10 million times more glamorous just stepping inside this candlelit restaurant attached to the swanky 39 Georgian-era hotel of the same name. No frills, no fuss retro-British favorites include ham-and-pea soup, old-school mince and potatoes, smoked haddock soufflé, and yummy sherry trifle. **Known for:** classy candlelit dining salon with British art on the walls; superprofessional service; cheery High Tea and Afternoon Tea. $ *Average main: £24* ✉ *69–71 Dean St., Soho* ☎ *020/7434–1775* ⊕ *www.deanstreettownhouse.com* Ⓜ *Oxford Circus, Tottenham Court Rd.* ✛ *3:D5.*

$
SRI LANKAN
FAMILY
Fodor's Choice
★
✕**Hoppers.** Curry fiends have gone mad for the cheap egg hopper pancakes (a Sri Lankan specialty) and paper-thin griddled dosas at this highly spiced, no-reservations Frith Street snuggery. Diners gorge on chili mutton rolls, curried duck hearts, and piles of steamed string hoppers dipped in spicy broth, coconut chutney, or onion-and-Maldives-fish-flakes relish. **Known for:** crispy egg hopper pancakes with coconut sambol; authentic Colombo-style cabin atmosphere; signature black pork kari curry. $ *Average main: £8* ✉ *49 Frith St., Soho* ⊕ *www.hopperslondon.com* Ⓜ *Tottenham Court Rd., Oxford Circus* ✛ *3:D4.*

$
THAI
Fodor's Choice
★
✕**Kiln.** Earthy northern Thai cuisine bursts out of the charcoal-fired kiln at this BBQ-focused wonderland in Soho. Overlook the open kitchen and you'll see sizzling cumin-dusted hogget skewers and charcoal-grilled chicken thigh bites, along with other village-style dishes that show influences from Laos, Myanmar, and the Yunnan province of China. **Known for:** open kitchen counter setup with charcoal grill and hot clay pots; awesome array of specially grown Thai, Burmese, and other Asian herbs and spices; popular cumin-dusted fatty hogget skewers. $ *Average main: £9* ✉ *58 Brewer St., Soho* ⊕ *www.kilnsoho.com* Ⓜ *Oxford Circus, Piccadilly Circus* ✛ *3:C5.*

$
INDIAN
FAMILY
✕**Kricket.** Upsized dishes of zingy Indian street food fly from the open kitchen at this Piccadilly party spot. Sit at the L-shaped, lava-topped counter and watch the chefs haul out bone marrow-smeared *kulcha* breads from the blazing clay tandoor alongside other funky dishes. **Known for:** pepped-up Indian street food faves; colonial cocktails in the raucous downstairs dining den; hip, young crowds. $ *Average main: £10* ✉ *12 Denman St., Piccadilly Circus* ☎ *No phone* ⊕ *www.kricket.co.uk* ☉ *Closed Sun.* Ⓜ *Piccadilly Circus* ✛ *3:C6.*

$ ✕ **Maison Bertaux.** Romantics and Francophiles cherish this quirky 1871
CAFÉ French pâtisserie, vintage tea parlor, and occasional pop-up art space,
FAMILY where nothing seems to have changed since the 1940s. Colorful pastries, tarts, croissants, and sweet cakes are still well loved and baked on-site. **Known for:** mesmerizing vintage French interiors; glamorous and eccentric owner; old-fashioned collection of creamy patisseries. $ *Average main: £8* ✉ *28 Greek St., Soho* ☎ *020/7437–6007* ⊕ *www. maisonbertaux.com* ▬ *No credit cards* Ⓜ *Leicester Sq.* ✛ *3:D5.*

$$ ✕ **The Palomar.** It's Jerusalem meets Palestine meets Beirut meets a funky
MIDDLE EASTERN scenester vibe at this Arab-Israeli spot off Chinatown. Sit at the open-kitchen zinc counter and down shots of *arak* while trading quips with the Middle Eastern chefs, who offer a medley of Levantine delights, including Yemeni-Jewish *kubaneh* bread, Palestinian steak tartare, Jerusalem truffled mushroom polenta, and tangy paprika-rich pork belly tagine with Israeli couscous. **Known for:** fun, Middle Eastern party atmosphere and free arak shots; lively pork pie–hatted chefs brigade in the open kitchen; popular Persian oxtail stew. $ *Average main: £16* ✉ *34 Rupert St., Piccadilly Circus* ☎ *020/7439–8777* ⊕ *www.thepalomar.co.uk* Ⓜ *Piccadilly Circus, Leicester Sq.* ✛ *3:D6.*

$$ ✕ **Rambla.** Dine curbside on Soho's busy Dean Street or lean in at the
TAPAS open kitchen counter at this popular elegant but casual tapas joint. Bril-
Fodor's Choice liantly cheap and exceptionally tasty Catalan-inspired small plates are
★ complemented by a fine all-Spanish wine list, which focuses on sherry, Cava, and wines from Catalunya. **Known for:** seafood and mountain-based Catalan small plates; braised oxtail canelones with hot Nevat goat cheese sauce; Catalan puddings for dessert. $ *Average main: £18* ✉ *64 Dean St., Soho* ☎ *020/7734–8428* ⊕ *www.ramblalondon.com* Ⓜ *Tottenham Court Road, Piccadilly Circus* ✛ *3:D5.*

$$$ ✕ **Social Eating House.** At Jason Atherton's underrated but brilliant
FRENCH French bistronomie Soho hangout, witty dishes like smoked duck's
FAMILY ham (made from cured duck's breast) and Scotch egg-and-chips are served alongside classics like the "CLT," consisting of white crabmeat, lettuce, and roast heritage tomato. The moodily lit bare-brick ground-floor salon is tricked out with dark parquet floors, antique mirrored ceilings, and red leather banquettes. **Known for:** vintage cocktails in the speakeasy lounge; affordable set lunches and extravagant tasting menus at the chef's table; signature boil-in-the-bag British wild mushrooms on toast. $ *Average main: £26* ✉ *58 Poland St., Soho* ☎ *020/7993–3251* ⊕ *www.socialeatinghouse.com* ⊙ *Closed Sun.* Ⓜ *Oxford Circus, Tottenham Court Rd.* ✛ *3:B4.*

$ ✕ **Spuntino.** Moody Edison bulbs, bluegrass tunes, a popcorn machine,
DINER and only 27 seats make this Theaterland speakeasy one of the coolest spots in town. Once seated, settle in with a Brooklyn Manhattan cocktail and dive into truffled egg toast before moving on to deep-fried grits, softshell crab, buttermilk fried chicken, or mini-Yankee sliders. **Known for:** cult collection of ground beef and pulled-pork sliders; hipster speakeasy scene; home-brewed hooch and killer rare whiskies. $ *Average main: £11* ✉ *61 Rupert St., Soho* ⊕ *www.spuntino.co.uk* Ⓜ *Piccadilly Circus* ✛ *3:C5.*

$ ✕ **temper.** Smokehouse maven Neil Rankin smashes the live fire meat
BARBECUE   scene at this Soho speakeasy-like basement joint. Sit at the central open
FAMILY   kitchen counter and feel the heat from the charcoal smoke pits, clay
ovens, and log-fired roasting spits before wolfing down nine-hour-
smoked Cabrito goat tacos. **Known for:** tough-looking but friendly
chef's brigade; hand-rolled tacos with smoked beef, lamb, and goat;
plenty of natural and low-intervention wines. ⑤ *Average main: £11*
✉ *25 Broadwick St., Soho* ☎ *020/3879–3834* ⊕ *www.temperrestaurant.
com* Ⓜ *Oxford Circus, Piccadilly Circus* ✛ *3:C4.*

$$ ✕ **10 Greek Street.** There may only be 28 table seats and nine counter
MODERN   stools at this stripped-down Modern European humdinger, but the con-
EUROPEAN   sistently great food, cheap wine, affable prices, and excellent service
more than make up for it. Once seated, expect simple starters and mains
like butternut ravioli with sage. **Known for:** buzzed-up foodie atmo-
sphere in a pared-back dining space; gutsy seasonal Modern European
mains; generous platters of house-cured charcuterie. ⑤ *Average main:
£21* ✉ *10 Greek St., Soho* ☎ *020/7734–4677* ⊕ *www.10greekstreet.
com* ☾ *Closed Sun.* Ⓜ *Tottenham Court Rd.* ✛ *3:D4.*

$$ ✕ **XU.** It feels like a cinematic reinterpretation of 1930s Taipei at this
TAIWANESE   glamorous jewel box on the edge of Chinatown. Peerless dishes like
Fodor's Choice   tomato and smoked eel cold soup and marinated *Shou Pa* chicken with
★   rice and white pepper are complemented by a tea kiosk and tea master.
Known for: Taiwanese classics like Char Siu Iberico pork; sparkling
Hong Yu cold brew tea; popular Taiwanese whisky. ⑤ *Average main:
£19* ✉ *30 Rupert St., Piccadilly* ☎ *020/3319–8147* ⊕ *www.xulondon.
com* Ⓜ *Piccadilly Circus, Leicester Sq.* ✛ *3:D5.*

COVENT GARDEN

$$ ✕ **Balthazar.** British restaurateur Keith McNally re-creates his famed
BRASSERIE   New York Parisian brasserie at this corner spot off Covent Garden.
FAMILY   The decor creates an enchanting backdrop to enjoy a classic French
brasserie menu of few surprises, including flavor-packed dishes like
macaroni and Gruyère cheese or ox cheek bourguignon. **Known for:**
Parisian-style grand café; handy prix-fixe, brunch, and Afternoon Tea
menus; classic French plats du jour. ⑤ *Average main: £23* ✉ *4–7 Russell
St., Covent Garden* ☎ *020/3301–1155* ⊕ *www.balthazarlondon.com*
Ⓜ *Covent Garden, Charing Cross* ✛ *3:F5.*

$$$ ✕ **Clos Maggiore.** Insist on a seat in the dreamy, white blossom–filled
FRENCH   conservatory at this warm, cozy, and seriously romantic Provençal
FAMILY   country-style inn in the heart of Covent Garden. Once inside, you'll
be wooed by unapologetically old-fashioned and refined French cuisine. **Known for:** one of London's most romantic restaurants; warren of blossom-filled conservatories and open wood-fired hideaways;
lunch and pre- and post-theater meal deals. ⑤ *Average main: £26* ✉ *33
King St., Covent Garden* ☎ *020/7379–9696* ⊕ *www.closmaggiore.com*
Ⓜ *Covent Garden* ✛ *3:F5.*

$ ✕ **Côte.** Where else can you find an amazing three-course French meal
BISTRO   in Covent Garden for £13? The Côte brasserie chain does the trick,
FAMILY   and offers a menu loaded with classic French favorites: crêpes with
mushrooms and Gruyère cheese, boeuf bourguignon, *moules marinières*
(mussels with white wine), and iced berries and white chocolate sauce.

14

Known for: part of a dependable chain of French brasseries; very reasonable pre- and post-theater deals; reliable French classics like moules marinères. $ *Average main: £13* ✉ *17–21 Tavistock St., Covent Garden* ☎ *020/7379–9991* ⊕ *www.cote.co.uk* Ⓜ *Covent Garden* ✛ *3:G5.*

$$$
BRITISH
FAMILY
Fodor'sChoice
★

✕ **The Ivy.** London's onetime most famous celebrity haunt and West End landmark is still so popular it receives over a thousand calls a day. Established as an Italian café in 1917, today it's where London's wealthiest dine on haddock and chips, Thai-baked sea bass, and good ole English classics like shepherd's pie and sticky toffee pudding. Known for: celebrity-filled history; famed house staples like grilled calf's liver; great people-watching. $ *Average main: £25* ✉ *1–5 West St., Covent Garden* ☎ *020/7836–4751* ⊕ *www.the-ivy.co.uk* Ⓜ *Covent Garden* ✛ *3:E5.*

$$$
SEAFOOD

✕ **J Sheekey.** This timelessly chic 1896 seafood haven is a discreet alternative to the more celebrity-focused eateries in the neighborhood. Sheekey charms with an inviting menu of snappingly fresh Atlantic prawns, pickled Arctic herrings, scallop, shrimp, and salmon burgers, or the famous Sheekey fish pie. Known for: low-key celebrity hideaway; old-school seafood menu; glamorous art deco oyster bar. $ *Average main: £27* ✉ *28–35 St. Martin's Ct., Covent Garden* ☎ *020/7240–2565* ⊕ *www.j-sheekey.co.uk* Ⓜ *Leicester Sq.* ✛ *3:E6.*

$$$
ITALIAN
FAMILY
Fodor'sChoice
★

✕ **Margot.** Served by seriously suave staff in bow ties and tuxedos, enjoy some of London's finest service at this effortlessly elegant Italian restaurant. Diners come for top pastas like *tagliolini*with Sicilian red prawns or roast octopus with *'nduja* and Umbrian lentils. Known for: unrivaled service; classic Milanese veal osso buco with saffron risotto; glitzy Covent Garden setting. $ *Average main: £26* ✉ *45 Great Queen St., Covent Garden* ☎ *020/3409–4777* ⊕ *www.margotrestaurant.com* Ⓜ *Covent Garden, Holborn* ✛ *3:G4.*

$$
TAPAS
FAMILY

✕ **Opera Tavern.** Ibérico pig's head terrine and Manchego mini cheeseburgers are a few of the outstanding hybrid Spanish and Italian tapas found at the overflowing Opera Tavern in Covent Garden. After enjoying a snack of crispy pigs' ears or guindilla peppers, opt for a gentle flow of rich venison empanadas, Italian Scotch eggs, or char-grilled Venetian-style sardines. Known for: winning fusion of Italian and Spanish tapas; informal waitstaff and boisterous atmosphere; signature Ibérico pork miniburgers. $ *Average main: £18* ✉ *23 Catherine St., Covent Garden* ☎ *020/7836–3680* ⊕ *www.saltyardgroup.co.uk/opera-tavern* Ⓜ *Covent Garden, Holborn* ✛ *3:G5.*

$$$
BRITISH
FAMILY
Fodor'sChoice
★

✕ **Rules.** Opened by Thomas Rule in 1798, London's oldest restaurant is still arguably its most beautiful. Resembling a High Victoriana bordello, here you can dig into classic traditional British fare like jugged hare, steak-and-kidney pie, or roast beef and Yorkshire pudding. Known for: the oldest restaurant in London; fancy, high-class game-focused menu; famous diners from Charles Dickens to the Prince of Wales. $ *Average main: £30* ✉ *35 Maiden La., Covent Garden* ☎ *020/7836–5314* ⊕ *www.rules.co.uk* 🕴 *Jacket required* Ⓜ *Covent Garden* ✛ *3:F6.*

$$$
BRITISH
FAMILY

✕ **Savoy Grill.** You can feel the history at this 1889 art deco hotel-dining powerhouse, which has wined and dined everyone from Oscar Wilde and Winston Churchill to Liz Taylor and Marilyn Monroe. Nowadays it caters to businesspeople and wealthy West End tourists who come for the Grill's famed table-side serving trolley, which might trundle up laden with hulking great roasts like beef Wellington, Suffolk rack of pork, or saddle of lamb. **Known for:** ravishing old-school dining salon; beef Wellington from the daily carvery trolley service; signature glazed omelet Arnold Bennett. ⑤ *Average main: £31* ⊠ *The Savoy, 100 Strand, Covent Garden* ☎ *020/7592–1600 for reservations only* ⊕ *www.gordonramsay.com/savoy-grill* Ⓜ *Charing Cross, Covent Garden* ✛ *3:G6.*

$$$
BRITISH
FAMILY
Fodor's Choice
★

✕ **Simpson's-in-the-Strand.** Head straight for the 28-day roast rib of Scottish beef and Yorkshire puddings carved table-side at this magnificent 1828 dining institution. Originally a cigar lounge, coffeehouse, and later a famed chess venue, it was once frequented by the likes of Sir Arthur Conan Doyle, Charles Dickens, and Vincent van Gogh. **Known for:** history as one of the city's most grand taverns; traditional steak-and-kidney pudding; roast beef and Welsh lamb served from the silver carving trolley. ⑤ *Average main: £28* ⊠ *100 Strand, Charing Cross* ☎ *020/7420–2111 restaurant reservations only* ⊕ *www.simpsonsin-thestrand.co.uk* Ⓜ *Charing Cross* ✛ *3:G6.*

14

$$$
ITALIAN
FAMILY
Fodor's Choice
★

✕ **Spring.** Australian chef Skye Gyngell worships the four seasons at her wildflower-filled dining salon in majestic Somerset House off the Strand. Housed in the former Inland Revenue's neoclassical 1856 New Wing, Spring offers healthy root-to-stem, produce-driven Italian dishes. **Known for:** homemade bread, butter, and ice cream; highly seasonal, sustainable, and ingredient-driven dishes; biodynamic Fern Verrow salads. ⑤ *Average main: £30* ⊠ *Somerset House, New Wing, Lancaster Pl., Covent Garden* ✛ *Turn right on entering courtyard at Somerset House from the Strand* ☎ *020/3011–0115* ⊕ *www.springrestaurant. co.uk* ☾ *No dinner Sun.* Ⓜ *Holborn, Charing Cross* ✛ *3:G6.*

$
MEXICAN
FAMILY

✕ **Wahaca.** Crowds come for the Mexican street food at this brightly colored Covent Garden subterranean foodie hot spot. Shared wooden bench seating and gaudy Mexican murals make for a bright and breezy setting, but it's the inexpensive and ethically sourced Mexican market-style tacos, enchiladas, quesadillas, burritos, and taquitos that pull in the budget-conscious. **Known for:** loud Mexican music and colorful basement setting; menu of relatively authentic Mexican tacos, quesadillas, and taquitos; cheap cocktails. ⑤ *Average main: £9* ⊠ *66 Chandos Pl., Covent Garden* ☎ *020/7240–1883* ⊕ *www.wahaca.co.uk* Ⓜ *Covent Garden* ✛ *3:F6.*

BLOOMSBURY, HOLBORN, AND FITZROVIA

The literary giants of the Bloomsbury set—from Virginia Woolf to E.M. Forster and Vanessa Bell—may be long gone but this bluestocking enclave (centered on the University of London and British Library) still excels at a cultured and pleasure-loving dining scene. Holborn, bordering Covent Garden, has some of those big, old-establishment hotel dining rooms, as well as a big, bright elegant shining star in The Delaunay on the Aldwych.

BLOOMSBURY

$$$
BRITISH

✕ **Noble Rot.** There's an old Amsterdam coffeehouse vibe at this dark and creaky wine bar and restaurant on historic Lamb's Conduit Street in Bloomsbury. Run by two wine buffs and cult wine magazine publishers, you'll find deceptively simple ingredient-driven British dishes like Whitstable oyster and Cornish turbot braised in oxidized 1998 Bâtard-Montrachet Grand Cru. **Known for:** paradise for oenophiles; unpretentious seasonal British and French wine-friendly fare; neat combos like smoked eel and Yorkshire rhubarb on soda bread. $ *Average main: £26* ✉ *51 Lamb's Conduit St., Bloomsbury* ☎ *020/7242–8963* ⊕ *www.noblerot.co.uk* Ⓜ *Holborn* ✛ *3:G1.*

HOLBORN

$$$
AUSTRIAN
FAMILY
Fodor's Choice
★

✕ **The Delaunay.** It's all *fin de siècle* Vienna at this evocative art deco–style grand café on the Aldwych near Covent Garden. Dishes on the majestic 60-item menu would do the Austro-Hungarian Empire proud—think Wiener schnitzel, Hungarian goulash, beef Stroganoff, and wonderful *würstchen* (frankfurters and hot dogs), served with sauerkraut and onions. **Known for:** elegant old-world Austro-Hungarian haunt; proper Holstein schnitzel and frankfurters; affordable set lunches. $ *Average main: £24* ✉ *55 Aldwych, Holborn* ☎ *020/7499–8558* ⊕ *www.thedelaunay.com* Ⓜ *Covent Garden, Holborn* ✛ *3:G4.*

FITZROVIA

$$$
MODERN BRITISH
FAMILY

✕ **Berners Tavern.** All the cool cats swing by this grand brasserie at Ian Schrager's insanely trendy London Edition hotel near Tottenham Court Road. Enter the monumental Edwardian dining salon, where you might swoon over a light lunch of ironbark pumpkin risotto or an evening dinner of Creedy Carver duck. **Known for:** knockout dining salon; cool back-lit cocktail bar; slow-roast Herdwick lamb with Wye Valley asparagus. $ *Average main: £28* ✉ *The London Edition, 10 Berners St., Fitzrovia* ☎ *020/7908–7979* ⊕ *www.bernerstavern.com* Ⓜ *Oxford Circus, Tottenham Court Rd.* ✛ *3:C3.*

$$
SEAFOOD

✕ **Bonnie Gull Seafood Shack.** It almost feels like you're seaside here at London's top seafood shack, where awesome fresh seafood (from Brixham brill to Shetland mussels) takes diners on a tour of the British Isles. Look up, and you'll spot an old ship's bell and captain's hat and a mini-raw bar of iced Palourde clams and Jersey oysters stashed inside an antique sea chest. **Known for:** fresh day-boat fish from around the British Isles; passionate service; popular Looe plaice with samphire and clams. $ *Average main: £23* ✉ *21A Foley St., Fitzrovia* ☎ *020/7436–0921* ⊕ *www.bonniegull.com* Ⓜ *Oxford Circus, Goodge St.* ✛ *3:B2.*

$$$
FRENCH
Fodor's Choice
★

✕ **Clipstone.** Exceptionally inventive dishes elevate this hipster casual joint to the top rank of London's mid-range gastro titans. With a focus on in-house curing, pickling, smoked meats, and heritage vegetables, expect a cavalcade of crudos, unlikely combinations, and classic gastronomy specialties. **Known for:** classic French dishes in a minimalist setting; lots of house-made, pickled, fermented, or cured extras; soothing blanquette de veau (veal ragout) and sweetbreads. $ *Average main: £27* ✉ *5 Clipstone St., Fitzrovia* ☎ *020/7637–0871* ⊕ *www.clipstonerestaurant.co.uk* ☙ *Closed Sun.* Ⓜ *Great Portland St.* ✛ *3:A1.*

$$$
MODERN
EUROPEAN
Fodor'sChoice
★

✕Portland. Consistently brilliant modern European fare in a low-key setting characterizes this restaurant on a one-way street just north of Oxford Circus. Marvel at the chef's brigade in the open kitchen before turning to a highly inventive seasonal produce–driven menu. **Known for:** gloriously edgy and inventive slew of veg-centric delights; a masterpiece game pithivier (pastry pie); artfully presented heritage carrots with goat's curd. ⑤ *Average main: £26* ✉ *113 Great Portland St., Fitzrovia* ☎ *020/7436–3261* ⊕ *www.portlandrestaurant.co.uk* Ⓜ *Oxford Circus* ✥ *3:A2.*

CLERKENWELL AND THE CITY

14

Historic and just beyond The City limits, chef-centric Clerkenwell is one of the most trendy and interesting quarters for London gastro-dining, which sets it in stark contrast to the adjacent City, which caters overwhelmingly to traditional business-focused dining.

$$
MODERN BRITISH

✕Anglo. Modern British bistronomy takes a giant leap forward at chef-patron Mark Jarvis's tasting menu mecca in the historic Hatton Garden jewelery quarter in Farringdon. Feast on the Brit-sourced seasonal foodie creations here, which are offered à la carte or as seven- or eight-course tasting menus at dinner. **Known for:** well-priced tasting menus for lunch and dinner; signature grated cheese and onion on malt toast; wacky desserts like lemon curd and horseradish. ⑤ *Average main: £19* ✉ *30 St Cross St., Clerkenwell* ☎ *020/7430–1503* ⊕ *www.anglorestaurant.com* ⊗ *Closed Sun. No lunch Mon.* Ⓜ *Farringdon* ✥ *2:E4.*

$
ISRAELI
FAMILY

✕Berber & Q - Shawarma Bar. Every night feels as crushed and crowded as downtown Tel Aviv at Exmouth Market's superb shawarma bar. Dip *chollah* toast into tahini-rich mezze and hummus spreads before delving into slow-cooked sumac and harissa-heavy lamb shawarmas. **Known for:** Tel Aviv–style hip hangout; wondrous char-grilled lamb and beef shawarmas; unmissable BBQ-ed cauliflower shawarma. ⑤ *Average main: £13* ✉ *45 Exmouth Market, Clerkenwell* ☎ *020/7837–1726* ⊕ *www.shawarmabar.co.uk* ⊗ *Closed Sun.* Ⓜ *Farringdon* ✥ *2:E3.*

$$
BRASSERIE
FAMILY

✕Blixen. Within a magnificent Kew Gardens–style tropical garden and plant conservatory, you'll find this stylish brasserie backing out onto Old Spitalfields Market. Housed in a converted former Victorian bank, Blixen offers evergreen European comfort food. **Known for:** captivating, palm-filled tropical conservatory; great cocktails in the basement bar; popular weekend brunches. ⑤ *Average main: £17* ✉ *65A Brushfield St., City of London* ☎ *020/7101–0093* ⊕ *www.blixen.co.uk* Ⓜ *Liverpool St.* ✥ *2:G2.*

$$$$
MODERN BRITISH

✕City Social. A largely corporate crowd comes here for the Manhattan-esque views of The City and chef Jason Atherton's masterful but straightforward cuisine. Impressed diners look out from level 24 of Tower 42 on a majestic panorama that takes in iconic buildings like The Gherkin and The Walkie Talkie. **Known for:** majestic panoramas of The City; gutsy steak and fish standards; suited financiers and corporate deal-maker crowd. ⑤ *Average main: £34* ✉ *Tower 42, 25 Old Broad St., City of London* ☎ *020/7877–7703* ⊕ *www.citysociallondon.com* ⊗ *Closed Sun. No lunch Sat.* Ⓜ *Liverpool St.* ✥ *2:G2.*

$$ **×Duck & Waffle.** Zoom up to the 40th floor of the Heron Tower and
MODERN BRITISH head straight for the cult signature dish of confit duck leg, Belgium
FAMILY waffle, fried duck egg, and mustard maple syrup for a taste of foodie
bliss. Open 24/7, with spectacular panoramas of The City, you might
satisfy the munchies with a foie gras breakfast, served all day, along-
side streaky bacon and homemade Nutella or an Elvis PB&J waffle
with banana brûlée. **Known for:** rare-to-London 24-hour service;
awe-inspiring panoramas of London's skyline; eponymous duck-
and-waffle dish. ⑤ *Average main: £19* ⊠ *Heron Tower, 110 Bishop-
sgate, City of London* ☎ *020/3640–7310* ⊕ *www.duckandwaffle.
com* Ⓜ *Liverpool St.* ✛ *2:G2.*

$$$ **×Luca.** You'll find a ballsy mix of modern Italian classics made with
MODERN ITALIAN top produce from the British Isles at this popular haunt in Clerken-
Fodor's Choice well. Sip a Negroni or Campari soda at the bar before exploring the
★ stylish main dining salon, pasta kitchen, secret garden, and stunning
glass-walled conservatory. **Known for:** edgy Italian pastas; cool and
glamorously designed brasserie; hip, design-conscious crowds. ⑤ *Average main: £30* ⊠ *88 St John St., Clerkenwell* ☎ *020/3859–3000* ⊕ *luca.
restaurant* Ⓜ *Farringdon* ✛ *2:F4.*

$$$ **×Moro.** Up from The City, you'll find Exmouth Market, a cluster of
MEDITERRANEAN cute indie boutiques, bookstores, vinyl shops, hardware stores, artisan
FAMILY bakeries, and more fine indie-spirited restaurants like this one. Lovingly
nurtured for over a decade by husband-and-wife chefs Sam and Sam
Clark, the menu includes a mélange of Spanish, Moroccan, and Moor-
ish North African flavors. **Known for:** loud and buzzy dining room
with booming acoustics; expressive Moorish delights; house yogurt
cake. ⑤ *Average main: £24* ⊠ *34–36 Exmouth Market, Clerkenwell*
☎ *020/7833–8336* ⊕ *www.moro.co.uk* ☾ *No dinner Sun.* Ⓜ *Far-
ringdon, Angel* ✛ *2:E3.*

$ **×Simpson's Tavern.** The City's oldest tavern and chop house was founded
BRITISH in 1757 and undoubtedly is every bit as raucous now as the day it
FAMILY opened. Approached via a cobbled alleyway, it draws diners who revel
in the old boarding school surroundings and are eager to down oodles
of claret and English tavern-style grub. **Known for:** lots of history,
with past diners from diarist Samuel Pepys to Charles Dickens; sig-
nature stewed cheese on toast; charming but old-fashioned service.
⑤ *Average main: £10* ⊠ *Ball Court, 38½ Cornhill, City of London*
☎ *020/7626–9985* ⊕ *www.simpsonstavern.co.uk* ☾ *Closed weekends.
No dinner* Ⓜ *Bank* ✛ *2:G2.*

$$ **×St. John.** Global foodie fanatics join Clerkenwell locals for the pio-
MODERN BRITISH neering nose-to-tail cuisine at this Puritan-esque converted smokehouse
FAMILY near Smithfield Market. Here the chef uses all scraps of a carcass—from
Fodor's Choice tongue and cheeks to tail and trotters—so brace for radically stark
★ signatures like bone-marrow-and-parsley salad. **Known for:** ground
zero of influential Modern British nose-to-tail dining; great wine list;
pig's-skin appetizer. ⑤ *Average main: £23* ⊠ *26 St. John St., Clerkenwell* ☎ *020/7251–0848* ⊕ *www.stjohnrestaurant.com* ☾ *No dinner Sun.*
Ⓜ *Farringdon, Barbican* ✛ *2:F4.*

$$$ ✕**Sweetings.** Established in 1889 not far from St. Paul's Cathedral, little
SEAFOOD seems to have changed since the height of the British Empire at this quirky eatery. Although there are some things Sweetings doesn't do (dinner, reservations, coffee, or weekends), it does, mercifully, do great seafood. **Known for:** fresh Billingsgate fish served at raised linen-covered counters; tankards of "Black Velvet" Guinness and champagne; popular potted shrimp and Dover sole. $ *Average main: £30* ⌂ *39 Queen Victoria St., City of London* ☎ *020/7248–3062* ⊕ *www.sweetingsrestaurant.co.uk* ⊘ *Closed weekends. No dinner* Ⓜ *Mansion House* ✛ *2:H6.*

EAST LONDON

14

An invasion of hipsters and foodies has transformed the once-bleak East End food scene into the city's most daring dining zone. Seek out new British breakout stars like BRAT or Lyle's in Shoreditch, or hunt down a nighttime food truck for an irreverent taste of the foodie underground.

$$$ ✕**Bistrotheque.** You'll need some help finding this East End fashionista
MODERN headquarters located down a side alley in hipster Bethnal Green. Once
EUROPEAN inside, check out the striking loft dining space and the Manchichi bar
FAMILY in its post-industrial chic setting, before polishing off light French and English dishes. **Known for:** classic choices like steak tartare and Croque Madame; weekend brunch with pancakes and maple syrup; resident pianist at brunch. $ *Average main: £25* ⌂ *23–27 Wadeson St., Bethnal Green* ☎ *020/8983–7900* ⊕ *www.bistrotheque.com* ⊘ *No dinner Sun.* Ⓜ *Bethnal Green* ✛ *2:H1.*

$$$ ✕**BRAT.** Welsh chef Tomos Parry brings his signature wood-grilled,
SPANISH whole roast Cornish turbot to this Basque-inspired hipster restaurant.
Fodor's Choice Expect other live fire smashes like aged Jersey beef chops and seared
★ leeks. **Known for:** meat-heavy dishes grilled in a variety of ways; noisy hipster atmosphere; heritage Welsh grain flour breads. $ *Average main: £26* ⌂ *1st Fl., 4 Redchurch St., Shoreditch* ⊕ *www.bratrestaurant.com* Ⓜ *Liverpool Street* ✛ *2:G1.*

$ ✕**E Pellicci.** It's all Cockney banter and full English breakfasts at this
CAFÉ tiny family-run café and onetime gangsters' lair near the East End's
FAMILY Brick Lane and Columbia Road markets. This rowdy hole-in-the-wall serves the greasy fry-ups Londoners still adore: copious scrambled eggs, bacon, sausages, baked beans, toast, tomatoes, fried mushrooms, black pudding, cabbage 'n' mash, and scorching hot tea. **Known for:** full cast of East End Cockney characters; copious full English breakfasts and builders' brew tea; cash-only cheap dishes. $ *Average main: £8* ⌂ *332 Bethnal Green Rd., Bethnal Green* ☎ *020/7739–4873* ⊕ *www.epellicci.com* ▭ *No credit cards* ⊘ *Closed Sun.* Ⓜ *Bethnal Green* ✛ *2:H1.*

$$ ✕**Lyle's.** Globally acclaimed Brit chef and co-owner James Lowe for-
MODERN BRITISH sakes heavy sauces and sorcery at this stripped-back, informal British
Fodor's Choice neobistronomy dining mecca in Shoreditch. Stark but highly inventive
★ locally sourced dishes may include house-cured cod with radiant nasturtium flowers or 24-hour Cornish Helford Estuary monkfish with wood sorrel and pick-your-own East Sussex greengages. **Known for:** highly modern and airy dining space; serious new-wave British neobistronomy; excellent cheese plates and wines by the glass. $ *Average main: £19*

✉ *Tea Bldg., 56 Shoreditch High St., East End* ✛ *Entrance on Bethnal Green Rd.* ☎ *020/3011–5911* ⊕ *www.lyleslondon.com* ◷ *Closed Sun. and bank holidays* Ⓜ *Shoreditch High St.* ✛ *2:G1.*

$$
MODERN
EUROPEAN
FAMILY

✕ **Merchants Tavern.** The legend on the front of this Hoxton restaurant reads "Merchants of Good Fortune," which neatly sums up the exceptional, smart-casual dining experience you'll encounter within. Seasonal, veg-focused hits from France, Italy, and Britain emerge from the open-counter kitchen housed in a former Victorian warehouse and onetime apothecary. **Known for:** eclectic Modern European cuisine; 1960s-style interior and open kitchen; rare-pink venison with Alsace bacon. Ⓢ *Average main: £20* ✉ *38 Charlotte St., Hoxton* ☎ *020/7060–5335* ⊕ *www.merchantstavern.co.uk* Ⓜ *Old St.* ✛ *2:G1.*

SOUTH OF THE THAMES

First mentioned in 1276 and believed to have existed in Roman times, Borough Market in Southwark on the South Bank is a firm favorite with tourists, chefs, and foodies alike. Open Wednesday and Thursday 10–5, Friday 10–6, and Saturday 8–5, this Dickensian location under moody Victorian wrought-iron railway arches at London Bridge is packed with food lovers eager to pick up the finest and freshest fruit, vegetables, cheese, and grub in town. There are more than 120 stalls, plus a bunch of nearby pubs, bars, restaurants, and specialty shops. Ever more groovy new eateries are springing up in nearby Bermondsey Street, just south of the Shard.

$$
BISTRO
FAMILY
Fodor's Choice
★

✕ **Casse-Croûte.** French tunes play in the background at this jaunty French bistro on Bermondsey Street near the Shard. The daily changing blackboard offers a limited three options per course menu of exceptional Gallic bistro classics and riffs—from *côte de boeuf* to glazed stuffed pig's trotters with mash. **Known for:** authentic Parisian-style neighborhood bistro; stuffed pig's trotters and côte de boeuf with French beans; delicious pastries with Chantilly cream. Ⓢ *Average main: £20* ✉ *109 Bermondsey St., Bermondsey* ☎ *020/7407–2140* ⊕ *www.cassecroute. co.uk* ◷ *No dinner Sun.* Ⓜ *London Bridge* ✛ *5:H2.*

$$$
MODERN FRENCH
FAMILY

✕ **Chez Bruce.** Top-notch French and Mediterranean cuisine, faultless service, and a winning wine list make this one of London's all-star favorite restaurants. At this cozy haunt overlooking Wandsworth Common, prepare for unfussy grown-up gastro wonders ranging from homemade charcuterie to lighter, simply grilled fish dishes. **Known for:** elegant neighborhood salon; luxe classics like lobster and scallop ravioli; impressive sommelier. Ⓢ *Average main: £27* ✉ *2 Bellevue Rd., Wandsworth Common, Battersea* ☎ *020/8672–0114* ⊕ *www.chezbruce.co.uk* Ⓜ *Overland: Wandsworth Common* ✛ *4:E6.*

$$
TAPAS

✕ **José.** Revered Spanish chef José Pizarro packs in diners at this tapas-and-sherry treasure trove on Bermondsey Street, just south of the Shard. With just 30 seats and no reservations, you'll be hard-pressed to find a spot after 6 pm, but it's worth the wait: the Spanish tapas dishes here are superb. **Known for:** notoriously long waits and large crowds; wondrous green padron peppers and Ibérico pork fillet; unique sherry menu. Ⓢ *Average main: £18* ✉ *104 Bermondsey St., Southwark* ☎ *020/7403–4902* ⊕ *www. josepizarro.com/jose-tapas-bar* Ⓜ *Borough, London Bridge* ✛ *5:H2.*

$$$
FRENCH
FAMILY

✕ **Le Pont de la Tour.** You'll find the winning combo of top-end French cuisine and smashing views of the River Thames, Tower Bridge, and the Tower of London at the storied Le Pont de la Tour. Enjoy favorites like seared duck foie gras with caramelized black fig and a touch of Madeira, or *recherché* roast Challans duck and herb-crusted rack of lamb with Provençal vegetables. **Known for:** stunning views of Tower Bridge and The City; lavish art deco main dining room; destination and celebration meals. ⑤ *Average main: £28* ✉ *36D Shad Thames, Bermondsey* ☎ *020/7403–8403* ⊕ *www.lepontdelatour.co.uk* Ⓜ *London Bridge, Tower Hill* ✛ *2:H6.*

$$
PORTUGUESE
Fodor's Choice
★

✕ **Londrino.** There's a sparse aesthetic here at chef Leandro Carreira's Portuguese food headquarters in the shadow of the Shard. Regional Portuguese riffs are as bold, stark, and Instagramable as any you'll find elsewhere. **Known for:** wood-fired regional Portuguese small plates; gutsy seafood dishes like octopus tentacle with red pepper miso; small-batch, Portuguese-focused wine list. ⑤ *Average main: £18* ✉ *36 Snowfields, Southwark* ☎ *020/3911–4949* ⊕ *www.londrino. co.uk* Ⓜ *London Bridge* ✛ *5:H2.*

$
ITALIAN
FAMILY
Fodor's Choice
★

✕ **Padella.** Sit at the galley kitchen counter at London's top pasta bar in Borough Market, and watch as the chefs toss and serve endless hot pans of authentic handmade Italian pasta. Seriously epic and amazingly cheap pasta dishes include egg-free Parmesan and black pepper-rich *pici cacio e pepe* from Tuscany, or devilishly addictive ricotta ravioli with a slick of sage butter. **Known for:** supercheap handmade Italian pasta; papardelle with eight-hour beef-shin ragù; fast-moving lines and no reservations. ⑤ *Average main: £7* ✉ *6 Southwark St., Borough* ⊕ *www. padella.co* Ⓜ *Borough, London Bridge* ✛ *5:H1.*

$$$$
MODERN BRITISH

✕ **Restaurant Story.** British chef-patron Tom Sellers storms the ramparts at this set-menu gastro mecca, with his conceptual take on intensively flavored, ingredient-led New British and New Nordic cuisine. Housed in a modish Scandinavian-inspired dining space, expect clever touches like edible nasturtium flowers or a surprise beef-dripping candle that melts into a silver candleholder, which you mop up with heritage grain sourdough throughout the meal. **Known for:** intricate and unhurried set meal extravaganzas; global foodie destination; signature beef dripping candle. ⑤ *Average main: £34* ✉ *199 Tooley St., Bermondsey* ☎ *020/7183–2117* ⊕ *www.restaurantstory.co.uk* ⊘ *Closed Sun. No lunch Mon.* Ⓜ *London Bridge* ✛ *2:H6.*

14

KENSINGTON, CHELSEA, KNIGHTSBRIDGE, AND BELGRAVIA

If you're fabulous, famous, wealthy, or preferably all three, chances are you'll be living—and dining—in one of these neighborhoods among London's world-class museums, royal parks, shops, hotels, historic monuments, fashion boutiques, and top restaurants. In Chelsea, made famous in the swingin' '60s, restaurants range from bijou boîtes to exclusive little froufrou places ideal for gossip, an Aperol, and a no-carb bite on the go. Over in upscale Knightsbridge, you'll find Harrods and the high end fashion boutiques of Sloane Street, plus a heap of platinum-class hotel-based restaurants. Come here for a celebratory dining experience, but don't expect bargains (unless it's lunchtime).

Nearby Kensington is a Victorian residential neighborhood with a wider range of restaurants, from French bistros to funky Persian hideaways.

KENSINGTON

$$$
JAPANESE

✕ **Yashin.** At this top London sushi bar off Kensington High Street, you can watch Japanese head chef and cofounder Yasuhiro Mineno tease, slice, tweak, and blowtorch his way to the freshest, funkiest, most colorful, and exquisite sushi, sashimi, salads, and carpaccio that you're likely to find this side of the East China Sea. Tofu-topped miso cappuccino comes in a Victorian cup and saucer, while delectable sushi spreads might mesmerize with ponzu-spiked salmon or Japanese sea bream with rice cracker dust. **Known for:** exquisite sushi and sashimi with the odd twist; 5- to 15-piece chef-decides omakase sets; superaffordable 5-piece salmon sushi lunch. ⑤ *Average main: £28* ⊠ *1A Argyll Rd., Kensington* ☎ *020/7938–1536* ⊕ *www.yashinsushi.com* Ⓜ *High St. Kensington* ✛ *4:B1.*

CHELSEA

$$$
FRENCH
FAMILY
Fodor's Choice
★

✕ **Elystan Street.** Former two-Michelin-starred chef and co-patron Phil Howard ditches the West End's typical high-end style and cuts loose at this more relaxed Chelsea *boîte.* Head for deeply flavored and immaculately burnished dishes in the lively salon tricked out with café curtains and Air Force blue chairs. **Known for:** Michelin-level cuisine in a relaxed salon; flawless lemon tart; convivial vibe enhanced by a smart wine list. ⑤ *Average main: £24* ⊠ *43 Elystan St., Chelsea* ☎ *020/7628–5005* ⊕ *www.elystanstreet.com* Ⓜ *S. Kensington* ✛ *4:E3.*

$$$
MODERN BRITISH
FAMILY

✕ **The Harwood Arms.** British game doesn't get much finer than at this game-lover's paradise (and London's only Michelin-star gastro-pub). Sample a catalog of awesome Sunday roasts or game like the popular carve-your-own whole roast lamb, pork, or beef joints with gravy and all the trimmings. **Known for:** standout Michelin-star grub in a gastro-pub setting; seasonal game from the pub's own hunting estate; Berkshire fallow deer. ⑤ *Average main: £26* ⊠ *27 Walham Grove, Chelsea* ☎ *020/7386–1847* ⊕ *www.harwoodarms.com* ☉ *No lunch Mon.* Ⓜ *Fulham Broadway* ✛ *4:A5.*

$$$
HUNAN
FAMILY

✕ **Hunan.** There's no printed menu at this quirky family-run Taiwanese stalwart situated a few blocks south of Sloane Square in Pimlico. Instead, diners simply state how spicy they like it, and sit back, relax, and chopstick their way through a succession of tasty tapas-size Hunan, Hakka, Cantonese, and Japanese-inspired dishes to share. **Known for:** unique menu-free Hunan dining experience; generous portions; tour de force procession of Taiwanese tapas-size delights. ⑤ *Average main: £23* ⊠ *51 Pimlico Rd., Pimlico, Chelsea* ☎ *020/7730–5712* ⊕ *www.hunanlondon.com* ☉ *Closed Sun.* Ⓜ *Sloane Sq.* ✛ *4:G3.*

KNIGHTSBRIDGE

$$$
SPANISH
FAMILY

✕ **Ametsa with Arzak Instruction.** At this modernist romp, lovers of all things Spain can bask in a fantasia of New Basque cuisine. Here diners enjoy the passionate service and marvel at high-spec riffs on traditional Basque dishes, like slow-cooked hen's eggs flecked with paprika-rich chistorra sausage, wild ceps, and chorizo, or lobster updated with a white cassava powder. **Known for:** modernist New Basque molecular gastronomy; stunning wavelike ceiling feature, with 7,000 spice-filled glass vials; jaw-dropping Fractal mead dessert. $ *Average main: £29* ⊠ *Halkin Hotel, 5 Halkin St., Knightsbridge* ☎ *020/7333–1234* ⊕ *www.comohotels.com/thehalkin/dining/ametsa* ☾ *Closed Sun. No lunch Mon.* Ⓜ *Hyde Park Corner, Knightsbridge* ✛ *4:G1.*

$$ ✕ **Bar Boulud.** United States–based French superchef Daniel Boulud
BRASSERIE combines the best of French high-end brasserie fare with a dash of
FAMILY superior Yankee gourmet burgers and fries at this popular hangout in the Mandarin Oriental. The knockout grazing menu has something for everyone, and the professional but informal waitstaff give out a convivial vibe. **Known for:** awesome beef, BBQ pork, and foie gras burgers; highly affordable set meals from noon until 6:30; global five-star hotel crowd. $ *Average main: £23* ⊠ *Mandarin Oriental Hyde Park, 66 Knightsbridge, Knightsbridge* ☎ *020/7201–3899 for reservations only* ⊕ *www.barboulud.com/london* Ⓜ *Knightsbridge* ✛ *4:F1.*

$$$$ ✕ **Dinner by Heston Blumenthal.** Splendidly revived old English gastron-
BRITISH omy dishes executed with ultramodern precision is the *schtick* here
FAMILY at chef Ashley Palmer-Watts's wildly popular eatery at the Mandarin
Fodor's Choice Oriental. As you take in views of Hyde Park, slice into options like the
★ Meat Fruit appetizer (circa 1500), a ball of ultrasmooth chicken liver parfait in a mandarin jelly. **Known for:** one of London's top destination dining spots overlooking Hyde Park; unique historically accurate dishes that span England's history; Sauternes-soaked brioche and pineapple tipsy cake for dessert. $ *Average main: £34* ⊠ *Mandarin Oriental Hyde Park, 66 Knightsbridge, Knightsbridge* ☎ *020/7201–3833* ⊕ *www.dinnerbyheston.com* Ⓜ *Knightsbridge* ✛ *4:F1.*

$$$ ✕ **Mari Vanna.** All of London's Russian expatriates squeeze into this fan-
RUSSIAN tasy dining salon in Knightsbridge, which overflows with a maximalist decor of vintage chandeliers, Tiffany lamps, *tchotchkes, cheburashkas,* and a Russian *pechka* stove. Snap into character with a horseradish vodka shot, then carb-up on pierogi sea bass savories, Siberian *pelmeni* (dumpling) soup, or smoked salmon blinis. **Known for:** fantastically kitsch prerevolution Russian dining room; tasty borscht, blinis, and beef Stroganoff; sweet crepes for dessert. $ *Average main: £28* ⊠ *The Wellington Court, 116 Knightsbridge, Knightsbridge* ☎ *020/7225–3122* ⊕ *www.marivanna.ru/london* Ⓜ *Knightsbridge* ✛ *4:F1.*

BELGRAVIA

$$$$ ✕ **Pétrus.** A talented Gordon Ramsay team conducts a flawless dining
MODERN FRENCH experience at this Michelin-starred haute cuisine restaurant in Knights-
FAMILY bridge. The dining salon may be a tad beige and dated, but between the impeccable food, assured sommelier, remarkable cheese board, and charming service, you've got a full-court gastro press. **Known for:** Gordon Ramsay's flagship London restaurant; 25-day Casterbridge beef fillet with Barolo sauce; fleet-footed and formidable service. $ *Average main: £32* ⊠ *1 Kinnerton St., Belgravia* ☎ *020/7592–1609* ⊕ *www.gordonramsayrestaurants.com/petrus* Ⓜ *Knightsbridge, Hyde Park Corner* ✛ *4:G1.*

14

NOTTING HILL AND BAYSWATER

Ever since Hugh Grant and Julia Roberts starred in *Notting Hill* and put the area on the global map, Notting Hill's had a reputation as London's most glamorous neighborhood, with its myriad boutiques, chic cafés, pâtisseries, restaurants, bars, pubs, and the famous Portobello Road Market's collection of antiques shops, vintage-clothing stands, and food stalls. Portobello is one of London's most popular street markets, so get there early on Saturday morning (the market is open 8–6) to beat the crowds. Peruse the antiques and vintage clothes stalls, and when you want to eat, head to the north end where you'll find fresh fruit-and-veg stalls, artisan bakeries, and rare Spanish olive and French cheese purveyors, plus numerous hot-food stalls peddling savory crêpes, gourmet hamburgers, spicy German chicken rolls, paella, Moroccan kebabs, and Malaysian noodles.

NOTTING HILL

$$$$
MODERN BRITISH
FAMILY
Fodor's Choice
★

✕ **Core by Clare Smyth.** Chef Clare Smyth's casual fine dining extravaganza in Notting Hill offers unlikely, must-try dishes like skin-on potato cooked in red seaweed and topped with trout roe, edible flowers, and fermented mini salt-and-vinegar crisps. Watch the kitchen through a floor-to-ceiling glass partition as they create the mesmerizing multicourse tasting menus. **Known for:** brilliant vegetable and fish dishes elevated to the highest levels; relaxed, smart, casual dining experience; three-, five-, or nine-course tasting menus. ⑤ *Average main: £34* ✉ *92 Kensington Park Rd., Notting Hill* ☎ *020/3937–5086* ⊕ *www.corebyclaresmyth.com* Ⓜ *Notting Hill Gate, Labroke Grove* ✛ *1:B1.*

$$$$
MODERN FRENCH
FAMILY
Fodor's Choice
★

✕ **The Ledbury.** Aussie chef Brett Graham wins hearts, minds, and some serious global accolades at this upbeat, no-dairy, no-carb modern French (with Pacific and British hints) dining landmark. Global gourmands will struggle to find a more inventive vegetable dish than Graham's ash-baked celeriac with hazelnut and wood sorrel, and it's impossible to best his ultrapretty, precise, and complex mains. **Known for:** vegetable-centric dishes like roast celeriac with smoked pheasant; excellent game like Berkshire roe buck with wild hops; fantastic desserts like figs with honey and sourdough ice cream. ⑤ *Average main: £40* ✉ *127 Ledbury Rd., Notting Hill* ☎ *0207/7792–9090* ⊕ *www.theledbury.com* ☉ *No lunch Mon. and Tues.* Ⓜ *Westbourne Park, Ladbroke Grove* ✛ *1:A4.*

$$
FRENCH
FAMILY
Fodor's Choice
★

✕ **Six Portland Road.** The ultimate neighborhood restaurant in west London's wealthy Holland Park section draws diners with its brilliant-but-understated French classics, relaxed service, and interesting, largely French Caves de Pyrene–sourced wines. Dive in for plump Cornish mussels with white wine sauce or perfectly matched Atlantic cod with creamed leeks, shrimps, and sea aster. **Known for:** intimate seating; unpretentious but pitch-perfect service; winning boutique wine list. ⑤ *Average main: £18* ✉ *6 Portland Rd., Notting Hill* ☎ *020/7229–3130* ⊕ *www.sixportlandroad.com* ☉ *Closed Mon. No dinner Sun.* Ⓜ *Holland Park* ✛ *1:B1.*

BAYSWATER

$ ✕ **Hereford Road.** A Bayswater favorite with the well-connected Notting
MODERN BRITISH Hill set, Hereford Road is renowned for its pared-down, pomp-free,
FAMILY and ingredient-driven seasonal British fare, with an emphasis on well-sourced regional British produce. Work your way through uncluttered combos like steamed mussels with cider and thyme, lemon sole with sea dulse, or English rice pudding with a dollop of strawberry jam. **Known for:** pared-back Modern British nose-to-tail dining; deceptively simple-sounding dishes like duck livers with watercress; famously affordable two- and three-course set lunches. $ *Average main: £15* ✉ *3 Hereford Rd., Bayswater* ☎ *020/7727–1144* ⊕ *www.herefordroad.org* Ⓜ *Bayswater, Queensway* ✛ *1:B4.*

14

REGENT'S PARK, HAMPSTEAD, AND ISLINGTON

Stucco-fronted Regent's Park and Islington attract a high-brow artsy crowd who love the slightly rough-and-rowdy neighborhood restaurants like Lemonia or Oldroyd. Meanwhile, farther north in leafy Hampstead, it's all Dick Turpin 17th-century wood-beam coach houses and inns with roaring fires, house ales, and trouser-busting Sunday lunches.

REGENT'S PARK

$$ ✕ **Lemonia.** Primrose Hill's favorite Greek Cypriot, the vine-decked,
GREEK taverna-style Lemonia is large and light, and always packed with hordes
FAMILY of hungry families and chic locals. Besides an endless supply of Hellenic small-dish meze dips, hot breads, and starters, there are rustic mains like moussaka or slow-baked *kleftiko* lamb in lemon. **Known for:** Greek holiday, taverna-style atmosphere; popular meze, moussaka, and grilled sea bass; great weekday set lunches. $ *Average main: £16* ✉ *89 Regent's Park Rd., Regent's Park* ☎ *020/7586–7454* ⊕ *www.lemonia. co.uk* ☾ *No dinner Sun.* Ⓜ *Chalk Farm* ✛ *1:F1.*

ISLINGTON

$$ ✕ **Bellanger.** Part neighborhood hangout and part city dining destina-
FRENCH tion, this stylish Belle Époque–style grand café offers everything from
FAMILY a cup of coffee and cake to full meals. Expect a menu full of Alsatian choucroute, *baeckeoffe* (casserole), and a tasty array of wafer-thin *tartes flambées.* **Known for:** hearty deep dishes of Coq au Riesling; thin-crust tartes flambées; variety of French sausages. $ *Average main: £16* ✉ *9 Islington Green, Islington* ☎ *020/7226–2555* ⊕ *www.bellanger.co.uk* Ⓜ *Angel* ✛ *2:F1.*

$$ ✕ **Oldroyd.** Islington's finest squeeze into this tiny neighborhood bis-
ITALIAN tro thanks to the groovy Italian food and warm and friendly service. Well-priced and ingredient-driven, the daily changing menu of seasonal small plates might wow with creamy Somerset Cardo cheese and grilled tardivo radicchio risotto. **Known for:** jam-packed space; earthy Italian fare like osso buco; popular Italian peas with goat cheese. $ *Average main: £16* ✉ *344 Upper St., Islington* ☎ *020/8617–9010* ⊕ *www.old-roydlondon.com* Ⓜ *Angel* ✛ *2:F1.*

THE THAMES UPSTREAM

These wealthy leafy suburbs may be under the Heathrow flight path and follow the meandering course of the River Thames, but there's nothing sleepy about the neighborhood dining scene here, which is becoming more and more "West End" in style and substance by the day. One fanatical maverick stands out: the bearded Mikael Jonsson, a self-taught Swedish obsessive genius, who knows his wild scallops from his foraged blueberries, and conjures up meals of staggering brilliance.

CHISWICK

$$$$
MODERN
EUROPEAN
Fodor's Choice
★

✕ **Hedone.** Only a loony or genius would serve an appetizer of half a Cévennes onion with a few pear shavings and beurre blanc, but luckily Swedish chef Mikael Jonsson falls triumphantly in the latter camp at his no-fixed-menu foodie haven in Chiswick. A former lawyer and food blogger, Jonsson's obsessive approach to the provenance of his largely British-sourced ingredients—often rare, wild, or foraged—means his daily changing dishes are some of the most vivid around. **Known for:** rare, wild, or forage-based destination dining; Isle of Mull hand-dived scallops, stonecrop, and sea aster; no menu means the multicourse dishes are left up to the chef. ⑤ *Average main: £38* ✉ *301–303 Chiswick High Rd., Chiswick* ☎ *020/8747–0377* ⊕ *www.hedonerestaurant. com* ⊗ *Closed Sun. and Mon.* Ⓜ *Chiswick Park* ✛ *1:A2.*

LONDON
DINING AND
LODGING ATLAS

KEY
☐ Hotels
■ Restaurants
■ Restaurant in Hotel
Ⓤ **WESTMINSTER** Station
London Underground
⇌ National Rail Connection

E   **F**   **G**   **H**

Lord's
Cricket
Ground

Lemonia

The Hide

**REGENT'S
PARK**

Inner Cir

Queen
Mary's
Gardens

Chester Rd

Outer Circle

1

Lodge Rd
Paveley St
Park Road
Outer Circle

Orchardson St
Lisson Grove
Church St
Possmore Rd
Balcombe St

York Br
Park Sq W

Meliá
White
House
Park Sq E
Park

**REGENT'S
PARK**

2

**SHERLOCK
HOLMES
MUSEUM**

Allsop Pl
**MADAME
TUSSAUDS**

Marylebone Rd

Park Crescent

Portland Pl

Ashmill St
Lisson St
Bell St
Penfold St

MARYLEBONE
Melcombe Pl

Dorset
Square
Hotel

Park Plaza
Sherlock Holmes
Hotel

BAKER STREET

Fischer's
Marylebone High St
Devonshire St

A5

EDGEWARE ROAD
Chapel St
Old Road
Edgeware Rd

York St
Crawford St
Seymour Pl
Montagu Sq
Gloucester Pl
Baker Street

22 York St.

Paddington St
Weymouth St

New Cavendish St
Wimpole St
Harley St

3

Praed St.
Star St
Sussex Gardens
Radnor Pl
Sussex Pl
Stanhope Ter
Norfolk
Hyde Park St

George St

Roganic

Thayer St

**The Golden
Hind**

**Les 110
de Taillevent**
Cavendish Pl
Cavendish
Square

Connaught St
The Sumner
A5
Zetter
Townhouse
Marylebone

Upper Berkeley St
Cumberland Pl
Hyatt Regency
London—
The Churchill

Wigmore St
James St

SELFRIDGES

Radisson Blu
Edwardian
Berkshire
Hotel

Henrietta Pl
A40
New Bond St

4

Parkwood
Hotel

MARBLE ARCH
Marble Arch
Park St

Oxford St
N. Audley St
Duke St
Davies St

Claridge's

**La Petite
Maison**

Bayswater Road

**SPEAKER'S
CORNER**

**The Colony
Grill Room**

**Hélène Darroze
at the Connaught**
The Connaught

Upper Brook St
Le Gavroche

Grosvenor
Square
Upper Grosvenor St

34
Scott's
S. Audley St
Mount St

Jamavar

Indian Accent
Berkeley
Sq.
Berkeley St

5

**HYDE
PARK**

Park Ln
Park Ln

MAYFAIR

Gymkhana
Brown's Hotel

Charles St
Chesterfield
Mayfair
Hotel
Curzon St

**Alain Ducasse
at The Dorchester**
The Dorchester

**CUT
at 45 Park Lane**

Kitty Fisher's

The Serpentine

Athenaeum Hotel and Apartments
Four Seasons Park Lane

Hertford St.

Piccadilly

Green
Park

6

0   500 yards
0   500 m

InterContinental London
Park Lane

Hamilton Pl.

E   **F**   **G**   **H**

E

Wynford St
Rodney St
Barnsbury St
Liverpool Rd
Essex Rd
Upper St
A104

Bellanger

Oldroyd

Colebrook Row
Noel Rd
City Road
Goswell Road
ANGEL Ⓤ

Donegal St
Pentonville Road

F

Inset: Shoreditch, Whitechapel and Bethnal Green

🚇 HOXTON 🚉   **CAMBRIDGE HEATH** 🚉
Hackney Rd.   Haggerston Park   Victoria Park Gardens
Courthouse Hotel–Shoreditch   **Bistrotheque**
Columbia Rd
Merchants Tavern   Gosset St.   Town Hall Hotel & Apartments
Old St.   **Ace Hotel London Shoreditch**   **BETHNAL GREEN**
Kingsland Rd
Shoreditch High St.
Great Eastern St.   Bethnal Green Rd.   **E Pellicci**
The Hoxton Shoreditch   **BRAT**   Weavers Fields
The Curtain   **Lyle's**   Vallance Rd.   **BETHNAL GREEN** 🚇🚉
SHOREDITCH HIGH ST. Ⓤ   Buxton St.   Cambridge Heath Rd.
Commercial St.
LIVERPOOL ST. 🚉Ⓤ   **WHITECHAPEL** Ⓤ🚉
Sun St. Passage   **Blixen**   Whitechapel Rd.   Sidney St.
Bishopsgate   **Andaz**   **Qbic London City**   Commercial Rd.
🚉Ⓤ London Wall   **Duck & Waffle**
Threadneedle St.   **ALDGATE** Ⓤ   Cannon St. Rd.
City Social   **Aldgate High St.**
Threadneedles Hotel   Minories   Leman St.
Simpson's Tavern   Mansell St.
Fenchurch St.
Ⓤ **Grange City Hotel**   **Apex City of London**   0   1/4 mi
MONUMENT   Ⓤ **TOWER HILL** 🚉   0   1/4 km
                                 Shoreditch, Whitechapel and Bethnal Green

G

A104
Lever St
Central St
St. John St
Spencer St
Percival St
Seward St
Moro
Berber & Q - Shawarma Bar
Exmouth Market
Skinner St
Bowling Green Ln
Farringdon
Goswell Road
Fann St
Luca
Aylesbury St
Clerkenwell Road
St. Johns St
The Rookery
Anglo   St. Cross St
FARRINGDON Ⓤ
Cowcross St
St. John
Charterhouse St
Long Ln
W Smithfield
Holborn Viaduct
Gray's Inn Rd
Halton Cross St
Greville St
High Holborn
A40
Leather Ln
Hatton Gdn
Little Britain
Giltspur St
Old Bailey
Ludgate Hill
ST. PAUL'S
Carter Ln
THE CITY
New Bridge St
Shoe Ln
St-Bride St
Fleet St
Mitre Ct
Tudor St
THE TEMPLE ◆
Temple Pl
Crowne Plaza London—The City
Victoria Embankment
Ⓤ **TEMPLE**
Queen Victoria St
BLACKFRIARS Ⓤ
Blackfriars Br

0   500 yards
0   500 m

RIVER   THAMES

H

OLD STREET Ⓤ
Bach St
Featherstone
Bunhill Row
Dufferin St
City Road
Whitecross St
Golden Ln
Old Street
Aldersgate St
Shoreditch, Whitechapel and Bethnal Green: see inset above →
Chiswell St
BARBICAN Ⓤ
BARBICAN CENTRE ◆
Silk St
Moore Ln
Moorfields
BARBICAN
MOORGATE Ⓤ
Beech St
Wood St
London Wall
Angel St
Gresham St
GUILDHALL ◆
Cable Street Inn □→
Cheapside
The Ned
BANK OF ENGLAND ◆
Watling St
BANK Ⓤ
King William St
Cannon St
Sweetings
Upper Thames St
CANNON ST. STATION 🚉
Le Pont de la Tour
CANNON STREET STATION
Southwark Br
Restaurant Story

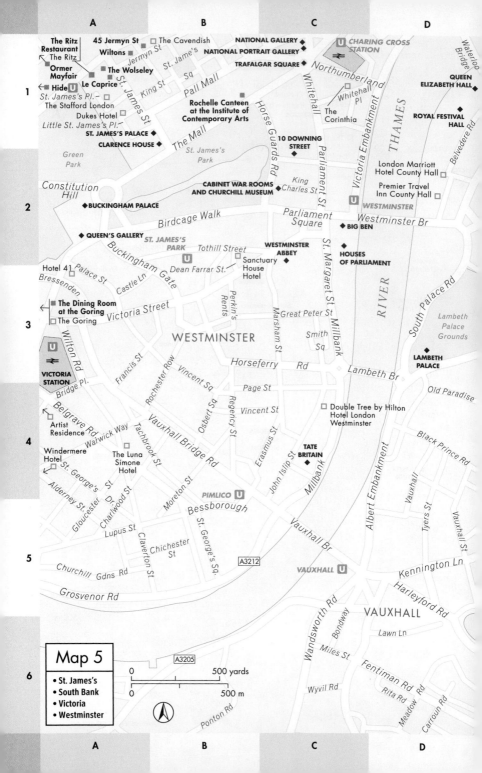

Map 5

- St. James's
- South Bank
- Victoria
- Westminster

A

The Ritz Restaurant
The Ritz
Ormer Mayfair
Le Caprice
Hide U
St. James's Pl.
The Stafford London
Dukes Hotel
Little St. James's Pl.
45 Jermyn St
Wiltons
The Wolseley
Jermyn St
King St
St. James's St

ST. JAMES'S PALACE ◆
CLARENCE HOUSE ◆

Green Park

Constitution Hill

◆ BUCKINGHAM PALACE

Birdcage Walk

◆ QUEEN'S GALLERY
Palace St
Hotel 41
Bressenden
The Dining Room at the Goring
The Goring
Wilton Rd
U
VICTORIA STATION
Bridge Pl.
Belgrave Rd
Artist Residence
Windermere Hotel
St. George's
Alderney St
Gloucester St
Drive Dr
Charlwood St
Lupus St
Churchill Gdns Rd
Grosvenor Rd

B

The Cavendish
St. Jame's
Sq
Pall Mall
Rochelle Canteen at the Institute of Contemporary Arts
The Mall
St. James's Park
ST. JAMES'S PARK
U
Tothill Street
Dean Farrar St.
Castle Ln
Buckingham Gate
Victoria Street
WESTMINSTER
Francis St
Rochester Row
Vincent Sq
Osbert St
Vauxhall Bridge Rd
Tachbrook St
The Luna Simone Hotel
Moreton St
PIMLICO U
Bessborough
Claverton St
Chichester St
St. George's Sq.
A3212
A3205

C

NATIONAL GALLERY ◆
NATIONAL PORTRAIT GALLERY ◆
TRAFALGAR SQUARE ◆
Whitehall
Northumberland
Whitehall Pl
The Corinthia
Horse Guards Rd
10 DOWNING STREET
Parliament St
King Charles St
CABINET WAR ROOMS AND CHURCHILL MUSEUM
Parliament Square
WESTMINSTER U
◆ BIG BEN
WESTMINSTER ABBEY ◆
St. Margaret St
Sanctuary House Hotel
Perkin's Rents
Great Peter St
Marsham St
Smith Sq
Horseferry Rd
Page St
Vincent St
Erasmus St
John Islip St
Millbank
TATE BRITAIN ◆
Vauxhall Br
VAUXHALL U
Wandsworth Rd
Bondway
Miles St
Wyvil Rd
Ponton Rd

D

U CHARING CROSS STATION
Waterloo Bridge
QUEEN ELIZABETH HALL
THAMES
ROYAL FESTIVAL HALL ◆
Belvedere Rd
Victoria Embankment
London Marriott Hotel County Hall
Premier Inn County Hall
WESTMINSTER
Westminster Br
HOUSES OF PARLIAMENT ◆
RIVER
South Palace Rd
Lambeth Palace Grounds
LAMBETH PALACE ◆
Lambeth Br
Old Paradise
Double Tree by Hilton Hotel London Westminster
Black Prince Rd
Albert Embankment
Vauxhall
Tyers St
Vauxhall St
Kennington Ln
Harleyford Rd
VAUXHALL
Lawn Ln
Fentiman Rd
Rita Rd
Meadow Rd
Carroun Rd

0   500 yards
0   500 m

1
2
3
4
5
6

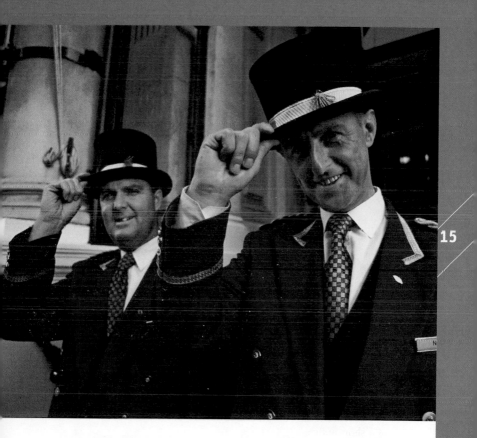

15

WHERE TO STAY

Visit Fodors.com for advice, updates, and bookings

Updated by
Toby Orton

If your invitation from Queen Elizabeth still hasn't shown up in the mail, no worries—staying at one of London's grande dame hotels is the next best thing to being a guest at the palace—and some say it's even better. Luckily there is no dearth of options where friendliness outdistances luxe; London has plenty of atmospheric places that won't cost a king's ransom.

That noted, until fairly recently it was extremely difficult to find a decent hotel in the center of town for less than £150 per night. Things have improved, thanks to a flurry of new mid-priced hotels that have sprung up in recent years. You'll still have to shop around for deals—never assume you'll be able to find somewhere good *and* cheap on short notice.

Of course, it's very different if money is no object. London has some of the very best and most luxurious hotels in the world. Freshly minted millionaires favor the rash of supertrendy hot spots like the Corinthia or ME London, while fashionistas gravitate toward Kit Kemp's super-stylish hotels like the Covent Garden and the Charlotte Street. But even these places have deals, and you can sometimes snag a bargain within reach of mere mortals, particularly in the off-season, or just be a spectator to all the glamour by visiting for afternoon tea, the most traditional of high-society treats.

Meanwhile, several mid-range hotels have dropped their average prices in response to the choppy waters of the global economy, which has pulled some fantastic places, such as Hazlitt's, the Rookery, and Town Hall, back into the affordable category. There's also a clutch of new, stylish, and supercheap hotels that are a real step forward for the city. The downside is that these places tend to be a little out of the way, but that's often a price worth paying. Another attractive alternative includes hotels in the Premier and Millennium chains, which offer sleek, modern rooms, lots of up-to-date conveniences, and sales that frequently bring room prices well below £100 a night.

At the budget level, London has come a long way in the last couple of years, with a familiar catch: to find a good, reasonably priced bed-and-breakfast, you must be prepared to look outside the very center of town. This means that you have to weigh the city's notoriously high transport costs against any savings—but on the plus side, the Tube can shuttle you out to even some far-flung suburbs in less than 20 minutes. If you're prepared to be just a little adventurous with your London base, you will be rewarded by a collection of unique and interesting B&Bs and small boutiques, in the kinds of neighborhoods real Londoners live in—places like the Cable Street Inn, the Main House, and the Church Street Hotel. If you're willing to fend for yourself, the city also has some great rental options.

But if you are interested in luxury, London is just the place. Although the image we love to harbor about Olde London Towne may be fast fading in the light of today's glittering city, when it comes time to rest your head, the old-fashioned clichés remain enticing. Choose one of London's heritage-rich hotels—Claridge's supplies perfect parlors; the Savoy has that river view—and you'll find that these fantasies can, and always will, be fulfilled.

15

PLANNING

RESERVATIONS

Yes, hotel reservations are an absolute necessity when planning your trip to London, so book your room as far in advance as possible. The further in advance you can book, the better a deal you're likely to get. Just watch out if you change your mind—cancellation fees can be hefty. On the other hand, it is possible to find some amazing last-minute deals at mid- to high-range places, but this is a real gamble, as you could just as easily end up paying full rate. Fierce competition means properties undergo frequent improvements, so when booking inquire about any ongoing renovations that may interrupt your stay.

CHECKING IN

Typical check-in and checkout times are 2 pm and 11 am, respectively. Many flights from North America arrive early in the morning, but having to wait six hours for a room after arriving jet-lagged at 8 am isn't the ideal way to start a vacation. Alert the hotel of your early arrival; large hotels can often make special early check-in arrangements, and almost all will look after your luggage in the meantime. Be prepared to drop your bags and strike out for a few hours. On the plus side, this can effectively give you a whole extra day for sightseeing.

HOTEL QUALITY

Note that rooms can vary considerably in a single hotel. If you don't like the room you're given, ask to see another. Hotels often renovate room by room—you might find yourself allocated a dark, unrenovated room, whereas bright, newly decorated quarters await just down the hall. Be prepared for the fact that, while smoking is now banned in public areas, this doesn't apply to hotel rooms; be firm and ask to change if you're given a smoking room and didn't request one.

BREAKFAST

Some hotels include breakfast in the price of the room. It ranges from a gourmet spread to what is known as the "full English" (one fried egg, two "bangers," or English-style sausage links, two thick slices of bacon, a grilled tomato, sautéed mushrooms or baked beans, and toast). In many budget hotels and B&Bs, this is the only hot breakfast available. Most expensive hotels (and the most imaginative small ones) may also offer pancakes, French toast, waffles, and omelets. Luckily, virtually all accommodations also offer packaged cereals, muffins, yogurt, and fresh fruit, so when the sausage-and-bacon brigade begins to wear you down, go continental.

FACILITIES

Keep in mind that some facilities come with the room rate while others cost extra. So, when pricing accommodations, always ask what's included. Modern hotels usually have air-conditioning, but B&Bs and hotels in older buildings often do not, and it is generally not the norm in London. Wi-Fi is common, but don't assume it's free (large hotels in particular can charge outrageous fees). If you want a double room, specify whether you want a double bed or a twin (two single beds next to each other). *All hotels listed here have private bathrooms unless otherwise noted.*

PRICES

If you're planning to visit in fall, winter, or early spring, start monitoring bargain rates online a few months before your trip and book whenever you see a good rate. Chains such as Hilton, Premier, and Millennium are known for their low-season sales during which prices can be as little as half the normal rate. And business-oriented hotels frequently have lower rates on weekends.

The exchange rate between the pound and the dollar is also unpredictable, so if it's looking good when you book, an advance-payment deal could end up saving you a decent amount of money. ■TIP→ The Visit London Accommodation Booking Service (www.visitlondon.com) offers a best-price guarantee. Also try the clearinghouse websites Late Rooms (www.laterooms.com), Booking (www.booking.com), and Last Minute (www.lastminute.com).

WHAT IT COSTS IN POUNDS			
$	$$	$$$	$$$$
Hotels	Under £125	£125–£250	£251–£400	Over £400

Prices in the reviews are the lowest cost of a standard double room in high season, including 20% V.A.T.

WHERE SHOULD I STAY?

	Neighborhood Vibe	Pros	Cons
Westminster, St. James's, and Royal London	This historic section is home to major tourist attractions like Buckingham Palace.	Central area near tourist sites; easy Tube access; considered a safe area to stay.	Mostly expensive lodging options; few good restaurants and entertainment venues nearby.
Mayfair and Marylebone	Traditional, old money; a mixture of the business and financial set with fashionable shops.	In the heart of the action; some of London's best hotels are found here.	Pricey part of town; the city-that-never-sleeps buzz makes peace and quiet hard to come by.
Soho and Covent Garden	A tourist hub with endless entertainment—this is party central for young adults.	Buzzing area with plenty to see and do; late-night entertainment abounds; wonderful shopping district.	Perhaps London's busiest (and noisiest) district after dark; few budget hotels.
Bloomsbury and Holborn	Diverse area that is part bustling business center and part tranquil respite with tree-lined streets and parks.	Easy access to Tube, and 15 minutes to city center; major sights, like the British Museum in Bloomsbury.	Holborn has busy and noisy streets; the area around King's Cross can be sketchy—particularly at night.
The City	London's financial district, where most of the city's banks and businesses are headquartered.	Extremely central with easy transportation access and great hotel deals.	The City can be as quiet as a tomb on weekends—even the pubs close.
East London	East of the city center, one of London's trendiest areas, with a great arts scene.	Great for art lovers, shoppers, and business execs with meetings in Canary Wharf.	Still a transitional area; parts of Hoxton can be a bit dodgy at night; 20-minute Tube ride from central London.
South of the Thames	South of the river is a vibrant cultural hub, centered on the South Bank, the Globe, and the Royal National Theatre.	South of the River is London's unofficial cultural quarter, and walking distance from the West End theaters.	You don't have to go very far from the South Bank before you hit some of London's dodgiest neighborhoods.
Kensington, Chelsea, Knightsbridge, and Belgravia	These are some of London's most upscale neighborhoods and a hub of London's tourist universe.	Diverse hotel selection; great area for meandering urban walks; London's capital of high-end shopping.	Depending on where you are, the nearest Tube might be a hike; residential area might be too quiet for some.
Notting Hill and Bayswater	This is an upscale, trendy area favored by locals, with plenty of good hotels.	Hotel deals abound if you know where to look; gorgeous greenery in Hyde Park.	Choose the wrong place and you may end up in a flea pit; residential area may be quiet.
Regent's Park and Hampstead	A mix of arty, fashionable districts with a villagelike feel in other places.	Some of London's most fashionable neighborhoods; easy to fall in love with.	Some distance from center; lack of hotel options.

15

HOTEL REVIEWS

Listed alphabetically by neighborhood. Use the coordinate (✛ 1:B2) at the end of each listing to locate a site on the corresponding map. To locate the property on a map, turn to the London Dining and Lodging Atlas at the end of the Where to Eat chapter. The first number after the symbol indicates the map number. Following that is the property's coordinate on the map grid.

Hotel reviews have been shortened. For full information, visit Fodors.com.

WESTMINSTER, ST. JAMES'S, AND ROYAL LONDON

WESTMINSTER

$$$$
HOTEL
Fodor's Choice
★

The Corinthia. The London outpost of the exclusive Corinthia chain is design heaven-on-earth, with levels of service that make anyone feel like a VIP. **Pros:** so much luxury and elegance you'll feel like royalty; exceptional spa with indoor pool; excellent fine dining options. **Cons:** prices jump to the stratosphere once the least expensive rooms sell out; not many special offers; not all room prices include breakfast. ⑤ *Rooms from: £500* ⊠ *Whitehall Pl., Westminster* ☎ *020/7930–8181* ⊕ *www.corinthia.com* ↪ *294 rooms* ⦿ *No meals* Ⓜ *Embankment* ✛ *5:C1.*

$$
HOTEL
FAMILY

DoubleTree by Hilton Hotel London Westminster. Spectacular views of the river, Big Ben, and the London Eye fill the floor-to-ceiling windows in this rather stark, steel-and-glass building steps from the Tate Britain, and a plethora of techy perks await inside. **Pros:** amazing views; flat-screen TVs and other high-tech gadgetry; can be surprisingly affordable for the location. **Cons:** small bedrooms; tiny bathrooms; TV has to be operated through a computer (confusing if you're not used to it). ⑤ *Rooms from: £175* ⊠ *30 John Islip St., Westminster* ☎ *020/7630–1000* ⊕ *www.doubletreewestminsterhotel.com* ↪ *460 rooms* ⦿ *Some meals* Ⓜ *Westminster, Pimlico* ✛ *5:C4.*

$$$$
HOTEL

The Goring. With Buckingham Palace just around the corner, this hotel, built in 1910 and now run by third-generation Gorings, has always been a favorite among discreet VIPs—including Kate Middleton's family on the night before her marriage to Prince William in 2011. **Pros:** elegant spacious rooms; overlooks Buckingham Palace; great attention to detail. **Cons:** price is still too high for what you get; interior's a bit fussy; the basic gym is small. ⑤ *Rooms from: £500* ⊠ *15 Beeston Pl., Grosvenor Gardens, Westminster* ☎ *020/7396–9000* ⊕ *www.thegoring.com* ↪ *75 rooms* ⦿ *Some meals* Ⓜ *Victoria* ✛ *5:A3.*

$$$$
HOTEL
Fodor's Choice
★

Hotel 41. With faultless service, sumptuous designer furnishings, and a sense of fun to boot, this impeccable hotel breathes new life into the cliché "thinks of everything," yet the epithet is really quite apt. **Pros:** impeccable service; beautiful and stylish; Buckingham Palace is on your doorstep. **Cons:** unusual design is not for everyone; expensive; the private bar can feel stuffy. ⑤ *Rooms from: £431* ⊠ *41 Buckingham Palace Rd., Westminster* ☎ *020/7300–0041* ⊕ *www.41hotel.com* ↪ *32 rooms* ⦿ *Free Breakfast* Ⓜ *Victoria* ✛ *5:A3.*

$$ ⛿ **Lime Tree Hotel.** In a central neighborhood where hotels veer from
HOTEL wildly overpriced at one extreme to grimy bolt-holes at the other, the
Lime Tree gets the boutique style just about right—and at a surprisingly reasonable cost for the neighborhood. **Pros:** lovely and helpful
hosts; great location; rooms are decent size. **Cons:** cheaper rooms are
small; some are up several flights of stairs and there's no elevator; lack
of amenities. ⑤ *Rooms from: £195* ✉ *135–137 Ebury St., Westminster*
☎ *020/7730–8191* ⊕ *www.limetreehotel.co.uk* ⬧ *25 rooms* ⊙ *Free
Breakfast* Ⓜ *Victoria, Sloane Sq.* ✛ *4:H2.*

$$ ⛿ **Sanctuary House Hotel.** This is a classic example of what the British
B&B/INN mean when they refer to an "inn"—a pub with bedrooms, albeit one of
better-than-average quality for London. **Pros:** cozy, authentic London
feel; friendly staff; "wow" location right in the heart of Westminster.
Cons: noise from pub; after-work crowd keeps the pub busy; dining
options are limited. ⑤ *Rooms from: £166* ✉ *33 Tothill St., Westminster* ☎ *020/7799–4044* ⊕ *www.sanctuaryhousehotel.co.uk* ⬧ *34 rooms*
⊙ *Free Breakfast* Ⓜ *St. James's Park* ✛ *5:B2.*

$$ ⛿ **Windermere Hotel.** This sweet and rather elegant old hotel, on the
HOTEL premises of London's first B&B (1881), is a decent, well-situated
FAMILY option. **Pros:** good location close to Victoria Station; free Wi-Fi; good
amenities for an old hotel of this size, including air-conditioning and
an elevator. **Cons:** rooms and bathrooms are tiny; traditional decor
might not suit all tastes; many major attractions are a 20-minute
walk away. ⑤ *Rooms from: £153* ✉ *142–144 Warwick Way, Westmin-
ster* ☎ *020/7834–5163* ⊕ *www.windermere-hotel.co.uk* ⬧ *19 rooms*
⊙ *Free Breakfast* Ⓜ *Victoria* ✛ *5:A4.*

ST. JAMES'S

$$$ ⛿ **Dukes Hotel.** At this small exclusive hotel in a discreet cul-de-sac,
HOTEL ample natural light brightens the classically elegant rooms. **Pros:**
famous martini bar; peaceful setting in a central location; excellent
restaurant. **Cons:** maybe a bit too quiet for some; price is still rather
high for what's available; the price of breakfast is steep. ⑤ *Rooms
from: £388* ✉ *35 St. James's Pl., St. James's* ☎ *020/7941–4840,
800/381–4702 in U.S.* ⊕ *www.dukeshotel.com* ⬧ *90 rooms* ⊙ *No
meals* Ⓜ *Green Park* ✛ *5:A1.*

$$$$ ⛿ **The Ritz.** If you're wondering if the *Downton Abbey*–style world of
HOTEL the old British upper class still exists, look no further than here; the Ritz
is as synonymous with London's high society and decadence today as
it was when it opened in 1906. **Pros:** historic luxury hotel; service at
every turn; iconic restaurant and bar. **Cons:** snooty service; tediously
old-fashioned dress code; located on a congested road. ⑤ *Rooms from:
£465* ✉ *150 Piccadilly, St. James's* ☎ *020/7493–8181* ⊕ *www.therit-
zlondon.com* ⬧ *136 rooms* ⊙ *No meals* Ⓜ *Piccadilly Circus* ✛ *5:A1.*

$$$$ ⛿ **The Stafford London.** This is a rare find: a posh hotel that's equal parts
HOTEL elegance and friendliness, and located in one of the few peaceful spots
Fodor'sChoice in the area, down a small lane behind Piccadilly. **Pros:** great staff; home
★ to one of London's original "American Bars"; quiet location. **Cons:**
traditional style is not to all tastes; perks in the more expensive rooms
could be more generous (free airport transfer, but one-way only; free
clothes pressing, but only one item per day); some rooms can feel small.

15

$ *Rooms from: £460* ⊠ *16–18 St. James's Pl., St. James's* ☎ *020/7493–0111* ⊕ *www.thestaffordlondon.com* ⪢ *106 rooms* ¹⊙¹ *Free Breakfast* Ⓜ *Green Park* ✢ *5:A1.*

MAYFAIR AND MARYLEBONE

MAYFAIR

$$$
HOTEL
⌖ **Athenaeum Hotel and Apartments.** This grand hotel overlooking Green Park offers plenty for the money: rooms are both comfortable and lavishly decorated, with deeply comfortable Hypnos beds, plasma-screen TVs, luxurious fabrics, and original contemporary artworks. **Pros:** peaceful park views; central location; great value for elegant setting. **Cons:** bathrooms are almost all small; some rooms can feel tiny; only some rooms come with park views. $ *Rooms from: £346* ⊠ *116 Piccadilly, Mayfair* ☎ *020/7499–3464* ⊕ *www.athenaeumhotel.com* ⪢ *164 rooms* ¹⊙¹ *Breakfast* Ⓜ *Green Park* ✢ *1:H6.*

$$$$
HOTEL
⌖ **Brown's Hotel.** Founded in 1837 by James Brown, Lord Byron's "gentleman's gentleman," this hotel occupying 11 Georgian town houses holds a treasured place in London society. **Pros:** elegant spaces; attentive service; good afternoon tea. **Cons:** even the most basic room is very pricey; renovation detracted from the hotel's historic atmosphere; low availability for the most basic rooms. $ *Rooms from: £540* ⊠ *34 Albemarle St., Mayfair* ☎ *020/7493–6020, 888/667–9477 in U.S.* ⊕ *www.roccofortehotels.com* ⪢ *117 rooms* ¹⊙¹ *Breakfast* Ⓜ *Green Park* ✢ *1:H5.*

$$$
HOTEL
⌖ **The Cavendish.** Located next door to Fortnum and Mason (one of the most luxurious department stores in the world), it seems appropriate that the Cavendish comes with a touch of Gilded Age history, a whiff of historical scandal, and a pleasant air of joie de vivre. **Pros:** sophisticated yet relaxed; great service; unbeatable location. **Cons:** guest rooms are small; some street noise; rooms near the elevator can be particularly noisy. $ *Rooms from: £285* ⊠ *81 Jermyn St., Mayfair* ☎ *020/7930–2111* ⊕ *www.thecavendish-london.co.uk* ⪢ *230 rooms* ¹⊙¹ *Breakfast* Ⓜ *Piccadilly* ✢ *5:B1.*

$$$
HOTEL
⌖ **Chesterfield Mayfair Hotel.** Deep in the heart of Mayfair, the former town house of the Earl of Chesterfield welcomes guests in wood-and-leather public rooms that match the dark-wood furnishings in the bedrooms—small but like fashion magazine spreads, with bold designer wallpaper or tones of fawn and gray. **Pros:** laid-back atmosphere; attentive service; great afternoon tea. **Cons:** prices rise sharply if you don't get the cheapest rooms; some rooms are tiny; restaurant is very expensive. $ *Rooms from: £260* ⊠ *35 Charles St., Mayfair* ☎ *020/7491–2622, 877/955–1515 in U.S.* ⊕ *www.chesterfieldmayfair.com* ⪢ *107 rooms* ¹⊙¹ *Breakfast* Ⓜ *Green Park* ✢ *1:H6.*

$$$$
HOTEL
FAMILY
Fodor's Choice
★
⌖ **Claridge's.** The well-heeled have been meeting—and eating—at Claridge's for generations, and the tradition continues in the original art deco public spaces of this superglamorous London institution. **Pros:** see-and-be-seen dining and drinking; serious luxury everywhere—this is an old-money hotel; famed history. **Cons:** better pack your designer wardrobe if you want to fit in with the locals; all that luxury means an expensive price tag; to protect the privacy of guests, photographs

are prohibited in some areas. $ *Rooms from: £550* ✉ *Brook St., May-
fair* ☎ *020/7629–8860, 866/599–6991 in U.S.* ⊕ *www.claridges.co.uk*
🛏 *203 rooms* ❄️ *Free Breakfast* Ⓜ *Bond St.* ✛ *1:H4.*

$$$$
HOTEL
FAMILY
Fodor'sChoice
★

🏨 **The Connaught.** A huge favorite of the "we wouldn't dream of staying
anywhere else" monied set since its opening in 1917, the Connaught has
many dazzlingly modern compliments to its famously historic delights.
Pros: legendary hotel; great for star-spotting; Michelin-starred dining.
Cons: history comes at a price; bathrooms are small; the superior king
room is small for the price. $ *Rooms from: £600* ✉ *Carlos Pl., Mayfair*
☎ *020/7499–7070, 866/599–6991 in U.S.* ⊕ *www.the-connaught.co.uk*
🛏 *121 rooms* ❄️ *Free Breakfast* Ⓜ *Bond St.* ✛ *1:H5.*

$$$$
HOTEL
Fodor'sChoice
★

🏨 **The Dorchester.** Few hotels this opulent manage to be as personable as the
Dorchester, which opened in 1939 and boasts a prime Park Lane location
with unparalleled glamour; gold leaf and marble adorn the public spaces,
and guest quarters are awash in English country house–art deco
style. **Pros:** historic luxury in 1930s building; lovely views of Hyde Park;
excellent spa. **Cons:** traditional look is not to all tastes; prices are sky-high;
some rooms are disappointingly small. $ *Rooms from: £592* ✉ *53 Park
La., Mayfair* ☎ *020/7629–8888* ⊕ *www.thedorchester.com* 🛏 *250 rooms*
❄️ *Free Breakfast* Ⓜ *Marble Arch, Hyde Park Corner* ✛ *1:H6.*

$$$$
HOTEL

🏨 **Four Seasons Park Lane.** A racy departure for the Four Seasons, this
hotel has an English clubhouse look with a dose of boudoir. **Pros:**
highly elegant rooms; excellent spa; lovely location next to Hyde Park.
Cons: not for strict traditionalists; haute design comes with high prices;
breakfast is an additional fee. $ *Rooms from: £750* ✉ *Hamilton Pl.,
Park La., Mayfair* ☎ *020/7499–0888* ⊕ *www.fourseasons.com/london*
🛏 *193 rooms* ❄️ *No meals* Ⓜ *Hyde Park Corner* ✛ *1:H6.*

$$$
HOTEL

🏨 **InterContinental London Park Lane.** Overlooking busy Hyde Park Corner
and the grounds of Buckingham Palace (much to the Queen's chagrin,
allegedly), this hotel's luxurious rooms are aimed at high-end business
travelers. **Pros:** great location; feel-like-a-million-dollars service; good
business facilities. **Cons:** no park views with standard rooms; prices
sky-high in midsummer; without the wow factor or history of some
similarly priced Park Lane hotels. $ *Rooms from: £350* ✉ *1 Hamilton
Pl., Park Ln., Mayfair* ☎ *020/7409–3131* ⊕ *parklane.intercontinental.
com* 🛏 *447 rooms* ❄️ *No meals* Ⓜ *Hyde Park Corner* ✛ *1:H6.*

$$$$
HOTEL
Fodor'sChoice
★

🏨 **The Langham.** Hotel pedigrees don't come much greater than this one;
built in 1865, the Langham was *the* original luxury hotel in the city,
all but inventing the very image of what a great London hotel looked
like. **Pros:** beautiful historic building; gorgeous and peaceful pool; great
restaurant and bar. **Cons:** price rises considerably once cheapest rooms
sell out; need to book ahead for the wildly popular Artesian Bar; some
modernized rooms don't share the building's historic charm. $ *Rooms
from: £450* ✉ *1C Portland Pl., Mayfair* ☎ *020/7636–1000* ⊕ *www.
langhamhotels.co.uk* 🛏 *378 rooms* ❄️ *Breakfast* Ⓜ *Oxford Circus*
✛ *2:A4.*

$$$
RENTAL
FAMILY

🏨 **No. 5 Maddox Street.** Just five minutes' walk from Oxford Street, this
is a great option for those who tire of traditional hotels: 12 luxury
suites—some with balconies and working fireplaces—filled with everything you could ever need, including a handy kitchen. **Pros:** cozy and

15

private; room service will deliver meals from local restaurants; guests have access to nearby health club. **Cons:** no elevator; no communal lobby can make you feel isolated; central location can (predictably) be noisy. $ *Rooms from: £311* ✉ *5 Maddox St., Mayfair* ☎ *020/7647–0200* ⊕ *www.living-rooms.co.uk/hotel/no5maddoxstreet* ⇆ *12 suites* ⦿⊙⦿ *No meals* Ⓜ *Oxford Circus* ✛ *3:A5.*

$$$
HOTEL
FAMILY

The Piccadilly London West End. This hotel couldn't be better situated for theater lovers; it's right in the famed West End district with three such venues within sight of the front door alone. **Pros:** unbeatable location; some thoughtful extras; attentive staff. **Cons:** noise is unavoidable; you're paying for the location rather than the amenities, and it shows; rooms are compact. $ *Rooms from: £275* ✉ *65–73 Shaftesbury Ave., Mayfair* ☎ *020/7871–6000, 877/898–1586 in U.S.* ⊕ *www.piccadillypremierlondon.co.uk* ⇆ *67 rooms* ⦿⊙⦿ *Breakfast* Ⓜ *Piccadilly Circus* ✛ *3:D5.*

$$
HOTEL

Radisson Blu Edwardian Berkshire Hotel. In a dangerously good location for shopaholics, with Oxford Street on the doorstep, the pleasant and well-run Radisson Berkshire offers a similar level of service to some of the more established hotels in the neighborhood, at a lower rate. **Pros:** great central location; good restaurant; free Wi-Fi. **Cons:** walk-in rate is still quite expensive; small bedrooms; some rooms suffer from street noise. $ *Rooms from: £239* ✉ *350 Oxford St., Mayfair* ☎ *020/7629–7474, 0800/374–411 toll-free in U.K., 800/333–3333 toll-free in U.S.* ⊕ *www.radissonblu-edwardian.com* ⇆ *149 rooms* ⦿⊙⦿ *Breakfast* Ⓜ *Bond St., Oxford Circus* ✛ *1:H4.*

$$
B&B/INN

22 York Street. This lovely Georgian town house has a cozy family feel, with polished pine floors and fetching antiques decorating the homey, individually furnished guest rooms. **Pros:** live out your London town-house fantasy; flexible check-in times; good location for shoppers. **Cons:** if you take away the great location, you're paying a lot for a B&B; not everyone enjoys socializing with strangers over breakfast; some guests won't enjoy the lack of anonymity. $ *Rooms from: £150* ✉ *22 York St., Mayfair* ☎ *020/7224–2990* ⊕ *www.22yorkstreet.co.uk* ⇆ *10 rooms* ⦿⊙⦿ *Free Breakfast* Ⓜ *Baker St.* ✛ *1:G3.*

MARYLEBONE

$$$
HOTEL
Fodor's Choice
★

Dorset Square Hotel. This fashionable boutique hotel occupies a charming old town house in one of London's most upscale neighborhoods. **Pros:** ideal location; lovely design; good afternoon tea. **Cons:** some rooms are small; no bathtub in some rooms; no gym. $ *Rooms from: £252* ✉ *39 Dorset Sq., Marylebone* ☎ *020/7723–7874* ⊕ *www.firmdalehotels.com* ⇆ *38 rooms* ⦿⊙⦿ *No meals* Ⓜ *Baker St.* ✛ *1:F2.*

$$$
HOTEL

Hyatt Regency London—The Churchill. Even though it's one of London's largest hotels, the Churchill is always abuzz with guests smiling at the perfection they find here, including warmly personalized service and calmly alluring guest rooms. **Pros:** comfortable and stylish; great dining and drinking, including a bottomless brunch; up to three can stay in one room. **Cons:** feels more geared to business than leisure travelers; lots of renovation; prices are steep. $ *Rooms from: £369* ✉ *30 Portman Sq., Marylebone* ☎ *020/7486–5800* ⊕ *londonchurchill.regency.hyatt.com* ⇆ *440 rooms* ⦿⊙⦿ *Breakfast* Ⓜ *Marble Arch* ✛ *1:G4.*

$$ **Park Plaza Sherlock Holmes Hotel.** Named in honor of the fictional
HOTEL detective who had his home on Baker Street, rooms here have a mas-
culine edge with lots of earth tones and pinstripe sheets (along with
hypermodern bathrooms stocked with fluffy bathrobes). **Pros:** nicely
decorated; international electrical outlets, including those that work
with American equipment; famous literary location. **Cons:** have to walk
through the bar to get to reception; not well soundproofed from the
noisy street; rooms on the small side. $ *Rooms from: £220 ✉ 108 Baker
St., Marylebone ☎ 0333/400–6136 ⊕ www.parkplazasherlockholmes.
com ➟ 119 rooms ⦿ Breakfast Ⓜ Baker St. ✛ 1:G3.*

$$ **The Sumner.** You can feel yourself relaxing the minute you enter this
HOTEL elegant Georgian town house. **Pros:** excellent location for shopping;
small enough that the staff know your name; attractive conservatory
and garden. **Cons:** services are limited; high prices; most rooms have
small bathrooms. $ *Rooms from: £180 ✉ 54 Upper Berkley St., Marble
Arch, Marylebone ☎ 020/7723–2244 ⊕ www.thesumner.com ➟ 20
rooms ⦿ Breakfast Ⓜ Marble Arch ✛ 1:F4.*

$$$ **Zetter Townhouse Marylebone.** No matter how hip the crowd here gets,
HOTEL the clientele is never likely to distract from the sumptuous decor of
Fodor's Choice this boutique hotel that is equal parts Tudor-style and Georgian flair,
★ with a pinch of steampunk for good measure. **Pros:** beautiful interior
design; cocktail bar that makes repeat visits a must; gorgeous rooms
that feel like you're on a movie set. **Cons:** atmosphere can feel too
trendy at times; prices are high considering the amenities; neighborhood
can be too quiet on weekends. $ *Rooms from: £290 ✉ 28-30 Seymour
St., Marylebone ☎ 020/7324–4544 ⊕ www.thezettertownhouse.com/
marylebone ➟ 24 rooms ⦿ No meals Ⓜ Marylebone ✛ 1:F4.*

SOHO AND COVENT GARDEN

SOHO

$$$ **Dean Street Townhouse.** Discreet and unpretentious—and right in the
HOTEL heart of Soho—this oh-so-stylish place has a bohemian vibe and an
Fodor's Choice excellent Modern British restaurant, hung with pieces by renowned
★ artists like Peter Blake and Tracy Emin. **Pros:** ultracool vibe; resembles
an upper-class pied-à-terre; great location in the heart of Soho. **Cons:**
some rooms are extremely small; rooms at the front of the building
can be noisy, especially on weekends; the crowd can often feel cooler-
than-thou. $ *Rooms from: £315 ✉ 69–71 Dean St., Soho ☎ 020/7434–
1775 ⊕ www.deanstreettownhouse.com ➟ 39 rooms ⦿ Free Breakfast
Ⓜ Leicester Sq., Tottenham Court Rd. ✛ 3:D5.*

$$$$ **Ham Yard Hotel.** Luxurious, playful, and riotously good fun, the
HOTEL Ham Yard Hotel is another property from the stable of London hotel
FAMILY designer extraordinaire, Kit Kemp. **Pros:** great design; excellent ser-
Fodor's Choice vice; fun facilities, including a bowling alley. **Cons:** rates can get very
★ pricey; some will find the scene at the hotel a little too trendy; with a
cinema, bowling alley, and spa on-site, you might not leave the hotel.
$ *Rooms from: £400 ✉ 1 Ham Yard, Soho ☎ 020/3642–2000 ⊕ www.
firmdalehotels.com/hotels/london/ham-yard-hotel ➟ 91 rooms ⦿ No
meals Ⓜ Piccadilly Circus ✛ 3:C6.*

15

$$$
HOTEL
Fodor's Choice
★

Hazlitt's. This disarmingly friendly place, full of personality, robust antiques, and claw-foot tubs, occupies three connected early 18th-century houses, one of which was the last home of essayist William Hazlitt (1778–1830). **Pros:** great for lovers of art and antiques; historic atmosphere with lots of small sitting rooms and wooden staircases; truly beautiful and relaxed. **Cons:** no in-house restaurant; breakfast costs extra; no elevators. ⑤ *Rooms from: £251* ⊠ *6 Frith St., Soho* ☎ *020/7434–1771* ⊕ *www.hazlittshotel.com* ⤳ *30 rooms* ⦿*No meals* Ⓜ *Tottenham Court Rd.* ✛ *3:D4.*

$$$
HOTEL

The Soho Hotel. This supertrendy hotel personifies Soho's enduring hipness with its artsy, urban chic vibe. **Pros:** small and sophisticated; excellent service; great restaurant. **Cons:** bar can be crowded and noisy on weeknights; some lower-level rooms lack the amenities of pricier rooms; expensive for a boutique hotel. ⑤ *Rooms from: £336* ⊠ *4 Richmond Mews, off Dean St., Soho* ☎ *020/7559–3000* ⊕ *www.firmdalehotels.com/hotels/london/the-soho-hotel* ⤳ *96 rooms* ⦿*Breakfast* Ⓜ *Tottenham Court Rd.* ✛ *3:C4.*

COVENT GARDEN

$$$
HOTEL
Fodor's Choice
★

Covent Garden Hotel. It's little wonder this is now the London home-away-from-home for off-duty celebrities, actors, and style mavens, with its Covent Garden location and guest rooms that are design-magazine stylish, using mix-and-match couture fabrics to stunning effect. **Pros:** great for star-spotting; supertrendy; basement cinema for movie buffs. **Cons:** you can feel you don't matter if you're not famous; location in Covent Garden can be a bit boisterous; only some rooms come with balcony views. ⑤ *Rooms from: £315* ⊠ *10 Monmouth St., Covent Garden* ☎ *020/7806–1000, 800/553–6674 in U.S.* ⊕ *www.firmdalehotels.com/hotels/london/covent-garden-hotel* ⤳ *58 rooms* ⦿*No meals* Ⓜ *Covent Garden* ✛ *3:E4.*

$$
HOTEL
Fodor's Choice
★

Henrietta Hotel. The stylish and hip will fit right in at this beautifully refined Covent Garden property. **Pros:** amazing bar and restaurant; beautiful boutique interiors; great location in the heart of Covent Garden. **Cons:** hip atmosphere and slick interiors won't be for everyone; standard rooms are on the small side; street noise can be a minor irritant. ⑤ *Rooms from: £213* ⊠ *14-15 Henrietta St., Covent Garden* ☎ *020/3794–5313* ⊕ *www.henriettahotel.com* ⤳ *18 rooms* ⦿*No meals* Ⓜ *Covent Garden* ✛ *3:F6.*

$$$
HOTEL
Fodor's Choice
★

ME London. A shiny fortress of luxury, the ME brings a splash of modern cool to a rather stuffy patch of the Strand. **Pros:** sleek and fashionable; full of high-tech comforts; stunning views from rooftop bar. **Cons:** design can sometimes verge on form over function; very small closets and in-room storage areas; the rooftop bar can get uncomfortably busy. ⑤ *Rooms from: £280* ⊠ *336 The Strand, Covent Garden* ☎ *0808/234–1953* ⊕ *www.melia.com* ⤳ *157 rooms* ⦿*Free Breakfast* Ⓜ *Covent Garden* ✛ *3:G5.*

$$$
HOTEL

One Aldwych. An Edwardian building, with an artsy lobby and understated blend of contemporary and classic, provides pure modern luxury in a great location for theaters and shopping. **Pros:** understated luxury; ultracool atmosphere; good deals and special offers, including big advance-booking discounts. **Cons:** all this luxury doesn't come cheap;

fashionable ambience is not always relaxing; rooms are relatively plain. $ *Rooms from: £378* ✉ *1 Aldwych, Covent Garden* ☎ *020/7300–1000* ⊕ *www.onealdwych.co.uk* ⇆ *105 rooms* ♚ *Breakfast* Ⓜ *Charing Cross, Covent Garden* ✣ *3:G5.*

$$$$ 🛏 **The Savoy.** One of London's most iconic hotels maintains its status at
HOTEL the top with winning attributes of impeccable service, stunning decor,
Fodor's Choice and a desirable location on the Strand. **Pros:** one of the top hotels in
★ Europe; iconic pedigree; Thames-side location. **Cons:** everything comes
with a price tag; street noise is surprisingly problematic, particularly
on lower floors; street can be too busy for some. $ *Rooms from: £504*
✉ *The Strand, Covent Garden* ☎ *020/7836–4343, 800/257–7544 in
U.S.* ⊕ *www.fairmont.com/savoy-london* ⇆ *268 rooms* ♚ *Free Break-
fast* Ⓜ *Covent Garden, Charing Cross* ✣ *3:G5.*

$$ 🛏 **Victory House.** Part of Sofitel's swankier, trendier MGallery brand, Vic-
HOTEL troy House brings a touch of Hollywood glamour to Leicester Square,
the home of movie premieres. **Pros:** great views of Leicester Square from
some rooms; complimentary smart phone for guests' use during their
stay; excellent location in the heart of the West End. **Cons:** noise from
Leicester Square can be a problem; low showers can be a struggle for
those over 6 feet; rates soar during high season. $ *Rooms from: £223*
✉ *14 Leicester Pl., West End* ☎ *0843/178–7190* ⊕ *www.victoryhousel-
ondon.com* ⇆ *86 rooms* ♚ *No meals* Ⓜ *Leicester Sq.* ✣ *3:D5.*

BLOOMSBURY, HOLBORN, AND FITZROVIA

BLOOMSBURY

$ 🛏 **Celtic Hotel.** This is a solid, dependable budget choice in an otherwise
HOTEL expensive district (close to the West End and British Museum), where
you'll be hard-pressed to find a better price. **Pros:** free Wi-Fi; good
location; bargain rates. **Cons:** no-frills approach means few extras; no
elevator; not all rooms have private bathrooms. $ *Rooms from: £105*
✉ *61–63 Guilford St., Bloomsbury* ☎ *020/7837–6737* ⊕ *www.stmarga-
retshotel.co.uk* ⇆ *35 rooms* ♚ *Breakfast* Ⓜ *Russell Sq.* ✣ *3:F1.*

$$$ 🛏 **Charlotte Street Hotel.** Tradition and modern flair are fused together in
HOTEL this superstylish retreat, a short walk from Oxford Street. **Pros:** elegant
Fodor's Choice and luxurious; great attention to detail; decent chance at finding a good
★ deal. **Cons:** the popular bar can be noisy; reservations essential for
the restaurant; some rooms are small considering the price. $ *Rooms
from: £306* ✉ *15–17 Charlotte St., Bloomsbury* ☎ *020/7806–2000,
800/553–6674 in U.S.* ⊕ *www.firmdalehotels.com* ⇆ *52 rooms* ♚ *No
meals* Ⓜ *Goodge St.* ✣ *3:C2.*

$ 🛏 **Grange Blooms Hotel.** In this white, Georgian town house hotel, just
HOTEL around the corner from the British Museum, traditionally styled rooms
are not too tiny by London standards, and those in the back look out
onto a leafy green garden. **Pros:** great location; overall good value;
excellent rates if you book early through the website. **Cons:** guests can
be bumped to sister hotel if fully booked; no air-conditioning; street
noise in some rooms. $ *Rooms from: £96* ✉ *7 Montague St., Blooms-
bury* ☎ *020/7323–1717, 800/2247–2643* ⊕ *www.grangehotels.com*
⇆ *27 rooms* ♚ *Some meals* Ⓜ *Russell Sq.* ✣ *3:F2.*

15

$$ ⌑ **Harlingford Hotel.** The most contemporary of the hotels around
HOTEL Bloomsbury's Cartwright Gardens offers sleek, quiet, and comfortable
bedrooms and perfectly appointed public rooms. **Pros:** good location;
friendly staff; private garden. **Cons:** rooms are small; no air-condition-
ing; no elevator. ⑤ *Rooms from: £140* ✉ *61–63 Cartwright Gardens,
Bloomsbury* ☎ *020/7387–1551* ⊕ *www.harlingfordhotel.com* ⇗ *43
rooms* ⦿ *Free Breakfast* Ⓜ *Russell Sq.* ✛ *2:C3.*

$ ⌑ **Jesmond Hotel.** This friendly little hotel is great value given the loca-
B&B/INN tion: a short walk from the British Museum in one direction, and Soho
and Covent Garden in the other. **Pros:** great location; friendly staff;
free Wi-Fi. **Cons:** some rooms are very small; nearly half have shared
bathrooms; decor is inoffensive but uninspiring. ⑤ *Rooms from: £90*
✉ *63 Gower St., Bloomsbury* ☎ *020/7636–3199* ⊕ *www.jesmondhotel.
org.uk* ⇗ *15 rooms* ⦿ *Breakfast* Ⓜ *Goodge St., Euston Sq., Warren
St., Russell Sq.* ✛ *3:C1.*

$$ ⌑ **Megaro.** Directly across the street from St. Pancras International Sta-
HOTEL tion, the snazzy, well-designed, modern rooms here surround guests
with startlingly contemporary style and amenities that include powerful
showers and espresso machines. **Pros:** comfortable beds; great location
for Eurostar travelers; short hop on Tube to city center. **Cons:** neighborhood isn't interesting; standard rooms are small; interiors may be a
bit stark for some. ⑤ *Rooms from: £210* ✉ *Belgrove St., King's Cross*
☎ *020/7843–2222* ⊕ *www.hotelmegaro.co.uk* ⇗ *57 rooms* ⦿ *Free
Breakfast* Ⓜ *King's Cross St. Pancras* ✛ *2:C2.*

$ ⌑ **The Ridgemount Hotel.** Mere blocks away from the British Museum and
B&B/INN London's West End theaters, this handsomely fronted guesthouse has
clean, neat, and plainly decorated rooms at bargain rates. **Pros:** good
location for theaters and museum; helpful staff; family rooms (accom-
modating up to five) are excellent value. **Cons:** decoration is basic; no
elevator; cheapest rooms have shared bathrooms. ⑤ *Rooms from: £98*
✉ *67 Gower St., Bloomsbury* ☎ *020/7636–1141* ⊕ *www.ridgemoun-
thotel.co.uk* ⇗ *32 rooms* ⦿ *Breakfast* Ⓜ *Goodge St.* ✛ *3:D1.*

$$$ ⌑ **St. Pancras Renaissance.** This stunningly restored Victorian land-
HOTEL mark—replete with gingerbread turrets and castlelike ornaments—
Fodor's Choice started as a love letter to the golden age of railways, and now it's one
★ of London's most sophisticated places to stay. **Pros:** unique and beauti-
ful; faultless service; close to the train station. **Cons:** very crowded bar
and restaurant; streets outside are busy 24/7; some cheaper rooms don't
include free Wi-Fi. ⑤ *Rooms from: £255* ✉ *Euston Rd., King's Cross*
☎ *020/7841–3540* ⊕ *www.marriott.com/hotels/travel/lonpr-st-pancras-
renaissance-hotel-london* ⇗ *245 rooms* ⦿ *Free Breakfast* Ⓜ *King's
Cross St. Pancras. National Rail: Kings Cross, St. Pancras* ✛ *2:C2.*

HOLBORN

$$$$ ⌑ **Rosewood London.** So striking it was featured in the movie *Howards
HOTEL End*, this landmark structure (built by the Pearl Assurance Company in
1914) now houses a beautiful hotel with a clubby atmosphere, subtly
elegant India Jane fabrics, and huge comfortable beds. **Pros:** gorgeous
romantic space; excellent restaurant; great spa. **Cons:** luxury comes at a
price; the area can be quiet on weekends; the rooms can't quite match the
splendor of the public areas. ⑤ *Rooms from: £450* ✉ *252 High Holborn,*

Holborn ☎ 020/7781–8888, 888/767–3966 in U.S. ⊕ www.rosewoodho-
tels.com/en/london ⤳ 306 rooms ⍥ Free Breakfast Ⓜ Holborn ✛ 3:G3.

$$ 🖾 **SACO Holborn.** Down a quiet backstreet, a 10-minute walk from
RENTAL the British Museum, these serviced apartments are spacious, modern,
FAMILY and extremely well equipped, including a kitchen with dishwasher
and washing machine. **Pros:** more independence than hotels; pleas-
ant and spacious accommodations; on-site parking. **Cons:** exterior is
dated; responsible for your own dining; the area is empty on week-
ends. 🅢 Rooms from: £250 ✉ Spens House, 72–84 Lamb's Conduit
St., Holborn ☎ 0330/202–0505 ⊕ www.sacoapartments.co.uk ⤳ 32
apartments ⍥ No meals Ⓜ Russell Sq. ✛ 3:G1.

FITZROVIA

$$$ 🖾 **The London Edition.** Style and image are the draw at the London Edi-
HOTEL tion Hotel, where Michelin-starred chefs and hip bars complement the
Fodor's Choice boutique property's sleek, contemporary design. **Pros:** very trendy; great
★ bars; beautifully designed bedrooms. **Cons:** rooms may feel small to
some; lobby can get crowded with trendsetters descending upon the bars
and nightclub; can at times feel more like an events space than a hotel.
🅢 Rooms from: £358 ✉ 10 Berners St., Fitzrovia ☎ 020/7781–0000
⊕ edition-hotels.marriott.com/london ⤳ 173 rooms ⍥ Free Breakfast
Ⓜ Oxford Circus ✛ 3:C3.

$$$ 🖾 **Sanderson Hotel.** At this fashionable and surreal urban spa in a con-
HOTEL verted 1950s textile factory, the lobby looks like a design museum;
bedrooms have sleigh beds and a mix of over-the-top Louis XV and
postmodern furnishings. **Pros:** excellent design; your every whim grati-
fied; unique afternoon tea. **Cons:** glass walls and sheer curtains are
all that separate the bathroom in some rooms; bar and restaurant
are so exclusive it's hard to get in; you need to book far in advance
to get lower rates. 🅢 Rooms from: £270 ✉ 50 Berners St., Fitzrovia
☎ 020/7300–1400 ⊕ www.sandersonlondon.com ⤳ 150 rooms ⍥ No
meals Ⓜ Oxford Circus, Tottenham Court Rd. ✛ 3:B3.

THE CITY

$$ 🖾 **Apex City of London.** At this sleek modern branch of the small Apex
HOTEL chain near the Tower of London, bedrooms are reasonably spacious,
with contemporary color schemes, 40-inch flat screen TVs, and little
sofas. **Pros:** great location; helpful staff; good advance-booking discounts. **Cons:** geared more to business than leisure travelers; price can
rise sharply during busy times; the neighborhood is hardly the most
buzzing on weekends. 🅢 Rooms from: £155 ✉ 1 Seething La., City
of London ☎ 020/7702–2020 ⊕ www.apexhotels.co.uk ⤳ 209 rooms
⍥ Breakfast Ⓜ Tower Hill ✛ 2:G2.

$$ 🖾 **Crowne Plaza London—The City.** Don't let the hotel's all-business
HOTEL appearance put you off: it's a polished operation, with stylish mini-
malist rooms, just steps from the Blackfriars Tube and train station
in one direction and bustling Fleet Street in the other. **Pros:** good rates
available with advance booking; devices in each room that allow access
to streaming services; two excellent dining options. **Cons:** neighbor-
hood is superbusy during the day and empty at night; breakfast not

15

included in the price of rooms; short Tube ride from main neighborhood sights. $ *Rooms from: £150* ✉ *19 New Bridge St., City of London* ☎ *0871/942–9190* ⊕ *www.cplondoncityhotel.co.uk* ⇲ *204 rooms* ❢⃝| *No meals* Ⓜ *Blackfriars* ✛ *2:F6.*

$$
HOTEL

⬚⃢ **Grange City Hotel.** With an eye on business, this sleek City hotel has everything the workaholic needs to feel right at home: chic bedrooms subtly decorated, modern furnishings, and plenty of space (by London standards). **Pros:** good-sized rooms; rates can drop considerably on weekends; women-friendly rooms are great for lone female travelers. **Cons:** a bit off the tourist track; some rooms overlook train platform; prices can soar midweek. $ *Rooms from: £167* ✉ *8–14 Cooper's Row, City of London* ☎ *020/7863–3700* ⊕ *www.grangehotels.com* ⇲ *307 rooms* ❢⃝| *Breakfast* Ⓜ *Tower Hill, Aldgate, Monument* ✛ *2:G2.*

$$
HOTEL
Fodor'sChoice
★

⬚⃢ **The Ned.** Bursting with eye-catching art deco design and achingly hip interiors, the Ned is as close to the glamour of the 1920s Jazz Age as you'll find in contemporary London. **Pros:** amazing variety of bars and restaurants, all of high quality; rooftop pool with views of St. Paul's Cathedral; beautiful interiors in all rooms. **Cons:** location in The City means public spaces get very busy after work; neighborhood is deserted on weekends; also doubles as a private members' clubs, so the vibe can get snooty. $ *Rooms from: £180* ✉ *27 Poultry, City of London* ☎ *020/3828–2000* ⊕ *www.thened.com* ⇲ *252 rooms* ❢⃝| *Free Breakfast* Ⓜ *Bank* ✛ *2:H5.*

$$
HOTEL
Fodor'sChoice
★

⬚⃢ **The Rookery.** A stylish period masterpiece in the heart of laid-back Clerkenwell, the Rookery is a luxury boutique hotel with a hefty dollop of *Downton Abbey* charm. **Pros:** helpful staff; free Wi-Fi; good deals in the off-season. **Cons:** breakfast costs extra; Tube ride to tourist sites; no restaurant in the hotel. $ *Rooms from: £210* ✉ *12 Peter's La., at Cowcross St., City of London* ☎ *020/7336–0931* ⊕ *www.rookeryhotel. com* ⇲ *33 rooms* ❢⃝| *No meals* Ⓜ *Farringdon* ✛ *2:F4.*

$$
HOTEL

⬚⃢ **Threadneedles Hotel.** The elaborate building housing this grand hotel in the financial district is a former bank, and the vast old banking hall—beautifully adapted as the lobby, with luxurious marble and mahogany panels—really sets the scene. **Pros:** lap of luxury; excellent service; a good variety of drinking and dining options. **Cons:** a bit stuffy for some tastes; can be at least three times more expensive weekdays; neighborhood is quiet at night. $ *Rooms from: £185* ✉ *5 Threadneedle St., City of London* ☎ *020/7657–8080* ⊕ *www.hotelthreadneedles.co.uk* ⇲ *74 rooms* ❢⃝| *Breakfast* Ⓜ *Bank* ✛ *2:G2.*

$$
HOTEL
Fodor'sChoice
★

⬚⃢ **The Zetter.** The five-story atrium, art deco staircase, and slick European restaurant hint at the delights to come in this converted warehouse—a breath of fresh air with its playful color schemes, elegant wallpapers, and wonderful views of The City from the higher floors. **Pros:** huge amounts of character; big rooms; free Wi-Fi. **Cons:** rooms with good views cost more; the contemporary style won't appeal to everyone; the property's best bar is across the street at the Zetter Townhouse. $ *Rooms from: £221* ✉ *86–88 Clerkenwell Rd., Clerkenwell* ☎ *020/7324–4444* ⊕ *www.thezetter.com* ⇲ *59 rooms* ❢⃝| *Free Breakfast* Ⓜ *Farringdon* ✛ *3:H1.*

EAST LONDON

$$ **Ace Hotel London Shoreditch.** The first European outlet of the superhip
HOTEL Ace hotel chain fits right into the scenery in achingly cool Shoreditch,
surrounded by galleries and on-trend boutiques every bit as style con-
scious as its own creatively minimalist interiors. **Pros:** extremely fash-
ionable; large and comfortable bedrooms; great bar. **Cons:** not everyone
will enjoy being surrounded by hipsters; street noise can be a prob-
lem; frustrating online booking system. ⑤ *Rooms from: £175 ⊠ 100
Shoreditch High St., Shoreditch* ☎ *020/7613–9800* ⊕ *www.acehotel.
com* ⇆ *258 rooms* ⎟⊙⎟ *Free Breakfast* Ⓜ *Shoreditch High St.* ✛ *2:G1.*

$$ **Andaz.** Swanky and upscale, this hotel sports a modern mascu-
HOTEL line design, and novel check-in procedure—instead of standing at
a desk, guests sit in a lounge while a staff member with a tablet
takes their information. **Pros:** nice attention to detail; no standing
in line to check in; "healthy minibars" are stocked with nuts, fruit,
and yogurt. **Cons:** sparse interior design is not for all; rates rise sig-
nificantly for midweek stays; busy, sometimes hectic neighborhood.
⑤ *Rooms from: £175 ⊠ 40 Liverpool St., East End* ☎ *020/7961–
1234, 800/492–8804 in U.S.* ⊕ *www.andaz.hyatt.com* ⇆ *269 rooms*
⎟⊙⎟ *Free Breakfast* Ⓜ *Liverpool St.* ✛ *2:G2.*

$$ **Cable Street Inn.** Wonderful modern art lines the walls of this former
B&B/INN Victorian pub a mile east of the Tower of London, which has been
Fodor's Choice beautifully restored and converted into a modern B&B. **Pros:** true one-
★ of-a-kind place; beautiful art; wonderful host. **Cons:** 20-minute journey
by DLR then Tube to the center; historic nature of the building makes
it unsuitable for those with mobility problems; with only three rooms,
availability can be low. ⑤ *Rooms from: £130 ⊠ 232 Cable St., East End*
☎ *020/7790–4019* ⊕ *www.cablestreetinn.co.uk* ⇆ *3 rooms* ⎟⊙⎟ *Break-
fast* Ⓜ *DLR: Shadwell* ✛ *2:H5.*

$$ **Courthouse Hotel – Shoreditch.** Housed within a beautifully restored
HOTEL former courthouse, this hip Shoreditch hotel contributes its own con-
temporary flair to the grand architectural style of the original building, with chic rooms that provide the perfect base to explore the
surrounding trendy neighborhood. **Pros:** great views over neighboring rooftops from the terrace; lively bar; excellent facilities including
cinema and bowling alley. **Cons:** not all rooms are located in the
historic former courthouse; a 20-minute Tube ride into central London; the size and scope of the public spaces can lead to some areas
feeling deserted. ⑤ *Rooms from: £175 ⊠ 335–337 Old St., Shoreditch*
☎ *020/3310–5555* ⊕ *www.shoreditch.courthouse-hotel.com* ⇆ *128
rooms* ⎟⊙⎟ *Breakfast* Ⓜ *Old Street* ✛ *2:G1.*

$$ **The Curtain.** For a classic hip Hoxton stay, it would only be right to
HOTEL choose a hotel crammed with exposed brick, heavy doses of industrial
chic, and stylish loft living appeal—a combination that The Curtain
presents from its location on the border of Shoreditch and The City.
Pros: rooftop pool great for summertime hangs; rooms feel spacious and
some come with terraces with great views; very trendy basement bar
and restaurant. **Cons:** bar and restaurant areas can get overcrowded;
some guests will find the industrial style a turnoff; area is renowned
for nightlife so don't expect quiet nights. ⑤ *Rooms from: £167 ⊠ 45*

15

Curtain Rd., Shoreditch ☎ *020/3146–4545* ⊕ *www.thecurtain.com* ⤹ *120 rooms* ⦿ *No meals* Ⓜ *Shoreditch High Street* ✛ *2:G1.*

$$
HOTEL
Fodor'sChoice
★

⬚ **The Hoxton Shoreditch.** The design throughout this trendy East London lodging is contemporary—but not so modern as to be absurd; in keeping with a claim to combine a country-lodge lifestyle with true urban living, a fire crackles in the lobby. **Pros:** cool vibe; neighborhood known for funky galleries and boutiques; huge weekend discounts. **Cons:** price skyrockets during the week; away from major tourist sights; cheapest rooms are called "shoeboxes" for a reason. ⑤ *Rooms from: £149* ⊠ *81 Great Eastern St., East End* ☎ *020/7550–1000* ⊕ *www.thehoxton.com/london/shoreditch/ hotels* ⤹ *210 rooms* ⦿ *Free Breakfast* Ⓜ *Shoreditch High St.* ✛ *2:G1.*

$
HOTEL

⬚ **Qbic London City.** A contrast to the superexpensive business hotels that proliferate in this part of the East End on the edge of The City, the Qbic is a modern and surprisingly affordable option in a trendy corner of town. **Pros:** free bike rentals; great value for money; environmentally friendly. **Cons:** a bit out of the way; not everyone will love the style; cheapest rooms have no windows. ⑤ *Rooms from: £88* ⊠ *42 Adler St., East End* ☎ *020/3021–1440* ⊕ *www.qbichotels.com* ⤹ *171 rooms* ⦿ *Breakfast* Ⓜ *Aldgate East* ✛ *2:H2.*

$$
HOTEL

⬚ **Town Hall Hotel and Apartments.** An art deco town hall, abandoned in the early 1980s and turned into a chic hotel 30 years later, is now a lively and stylish place, with the best of the building's elegant original features intact. **Pros:** beautifully designed; lovely staff; big discounts on weekends. **Cons:** the area is far from the major sights; a 15-minute Tube ride from central London; some rooms choose style over function. ⑤ *Rooms from: £185* ⊠ *Patriot Sq., Bethnal Green, East End* ☎ *020/7871–0460* ⊕ *www.townhallhotel.com* ⤹ *90 rooms* ⦿ *Free Breakfast* Ⓜ *Bethnal Green* ✛ *2:H1.*

SOUTH OF THE THAMES

$
HOTEL
Fodor'sChoice
★

⬚ **Church Street Hotel.** Like rays of sunshine in gritty south London, the rooms at this Camberwell hotel are decorated in rich bold tones, and authentic Central American touches like elaborately painted crucifixes, tiles handmade in Guadalajara, and homemade iron bed frames. **Pros:** unique and arty; great breakfasts; closer to central London than it might appear. **Cons:** would suit adventurous young people more than families; a mile from a Tube station (though bus connections are handier); some rooms have shared bathrooms. ⑤ *Rooms from: £90* ⊠ *29–33 Camberwell Church St., Camberwell, South East London* ☎ *020/7703–5984* ⊕ *www. churchstreethotel.com* ⤹ *31 rooms* ⦿ *Free Breakfast* Ⓜ *Oval St.* ✛ *5:H6.*

$
HOTEL

⬚ **CitizenM London Bankside.** High-concept, high-tech, and supertrendy, the CitizenM chain has a unique selling point—nearly everything at the hotel is self-service, and that includes check-in and breakfast. **Pros:** great budget concept; stylish and modern; no waiting in line for checkout. **Cons:** only really qualifies as "budget" on certain nights (price is higher midweek); might be too much technology for some; rooms are compact. ⑤ *Rooms from: £112* ⊠ *20 Lavington St., Bankside* ☎ *020/3519–1680* ⊕ *www.citizenm.com/destinations/london/london-bankside-hotel* ⤹ *192 rooms* ⦿ *No meals* Ⓜ *Southwark* ✛ *5:G1.*

$$ ⊡ **The LaLit London.** A stone's throw from City Hall and just down the
HOTEL   road from Tower Bridge, this luxurious hotel plays on the building's for-
mer incarnation as a historic grammar school to create a unique board-
ing experience where rooms are known as "classrooms" and meeting
spaces as "laboratories". **Pros:** set in a beautiful historic building; close
to the Tower of London and the South Bank; complimentary minibar in
all rooms. **Cons:** basic rooms are much smaller than their more expen-
sive counterparts; neighborhood a bit slow on weekends; the junction
outside can get noisy. ⑤ *Rooms from: £220* ⊠ *181 Tooley St., London
Bridge* ☎ *020/3765–0000* ⊕ *www.thelalit.com/the-lalit-london* ➴ *70
rooms* ❍ *Breakfast* Ⓜ *London Bridge* ✛ *5:H2.*

$$ ⊡ **London Bridge Hotel.** Steps away from the London Bridge rail and
HOTEL   Tube stations, and handy for the South Bank, this thoroughly modern
stylish hotel is popular with business travelers, but leisure travelers find
it just as appealing. **Pros:** good location for visiting South Bank attractions; free Wi-Fi; good deals available online in the off-season. **Cons:**
small bedrooms; prices rise by £100 or more midweek; area is filled
with crowds on evenings and weekends. ⑤ *Rooms from: £190* ⊠ *8–18
London Bridge St., Southwark* ☎ *020/7855–2200* ⊕ *www.london-
bridgehotel.com* ➴ *141 rooms* ❍ *Breakfast* Ⓜ *London Bridge* ✛ *5:H1.*

$$$ ⊡ **London Marriott Hotel County Hall.** This grand hotel on the Thames
HOTEL   enjoys perhaps the most iconic view in the city—right next door is the
London Eye, and directly across the Thames are the Houses of Parlia-
ment and Big Ben. Until the 1980s this building was the seat of London's
government, and the public areas are suitably grand, full of pedimented
archways, bronze doors, and acres of polished mahogany. **Pros:** handy
for South Bank arts scene, London Eye, and Westminster; great pool;
good weekend discounts. **Cons:** interior design can be overdone for
some tastes; rooms facing the river cost extra; high summer midweek
rates are just ridiculous. ⑤ *Rooms from: £291* ⊠ *London County Hall,
Westminster Bridge Rd., South Bank* ☎ *020/7928–5200, 888/236–2427
in U.S.* ⊕ *www.marriott.com/hotels/travel/lonch-london-marriott-hotel-
county-hall* ➴ *206 rooms* ❍ *Breakfast* Ⓜ *Westminster, Waterloo.
National Rail: Waterloo* ✛ *5:D2.*

$$$ ⊡ **The Mondrian.** A quirky yet sophisticated addition to the burgeoning
HOTEL   South Bank, the Mondrian is a fun callback to the area's docklands
Fodor's Choice   history. **Pros:** excellent bars and restaurants; beautiful river views; short
★   riverside walk to Tate Modern and Shakespeare's Globe. **Cons:** river-
view rooms are pricey (of course); public areas, outside the lobby and
bars, are a little bland; standard rooms are small. ⑤ *Rooms from: £256*
⊠ *Sea Containers House, 20 Upper Ground, Southwark* ☎ *020/3747–
1000* ⊕ *www.morganshotelgroup.com/mondrian/mondrian-london*
➴ *359 rooms* ❍ *Free Breakfast* Ⓜ *Blackfriars, Southwark* ✛ *5:F1.*

$ ⊡ **Premier Travel Inn County Hall.** The small but nicely decorated rooms
HOTEL   at this budget choice share the same County Hall complex as the fan-
FAMILY   cier London Marriott Hotel County Hall, and though it has none of
the spectacular river views, and facilities are more basic, the selling
point is the same convenient location at a fraction of the price. **Pros:**
fantastic location for the South Bank; bargains to be had if you book
in advance; kids (sharing with adults) stay free. **Cons:** limited services;

15

cookie-cutter chain-hotel atmosphere; on a busy road. $ *Rooms from: £108* ⊠ *County Hall, Belvedere Rd., South Bank* ☎ *0871/527–8648* ⊕ *www.premierinn.com* ⌨ *318 rooms* ❤️ *Breakfast* Ⓜ *Westminster, Waterloo. National Rail: Waterloo* ✛ *5:D2.*

$$$$
HOTEL
Fodor's Choice
★

🔆 **The Shangri-La Hotel, at The Shard.** With its floor-to-ceiling windows, the city's highest cocktail bar and infinity pool, and unrivaled views of the London skyline from 1,016 feet above the South Bank of the Thames, the Shangri-La has become one of London's most chic addresses. **Pros:** matchless views; excellent service; superb restaurants and cocktail bar. **Cons:** a design flaw allows some guests to see into their neighbor's rooms at night; decor may feel cold to some; restaurant, bar, and elevator often overcrowded due to popularity of the view. $ *Rooms from: £468* ⊠ *31 St. Thomas St., South Bank* ☎ *0207/234–8000* ⊕ *www.the-shard.com/shangri-la* ⌨ *202 rooms* ❤️ *No meals* Ⓜ *London Bridge Station* ✛ *5:H1.*

KENSINGTON, CHELSEA, KNIGHTSBRIDGE, AND BELGRAVIA

KENSINGTON

$$
HOTEL
Fodor's Choice
★

🔆 **Ampersand.** A sense of style emanates from every surface of this sumptuous hotel in the heart of Kensington, and the playful vintage vibe lends the property a refreshingly down-to-earth feel in a neighborhood that can feel stodgy. **Pros:** flawless design; great service; good restaurant. **Cons:** ground-floor rooms can be noisy; breakfast is not included in the price of a room; the area swarms with tourists visiting the museums on weekends. $ *Rooms from: £216* ⊠ *10 Harrington Rd., Kensington* ☎ *020/7589–5895* ⊕ *www.ampersandhotel.com* ⌨ *111 rooms* ❤️ *No meals* Ⓜ *Gloucester Rd.* ✛ *4:D2.*

$$
HOTEL

🔆 **Ashburn Hotel.** A short walk from Gloucester Road Tube station and within walking distance of Harrods and the Kensington museums, the Ashburn is one of the better "boutique" hotels in this part of town. **Pros:** friendly atmosphere; free Wi-Fi; different turndown gift every night. **Cons:** summer prices sometimes hike the cost; some rooms on the small side; immediate vicinity lacks a little life. $ *Rooms from: £144* ⊠ *111 Cromwell Rd., Kensington* ☎ *020/7244–1999* ⊕ *www.ashburnhotel.co.uk* ⌨ *38 rooms* ❤️ *Free Breakfast* Ⓜ *Gloucester Rd.* ✛ *4:C2.*

$
HOTEL

🔆 **easyHotel South Kensington.** London's original "pod hotel" has tiny rooms with a double bed, private shower room, and little else—each brightly decorated in the easyGroup's trademark orange and white (to match their budget airline easyJet). **Pros:** amazing rates; safe and decent-enough space; good location. **Cons:** not for the claustrophobic—rooms are truly tiny and most have no windows; six floors and no elevator; Wi-Fi is not included in the price of rooms. $ *Rooms from: £42* ⊠ *14 Lexham Gardens, Kensington* ☎ *07951/440134* ⊕ *www.easyhotel.com* ⌨ *34 rooms* ❤️ *No meals* Ⓜ *Gloucester Rd.* ✛ *4:B2.*

$$
HOTEL
Fodor's Choice
★

🔆 **The Gore Hotel.** Just down the road from the Albert Hall, this gorgeous friendly hotel has a luxurious mixture of the comfortable and the extraordinary. **Pros:** gorgeously designed and spacious rooms; outstanding attentive service; air-conditioning in all rooms. **Cons:** some old-fashioned interiors; bar can be noisy; a 10-minute walk to the nearest Tube station. $ *Rooms from: £187* ⊠ *190 Queen's Gate, Kensington*

☎ *020/7584–6601, 888/757–5587 in U.S* ⊕ *www.gorehotel.com* ⤵ *50 rooms* |O| *Breakfast* Ⓜ *Gloucester Rd.* ✛ *4:D1.*

$ 🏨 **Kensington House Hotel.** A short stroll from High Street Kensington
HOTEL and Kensington Gardens, this refurbished 19th-century town house has streamlined contemporary rooms with large windows letting in plenty of light and comfortable beds with luxurious fabrics and soft comforters. **Pros:** attractive design; relaxing setting; free Wi-Fi. **Cons:** rooms are on the small side; bathrooms are minuscule; room decor might feel quite plain to some. ⑤ *Rooms from: £120* ✉ *15–16 Prince of Wales Terr., Kensington* ☎ *020/7937–2345* ⊕ *www.kenhouse.com* ⤵ *41 rooms* |O| *Free Breakfast* Ⓜ *High Street Kensington* ✛ *4:C1.*

$$ 🏨 **London Marriott Kensington.** A big favorite for the business crowd,
HOTEL this pleasant modern outpost of the Marriott megachain is just one of several big-name hotels on busy Cromwell Road. **Pros:** friendly efficient service, good neighborhood; one-minute Tube ride to Kensington museums. **Cons:** business ambience feels impersonal; bedrooms are on the small side; unattractive location on busy Cromwell Road. ⑤ *Rooms from: £164* ✉ *147 Cromwell Rd., Kensington* ☎ *020/7973–1000* ⊕ *www.marriott.com/hotels/travel/lonlm-london-marriott-hotel-kensington* ⤵ *216 rooms* |O| *Some meals* Ⓜ *Earl's Ct., Gloucester Rd.* ✛ *4:B2.*

$$$ 🏨 **The Milestone Hotel.** This pair of intricately decorated Victorian town
HOTEL houses overlooking Kensington Palace and Gardens is an intimate luxu-
Fodor's Choice rious alternative to the city's more famous high-end hotels, offering
★ thoughtful hospitality and sumptuous distinctive rooms full of antiques. **Pros:** beautiful and elegant; big rooms, many with park views; excellent location. **Cons:** actual room rate discounts are rare; luxury and elegance comes at a high price; some guests might find the decor a little over-the-top. ⑤ *Rooms from: £320* ✉ *1 Kensington Ct., Kensington* ☎ *020/7917–1000* ⊕ *www.milestonehotel.com* ⤵ *62 rooms* |O| *Breakfast* Ⓜ *High Street Kensington* ✛ *4:C1.*

$$ 🏨 **Millennium Gloucester.** With a Tube station opposite and Kensington's
HOTEL many attractions nearby, this hotel is both convenient and alluring. **Pros:** great location; elegant design; good deals available if you book in advance. **Cons:** lighting in some bedrooms is a bit too subtle; bathrooms are relatively small; the modestly decorated rooms will appeal more to business travelers. ⑤ *Rooms from: £131* ✉ *4–18 Harrington Gardens, Kensington* ☎ *020/7373–6030* ⊕ *www.millenniumhotels.co.uk* ⤵ *610 rooms* |O| *Breakfast* Ⓜ *Gloucester Rd.* ✛ *4:C2.*

$$ 🏨 **The Nadler Kensington.** Known as an "aparthotel," this creamy white
HOTEL Georgian town house offers a useful compromise between full-service hotel and the freedom of self-catering in the form of comfortable rooms with a stylish modern look and tiny kitchenettes. **Pros:** handy mini-kitchens; free Wi-Fi; televisions can stream content from your tablet or phone. **Cons:** basic rooms are small; breakfast is served to the room only; 15-minute Tube ride to central London. ⑤ *Rooms from: £130* ✉ *25 Courtfield Gardens, South Kensington* ☎ *020/7244–2255* ⊕ *www.nadlerhotels.com* ⤵ *65 rooms* |O| *No meals* Ⓜ *Earl's Ct.* ✛ *4:B3.*

15

$$$
HOTEL
Fodor's Choice
★

⌖ **Number Sixteen.** Rooms at this lovely luxury guesthouse, just around the corner from the Victoria & Albert Museum, look like they come from the pages of *Architectural Digest,* and the delightful garden is an added bonus. **Pros:** just the right level of helpful service; interiors are gorgeous; the afternoon tea is excellent. **Cons:** no restaurant; small elevator; the intimate nature of the small boutique hotel won't appeal to everyone. ⑤ *Rooms from: £288* ✉ *16 Sumner Pl., South Kensington* ☎ *020/7589–5232, 888/559–5508 in U.S.* ⊕ *www.firmdale.com* ⌦ *41 rooms* ⦿ *Free Breakfast* Ⓜ *South Kensington* ✚ *4:D2.*

$$
HOTEL

⌖ **The Pelham Hotel.** One of the first and most stylish of London's famed "boutique" hotels, this still-chic choice is but a short stroll away from the Natural History, Science, and Victoria & Albert museums. **Pros:** great location for museum-hopping; elegant interior design; lovely staff. **Cons:** taller guests will find themselves cursing the top-floor rooms with sloping ceilings; some rooms are on the small side given the price; some suites are only accessible via the stairs. ⑤ *Rooms from: £200* ✉ *15 Cromwell Pl., South Kensington* ☎ *020/7589–8288, 888/757–5587 in U.S.* ⊕ *www.pelhamhotel.co.uk* ⌦ *52 rooms* ⦿ *Free Breakfast* Ⓜ *South Kensington* ✚ *4:D2.*

$
HOTEL

⌖ **The Rockwell.** Despite being on the notoriously traffic-clogged Cromwell Road, this excellent little place is one of the best boutique hotels in this part of London—and windows have good soundproofing. **Pros:** large bedrooms; stylish surroundings; helpful staff. **Cons:** on a busy road; 20-minute Tube ride to central London; street noise is a potential problem. ⑤ *Rooms from: £108* ✉ *181 Cromwell Rd., South Kensington* ☎ *020/7244–2000* ⊕ *www.therockwell.com* ⌦ *40 rooms* ⦿ *Free Breakfast* Ⓜ *Earl's Ct.* ✚ *4:B2.*

CHELSEA

$$
B&B/INN
FAMILY

⌖ **At Home Inn Chelsea.** King's Road and the rest of superrich Chelsea is just a short stroll from this delightfully informal B&B, and you'd be hard-pressed to find a better room in this neighborhood for the price. **Pros:** picturesque top floor terrace; short Tube ride to tourist sites; can be booked as a whole apartment. **Cons:** only accessible via the owners' own apartment's main entrance; few extras; only two guest rooms available. ⑤ *Rooms from: £125* ✉ *5 Park Walk, Chelsea* ☎ *07790/844–008* ⊕ *www.athomeinnchelsea.com* ⌦ *2 rooms* ⦿ *Free Breakfast* Ⓜ *Fulham Broadway* ✚ *4:D4.*

$$$
HOTEL
FAMILY
Fodor's Choice
★

⌖ **The Draycott.** This elegant yet homey boutique hotel near Sloane Square is the stuff London dreams are made on—if your dream is to live like a pleasantly old-fashioned, impeccably mannered, effortlessly stylish Chelsea lady or gentleman. **Pros:** lovely traditional town house; great service; discreet and peaceful. **Cons:** no restaurant or bar; single rooms are very small; elevator is tiny. ⑤ *Rooms from: £286* ✉ *26 Cadogan Gardens, Chelsea* ☎ *020/7730–0236* ⊕ *www.draycotthotel.com* ⌦ *35 rooms* ⦿ *Free Breakfast* Ⓜ *Sloane Sq.* ✚ *4:F3.*

$
HOTEL

⌖ **myhotel chelsea.** Rooms at this small chic charmer—tucked away down a side street in an upscale neighborhood—are bijou tiny but sophisticated, with colorful pastel throws atop crisp white down comforters. **Pros:** stylish rooms made for relaxation; good neighborhood; healthy dining options. **Cons:** tiny rooms; not much food variety at on-site café; relaxed style not for everyone. ⑤ *Rooms from: £93 ⊠ 35 Ixworth Pl., Chelsea* ☎ *020/7225–7500* ⊕ *www.myhotels.com* ↩ *54 rooms* ⦿*| Breakfast* Ⓜ *South Kensington* ⊹ *4:E3.*

$$$
HOTEL
Fodor'sChoice
★

San Domenico House. Discreet, beautiful, and exceptionally well run, this converted Chelsea town house makes for a restful hideaway. **Pros:** unique and beautiful design; great neighborhood, with the King's Road and Saatchi Gallery a short walk away; exceptional service. **Cons:** no bar or restaurant; no breakfast included for the (still pretty expensive) cheapest rates; only some rooms have bathtubs. ⑤ *Rooms from: £270 ⊠ 29–31 Draycott Pl., Chelsea* ☎ *020/7581–5757* ⊕ *www.sandomenicohouse.com* ↩ *19 rooms* ⦿*| Breakfast* Ⓜ *Sloane Sq.* ⊹ *4:F3.*

KNIGHTSBRIDGE

$$
HOTEL

The Beaufort. This gracious boutique hotel is a favorite entry in the little black books of many a visiting high-society fashionista—Harrods is the merest toss of a diamond from the front door. **Pros:** gorgeous interiors; friendly and professional staff; complimentary daily afternoon tea. **Cons:** standard doubles are much smaller than the price might indicate; the sights of the West End are a 20-minute Tube ride away; no restaurant on-site. ⑤ *Rooms from: £230 ⊠ 33 Beaufort Gardens, Knightsbridge* ☎ *020/7584–5252* ⊕ *www.thebeaufort.co.uk* ↩ *22 rooms* ⦿*| Breakfast* Ⓜ *Knightsbridge* ⊹ *4:F1.*

$$$$
HOTEL
FAMILY
Fodor'sChoice
★

The Berkeley. Convenient for Knightsbridge shopping, the very elegant Berkeley is known for its renowned restaurants and luxuries that culminate—literally—in a splendid penthouse swimming pool. **Pros:** lavish and elegant; attentive service; great drinking and dining options. **Cons:** you'll need your best designer clothes to fit in; even the cheapest rooms are expensive; while beautiful, the style is very traditional. ⑤ *Rooms from: £440 ⊠ Wilton Pl., Knightsbridge* ☎ *020/7235–6000, 800/637–2869 in U.S.* ⊕ *www.the-berkeley.co.uk* ↩ *190 rooms* ⦿*| Free Breakfast* Ⓜ *Knightsbridge* ⊹ *4:G1.*

$$$
HOTEL

The Capital Hotel. Nothing is ever too much at this elegant hotel that was formerly a private house; mattresses are handmade, sheets are 450-thread count, bathrooms are marble, and everything is done in impeccable taste. **Pros:** beautiful space; handy for shopping at Harrods; excellent restaurant. **Cons:** breakfast is expensive; cheaper rooms are small for the price; neighborhood can be pricey. ⑤ *Rooms from: £290 ⊠ 22–24 Basil St., Knightsbridge* ☎ *020/7589–5171, 800/926–3199 in U.S.* ⊕ *www.capitalhotel.co.uk* ↩ *49 rooms* ⦿*| Breakfast* Ⓜ *Knightsbridge* ⊹ *4:F1.*

$$$
HOTEL
Fodor'sChoice
★

Egerton House. A sensationally soigné and chic space that feels like your own private London home, this hotel has some truly luxuriant design touches, including guest rooms lavishly decorated with rich fabrics and a knockout white-on-gold dining room. **Pros:** lovely staff; magnificent interiors; striking art. **Cons:** some style touches are a little too froufrou; sensory overload from the decor of some rooms; the traditional elegance won't appeal to everyone. ⑤ *Rooms from: £290 ⊠ 17–19 Egerton Terr., Knightsbridge* ☎ *020/7589–2412, 877/955–1515 in U.S.* ⊕ *www.redcarnationhotels.com* ↩ *29 rooms* ⦿*| Free Breakfast* Ⓜ *Knightsbridge, South Kensington* ⊹ *4:F2.*

15

$$$$
HOTEL
Fodor's Choice
★

🏨 **The Lanesborough.** Beautiful, traditional, and luxurious, the Lanes-borough is like a gilded cocoon for the seriously wealthy that exudes a spectacular richness, from the design-magazine perfection of the bed-rooms to the magnificent 19th-century antiques. **Pros:** beautiful and historic; great service; your wish is their command—there's even an in-house butler. **Cons:** prices are extraordinary; might be too fancy for some; Hyde Park Corner is often clogged with heavy traffic. $ *Rooms from: £635 ⌧ Hyde Park Corner, Knightsbridge ☎ 020/7259–5599, 800/999–1828 in U.S. ⊕ www.lanesborough.com ▤ No credit cards ⇨ 95 rooms ⦿ Breakfast Ⓜ Hyde Park Corner ✛ 4:G1.*

$$$$
HOTEL
Fodor's Choice
★

🏨 **Mandarin Oriental Hyde Park.** Built in 1880, the Mandarin Oriental welcomes you with one of the most exuberantly Victorian facades in town, then fast-forwards you to high-trend modern London, thanks to striking and luxurious guest rooms filled with high-tech gadgets. **Pros:** great shopping at your doorstep; amazing views of Hyde Park; excellent service. **Cons:** nothing comes cheap; you must dress up for dinner (and lunch and breakfast); located on a traffic-clogged stretch of Knightsbridge. $ *Rooms from: £720 ⌧ 66 Knightsbridge, Knights-bridge ☎ 020/7235–2000 ⊕ www.mandarinoriental.com/london ⇨ 181 rooms ⦿ Free Breakfast Ⓜ Knightsbridge ✛ 4:F1.*

BELGRAVIA

$$
HOTEL
Fodor's Choice
★

🏨 **Artist Residence.** As packed with character and charm as they come, this artsy boutique hotel oozes bohemian sophistication. **Pros:** romantic and charming; close to Victoria Station; great staff. **Cons:** the wrong side of Victoria for most attractions; stairs to climb; the rustic chic won't appeal to more traditional tastes. $ *Rooms from: £170 ⌧ 52 Cambridge St., Belgravia ☎ 020/7931–8946 ⊕ www.artistresidence-london.co.uk ⇨ 10 rooms ⦿ Breakfast Ⓜ Victoria, Pimlico ✛ 5:A4.*

$$
B&B/INN

🏨 **B&B Belgravia.** At this modern guesthouse near Victoria Station, a clean, chic white color scheme, simple modern furniture, and a lounge where a fire crackles away in the winter are all geared to homey com-forts. **Pros:** nice extras like free use of a laptop in hotel lounge; coffee and tea always available; superb value for money in a vibrant area. **Cons:** rooms and bathrooms are small; can be noisy, especially on lower floors; great value means no frills. $ *Rooms from: £129 ⌧ 64–66 Ebury St., Belgravia ☎ 020/7259–8570 ⊕ www.bb-belgravia.com ⇨ 28 rooms ⦿ Breakfast Ⓜ Sloane Sq., Victoria ✛ 4:H2.*

$
HOTEL

🏨 **The Luna Simone Hotel.** This delightful and friendly little family-run hotel, a short stroll from Buckingham Palace, is a real find for the price in central London. **Pros:** friendly and well run; family rooms are out-standing value; superb location. **Cons:** tiny bathrooms; thin walls; no elevator or air-conditioning. $ *Rooms from: £120 ⌧ 47–49 Belgrave Rd., Belgravia ☎ 020/7834–5897 ⊕ www.lunasimonehotel.com ⇨ 36 rooms ⦿ Breakfast Ⓜ Pimlico, Victoria ✛ 5:A4.*

$
RENTAL

🏨 **Studios@82.** A great little side operation from B&B Belgravia, these self-catering apartments present a fantastic value. **Pros:** great rates; lovely location; all the independence of self-catering. **Cons:** lots of stairs and no elevator; check-in is at B&B Belgravia, six doors down the street; can be subject to street noise. $ *Rooms from: £120 ⌧ 82 Ebury St.,*

Belgravia ☎ *020/7259–8570* ⊕ *www.bb-belgravia.com* ➫ *9 apartments* †⊚| *Breakfast* Ⓜ *Knightsbridge* ✛ *4:H2.*

NOTTING HILL AND BAYSWATER

NOTTING HILL

$$ ⊡ **The Main House.** A stay in this delightfully welcoming B&B feels more
B&B/INN like sleeping over at a friend's house than a stay in a hotel—albeit a par-
Fodor'sChoice ticularly wealthy and well-connected friend. **Pros:** unique and unusual
★ place; charming and helpful owners; room prices decrease for longer
stays. **Cons:** three-night minimum stay is restrictive; few in-house ser-
vices; decor not for everyone. ⑤ *Rooms from: £150* ✉ *6 Colvile Rd.,
Notting Hill* ☎ *020/7221–9691* ⊕ *www.themainhouse.com* ➫ *4 rooms*
†⊚| *Free Breakfast* Ⓜ *Notting Hill Gate* ✛ *1:A4.*

$$ ⊡ **The Portobello Hotel.** One of London's quirkiest hotels, the little Porto-
HOTEL bello (formed from two adjoining Victorian houses) has attracted scores
of celebrities to its small but stylish rooms over the years, and the decor
reflects these hip credentials with joyous abandon. **Pros:** stylish and
unique; pets are allowed; guests have use of nearby gym and pool. **Cons:**
all but the priciest rooms are quite small; may be too eccentric for some;
a 25-minute Tube ride into central London. ⑤ *Rooms from: £205* ✉ *22
Stanley Gardens, Notting Hill* ☎ *020/7727–2777* ⊕ *www.portobello-
hotel.com* ➫ *21 rooms* †⊚| *Free Breakfast* Ⓜ *Notting Hill Gate* ✛ *1:A5.*

BAYSWATER

$$ ⊡ **Colonnade.** Near a canal filled with colorful "narrowboats" in the Little
HOTEL Venice neighborhood, this lovely town house offers individually styled
rooms, some of which are split-level; others have balconies filled with rich
brocades, velvets, and antiques. **Pros:** beautifully decorated; unique and
little-known part of London by the Regent's Canal; free Wi-Fi. **Cons:** you
have to go through shoddier parts of town to get here; rooms are small;
not the closest location for visiting major sights. ⑤ *Rooms from: £135*
✉ *2 Warrington Crescent, Bayswater* ☎ *020/7286–1052* ⊕ *www.colon-
nadehotel.co.uk* ➫ *43 rooms* †⊚| *Breakfast* Ⓜ *Warwick Ave.* ✛ *1:C2.*

$ ⊡ **London House Hotel.** Set in a row of white Georgian town houses,
HOTEL this excellent budget option in hit-or-miss Bayswater is friendly, well
run, and spotlessly clean. **Pros:** friendly and efficient; emphasis on
value; good location. **Cons:** basement rooms lack sunlight; smallest
rooms are tiny; the area isn't quite as vibrant as neighboring Notting
Hill. ⑤ *Rooms from: £110* ✉ *81 Kensington Garden Sq., Bayswater*
☎ *020/7243–1810* ⊕ *www.londonhousehotels.com* ➫ *103 rooms*
†⊚| *Free Breakfast* Ⓜ *Queensway, Bayswater* ✛ *1:B4.*

$$ ⊡ **Parkwood Hotel.** Just seconds from Hyde Park in one of London's
B&B/INN swankiest enclaves, this sweet little guesthouse is an oasis of value, with
warm and helpful hosts and bright guest rooms that are simply furnished
with pastel color schemes and reproduction antique beds. **Pros:** lovely
hosts; free Wi-Fi; hotel guarantees to match or beat rate of any other hotel
of its class in the area. **Cons:** often booked up in advance; no elevator and
no ground-floor bedrooms; front-facing rooms can be noisy. ⑤ *Rooms
from: £140* ✉ *4 Stanhope Pl., Bayswater* ☎ *020/7402–2241* ⊕ *www.lon-
don-parkwood.com* ➫ *16 rooms* †⊚| *Breakfast* Ⓜ *Marble Arch* ✛ *1:F4.*

15

$$ ☲ **Space Apart Hotel.** These studio apartments near Hyde Park are done in
RENTAL   soothing tones of white and gray, with polished wood floors and attractive modern kitchenettes equipped with all you need to make small meals. **Pros:** especially good value; the larger suites have space for four people; handy location. **Cons:** no in-house restaurant or bar; two-night minimum stay; standard apartments are small. $ *Rooms from: £160* ✉ *36–37 Kensington Gardens Sq., Bayswater* ☎ *020/7908–1340* ⊕ *www.aparthotel-london.co.uk* ⬎ *30 rooms* ¶◎¶ *No meals* Ⓜ *Bayswater* ✛ *1:B4.*

REGENT'S PARK, HAMPSTEAD, AND ISLINGTON

REGENT'S PARK

$$ ☲ **Meliá White House.** Converted from a beautiful modernist 1930s
HOTEL   apartment block, this stylish hotel is filled with nods to its prewar origins.
FAMILY   **Pros:** great location near Regent's Park and Oxford Street; good restaurant; families are well treated—kids get a gift on arrival. **Cons:** classic rooms are small; the vast size means a stay lacks the intimacy of smaller hotels; bathrooms are generally tiny. $ *Rooms from: £189* ✉ *Albany St., Regent's Park* ☎ *020/7391–3000* ⊕ *www.melia.com/en/hotels/united-kingdom/london/melia-white-house* ⬎ *700 rooms* ¶◎¶ *Some meals* Ⓜ *Great Portland St.* ✛ *1:H2.*

HAMPSTEAD

$ ☲ **Glenlyn Guest House.** An excellent option for travelers who don't mind
B&B/INN   being a long Tube ride away from the action, this converted Victorian town house offers a high standard of accommodation a few miles north of Hampstead. **Pros:** comfortable and friendly; you get more for your money than you would in central London; five-minute walk to Tube station. **Cons:** you have to factor in the cost and inconvenience of a half-hour Tube ride to central London; no in-house restaurant; room decor is simple yet uninspiring. $ *Rooms from: £81* ✉ *6 Woodside Park Rd., Hampstead* ☎ *020/8445–0440* ⊕ *www.glenlynhotel.com* ⬎ *24 rooms* ¶◎¶ *Free Breakfast* Ⓜ *Woodside Park* ✛ *1:D1.*

$ ☲ **The Hide.** This cozy, chic little hideaway is exceptional value for money
HOTEL   and exceeds virtually anything you could hope to find in central London for the price; the downside is that the half-hour Tube ride to and from town can be exhausting after a long day of sightseeing. **Pros:** excellent value; great service; free Wi-Fi. **Cons:** far from the center; somewhat dull neighborhood; no restaurant on-site. $ *Rooms from: £105* ✉ *230 Hendon Way, Hendon, Hampstead* ☎ *020/8203–1670* ⊕ *www.thehide-london.com* ⬎ *23 rooms* ¶◎¶ *Free Breakfast* Ⓜ *Hendon Central* ✛ *1:H1.*

$ ☲ **La Gaffe.** The name of this simple B&B means "the mistake" in Ital-
B&B/INN   ian, and is also the punchline to the unlikely tale of how the original husband-and-wife proprietors met in the 1950s—but it also rather neatly chimes with the Cockney term "gaff," meaning a simple cozy residence. **Pros:** unusual place with a cheerful atmosphere; great price; comes with the convenience of a traditional Italian restaurant below. **Cons:** few services; no elevator; outside city center. $ *Rooms from: £110* ✉ *107–111 Heath St., Hampstead* ☎ *020/7435–8965* ⊕ *www.lagaffe.co.uk* ⬎ *18 rooms* ¶◎¶ *Breakfast* Ⓜ *Hampstead* ✛ *1:D1.*

NIGHTLIFE

Updated
by Alex
Wijeratna

There isn't a London nightlife scene—there is a multitude of them. As long as there are crowds for obscure teenage rock bands, Dickensian-style pubs, comedy cabarets, cocktail lounges, and swing dance nights, someone will create clubs and venues for them in London. The result? London has become a veritable utopia for excitement junkies, culture fiends, and those who—simply put—like to party.

Nearly everyone who visits London these days is mesmerized by the city's energy, which reveals itself in layers. Whether you prefer rhythm and blues with fine French food, the gritty guitar-riff music of Camden Town, the craft beers of East London, a pint and a gourmet pizza at a local gastro-pub, or swanky heritage cocktails and sushi at London's sexiest subterranean lair, London is sure to feed your fancy.

PLANNING

GETTING AROUND

London's nightlife has been given a big boost with six Night Tube lines serving central London (see ⊕ *www.tfl.gov.uk* for details) that run all night on Friday and Saturday, making getting home after a night out cheaper and easier than ever before. The rest of the network stops running around 12:30 am Monday through Saturday and midnight on Sunday. Night buses are largely safe and reliable but far slower than taxis, as you'd expect. The best place to hail a black taxi is at the front door of one of the major hotels; or find a licensed local minicab firm on the Transport for London website. Avoid unlicensed taxis or minicabs that tout for business around closing time.

PUBS

Pubs are where Londoners go to hang out, see and be seen, act out the drama of life, and, for some, drink themselves into varying degrees of oblivion. The pub is still a vital part of London life, though many of the traditions of the pub experience are evolving. There are few better places to meet Londoners in their local habitat. There are somewhere around 4,000 pubs in London; some are dark and woody, others plain and functional, a few still have original Victorian etched glass, Edwardian panels, and art nouveau carvings.

Not long ago, before the smoking ban, pubs tended to be smoky, male-dominated places with a couple of ubiquitous beers on tap and the only available food a packet of salt-and-vinegar-flavor crisps (potato chips). All that has changed. Gastro-pub fever swept through London around the turn of the 21st century and at many places, char grills are installed in the kitchen and inventive pub grub is on the menu. A new wave of enthusiasm for craft beers and microbreweries is now having a similar effect on the liquid offerings.

The big decision is what to drink. The beer of choice among Britons has traditionally been **"bitter,"** lightly fermented, with an amber color, and getting its bitterness from hops. It's usually served at cellar temperature (that is, cooler than room temperature but neither chilled, nor, as common misconception would have it, warm). **Real ales,** served from wooden kegs and made without chilling, filtering, or pasteurization, are flatter than other bitters and are enjoying a renaissance. Many small London breweries have sprung up in recent years, and bottled designer and American beers can be found in most bars across London. **Stouts,** like Guinness, are a meal in themselves and something of an acquired taste—they have a dark, caramel-infused flavor and look like thickened flat Coke with a frothy top. Chilled continental **lagers,** most familiar to American drinkers, are light in color and carbonated. ■TIP→ The most commonly served lagers in Britain are from continental Europe.

Many English pubs are owned by chains such as Fullers, Nicholson's, or Samuel Smith, and are tenanted, meaning that they are run on a sort of franchise basis. Most are not obviously branded and retain at least some independence. Independently owned pubs, sometimes called "free houses," tend to offer a more extensive selection of beer. Other potations available include apple-based **ciders,** ranging from sweet to dry and from alcoholic to very alcoholic (Irish cider, served over ice, is now also ubiquitous), and **shandies,** a refreshing mix of beer and lemonade. Friendly pubs will usually be happy to give you a taste of the brew of your choice before you order.

LIQUOR AND SMOKING LAWS
Laws now allow London drinking establishments to extend their opening hours beyond the traditional 11 pm closing, and smoking is banned. Most pubs and bars still close by midnight or a few short hours later.

CHILDREN IN PUBS
As pubs increasingly emphasize what's coming out of the kitchen alongside what's flowing from the tap, bringing the kids is more of an option. The law dictates that children ages 14–17 may enter a pub but are not permitted to purchase or drink alcohol, and children under 14 are not permitted in the bar area of a pub unless the pub has a "children's certificate" and the kids are accompanied by an adult. Some pubs have a section set aside for families, especially during the day, but many don't allow children in the evening.

16

WHAT TO WEAR

As a general rule, you won't see too many people in the upscale London nightspots wearing jeans and sneakers. People are more likely to dress down for an evening in the pub.

FIND OUT WHAT'S PLAYING WHERE

Because today's cool spot is often tomorrow's forgotten or closed venue, check the weekly listings in the *Evening Standard* (⊕ *www.standard. co.uk*) and especially *Time Out* (⊕ *www.timeout.com/london*). Other websites to consult are ⊕ *www.londontown.com* or ⊕ *www.allinlondon.co.uk*. Although most clubs are frequented by those under 30, there are plenty of others that are popular with patrons of all ages and types. One particularly useful website for clubs and club nights is ⊕ *www. residentadvisor.net*.

Door and bar staff are hawkish about underage drinking, so take photo ID with you on a night out.

NIGHTLIFE REVIEWS

WESTMINSTER AND ST. JAMES'S

Elegant drinking holes catering to London's political and social elites abound in these central neighborhoods. Streets that are thronged with tourists and workers by day quiet down by evening, leaving the area to its few residents and a handful of sophisticated drinkers and diners.

WESTMINSTER

BARS

FAMILY   **Cinnamon Club.** In the ground floor of what was once the Reading Room of the old Westminster Library, the book-lined Library Bar of this contemporary Indian restaurant (the curries are superb) has Indian-theme cocktails (mango mojitos, "Delhi mules"), delicious bar snacks, and a clientele that includes thrusting young politicos and apparatchiks. ⊠ *The Old Westminster Library, 30–32 Great Smith St., Westminster* ☎ *020/7222–2555* ⊕ *www.cinnamonclub.com* Ⓜ *St James's, Westminster.*

FAMILY   **Gordon's Wine Bar.** Nab a rickety candelit table in the atmospheric, 1890s
Fodor's Choice   low-slung brick vaulted cellar interior of what claims to be the oldest
★   wine bar in London, or fight for standing room in the long pedestrian-only alley garden that runs alongside it. Either way, the mood is always cheery as a diverse crowd sips on more than 60 different wines, ports, and sherries. Tempting cheese and meat plates are great for sharing. ⊠ *47 Villiers St., Westminster* ☎ *020/7930–1408* ⊕ *gordonswinebar. com* Ⓜ *Charing Cross, Embankment.*

ST. JAMES'S

BARS

FAMILY   **American Bar.** Festooned with a chin-dropping array of old club ties, vin-
Fodor's Choice   tage signed celebrity photographs, sporting mementos, model airplanes
★   and baseball caps, this sensational hotel cocktail bar has superb martinis and manhattans. The name dates from the 1930s, when hotel bars in

London started to cater to growing numbers of Americans crossing the Atlantic in ocean liners, and in the 1970s, when a customer left a small carved wooden eagle, the collection of paraphernalia was started. ⊠ *The Stafford, 16–18 St. James's Pl., St. James's* ☎ *020/7493–0111* ⊕ *www.thestaffordlondon.com* Ⓜ *Green Park.*

MAYFAIR

Bars in this upscale central neighborhood—many of which can be found within luxury hotels—attract a polished crowd. Cocktails, fine wines, and rare aged spirits are the tipples of choice. Even the pubs tend to be as upscale as the people who frequent them, but you'll also find plenty of informal establishments with a lot of character.

BARS

Claridge's Bar. This elegant Mayfair meeting place remains unpretentious even when it brims with beautiful people. The bar has an art deco heritage made hip by the sophisticated touch of designer David Collins. A library of rare champagnes and brandies as well as a delicious choice of traditional and exotic cocktails—try the Flapper or the Black Pearl—will occupy your taste buds. Request a glass of vintage Cristal in the darkly moody leather-walled 36-seat Fumoir. ⊠ *Claridge's, 55 Brook St., Mayfair* ☎ *020/7629–8860* ⊕ *www.claridges.co.uk* Ⓜ *Bond St.*

Fodor'sChoice ★ **Connaught Bar.** The walls are platinum silver leaf and everything's all buffed and burnished at this glamorous David Collins–designed 1920s Irish Cubist-inspired shimmering cocktail lounge at the Connaught. Hail the famous martini trolley for a classic dry martini or sip signatures like a Ron Zacapa rum-based Vieux Connaught, which is presented on a mirrored tray with a swirl of saffron smoke. ⊠ *The Connaught, Carlos Place, Mayfair* ☎ *020/7314–3419* ⊕ *www.the-connaught.co.uk* ☞ *No reservations* Ⓜ *Green Park, Marble Arch.*

Fodor'sChoice ★ **Mr Fogg's Residence.** Explorers of all stripes will be captivated by this Jules Verne–inspired town house cocktail parlor, which is chock-full of the weathered maps, hunting trophies, taxidermy, suspended penny-farthings, and *Around the World in 80 Days* globe-trotting detritus of eccentric fictional Victorian British adventurer, Phileas J Fogg. Expect Victorian tipples and gin-based Afternoon "Tipsy teas" from staff in bow ties and sporting curly waxed mustaches. ⊠ *15 Bruton La., Mayfair* ☎ *020/7036–0608* ⊕ *www.mr-foggs.com* ☑ *Free* Ⓜ *Green Park, Oxford Circus.*

PUBS

FAMILY **The Punch Bowl.** In a quiet corner of Mayfair, the cozy little Punch Bowl has a worn wood floor and well-spoken staff. The pub dates to 1729 and the interior remains steadfastly old-fashioned, with a painting of Churchill, candles, polished dark wood, and engraved windows. Try the place's own ale, made specially in Scotland by Caledonian. A dining area at the rear buzzes at lunchtime with locals who come for the upscale English pub food, and there's a fancier restaurant upstairs. ⊠ *41 Farm St., Mayfair* ☎ *020/7493–6811* ⊕ *www.punchbowllondon.com* Ⓜ *Green Park, Bond St.*

16

JAZZ AND BLUES

Jazz in London is having a moment, with a crop of hometown stars like band leader Shabaka Hutchins electrifying the scene. You can expect anything from danceable smooth tunes played at a dapper supper club to groovy New Orleans–style blues to exotic world-beat rhythms, which can be heard at some of the edgier, less central venues throughout the capital. Head to the granddaddy of them all, **Ronnie Scott's**, in Soho for the big-time jazz giants. Other top jazz and blues clubs include the **Jazz Café, 606 Club,** the **Vortex, Pizza Express Jazz Club, Nightjar, Scarfe's Bar, Boisdale,** and **The Blues Kitchen** in Camden. London also hosts the city-wide **London Jazz Festival** (⊕ www.efglondon-jazzfestival.org.uk) in November, which showcases top and emerging artists in experimental jazz.

SOHO AND COVENT GARDEN

The center of town is famous for its vibrant gay scene, atmospheric music, cabaret venues, and acclaimed comedy clubs. Traditional British "boozers" stand side by side with informal continental-style drinking dens. Drop in for a late drink and you may find yourself rubbing shoulders with musicians and actors from the West End's 50-odd theaters. In Covent Garden, recent bar openings have also added extra buzz.

SOHO

BARS

Fodor's Choice ★
Bar Américain. The beaux art interior of this underground bar just north of Piccadilly Circus is so opulent and glamorous that you'd be forgiven for thinking it had been here since the 1930s. In fact it's a relatively new arrival and has been a hit since it opened in 2012, along with the Brasserie Zédel and racy The Crazy Coqs Cabaret & Bar that share the premises. The cocktails aren't quite as imaginative or accomplished as they might be, but the beaux arts surroundings make up for what the drinks don't quite deliver. ⊠ *20 Sherwood St., Soho* ☎ *020/7734–4888* ⊕ *www.brasseriezedel.com* Ⓜ *Piccadilly Circus.*

Fodor's Choice ★
The Blind Pig. Chances are you won't have heard of half the ingredients on the cocktail menu at this dark and sultry bar above Jason Atherton's smart casual restaurant, Social Eating House in Soho, but the sense of mystery only adds to the experience. So, too, do the antique mirrored ceilings and copper-topped bar, the delectable small plates (like black pepper prawn crackers and macaroni and cheese with shaved mushroom)—and the knowledge that you've nabbed a seat at one of the coolest spots in Soho. ⊠ *58 Poland St., Soho* ☎ *020/7993–3251* ⊕ *www.socialeatinghouse.com* Ⓜ *Oxford Circus, Tottenham Court Rd.*

Experimental Cocktail Club. It's easy to miss the unmarked shabby chic black door with a scuffed wash of red paint on Chinatown's hectic main drag Gerrard Street, but once you finally find it and make your way past the hard-to-please doorman, you'll be in a secret three-floor speakeasy-style cocktail bar that is also one of London's coolest bars. With a lively crowd, creative cocktails, subtle lighting, and a DJ spinning smooth sounds, the vibe is laid-back, sexy, Parisian cool. ✉ *13A Gerrard St., Chinatown* ✛ *Look for unmarked scuffed black and red door* ☎ *020/7434–3559* ⊕ *www.experimentalcocktailclublondon.com* 🖃 *£5 cover charge after 11 pm* Ⓜ *Leicester Sq., Piccadilly Circus.*

Mark's Bar. At bon vivant Mark Hix's relaxed basement Soho haunt, you can knock back decidedly British cocktails (from age-old recipes) like the Britz Spritz or a Full English Negroni or stick to the resplendent Punch Bowls, perfectly executed classic cocktails, or British ales. The bar is tucked below the modern British restaurant Hix Soho. The atmosphere is clubby, with kilim rugs, suede poufs, a low bar, and worn large leather Chesterfields. For fare, there are first-rate bar snacks, including oysters, pork crackling with rhubarb sauce, and Scotch quails eggs. ✉ *66–70 Brewer St., Soho* ☎ *020/7292–3518* ⊕ *www.hixrestaurants. co.uk* Ⓜ *Piccadilly Circus, Oxford Circus.*

COMEDY

Amused Moose Comedy. This roving West End comedy night group is often considered the best place to see breaking talent as well as household names doing "secret" shows. Ricky Gervais, Eddie Izzard, and Russell Brand are among those who have graced the Amused Moose stage, and every summer a handful of the Edinburgh Fringe comedians preview here. The bar is open late (and serves food), and there's a DJ and dancing after the show. Tickets are often discounted with a printout from their website, and shows are mainly on Saturday. ✉ *Karma Sanctum Hotel, 20 Warwick St., Soho* ☎ *020/7287–3727* ⊕ *www. amusedmoose.com* 🖃 *£12 and up* Ⓜ *Oxford Circus, Piccadilly Circus.*

Fodor's Choice ★ **The Comedy Store.** Before heading off to prime time, some of the United Kingdom's funniest stand-ups cut their teeth here, at what's considered the birthplace of alternative comedy. Comedy Store Players, a team with six comedians doing improvisation with audience suggestions, entertain on Wednesday and Sunday; the Cutting Edge steps in with a topical take every Tuesday; and Thursday, Friday, and Saturday have the best stand-up acts. There's also a bar with food. You must be over 18 to enter. ✉ *1A Oxendon St., Soho* ☎ *020/7024–2060 for tickets and booking* ⊕ *www.thecomedystore.co.uk* 🖃 *£16–£25* Ⓜ *Piccadilly Circus, Leicester Sq.*

ECLECTIC MUSIC

The 100 Club. Since this small club opened in 1942, many of the greats have played here, from Glenn Miller and Louis Armstrong to The Who, The Damned, The Clash, and the Sex Pistols. Saved from closure in 2010 by a campaign led by Sir Paul McCartney, the legendary space now reverberates to jazz, '60s R&B, and northern soul. ✉ *100 Oxford St., Soho* ☎ *020/7636–0933* ⊕ *www.the100club.co.uk* 🖃 *£10–£26* Ⓜ *Oxford Circus, Tottenham Court Rd.*

Phoenix Artist Club. Nonmembers can gain free entry before 9 pm at this legendary West End open-mic musical theater, cabaret, impromptu arts review, brasserie, and late-night private members' club of boozed-up thespians, critics, Soho habitués, and showbiz chorus-line divas. You might catch a raunchy cabaret, see a Theaterland star jump up for the "Gotta Sing" Thursday night open-mic sessions, or be transported by

16

the anecdotes of a fading onetime movie star raconteur. ⊠ *1 Phoenix St., Soho* ☎ *020/7836–1077* ⊕ *www.phoenixartistclub.com* Ⓜ *Tottenham Court Rd., Covent Garden.*

GAY AND LESBIAN

The Friendly Society. An unremarkable-looking door in a Soho alleyway leads down some dingy steps into one of the most fun LGBTQ joints in the neighborhood. Hopping with activity almost any night of the week, the place is known for its welcoming atmosphere to everyone—gay, trans, questioning, or straight. The interior alone—including garden gnome stools and a ceiling covered in Barbie dolls and disco balls—is enough to lift the spirits. ⊠ *79 Wardour St., Soho* ☎ *020/7434–3804* Ⓜ *Leicester Sq., Tottenham Court Rd.*

She. This basement club, part of the popular Ku group of gay venues, is a recent arrival on the Soho scene. It welcomes a mostly young lesbian crowd for informal cocktails early in the evening followed by dancing—of the pop and house variety—later on. The vibe is fun and friendly, especially on the last Thursday of each month, when She hosts London's only drag-king open-mic night. ⊠ *23A Old Compton St., Soho* ☎ *020/7437–4303* ⊕ *www.she-soho.com* 🎫 *£5 cover Fri. and Sat. after 9 pm* Ⓜ *Leicester Sq., Piccadilly Circus.*

The Yard. A corridor of kitsch leads to a surprisingly laid-back bar and spacious terrace at The Yard. This oasis of calm in the middle of Soho attracts a mixed, friendly crowd. ⊠ *57 Rupert St., Soho* ☎ *020/7437–2652* ⊕ *www.yardbar.co.uk* Ⓜ *Piccadilly Circus.*

JAZZ AND BLUES

Ain't Nothin' But... This sweaty fun place off Carnaby Street does exactly what its name suggests. Local blues musicians, as well as some notable names, squeeze onto the tiny stage and there's good bar food of the chili-and-gumbo variety. Most weekday nights there's no cover. ⊠ *20 Kingly St., Soho* ☎ *020/7287–0514* ⊕ *www.aintnothinbut.co.uk* 🎫 *£7 cover Fri. and Sat. after 8:30 pm* Ⓜ *Oxford Circus, Piccadilly Circus.*

Pizza Express Jazz Club. One of the United Kingdom's most ubiquitous pizza chains also runs a leading Soho jazz venue. The dimly lighted restaurant hosts both established and emerging top-quality international jazz acts every night, with food available in the downstairs venue (as opposed to the upstairs restaurant) around 90 minutes before stage time. The Italian-style thin-crust pizzas are about what you'd expect from a major chain. ⊠ *10 Dean St., Soho* ☎ *020/7439–4962 for the jazz club, 020/7437–9595 for restaurant* ⊕ *www.pizzaexpresslive.com* 🎫 *£16–£38* Ⓜ *Tottenham Court Rd.*

Fodor's Choice ★ **Ronnie Scott's.** London's best-known jazz club has attracted the biggest names—from Stan Getz to Count Basie and Ella Fitzgerald—since opening in 1959. It's usually crowded and hot, but the food and service are better than they used to be. The cool mood can't be beat, even since the sad departure of the eponymous founder and saxophonist. Shows take place every night, with additional late gigs on Friday and Saturday. Reservations are recommended. ⊠ *47 Frith St., Soho* ☎ *020/7439–0747* ⊕ *www.ronniescotts.co.uk* 🎫 *£24–£55* Ⓜ *Leicester Sq.*

PUBS

FAMILY **The Dog and Duck.** A beautiful example of a late-19th-century London pub, the Dog and Duck has a well-preserved Heritage-listed interior furnished with glazed tiles, mirrors, and polished wood, though it's often so packed that it's hard to get a good look. There's a decent selection of real ales at the bar and a restaurant serving outstanding ale-battered fish-and-chips. The cozy upstairs dining room is named for writer George Orwell, who frequented this spot. ⊠ *18 Bateman St., Soho* ☎ *020/7494–0697* ⊕ *www.nicholsonspubs.co.uk* Ⓜ *Tottenham Court Rd.*

The French House. In the pub where the French Resistance under Charles de Gaulle convened during World War II, Soho hipsters, artists, and eccentrics now rub shoulders with theater people and the literati. More than shoulders, actually, because this tiny, tricolor-waving, photo-lined pub is almost always packed. In the French style, beer is served in half-pints only. If you're around on July 14, you can join in the rapturous Bastille Day celebrations. ⊠ *49 Dean St., Soho* ☎ *020/7437–2477* ⊕ *www.frenchhousesoho.com* Ⓜ *Leicester Sq., Tottenham Court Rd.*

COVENT GARDEN

BARS

Fodor's Choice
★ **Beaufort Bar.** Things could hardly get more glamorous than at the Savoy's lesser-known Beaufort Bar—a black-and-gold art deco master class with dramatic lighting that has vintage champagne and a spread of heritage cocktails. Dark and sultry and with a rising cabaret stage once graced by Gershwin and Josephine Baker, this venue has nightly live jazz piano music beginning at 7 pm. ⊠ *The Savoy, Strand, Covent Garden* ☎ *020/7420–2111 for reservations only* ⊕ *www.fairmont.com/savoy-london* Ⓜ *Charing Cross, Covent Garden.*

FAMILY **Terroirs.** Specializing in low-intervention "natural wines" (organic, unfiltered, and sustainably produced with minimal added ingredients), Terroirs wine bar has an unusually careful selection of 260 wines from small French and Italian artisan winemakers. These are served, along with delicious, relatively simple wine-friendly dishes—charcuterie, tapas, cheese, and more substantial French-inspired dishes—at a bar and bare oak tables surrounded by whitewashed walls and wooden floors. ⊠ *5 William IV St., Covent Garden* ☎ *020/7036–0660* ⊕ *www.terroirswinebar.com* Ⓜ *Charing Cross.*

GAY AND LESBIAN

Heaven. With the best light show on any London dance floor, Heaven is unpretentious, loud, and huge, with a labyrinth of rooms, bars, and live-music parlors. Thursday through Saturday nights it's all about the G-A-Y club and comedy nights. Check in advance about live performances—they can take place any night of the week. If you go to just one gay club in London, Heaven should be it. ⊠ *Under the Arches, Villiers St., Covent Garden* ☎ *020/7930–2020 24-hr ticket line* ⊕ *www.heavennightclub-london.com* 🎟 *£15–£26* Ⓜ *Charing Cross, Embankment.*

16

PUBS

FAMILY **The Harp.** This is the sort of friendly flower-decked locale you might find on some out-of-the-way backstreet, except that it's right in the middle of town, between Trafalgar Square and Covent Garden. As a result, The Harp can get crowded, especially because it was recently named British pub of the year by the Campaign for Real Ale, but the squeeze is worth it for the excellent beer and cider (there are usually 10 carefully chosen ales, often including a London microbrew, plus 10 ciders and perries) and a no-frills menu of high-quality British sausages, cooked behind the bar. ⊠ *47 Chandos Pl., Covent Garden* ☎ *020/7836–0291* ⊕ *www.harpcoventgarden.com* Ⓜ *Charing Cross.*

Lamb & Flag. This refreshingly ungentrified 17th-century pub was once known as the Bucket of Blood because the upstairs room and front yard were used as a ring for winner-takes-all bare-knuckle boxing contests. Now it's a friendly (and *bloodless*) place, serving food and real ale. It's on the edge of Covent Garden, up a hidden alley off Garrick Street. ⊠ *33 Rose St., Covent Garden* ☎ *020/7497–9504* ⊕ *www.lambandflag-coventgarden.co.uk* Ⓜ *Covent Garden.*

BLOOMSBURY, HOLBORN, FITZROVIA, AND ISLINGTON

The gorgeous pubs of Bloomsbury attract tourists in the daytime and huge crowds of after-work drinkers in the early evening. They tend to quiet down as the night advances, making this a great spot for a relaxing night out. The redevelopment of the area around King's Cross St. Pancras Station has especially invigorated the nightlife scene here. Fitzrovia, meanwhile, manages to blend sophistication, informality, and a certain edginess that's not found elsewhere in the center of town.

Exmouth Market and Upper Street are the main nightlife hot spots in Islington, just north and east of central London. The fun informal bars here make it a reliable choice for going out.

BLOOMSBURY
PUBS

FAMILY **The Lamb.** Charles Dickens and his contemporaries drank here, but today's enthusiastic clientele make sure this intimate and eternally popular pub avoids the pitfalls of feeling too old-timey. One interesting feature: for private chats at the bar, you can close a delicate etched-glass "snob screen" to the bar staff, opening it only when you fancy another pint. ⊠ *94 Lamb's Conduit St., Bloomsbury* ☎ *020/7405–0713* ⊕ *www.thelamblondon.com* Ⓜ *Russell Sq.*

HOLBORN
BARS

FAMILY
Fodor'sChoice
★ **Scarfes Bar.** Settle in with Indian-inspired bar snacks and complimentary nightly jazz and other entertainment at the Rosewood's impossibly glamorous Scarfes Bar—a cross between an Edwardian gentleman's club and a Downton Abbey drawing room. Sit on sofas by a roaring log fire or sink into velvet armchairs and explore the collection of over 400 gins and 30 assorted tonics. Be sure to check out London-born artist (and the bar's namesake) Gerald Scarfe's paintings and political cartoons

adorning the walls. ✉ *The Rosewood, 252 High Holborn, Holborn* ☎ *020/3747–8670* ⊕ *www.scarfesbar.com* Ⓜ *Holborn.*

PUBS

FAMILY **Museum Tavern.** Across the street from the British Museum in Bloomsbury, this friendly and classy Victorian pub makes an ideal resting place after the rigors of the culture trail. Karl Marx unwound here after a hard day in the British Museum Library. He could have spent his *kapital* on any of around 15 well-kept beers available on tap. ✉ *49 Great Russell St., Bloomsbury* ☎ *020/7242–8987* ⊕ *www.greeneking-pubs.co.uk/ pubs/greater-london/museum-tavern* Ⓜ *Tottenham Court Rd., Holborn.*

FAMILY **Princess Louise.** This fine popular pub is an exquisite museum piece of a Victorian interior, with glazed tiles and intricately engraved glass screens that divide the bar area into cozy little annexes. It's not all show, either. There's a good selection of excellent-value Yorkshire real ales from Samuel Smith's brewery. ✉ *208 High Holborn, Holborn* ☎ *020/7405–8816* ⊕ *www.princesslouisepub.co.uk* Ⓜ *Holborn.*

FAMILY **The Queens Larder.** The royal associated with this tiny pub is Queen Charlotte, who is said to have stored food here for her "mad" husband, George III, when he was being treated nearby. The interior preserves its antique feel, with dark wood and old posters, and in the evenings fills up quickly with office workers, pediatricians, and students. In good weather, you might prefer to grab one of the seats outdoors. ✉ *1 Queen's Sq., Bloomsbury* ☎ *020/7837–5627* ⊕ *www.queenslarder. co.uk* Ⓜ *Russell Sq., Holborn.*

FITZROVIA

BARS

Fodor's Choice **Artesian.** They don't take reservations at this jewel box of a cocktail ★ bar at the Langham hotel, but you can order a drink while you wait for a chic mirror-top table surrounded by some of the most beautiful people in London. The cocktails—highly innovative creations involving ingredients like sandalwood, Mexican raicilla, and Japanese salt seasoning—are pricey, but service is top-notch, making this a nightlife experience that's hard to fault. After 6 pm it's for ages 18 and over only. ✉ *The Langham, 1C Portland Pl., Fitzrovia* ☎ *020/7636–1000* ⊕ *www. artesian-bar.co.uk* Ⓜ *Oxford Circus, Goodge St.*

Fodor's Choice **The London Edition bars.** Visitors to Ian Schrager's London Edition hotel ★ are spoiled for choice when it comes to bars. High ceilings, eclectic artwork, and innovative cocktails can be found at the all-day Berners Tavern and in the Lobby Bar, which opens in the evening. You'll need a reservation to get into the cozy wood-paneled and open-fire Punch Room, but the bar's reinventions of traditional punches (the type favored by pirates and privateers) and the exemplary service are well worth the extra effort. On the weekend there's dancing until late in the more informal Basement (guest list only; visit ⊕ *www. basementldn.com* for the current lineup). ✉ *10 Berners St., Fitzrovia* ☎ *020/7781–0000* ⊕ *www.editionhotels.com/london* Ⓜ *Tottenham Court Rd., Oxford Circus.*

16

ISLINGTON

BARS

69 Colebrooke Row. This elegant faux speakeasy must be London's tiniest cocktail lounge. Book one of the handful of tables or a seat at the diminutive bar to sample perfectly made twists on classic cocktails, like the panettone bellini, which uses a purée of the sweet Italian bread instead of peach. Staff are immaculate but approachable. ⊠ *69 Colebrooke Row, Islington* ☎ *07540/528–593* ⊕ *www.69colebrookerow. com* Ⓜ *Angel.*

ECLECTIC MUSIC

FAMILY **Union Chapel.** The beauty of this sublime old chapel and its impressive multicultural not-for-profit programming make this spot one of London's best musical venues, especially for acoustic shows. Performers have included Björk, Beck, and Goldfrapp, although now you're more likely to hear lower-key alternative country, world music, and jazz, alongside poetry and literary events, film screenings, and stand-up comedy gigs. ⊠ *Union Chapel, Compton Terr., Islington* ☎ *020/7226–1686 for venue (no box office; ticket sales numbers vary with each event)* ⊕ *www.unionchapel.org.uk* 🎫 *Free–£35* Ⓜ *Highbury & Islington.*

THE CITY

Workers from The City's many finance firms pour into the neighborhood's pubs at the end of the day, but by 8 pm the party is pretty much over and you'll have no trouble finding a place to sit. It's always worth ducking down a side street, as this is where some of the area's most interesting drinking establishments can be found.

BARS

Café Kick. This homey Iberian-vibe café and sports bar on Exmouth Market is open all day for meals, snacks, coffee, and cocktails. Decked with vintage global football paraphernalia, it's famous for its Bonzini foosball tables, which give the place a fun informal environment. Deals are available on "cocktails of the month" and house beers during happy hour (4–7). You can reserve foosball tables in advance. ⊠ *43 Exmouth Market, Clerkenwell* ☎ *020/7837–8077* ⊕ *www.cafekick. co.uk* Ⓜ *Angel.*

PUBS

FAMILY **The Blackfriar.** A step from Blackfriars Tube station, this spectacular
Fodor's Choice pub has an Arts and Crafts interior that is entertainingly, satirically
★ ecclesiastical, with inlaid mother-of-pearl, wood carvings, stained glass, and marble pillars all over the place. Under finely lettered temperance tracts on view just below the reliefs of monks, fairies, and friars, there is a nice group of ales on tap from independent brewers. The 20th-century poet Sir John Betjeman once led a successful campaign to save the pub from demolition. ⊠ *174 Queen Victoria St., City of London* ☎ *020/7236–5474* ⊕ *www.nicholsonspubs.co.uk* Ⓜ *Blackfriars.*

FAMILY **Craft Beer Co.** With 37 beers on tap and 350 more in bottles (one brewed exclusively for the Craft Beer Company), the main problem here is knowing where to start. Luckily, friendly and knowledgeable staff are happy to advise or give tasters—or why not sign up for a guided tasting session? A huge chandelier and a mirrored ceiling lend antique charm to the interior, and a smattering of tourists and beer pilgrims break up the crowds of Leather Lane workers and locals. ⊠ *82 Leather La., Clerkenwell* ☎ *020/7404–7049* ⊕ *www.thecraftbeerco.com* Ⓜ *Chancery La.*

FAMILY

Fodor'sChoice ★

Jerusalem Tavern. Loved by Londoners and owned by the well-respected St. Peter's Brewery in Suffolk, the Jerusalem Tavern is one-of-a-kind: small, historic, atmospheric, and endearingly eccentric. Antique Delft-style tiles meld with wood and concrete in a converted watchmaker and jeweler's shop dating back to the 18th century. The beer, both bottled and on tap, is some of the best available anywhere in London. It's often busy, especially after work. ⊠ *55 Britton St., Clerkenwell* ☎ *020/7490–4281* ⊕ *www.stpetersbrewery.co.uk/london-pub* Ⓜ *Farringdon.*

FAMILY

Ye Olde Cheshire Cheese. Yes, this pub on Fleet Street is full of tourists, but it deserves a visit for more than its popularity. It's extremely historic, dating to 1667, the year after the Great Fire of London. The most frequented pub of Dr. Johnson's and Charles Dickens's many locals, it has sawdust-covered floors, low wood-beam ceilings, and the 14th-century crypt of Whitefriars' Carmelite monastery under the cellar bar. Food is served in the Chop Room—one of London's earliest steak houses. ⊠ *145 Fleet St., City of London* ☎ *020/7353–6170* ⊗ *Closed Sun. from 4* Ⓜ *Blackfriars.*

FAMILY

Ye Olde Mitre. Hidden off the side of 8 Hatton Gardens (and notoriously hard to find), this cozy pub's roots go back to 1546, though it was rebuilt around 1782. Originally built for the staff of the Bishop of Ely, whose London residence was next door, it remained officially part of Cambridgeshire until the 20th century. Elizabeth I was once spotted dancing round a cherry tree here with a dashing young beau. Now it's a friendly little labyrinthine place, with a fireplace, well-kept ales, wooden beams, and traditional bar snacks. ⊠ *1 Ely Ct., City of London* ⊹ *Off 8 Hatton Gardens* ☎ *020/7405–4751* ⊕ *www.yeoldemitreholburn.co.uk* ⊗ *Closed weekends* Ⓜ *Chancery La.*

FAMILY

Ye Olde Watling. This busy corner pub has been rebuilt at least three times since 1666. One of its incarnations was as the drawing office for Sir Christopher Wren, who used it while building nearby St. Paul's Cathedral. The ground floor is a laid-back pub, while the upstairs houses an atmospheric restaurant, complete with wooden beams and trestle tables, and offering a basic English pub menu, such as fish-and-chips, and Gloucester old-spot sausages. ⊠ *29 Watling St., City of London* ☎ *020/7248–8935* ⊕ *www.nicholsonspubs.co.uk* Ⓜ *Mansion House.*

16

EAST LONDON

East London's bar scene is ever evolving, with the trendy hipster crowd constantly pushing farther east in search of the next big thing. Shoreditch has bars and clubs to suit nearly all tastes these days, while Dalston, the neighborhood to its north, attracts an edgier, younger clientele. In historic neighborhoods such as Spitalfields and Wapping, there's a cozy old drinking den around practically every corner.

BARS

Birthdays. Dalston is probably London's hippest neighborhood for night-life right now, and this stark industrial bar near the top of the main drag is as hot as it gets. Join the youngish crowd for craft beers and high-end fried chicken and burgers. There's a club in the basement that hosts DJs and edgy live gigs. ⊠ *33.–35 Stoke Newington Rd., Dalston* ☎ *020/7739–7033* ⊕ *www.birthdaysdalston.com* ✉ *Bar free, club £7–£16* Ⓜ *Overground: Dalston Kingsland, Dalston Junction.*

DANCE CLUBS

XOYO. Big international DJs regularly play at this cool Shoreditch spot that's on a small side street off the main drag. The interior is industrial chic, with some banquet seating in the relaxed upstairs room and a downstairs that's a bit more hard-core. A youngish crowd dances the night away on the weekend, while weeknight live gigs attract a more diverse bunch. ⊠ *32–37 Cowper St., Shoreditch* ☎ *020/7608–2878* ⊕ *www.xoyo.co.uk* ✉ *Club nights £14–£25; gig ticket prices vary* Ⓜ *Old St.*

ECLECTIC MUSIC

Fodor's Choice ★ **Cafe Oto.** A relaxed café by day, and London's leading venue for experi-mental music by night, Cafe Oto is a Dalston institution. Its program-ming of free jazz, avant-garde electronica, and much more is enough of a draw that it regularly sells out, with music fans steaming up the windows and spilling out onto the pavement and road outside to smoke during breaks. Healthy Japanese food is served in the daytime, before customers are kicked out at 5:30 pm to make way for sound checks. It's open as a bar (no cover) on nights when no concerts are taking place. ⊠ *18–22 Ashwin St., Dalston* ⊕ *www.cafeoto.co.uk* ✉ *Café free, concerts free–£30* Ⓜ *Overground: Dalston Junction.*

PUBS

Callooh Callay. Cocktails are tasty, well-executed classics, and there's also a selection of unique instant-classics at this eccentric Hoxton bar where the bells and whistles are left to the decor. There's a secret hidden bar accessed Narnia-like through a wardrobe and an upstairs rock-themed 'Palace of Humbug' bar where VLPs (Very Lovely People) can hide away. ⊠ *65 Rivington St., Hoxton* ☎ *020/7739–4781* ⊕ *www.cal-loohcallaybar.com* Ⓜ *Old St.*

Nightjar. The feel is moody, Prohibition-era '20s Chicago at this fabu-lously low-lit tin-tiled ceiling speakeasy and basement jazz cocktail bar in Shoreditch. Book a table or chance it on the door at this no-standing venue, where live jazz and swing bands nightly keeps things lively. ⊠ *129 City Rd., Hoxton* ☎ *020/7253–4101* ⊕ *www.barnightjar.com* ✉ *£5–£8 music cover charge* Ⓜ *Old St.*

FAMILY
Fodor's Choice ★ **Prospect of Whitby.** Named after a collier ship, this is one of London's oldest riverside pubs, dating to around 1520. Although a regular for Dickens, Pepys, Samuel Johnson, and the American artist James Whistler, once upon a time it was called the Devil's Tavern because of the lowlifes—sailors, smugglers, footpads, and cutthroats—who congregated here. With a 400-year-old flagstone floor and ornamented with pewter ware and nautical objects, this much-loved "boozer"

has a terrace with views of the Thames, from where boat trips often point it out. ✉ *57 Wapping Wall, East End* ☎ *020/7481–1095* ⊕ *www.greeneking-pubs.co.uk/pubs/greater-london/prospect-of-whitby* Ⓜ *Wapping. DLR: Shadwell.*

FAMILY **The Ten Bells.** Although the number of bells in its name has varied between 8 and 12, depending on how many bells were used by neighboring Christ Church, Spitalfields, this pub retains it original mid-Victorian interior and original tiles, including a frieze depicting the area's French Huguenot silk weaving tradition on the north wall and particularly fine floral tiling on two others. Urban legend says that Jack the Ripper's third victim, Annie Chapman, had a drink here before meeting her gory end. The pub is also depicted in Alan Moore's acclaimed graphic novel *From Hell.* ✉ *84 Commercial St., Spitalfields* ☎ *020/7247–7532* ⊕ *www.tenbells.com* Ⓜ *Liverpool St.*

Worship Street Whistling Stop. Slip back in time to 19th-century London with craft beers and bitters-loaded "ginaissance" cocktails from London's young independent distillers in this Dickensian cocktail-lab-meets-gin-palace in Shoreditch. Descend the narrow staircase to a lively Victorian saloon kitted out with glazed wood panelling, exposed brickwork, various Victoriana, and mismatched 19th-century furniture. ✉ *63 Worship St., Shoreditch* ☎ *020/7274–0015* ⊕ *www.whistlingshop.com* Ⓜ *Liverpool St., Old St.*

16

SOUTH OF THE THAMES

Recent years have seen an explosion in south London nightlife, including the gentrification of Brixton, the artistic colonization of Peckham, and the continuing popularity of Vauxhall's gay clubs. Head to the area around Borough Market—one of London's oldest neighborhoods—for lively historic pubs where locals and tourists jostle for craft ales and gourmet snacks.

BARS

Fodor's Choice ★ **Aqua Shard.** This classy bar on level 31 of the Shard, London's most iconic skyscraper and the tallest building in the United Kingdom (fourth in Europe), is worth a visit for the phenomenal views alone. The cocktail list is pretty special, too—big on fruit purées and unusual bitters. No reservations are taken in the bar, so be prepared to wait during busy periods. ✉ *The Shard, 31 St. Thomas St., Level 31, London Bridge* ☎ *020/3011–1256* ⊕ *www.aquashard.co.uk* Ⓜ *London Bridge.*

FAMILY **Three Eight Four.** Epitomizing a new breed of Brixton bar, Three Eight Four mixes up inventive cocktails. The menu changes seasonally but always involves boutique spirits and unusual mixing techniques—try the Nightshade, which comes with a pipette that you use to add the final ingredient (crème de cassis) yourself. Bare lightbulbs and brick walls seem to be the style of choice for lots of cool London bars these days, but this place manages it with particular panache. A delectable selection of small dishes is also available. ✉ *384 Coldharbour La., Brixton* ☎ *020/3417–7309* ⊕ *www.threeeightfour.com* Ⓜ *Brixton.*

PUBS

FAMILY   **Anchor & Hope.** One of London's most popular gastro-pubs, the Anchor & Hope doesn't take reservations (except for the three-course prix-fixe Sunday lunch that begins at 12:30 pm). Would-be diners snake around the red-wall, wood-floor pub, kept happy by some good real ales and a fine wine list as they wait for at least 45 minutes for a table; get there by 6 pm, and you're in with a chance of being seated right away. The excellent, meaty food is old-fashioned English—for instance, salt cod, tripe, and chips (fries)—with a few modern twists. ✉ *36 The Cut, South Bank* ☎ *020/7928–9898* ⊕ *www.anchorandhopepub.co.uk* Ⓜ *Southwark.*

FAMILY   **George Inn.** Shakespeare drank in what is now London's last remaining galleried inn and Dickens featured the place in *Little Dorrit.* Now owned by the National Trust, the George Inn has a cobblestone courtyard where Shakespeare's plays were regularly performed; inside several small, completely untouched 18th-century low-ceilinged rooms lead to a so-so restaurant and the cozy Parliament Bar. ✉ *77 Borough High St., South Bank* ☎ *020/7407–2056* ⊕ *www.greeneking-pubs.co.uk/pubs/ greater-london/george-southwark* Ⓜ *London Bridge.*

FAMILY   **The Market Porter.** Opposite the foodie treasures of Borough Market, this atmospheric pub opens at 6 am (weekdays) for the market stallholders, and always seems busy. Remarkably, the place manages to remain relaxed, with helpful staff and happy customers spilling out onto the road right through the year. The wide selection of real ales is lovingly tended (and you'll find an astonishing number of pump badges and beer mats covering the ceiling and walls). The pub was transformed into the set of the "Third Hand Emporium" in *Harry Potter and the Prisoner of Azkaban.* ✉ *9 Stoney St., Borough* ☎ *020/7407–2495* ⊕ *www.the-marketporter.co.uk* Ⓜ *London Bridge.*

FAMILY   **The Mayflower.** This deeply atmospheric 17th-century riverside inn
Fodor's Choice   (rebuilt in the following century) has exposed beams, model tall masts,
★   and a terrace near the onetime berth of the famous ship on which the 102 Pilgrims sailed in 1620 to what became the American colonies. The pub has a heated jetty where customers can sit outside, or they can opt to enjoy the ancient wood-beam interiors, which can get quite packed with sightseers. Those with *Mayflower* family connections are invited to sign "The *Mayflower* Descendants" book. ✉ *117 Rotherhithe St., South East London* ☎ *020/7237–4088* ⊕ *www.mayflowerpub.co.uk* Ⓜ *Overground: Rotherhithe.*

KENSINGTON, CHELSEA, KNIGHTSBRIDGE, AND BELGRAVIA

The pages of high-society magazines are full of photographs of gorgeous young people dancing the night away at clubs—many of which are members only—in these famously swanky neighborhoods. Dress up and be prepared to splurge. Pubs here range from classy modern affairs with impressive wine lists and shared plates to tiny local institutions guaranteed to make you feel like you've stepped back into time.

KENSINGTON
PIANO BARS/LOUNGES
Piano Kensington. Grab a cocktail at the tiny bar and fight your way in to grab a prime spot around the piano for a night of riotous fun at this compact Kensington joint. The talented pianists that play here six nights a week somehow know every song requested by this surprisingly diverse crowd, and it's clear they're having a great time, too. Table bookings recommended. ⊠ *106 Kensington High St., Kensington* ☎ *020/7938–4664* ⊕ *www.pianokensington.com* Ⓜ *High St. Kensington.*

CHELSEA
JAZZ AND BLUES
FAMILY
Fodor'sChoice
★
606 Club. This Chelsea jazz club has been doing things speakeasy-style since long before it became a nightlife trend in London. Buzz the door and you'll find a basement venue showcasing mainstream and contemporary jazz by well-known U.K.-based musicians. You must eat a meal in order to consume alcohol, so allow for an extra £30. Reservations are advisable. Lunchtime jazz takes place on select Sundays; call ahead. ⊠ *90 Lots Rd., Chelsea* ☎ *020/7352–5953* ⊕ *www.606club.co.uk* 🖾 *£10–£12 music charge added to bill* Ⓜ *Fulham Broadway. Overground: Imperial Wharf.*

PUBS
FAMILY
The Anglesea Arms. This traditional, family-friendly Chelsea pub has a large terrace out front that's ideal for resting your weary feet after a shopping spree on the King's Road or a culture-packed afternoon at the great Victorian museums of South Kensington. A menu of pub-grub classics, plus fancier dishes like fresh fish or shoulder of lamb, is available both in the bar and in the more refined dining room upstairs. You'll find six lovingly tended ales on tap, and a wine list with a largely French focus. ⊠ *15 Selwood Terr., Chelsea* ☎ *020/7373–7960* ⊕ *www.angleseaarms.com* Ⓜ *South Kensington.*

KNIGHTSBRIDGE
BARS
The Blue Bar at the Berkeley Hotel. With low-slung dusty-blue walls and Edwardian plasterwork, this black onyx hotel bar at the Berkeley is ever so slightly sexy. Immaculate service, an excellent seasonal cocktail list and a trendy David Collins design make this an ideal spot for a romantic tête-à-tête, complete with jazzy music in the background. ⊠ *The Berkeley, Wilton Pl., Knightsbridge* ☎ *020/7235–6000* ⊕ *www.the-berkeley.co.uk* Ⓜ *Knightsbridge, Hyde Park Corner.*

BELGRAVIA
PUBS
FAMILY
The Grenadier. Tricky to find off a majestic Victorian stucco square, the 1720 building was originally the officers' mess for the First Royal Regiment of Foot Guards whose barracks were next door. Opened as a pub in 1818 and renamed after the Grenadier Guards, now it's adorned with antique Guards cartoons and memorabilia, and *may* be haunted by a subaltern named Cedric. Turn up on the annual Regimental Remembrance Day for a colorful army veterans' gathering. ⊠ *18 Wilton Row, Belgravia* ☎ *020/7235–3074* ⊕ *www.greeneking-pubs.co.uk/pubs/greater-london/grenadier* Ⓜ *Knightsbridge, Hyde Park Corner.*

16

FAMILY **The Nag's Head.** The landlord of this idiosyncratic little mews pub in Belgravia runs a tight ship, and no cell phones are allowed. The lovingly collected artifacts (including antique penny arcade games) that decorate every inch of the place, high-quality beer, and old-fashioned pub grub should provide more than enough distraction. ✉ *53 Kinnerton St., Belgravia* ☎ *020/7235–1135* Ⓜ *Knightsbridge, Hyde Park Corner.*

NOTTING HILL

The focus is more on bars than clubs in this west London neighborhood, although late-night fun is on offer at a few notable exceptions. In general, you can expect a young moneyed crowd making this their first stop on a wild night out elsewhere. The line between pub and bar is frequently blurred here, with an emphasis on good—often haute—food, sleek style, and extensive wine lists.

BARS

Fodor's Choice **Beach Blanket Babylon.** In a Victorian mansion house close to Portobello
★ Market, this always-packed bar is distinguishable by its eclectic indoor–outdoor spaces with Gaudí-esque curves and snug corner spaces—like a candlelit fairy-tale grotto, folly, or a medieval dungeon. A sister restaurant-bar-gallery offers a slightly more modern take on similar themes in an ex-warehouse in Shoreditch (*19–23 Bethnal Green Rd.; 020/7749–3540*). ✉ *45 Ledbury Rd., Notting Hill* ☎ *020/7229–2907* ⊕ *www.beachblanket.co.uk* Ⓜ *Notting Hill Gate.*

FAMILY **Electric Diner.** A huge selection of bottled beers and quirky twists on classic cocktails (Courvoisier, mint, and champagne anyone?) are the attractions at this bar and diner next to Notting Hill's famed Electric Cinema on Portobello Road. Run by the people behind the members-only Soho House, the place exudes the same effortless mixture of posh and cool, but it is open to anyone and everyone. Sit in the window and watch the world go by along Portobello, or opt for one of the luxury takes on classic diner fare at a booth in the moody, vaulted interior. ✉ *191 Portobello Rd., Notting Hill* ☎ *020/7908–9696* ⊕ *www.electric-diner.com* Ⓜ *Ladbroke Grove.*

PUBS

FAMILY **The Cow.** Crowds head to this boho-chic mix of fun, haute seafood, and friendly retro style for Guinness and rock oysters, either enjoying them in the unpretentious downstairs saloon bar or the more formal dining rooms upstairs. The pub food is all excellent, though pricey, with lots of fresh seafood platters, pies, and steaks. The atmosphere's always warm, welcoming, and buzzing. ✉ *89 Westbourne Park Rd., Notting Hill* ☎ *020/7221–0021* ⊕ *www.thecowlondon.co.uk* Ⓜ *Westbourne Park, Royal Oak.*

REGENT'S PARK AND HAMPSTEAD

London's villagelike northern neighborhoods all boast fantastic local boozers where you can easily while away an afternoon. Camden Town has more of a buzz and attracts a younger international crowd with its dance clubs and music venues. Every genre is covered, from folk and pop to jazz and world music, with interesting gigs taking place every night of the week.

REGENT'S PARK
DANCE CLUBS
KOKO. Once known as Camden Palace, this legendary Victorian theater venue has seen acts from Charlie Chaplin to Madonna, and genres from punk to acid house rave. Furnished with lush reds that make it not unlike a cockney Moulin Rouge, this is still one of London's most stunning venues. Sounds of live indie rock, cabaret, funky house, and club classics keep the big dance floor moving, even when it's not heaving. ⊠ *1A Camden High St., Camden Town* ☎ *020/7388–3222* ⊕ *www.koko.uk.com* ☎ *£6–£33* Ⓜ *Mornington Crescent.*

ECLECTIC MUSIC
FAMILY **Roundhouse.** This 1840s former London and Birmingham Railway terminus and onetime gin warehouse in Chalk Farm now hosts some of the most atmospheric medium-scale rock and pop gigs in the capital, plus a varied program of circus, theater, contemporary dance, and the occasional art installation. There's a good restaurant on the first floor, and in the summer the terrace bar is transformed into a popular "urban beach," complete with sand. ⊠ *Chalk Farm Rd., Chalk Farm* ☎ *0300/6789–222* ⊕ *www.roundhouse.org.uk* ☎ *£5–£40* Ⓜ *Chalk Farm.*

JAZZ AND BLUES
Fodor's Choice ★ **Jazz Café.** A palace of cool in bohemian Camden, this remains an essential hangout for fans of both the mainstream end of the jazz repertoire and hip-hop, funk, world music, and Latin fusion. It's also the unlikely venue for "I Love the 80s Vs I Love the 90s" on Saturday night. Book ahead if you want a prime table in the balcony restaurant overlooking the stage. ⊠ *5 Parkway, Camden Town* ☎ *020/7485–6834 for venue info, 020/7485–6834 for tickets (Ticketmaster)* ⊕ *www.thejazzcafelondon.com* ☎ *£6–£35* Ⓜ *Camden Town.*

ROCK
The Camden Assembly. At one of the finest small clubs in the capital, punk, indie guitar, and new metal rock attract a nonmainstream crowd. Weekend club nights upstairs host DJs (and live bands) who rock the decks. ⊠ *49 Chalk Farm Rd., Camden Town* ☎ *020/7424–0800 for venue, 020/7424–0800 for tickets* ⊕ *www.camdenassembly.com* ☎ *Free–£14* Ⓜ *Chalk Farm.*

The Forum. The best up-and-coming and medium-to-big-name rock performers consistently play at this 2,000-capacity club. It's a converted 1920 art deco movie theater, with a balcony overlooking the grungy dance floor. ⊠ *9–17 Highgate Rd., Kentish Town* ☎ *0844/477–2000 for tickets* ☎ *£12–£60* Ⓜ *Kentish Town.*

HAMPSTEAD
PUBS
FAMILY **The Holly Bush.** A short walk up the hill from Hampstead Tube station, the friendly Holly Bush was a country pub before London spread this far north. It retains something of a rural feel, with stripped wooden floors, tobacco-color walls, and an open fire, and is an intimate place to enjoy great ales and organic and free-range pub food. Try the homemade pork scratchings (crispy rinds) and pickled eggs, and don't miss the hot cider

16

in the wintertime. ⊠ *22 Holly Mount, Hampstead* ☎ *020/7435–2892* ⊕ *www.hollybushhampstead.co.uk* Ⓜ *Hampstead.*

FAMILY **The Spaniards Inn.** Ideal as a refueling point when you're on a hike in
Fodor'sChoice Hampstead Heath, this historic, country-style, oak-beam pub has a gor-
★ geous garden—the scene of the tea party in Dickens's *Pickwick Papers.*
Dick Turpin, the infamous highwayman, frequented the 1585 inn before
Dickens's time, and the great poets Shelley, Keats, Blake, and Byron
hung out here as well. The place is extremely popular, especially on Sunday, when Londoners roll in. It's canine-friendly, too—there's even a dog
wash in the garden. ⊠ *Spaniards Rd., Hampstead* ☎ *020/8731–8406*
⊕ *www.thespaniardshampstead.co.uk* Ⓜ *Hampstead.*

THE THAMES UPSTREAM

A pint in a riverside pub is a London must, and the capital's western
reaches (including the Richmond and Hammersmith neighborhoods)
offer some truly picturesque drinking opportunities. Pick a traditional
establishment and you'll feel like you've ventured far from the Big Smoke.

RICHMOND
PUBS
FAMILY **Roebuck.** Perched on top of Richmond Hill, the Roebuck has perhaps
the best view of any pub in London. The most sought-after seats are the
benches found directly across the road, which look out over the Thames
as it winds its way into the countryside below. Friendly and surprisingly
unpretentious, given its lofty surrounds, it is well worth the long climb
up the hill from the center of Richmond. ⊠ *130 Richmond Hill, Richmond* ☎ *020/8948–2329* ⊕ *www.greeneking-pubs.co.uk* Ⓜ *Richmond.*

HAMMERSMITH
PUBS
FAMILY **The Dove.** Read the list of famous ex-regulars, from Charles II and Nell
Fodor'sChoice Gwynn to Ernest Hemingway and Dylan Thomas, as you wait for a beer
★ at this smart, comely, and popular 16th-century Thames riverside pub
on the Upper Mall towpath in Hammersmith. If—as is often the case—
the Dove is too full, stroll upstream along the bank to the Old Ship
or Blue Anchor. ⊠ *19 Upper Mall, Hammersmith* ☎ *020/8748–9474*
⊕ *www.dovehammersmith.co.uk* Ⓜ *Hammersmith.*

17

PERFORMING ARTS

National Theatre

Updated by
Jo Caird

"All the world's a stage," said Shakespeare, immortal words heard for the first time right here in London. And whether you prefer your theater, music, and art classical or modern, or as contemporary twists on time-honored classics, you'll find that London's vibrant cultural scene more than holds its own on the world stage.

Divas sing original-language librettos at the Royal Opera House, Shakespeare's plays are brought to life at the reconstructed Globe Theatre, and challenging new writing is produced at the Royal Court. Whether you feel like basking in the lighthearted extravagance of a West End musical or taking in the next shark-in-formaldehyde at the White Cube gallery, the choice is yours.

There are international theater festivals, innovative music festivals, and critically acclaimed seasons of postmodern dance. Short trip or long, you'll find the cultural scene in London is ever-changing, ever-expanding, and ever-exciting.

No matter where you head, London's art and performing arts scenes have been setting global trends for decades—and even for centuries, when you count Shakespearean theater and Handel oratorios. Fringe theater, classical ballet, participatory chorales: you name it, and London probably did it first (and often still does it best).

PLANNING

FIND OUT WHAT'S PLAYING WHERE

To find out what's showing now, the free weekly magazine *Time Out* (issued every Tuesday outside major stations and around the city; also online at ⊕ *www.timeout.com*) is invaluable.

The free *Evening Standard* carries listings, many of which are also available online at ⊕ *www.standard.co.uk*. *Metro*, London's other widely available free newspaper, is also worth checking out, as are many Sunday papers, and the Saturday *Telegraph*, *Guardian*, and *Times*.

The website ⊕ *www.whatsonstage.com* is an invaluable resource for theater listings.

There are hundreds of small private galleries all over London with interesting work by famous and emerging artists. The bimonthly free pamphlet "new exhibitions of contemporary art" (⊕ *www.newexhibitions.com*), available at most galleries, lists and maps nearly 200 art spaces in London.

FESTIVALS AND EVENTS

BFI London Film Festival. More than 200 feature films, many of them world or European premieres, plus shorts and artist talks, grace the program of the BFI London Film Festival, which takes place over 12 days every October. The big movie theaters in Leicester Square are the focus for the galas and major releases, but you can catch screenings at a total of 15 other venues across town, including unusual locations like the National Gallery. Booking ahead advised. ⊠ *London* ☏ *020/7928–3232* ⊕ *whatson.bfi.org.uk/lff* ⊑ *£9–£40.*

Dance Umbrella. The biggest annual performing arts event in London is Dance Umbrella, a 20-day festival in October that hosts international and British-based artists at venues across the city. ⊠ *London* ☏ *020/7257–9380* ⊕ *www.danceumbrella.co.uk* ⊑ *Free–£28.*

Fodor's Choice ★

Frieze London. A glamorous contemporary art fair, Frieze London brings the crème de la crème of the international art world to London each October. Its sister show, Frieze Masters, is a 15-minute walk across Regent's Park and focuses on art from the ancient world through the late 20th century. For the two events combined, hundreds of galleries exhibiting thousands of artworks—everything from Old Masters to Rachel Whiteread—fill two huge pop-up spaces in the park. The food and drink available on-site is pricey but excellent, and there's a compelling program of artist and curator talks. ⊠ *Regent's Park, Regent's Park* ☏ *020/3372–6111* ⊕ *www.frieze.com/fairs/frieze-london* ⊑ *Combined ticket £52* Ⓜ *Regent's Park, Baker St., Great Portland St.*

FAMILY

London Jazz Festival. Come November, international jazz superstars rub shoulders with upcoming local talent and cutting-edge bands at 60 venues across the city during the 10 days of the London Jazz Festival. A varied program of around 350 performances, including free concerts and gigs for toddlers, means both jazz connoisseurs and those new to the genre will find plenty to enjoy. ⊠ *London* ⊕ *www.efglondonjazzfestival.org.uk* ⊑ *Free–£65.*

Meltdown. The wildly eclectic and very cool Meltdown Festival takes place in June at the Southbank Centre. It's curated by a different big-name artist each year (e.g., M.I.A. in 2017 and Robert Smith in 2018), so you never have any idea what to expect until the program comes out. ⊠ *Belvedere Rd., South Bank* ☏ *020/3879–9555* ⊕ *www.southbankcentre.co.uk* ⊑ *Free–£65* Ⓜ *Waterloo, Embankment.*

Vault Festival. This six-week extravaganza of fringe theater and stand-up comedy is a chance to see some of the U.K.'s most innovative and engaging performers. The atmosphere in the eerie tunnels beneath Waterloo Station (where the Vault Festival takes place) is always

17

buzzing. ⊠ *The Vaults, Leake St., South Bank* ☎ *07598/676–202* ⊕ *www.vaultfestival.com* 🎫 *£5–£26.50* Ⓜ *Waterloo.*

PERFORMING ARTS REVIEWS

ST. JAMES'S AND WESTMINSTER

Wander the streets of this chic central London neighborhood—home to aristocrats in the 17th century—to discover small commercial galleries, fine-art auction houses, and antiques dealers mixed in among the high-end tailors and gentlemen's clubs.

ART GALLERIES

Institute of Contemporary Arts (*ICA*). Housed in an elegant John Nash–designed Regency terrace, the ICA's two galleries have changing exhibitions of contemporary visual art. The ICA also programs performances, underground and vintage movies, talks, and photography, and there's an excellent arts bookstore, a cafeteria run by top chef Margot Henderson, and a funky bar. ⊠ *The Mall, St. James's* ☎ *020/7930–3647* ⊕ *www.ica. org.uk* 🎫 *£1, cinema tickets £6–£11* ☉ *Closed Mon.* Ⓜ *Charing Cross, Piccadilly Circus.*

White Cube. The English role in the exploding contemporary art scene has been major, thanks in good portion to Jay Joplin's influential gallery, which has regularly moved around London since 1993. This striking modern concrete structure was the first freestanding building to be built in the area for 30 years when it opened in 2006. It is home base for an array of British artists who have won the Turner Prize, including Damien Hirst, Tracey Emin, and Gary Hume. ⊠ *25–26 Mason's Yard, St. James's* ☎ *020/7930–5373* ⊕ *www.whitecube.com* 🎫 *Free* ☉ *Closed Sun. and Mon.* Ⓜ *Green Park, Piccadilly Circus.*

CLASSICAL MUSIC

St. John's Smith Square. Chamber music, organ recitals, and orchestral concerts are held at this baroque church behind Westminster Abbey. There are three or four lunchtime recitals a month. ⊠ *Smith Sq., Westminster* ☎ *020/7222–1061* ⊕ *www.sjss.org.uk* 🎫 *Free–£60* Ⓜ *Westminster.*

MAYFAIR AND MARYLEBONE

The historic center of the London art world, Mayfair has a thriving gallery scene that has undergone a renaissance in recent years. With East End gallerists relocating to central London and a number of top international galleries opening new premises here, there's a real buzz about the place. Directly north of Mayfair, Marylebone has more of a village atmosphere, with a few choice galleries and arts institutions dotted around.

MAYFAIR

ART GALLERIES

Marlborough Fine Art. This veteran of the Mayfair art scene has been presenting exhibitions by masters old and new since it was founded in 1946. Great living artists like Paula Rego and Frank Auerbach, plus exhibitions of graphic works from a whole host of starry names, are showcased in the main first floor space, while the contemporary gallery on the second floor puts the spotlight on a younger generation of artists from the U.K. and abroad. ✉ *6 Albermarle St., Mayfair* ☎ *020/7629–5161* ⊕ *www.marlboroughfineart.com* ✆ *Free* ⊙ *Closed Sun.* Ⓜ *Green Park, Piccadilly Circus.*

MARYLEBONE

ART GALLERIES

Lisson. Owner Nicholas Logsdail represents about 50 blue-chip artists, including the minimalist Sol LeWitt and performance artist Marina Abramović, at one of the most respected galleries in London. The gallery is most associated with New Object sculptors like Anish Kapoor and Richard Deacon, many of whom have won the Turner Prize. There's another branch down the road at 27 Bell Street. ✉ *52 Bell St., Marylebone* ☎ *020/7724–2739* ⊕ *www.lissongallery.com* ✆ *Free* ⊙ *Closed Sun.* Ⓜ *Edgware Rd., Marylebone.*

CLASSICAL MUSIC

FAMILY

Fodor'sChoice

★

Wigmore Hall. London's most beautiful venue for chamber music also happens to boast near-perfect acoustics. The hall has a rich history, including hosting the premieres of a number of works by the British composer Benjamin Britten, and today attracts leading ensembles from all over the world. The varied program contains lunchtime and Sunday morning concerts, plus workshops and concerts for babies and toddlers. ✉ *36 Wigmore St., Marylebone* ☎ *020/7935–2141* ⊕ *www.wigmore-hall.org.uk* ✆ *£18–£50* Ⓜ *Bond St.*

SOHO AND COVENT GARDEN

London's hip center has it all, from multiplexes playing the biggest blockbuster movies to niche contemporary art galleries tucked away in backstreets, and from world-famous opera houses to sultry cabaret joints.

SOHO

ART GALLERIES

Fodor'sChoice

★

Photographer's Gallery. Britain's first and foremost photography gallery programs cutting-edge and provocative exhibitions. The prestigious Deutsche Börse Photography Prize is exhibited and awarded here annually. The gallery also has a print sales room, a bookstore, and a café-bar—a great spot to escape the bustle of nearby Oxford Street. ✉ *16–18 Ramillies St., Soho* ☎ *020/7087–9300* ⊕ *www.thephotographersgallery.org.uk* ✆ *Free until noon; £4 thereafter* Ⓜ *Oxford Circus.*

Sadie Coles HQ. Containing the work of important British and international artists such as Sarah Lucas and Wilhelm Sasnal, this light-filled art space overlooking busy Regent Street marked a major expansion for

17

respected British gallerist Sadie Coles when it opened in fall 2013. ⊠ *62 Kingly St., Soho* ☎ *020/7493–8611* ⊕ *www.sadiecoles.com* ⟳ *Closed Sun. and Mon.* Ⓜ *Oxford Circus, Piccadilly Circus.*

FILM

Curzon Soho. This popular, comfortable movie theater runs a vibrant and artsy program of mixed repertoire and mainstream films, with a good calendar of director talks and other events, too. The bar is great for a quiet drink, even when Soho is crawling with people. There are further Curzon branches in Mayfair, Bloomsbury, Aldgate, Victoria, Wimbledon, and Richmond. ⊠ *99 Shaftesbury Ave., Soho* ☎ *0330/500–1331* ⊕ *www. curzoncinemas.com* 🎫 *£10.50–£16* Ⓜ *Piccadilly Circus, Leicester Sq.*

FAMILY **Prince Charles Cinema.** This repertory movie theater right off Leicester Square offers you a chance to catch up with independent features, documentaries, and even blockbusters you may have missed. A second screen upstairs shows newer movies at more usual West End prices. This is where the "sing-along screening" took off; come in character and warble along to *The Sound of Music, Grease, The Rocky Horror Picture Show,* and others. ⊠ *7 Leicester Pl., Soho* ☎ *020/7494–3654* ⊕ *www.princecharlescinema.com* 🎫 *£9–£12; sing-alongs £16* Ⓜ *Leicester Sq., Piccadilly Circus.*

THEATER

Soho Theatre. This sleek theater in the heart of Soho is devoted to fostering new work and is a prolific presenter of plays by emerging writers, comedy performances, cabaret shows, and other entertainment. The bar is always buzzing. ⊠ *21 Dean St., Soho* ☎ *020/7478–0100* ⊕ *www. sohotheatre.com* 🎫 *£10–£30* Ⓜ *Tottenham Court Rd.*

COVENT GARDEN

PERFORMING ARTS CENTERS

The London Coliseum. A veritable architectural extravaganza of Edwardian exoticism, the baroque-style theater has a magnificent auditorium and a rooftop glass dome with a bar and great views. As one of the city's most venerable theaters, the Coliseum functions mainly as the home of the English National Opera, which produces innovative opera, sung in English, for lower prices than the Royal Opera House. In recent years the company also has presented musicals, sometimes featuring star opera singers. During opera's off-season (including summertime and during winter holidays), the house hosts the English National Ballet (⊕ *www.ballet.org.uk*) and other troupes. Guided tours offering fascinating insights into the architecture and history of the building take place on selected dates at 11 am and 2 pm. ⊠ *St. Martin's La., Covent Garden* ☎ *020/7845–9300* ⊕ *www.eno.org* 🎫 *Opera £12–£125, ballet £14–£79, tours £10* Ⓜ *Leicester Sq., Charing Cross.*

OPERA

Fodor's Choice **Royal Opera House.** Along with Milan's La Scala, New York's Metropolitan, and the Palais Garnier in Paris, this is one of the world's great opera ★ houses. The resident troupe has mounted spectacular productions in the past, while recent productions have tended toward more contemporary operas. Whatever the style of the performance, the extravagant theater delivers a full dose of opulence. The famed Royal Ballet performs classical and contemporary repertoire here, too, and smaller-scale works of both opera and dance are presented in the Linbury Studio Theatre and Clore Studio Upstairs. A small allocation of tickets for each performance of main stage productions for the week ahead—even those that are sold out—goes on sale online at 1 pm every Friday. ■TIP→ *If you wish to see the hall but are not able to procure a ticket, you can join a backstage tour or one of the less frequent tours of the auditorium; they book up several weeks in advance.* BP Big Screens is the ROH's summer series of live relays of its opera and ballet productions; screenings are free and take place outdoors in public spaces all over the country, including Trafalgar Square. ⊠ *Bow St., Covent Garden* ☎ *020/7304–4000* ⊕ *www.roh.org.uk* ⊠ *Performances £4–£280; tours £10–£15* Ⓜ *Covent Garden.*

BLOOMSBURY AND HOLBORN

Once the heart of fashionable literary London, there's still an air of refinement about this neighborhood. A handful of small theaters with links to the colleges with campuses in the area create a vibrant small-scale performance scene with theater, dance, and stand-up comedy.

CLASSICAL MUSIC

Kings Place. The cultural jewel among the huge developments near the Eurostar terminal in King's Cross, this airy concert venue is the permanent home of the London Sinfonietta and the Orchestra of the Age of Enlightenment. Kings Place presents a hugely varied cultural calendar of jazz, comedy, folk, and political and literary lectures, plus two gallery spaces. ⊠ *90 York Way, King's Cross* ☎ *020/7520–1490* ⊕ *www.kingsplace.co.uk* ⊠ *£10–£70* Ⓜ *King's Cross.*

DANCE

Peacock Theatre. Sadler's Wells's West End annex, this modernist theater near the London School of Economics (which uses it as a lecture hall during the day) focuses on younger companies and it shows in popular dance genres like flamenco, tango, and hip-hop. ⊠ *Portugal St., Holborn* ☎ *020/7863–8222* ⊕ *www.peacocktheatre.com* ⊠ *£12–£45* Ⓜ *Holborn.*

The Place. The Robin Howard Dance Theatre at The Place is London's only theater dedicated to contemporary dance, and with tickets often under £20 (performances by student dancers, for example, cost just £15), it's good value, too. The "Resolution" festival in January and February is the United Kingdom's biggest platform event for new choreographers. ⊠ *17 Duke's Rd., Bloomsbury* ☎ *020/7121–1100* ⊕ *www.theplace.org.uk* ⊠ *£10–£25* Ⓜ *Euston.*

17

ISLINGTON

Close to central London, yet with its own unique atmosphere, this neighborhood is home to a handful of renowned theaters and music venues that make the short journey northeast well worth the effort.

ART GALLERIES

Victoria Miro Gallery. This large, important commercial gallery, in a former furniture factory, has exhibited some of the biggest names on the British contemporary art scene: Grayson Perry, the Chapman Brothers, and Peter Doig, to name a few. Some exhibitions spill out into the gallery's garden. It also brings in exciting talent from abroad. There's another branch in Mayfair. ⊠ *16 Wharf Rd., Islington* 🕾 *020/7336–8109* ⊕ *www.victoria-miro.com* 🖃 *Free* Ⓜ *Old St., Angel.*

DANCE

FAMILY

Fodor'sChoice

★

Sadler's Wells. Head to this gleaming building, which opened in 1998 and is the seventh on the site in its 300-year history, to see performances by leading classical and contemporary dance companies. Matthew Bourne's New Adventures is in residence, and the little Lilian Baylis Studio hosts avant-garde work. ⊠ *Rosebery Ave., Islington* 🕾 *020/7863–8000* ⊕ *www.sadlerswells.com* 🖃 *£12–£45* Ⓜ *Angel.*

THEATER

Almeida Theatre. This Off West End venue, helmed by director Rupert Goold, premiers excellent new plays and exciting twists on the classics, often featuring high-profile actors. There's a good café and a licensed bar that serves "sharing dishes," as well as tasty main courses. ⊠ *Almeida St., Islington* 🕾 *020/7359–4404* ⊕ *www.almeida.co.uk* 🖃 *£10–£40* Ⓜ *Angel, Highbury & Islington.*

FAMILY

Little Angel Theatre. Innovative puppetry performances for children and adults have been taking place in this adorable former temperance hall since 1961. ⊠ *14 Dagmar Passage, Islington* 🕾 *020/7226–1787* ⊕ *www. littleangeltheatre.com* 🖃 *£5–£15* Ⓜ *Angel, Highbury & Islington.*

THE CITY

It may seem at first glance like the denizens of London's financial center are far too busy to take time out for culture, but look a little closer: arts events are taking place all over, courtesy of a number of acclaimed annual festivals. Art exhibits in empty offices and chamber performances in historic churches are regular occurrences.

PERFORMING ARTS CENTERS

FAMILY

Barbican Centre. Opened in 1982, the Barbican is an enormous Brutalist concrete maze that Londoners either love or hate—but its importance to the cultural life of the capital is beyond dispute. At the largest performing arts center in Europe, you could listen to Elgar, see 1960s photography, and catch German animation with live accompaniment, all in one day. The main concert hall, known for its acoustics, is most famous as the home of the London Symphony Orchestra. The Barbican is also a frequent host to the BBC Symphony Orchestra. Architecture tours take place several times a week. ⊠ *Silk St., City of London* 🕾 *020/7638–8891*

⊕ www.barbican.org.uk ✉ Art exhibits free–£14.50, cinema £6–£14, theater and music £10–£85, tours £12.50 Ⓜ Barbican.

EAST LONDON

Artists and other creative types, no longer able to afford central London rents, have been making their way eastward for years. It began in Shoreditch, but as rents increased there, too, neighborhoods farther and farther out have taken on these new residents. Go gallery hopping in Vyner Street in Bethnal Green or catch a hip band in action at one of Shoreditch's myriad music venues.

PERFORMING ARTS CENTERS

Fodor'sChoice ★ **Wilton's.** Arguably London's most atmospheric cultural space, Wilton's has been entertaining the crowds since 1743, first as an alehouse, then as a music hall. It now hosts gigs, talks, theater performances, movie screenings (often with live scores), and swing-dance evenings. The cozy Mahogany Bar, the oldest part of the building, serves a good range of quality local ales, along with snacks and meals that change according to what's playing in the theater. There's a cocktail bar upstairs, in what was once the artists' green room. *⊠ Graces Alley, East End ☎ 020/7702–2789 ⊕ www.wiltons.org.uk ✉ £10–£35 Ⓜ Aldgate East, Tower Hill.*

THEATER

FAMILY **Hackney Empire.** The history of this treasure of a theater is drama in its own right. Charlie Chaplin is said to have appeared at Hackney Empire during its days as a thriving variety theater and music hall in the early 1900s. The theater now hosts traditional family entertainment and variety shows, opera, music, musical theater, dance, and drama, often with a multicultural slant. Its annual Christmas pantomime show is legendary. *⊠ 291 Mare St., Hackney ☎ 020/8985–2424 ⊕ www.hackneyempire. co.uk ✉ £5–£65 Ⓜ Overground: Hackney Central.*

17

SOUTH OF THE THAMES

The South Bank and its easterly near neighbor Bankside together make up one of the richest areas in London when it comes to arts and entertainment. Whether you want to watch a play, hear a concert, or see an art exhibit, you won't have to wander far to find something top class. Venture a little farther into south London for a sprinkling of fringe theaters that act as incubators for the capital's mainstream theater scene.

FILM

FAMILY **BFI London IMAX Cinema.** The British Film Institute's glazed drum-shaped IMAX theater (now, confusingly, operated by Odeon) has the largest screen in the United Kingdom (approximately 75 feet wide and the height of five double-decker buses). It shows state-of-the-art 2-D and 3-D films. *⊠ 1 Charlie Chaplin Walk, South Bank ☎ 0330/333–7878 ⊕ www.bfi.org.uk/imax ✉ £15–£25 Ⓜ Waterloo.*

FAMILY **BFI Southbank.** With the best repertory programming in London, the three movie theaters and studio here are effectively a national film center run by the British Film Institute. More than 1,000 titles are screened each year, with art-house, foreign, silent, overlooked, classic, noir, and short films favored over recent Hollywood blockbusters. The center also has a gallery, bookshop, and "mediatheque" where visitors can watch film and television from the National Archive for free (closed Monday). This is one of the venues for the BFI London Film Festival; throughout the year there are minifestivals, seminars, and guest speakers. ■TIP➔ The BFI Bar & Kitchen, toward the back of the building, is a great secret spot for a drink. ✉ *Belvedere Rd., South Bank* 🕾 *020/7928–3232* ⊕ *www.bfi.org.uk* 🎫 *£10–£17* Ⓜ *Waterloo.*

PERFORMING ARTS CENTERS

FAMILY **The Scoop.** This open-air amphitheater next to the Thames at City Hall hosts free theater performances, film screenings (including live relays from the Royal Opera House), live music, circus and dance workshops, and talks every night in June, July, and August. Theater productions are often family-friendly tellings of classic Greek plays, with postshow chats taking place on select dates. ✉ *Queens Walk, London Bridge* 🕾 *020/7240–0344* ⊕ *www.thelondonriviera.com* 🎫 *Free* Ⓜ *London Bridge, Tower Hill.*

FAMILY

Fodor'sChoice

★

Southbank Centre. The public has never really warmed to the Southbank Centre's hulking concrete buildings (beloved by architecture aficionados), products of the Brutalist style popular when the center was built in the 1950s and '60s—but all the same, the masses flock to the concerts, recitals, festivals, and exhibitions held here, Europe's largest arts center. The **Royal Festival Hall** is truly a People's Palace, with seats for 2,900 and a schedule that ranges from major symphony orchestras to pop stars. The smaller **Queen Elizabeth Hall** is more classically oriented. It contains the **Purcell Room,** which hosts lectures and chamber performances. For art, head to the **Hayward Gallery,** which hosts shows on top contemporary artists such as Anthony Gormley and Cy Twombly. The Queen Elizabeth Hall and Hayward Gallery reopened in early 2018 following a major renovation and are looking and sounding better than ever. The center's riverside street level has a terrific assortment of restaurants and bars, though you'll need to head to The Cut, just south of here, for independent eateries. ✉ *Belvedere Rd., South Bank* 🕾 *020/3879–9555* ⊕ *www.southbankcentre.co.uk* 🎫 *Free–£120* Ⓜ *Waterloo, Embankment.*

THEATER

Fodor'sChoice

★

Battersea Arts Centre (*BAC*). Battersea Arts Centre has a reputation for producing innovative new work as well as hosting top alternative stand-up comics. Performances take place in quirky spaces all over this atmospheric former town hall. Check out Scratch events, low-tech theater where the audience provides feedback on works-in-progress. Entry for Scratch events is pay-what-you-can (minimum £3). The bar, which serves snacks and sharing plates, is open all day. ✉ *176 Lavender Hill, Battersea* 🕾 *020/7223–2223* ⊕ *www.bac.org.uk* 🎫 *Pay what you can (£3 suggested)–£30* Ⓜ *National Rail: Clapham Junction.*

The Bridge Theatre. This gleaming new theater on the banks of the River Thames by Tower Bridge is the brainchild of director Nicholas Hytner and producer Nick Starr, who together oversaw a golden age at the National Theatre before handing over the reins to current artistic

CONTEMPORARY ART: LONDON TODAY

In the 21st century, the focus of the city's art scene has shifted from the past to the future. Helped by the prominence of Tate Modern, London's contemporary art scene has never been so high profile. In publicly funded exhibition spaces like the Barbican Gallery, the Hayward Gallery, and the Institute of Contemporary Arts, London now has a modern art environment on par with that of Bilbao and New York. The so-called Young British Artists (YBAs, although no longer that young) Damien Hirst, Tracey Emin, and others are firmly planted in the public imagination. The celebrity status of British artists has a lot to do with the annual Turner Prize, which always stirs up controversy in the media during the display of the work, usually at Tate Britain.

Depending on who you talk to, the Saatchi Gallery is considered to be either the savior of contemporary art or the wardrobe of the emperor's new clothes. After a couple of moves it is now ensconced in the former Duke of York's barracks off Chelsea's King's Road.

The South Bank's Tate Modern may house the giants of modern art, but east London is where the innovative action is. There are dozens of galleries in the fashionable spaces around Old Street, and the truly hip have already moved even farther afield, to areas such as Bethnal Green, to the east, and Peckham, to the south. The Whitechapel Art Gallery and Jay Jopling's influential White Cube, with branches in Bermondsey and St. James's, remain essential parts of the new art establishment and continue to show exciting work by emerging British artists.

On the first Thursday of every month, more than 130 museums and galleries in east London stay open late and host talks, workshops, and other events (more information at ⊕ www.firstthursdays.co.uk).

director Rufus Norris in 2015. The program at this totally adaptable space is a blend of the classics (Hytner's *Julius Caesar* was a huge hit in 2018) and riskier new works through big-name actors (e.g., Ben Whishaw, Laura Linney) are a constant. ⊠ *3 Potters Fields Park, London Bridge* ☎ *033/3320–0051* ⊕ *www.bridgetheatre.co.uk* 🎫 *£15–£90* Ⓜ *London Bridge, Tower Hill.*

FAMILY
Fodor's Choice
★

National Theatre. When this theater designed by Sir Denys Lasdun opened in 1976, Londoners weren't all so keen on the low-slung Brutalist block. Prince Charles described it as "a clever way of building a nuclear power station in the middle of London without anyone objecting." But whatever its merits or demerits, the National Theatre's interior spaces are worth a visit. Interspersed with the three theaters—the 1,150-seat Olivier, the 890-seat Lyttelton, and the 450-seat Dorfman—is a multilayered foyer with exhibitions, bars, restaurants, and free entertainment. Musicals, classics, and plays are performed by top-flight professionals, and they sometimes give talks as well. Backstage, costume, and architecture tours are available. The Clore Learning Centre offers courses and events on all aspects of theater making, and you can watch staff at work in the backstage workshops from the Sherling High-Level Walkway. Each weekend in August, the River Stage Festival presents live music, dance, workshops, and DJ sets in the area in front of the theater. ✉ *Belvedere Rd., South Bank* ☎ *020/7452–3000* ⊕ *www.nationaltheatre.org.uk* 🎫 *£15–£72, tours £11–£12.50* Ⓜ *Waterloo.*

The Old Vic. In 2015 Matthew Warchus, the director behind *Matilda the Musical,* took over as artistic director at this grand old theater, the former haunting grounds of such stage legends as John Gielgud, Vivien Leigh, Peter O'Toole, Richard Burton, and Judi Dench. The venue had suffered decades of financial duress before being brought under the ownership of a dedicated trust headed by its previous artistic director, actor Kevin Spacey. Notwithstanding a bumpy period in the wake of numerous allegations of inappropriate behavior leveled at Spacey as a result of the #MeToo movement, The Old Vic is now in great shape, secure for the future and producing some of the best theater in London. ✉ *The Cut, Southwark* ☎ *0844/871–7628* ⊕ *www.oldvictheatre.com* 🎫 *£10–£65* Ⓜ *Waterloo, Southwark.*

Shakespeare's Globe Theatre. *See full listing in Chapter 8: South of the Thames.*

Southwark Playhouse. This impressive little theater, in what was once a car showroom, produces award-winning new musicals and gritty drama for a fraction of the cost of the West End. The bar-café is good, too, which is fortunate—the surrounding area is something of a culinary no-man's-land. ✉ *77–85 Newington Causeway, Borough* ☎ *020/7407–0234* ⊕ *www. southwarkplayhouse.co.uk* 🎫 *£12–£25* Ⓜ *Borough, Elephant & Castle.*

FAMILY **Unicorn Theatre.** Dedicated to innovative work for young audiences, this modern theater hosts plays, musicals, and interactive theater for everyone from toddlers on up. Inclusivity is a major focus, with performances for those with visual and hearing and other impairments taking place regularly. ✉ *147 Tooley St., Borough* ☎ *020/7645–0560* ⊕ *www.unicorntheatre.com* 🎫 *£8–£22* Ⓜ *London Bridge.*

Young Vic. At this Waterloo theater, big names perform alongside young talent, often in daring innovative productions of classic plays that appeal to a more diverse audience than is traditionally found on the London scene. Good food is served all day at the bustling bar. ✉ *66 The Cut, Waterloo, South Bank* ☎ *020/7922–2922* ⊕ *www.youngvic. org* 🎫 *£10–£40* Ⓜ *Southwark, Waterloo.*

KENSINGTON AND CHELSEA

These refined neighborhoods just west of central London have a wide variety of galleries and performance spaces, with several located within the area's large public green spaces.

KENSINGTON
CLASSICAL MUSIC
Cadogan Hall. Once a church, this spacious venue is home to the Royal Philharmonic Orchestra, and the English Chamber Orchestra performs here regularly. The hall also hosts a wide range of choral and chamber concerts, plus the occasional folk, rock, and world-music

gig. ⊠ *5 Sloane Terr., Kensington* ☎ *020/7730–4500* ⊕ *www.cado-ganhall.com* ☏ *Free–£100* Ⓜ *Sloane Sq.*

Fodor's Choice **Royal Albert Hall.** Opened in 1871, this splendid iron-and-glass-domed
★ auditorium hosts everything from pop and classical headliners to
Cirque du Soleil, awards ceremonies, and sumo wrestling championships, but it is best known for the annual July–September BBC
Promenade Concerts. Bargain-price standing-room (or promenading
or sitting-on-the-floor) tickets for "the Proms" are sold on the night
of the concert. The circular 5,272-seat auditorium has a terra-cotta
exterior surmounted by a mosaic frieze depicting figures engaged in
cultural pursuits. The hall is open most days for daytime guided tours
and Tuesday through Sunday for afternoon tea. ⊠ *Kensington Gore,
Kensington* ☎ *0207/589–8212* ⊕ *www.royalalberthall.com* ☏ *£6–
£90; tours £13.25* Ⓜ *South Kensington.*

OPERA

FAMILY **Opera Holland Park.** In summer, well-loved operas and imaginative
productions of lesser-known works are presented under a spectacular
canopy against the remains of Holland House, one of the first great
houses built in Kensington. The company has successfully branched
out into opera for families in recent years, too. There are 1,000 tickets
offered free to those ages 7–18 every season. Tickets go on general sale
in April (earlier for members). ⊠ *Holland Park, Kensington High St.,
Kensington* ☎ *0300/999–1000 for box office (opens Apr.), 020/3846–
6222 for inquiries* ⊕ *www.operahollandpark.com* ☏ *£20–£80* Ⓜ *High
Street Kensington, Holland Park.*

CHELSEA

THEATER

Royal Court Theatre. Britain's undisputed epicenter of new theatrical
works, the Court continues to produce gritty British and international
drama. Don't miss the best deal in town: four 10-pence standing tickets
go on sale one hour before each performance (of sold-out shows), and
£12 tickets are available on Monday. Backstage and building tours
take place at 11:30 am on the first or second Saturday of the month.
⊠ *Sloane Sq., Chelsea* ☎ *020/7565–5000* ⊕ *www.royalcourttheatre.
com* ☏ *£12–£49; tours £9* Ⓜ *Sloane Sq.*

NOTTING HILL

This cosmopolitan west London neighborhood, shown to advantage
in the 1999 film of the same name, is best known for the Notting
Hill Carnival, a lively music-focused street festival that takes over
the wider area on the final weekend of August each year. There's a
year-round culture scene, too, catering mainly to the neighborhood's
trendy young professionals.

FILM

FAMILY **The Electric Cinema.** This refurbished Portobello Road art house screens
mainstream and international movies. The emphasis is on comfort,
with leather sofas for two, armchairs, coffee tables for your wine and
appetizers, and even double beds in the front row. The Electric also has

17

another movie theater in east London on Redchurch Street, with sofas and wine coolers. ✉ *191 Portobello Rd., Notting Hill* ☎ *020/7908–9696* ⊕ *www.electriccinema.co.uk* 🎬 *£17.50–£22.50* Ⓜ *Ladbroke Grove, Notting Hill Gate.*

REGENT'S PARK AND HAMPSTEAD

Leafy north London has long been a stomping ground for the capital's cultural elite—stroll through Primrose Hill and you're practically guaranteed to spot a film star or musician—but there's diversity here, too. Camden Town is justifiably famous for its indie music scene, while respected fringe theaters in Swiss Cottage and Kilburn don't shy away from major topics.

REGENT'S PARK

THEATER

FAMILY **Open Air Theatre.** Works by Shakespeare have been performed here
Fodor's Choice every summer (from mid-May to mid-September) since 1932, with
★ casts including luminaries such as Vivien Leigh, Dame Judi Dench, and Damien Lewis. Today the theater also mounts productions of classic plays, musicals, and shows for family audiences among its four annual productions. *A Midsummer Night's Dream* is the one to catch, if it's on—never has that enchanted Greek wood been better evoked, especially when enhanced by genuine birdsong and a rising moon. There's a covered restaurant for pretheater dining, an informal café, and, of course, a bar. You also can order picnic hampers in advance. The park can get chilly, so bring a blanket. Performances proceed rain or shine (umbrellas aren't allowed) with refunds only in case of a very heavy downpour. ✉ *Inner Circle, Regent's Park* ☎ *0844/826–4242* ⊕ *www.openairtheatre.com* 🎬 *£25–£59* Ⓜ *Baker St., Regent's Park.*

HAMPSTEAD

FILM

FAMILY **Everyman Cinema.** Kick off your shoes, curl up on the large comfy sofas, and have tapas and champagne brought to you in front of classic, foreign, cutting-edge, and Hollywood titles. This venue also screens the Metropolitan Opera live from New York, and is a popular place for Hampstead denizens to bring their kids. Other branches around London also tend to offer a movie experience a cut above average. ✉ *5 Holly Bush Vale, Hampstead* ☎ *0871/906–9060* ⊕ *www.everymancinema.com* 🎬 *£16.90–£19.90* Ⓜ *Hampstead.*

THEATER

FAMILY **Kiln Theatre.** Committed to representing the cultural diversity of its community, the Kiln (known as the Tricycle until its reopening after a major refurbishment in 2018) shows the best in black, Irish, Jewish, Asian, and South African drama, and also promotes new work. There is a movie theater, too: expect top-quality new European and international cinema, including films from the United States, occasionally screened at film festivals the theater organizes. Discounted movie tickets are available on Monday. ✉ *269 Kilburn High Rd., Kilburn* ☎ *020/7328–1000* ⊕ *www.kilntheatre.com* 🎬 *Theater £10–£33, movies £5–£12* Ⓜ *Kilburn.*

SHOPPING

Updated by
Ellin Stein

The keyword of London shopping has always been "individuality," whether expressed in the superb custom tailoring of Savile Row, the nonconformist punk roots of quintessential British designer Vivienne Westwood, or the unique small stores that purvey their owners' private passions—be they paper theaters, toy soldiers, or buttons. This tradition is under threat from the influx of chains (global luxury, domestic mid-market, and international youth), but the distinctively British mix of quality and originality, tradition, and character remains.

You can try on underwear fit for a queen at Her Majesty's lingerie supplier, track down a leather-bound Brontë classic at an antiquarian bookseller, or find a bargain antique on Portobello Road. Whether you're just browsing—there's nothing like the size, variety, and sheer theater of London's street markets to stimulate the acquisitive instinct—or on a fashion-seeking mission, London shopping offers something for all tastes and budgets.

Although it's impossible to pin down one particular look that defines the city, London style tends to fall into two camps: one is the quirky, somewhat romantic look exemplified by homegrown designers like Matthew Williamson, Jenny Packham, Vivienne Westwood, and Lulu Guinness; the other reflects Britain's celebrated tradition of classic knitwear and suiting, with labels like Jaeger, Pringle, and Brora, while Oswald Boateng, Paul Smith, and Richard James take tradition and give it a very modern twist. Traditional bespoke men's tailoring can be found in the upscale gentlemen's shops of Jermyn Street and Savile Row—there's no better place in the city to buy custom-made shirts and suits—while the handbags at Mulberry, Asprey, and Anya Hindmarch are pure classic quality. If your budget can't stretch that far, no problem; the city's chain stores like Topshop, Zara, and H&M, aimed at the younger end of the market, are excellent places to pick up designs copied straight from the catwalk at a fraction of the price, while mid-market chains like Reiss, Jigsaw, and L.K. Bennett offer smart design and better quality for the more sophisticated shopper.

If there's anything that unites London's designers, it's a commitment to creativity and originality, underpinned by a strong sense of heritage. This combination of posh and rock 'n' roll sensibilities turns up in everyone from Terence Conran, who revolutionized product and houseware design in the '60s (and is still going strong), to Alexander McQueen, who combined the punk aesthetic with the rigor of couture. You'll see it in fanciful millinery creations by Philip Treacy and Stephen Jones, and in the work of imaginative shoemakers Nicholas Kirkwood, United Nude, and Terry de Havilland—and it keeps going, right through to current hot designers Erdem, Christopher Kane, Victoria Beckham, and up-and-coming names like Shrimps, Duro Olowu, and Molly Goddard.

One reason for London's design supremacy is the strength of local fashion college Central St. Martin's, whose graduates include Conran, Kane, McQueen, his successor at his eponymous label—and designer of the Duchess of Cambridge's wedding dress—Sarah Burton, and Stella McCartney's equally acclaimed successor at Céline, Phoebe Philo.

To find the McQueens and McCartneys of tomorrow, head for the independent boutiques of the East End and Bermondsey. If anything, London is even better known for its vibrant street fashion than for its high-end designers. Stock up from the stalls at Portobello, Camden, and Spitalfields markets.

Aside from bankrupting yourself, the only problem you may encounter is exhaustion. London's shopping districts are spread out over the city, so do as savvy locals do: plan your excursion with military precision, taking in only one or two areas in a day, and stopping for lunch with a glass of wine or for a pint at a pub.

18

PLANNING

OPENING HOURS

Most shops are open from about 9:30 or 10 am to 6 or 6:30 pm. Larger department stores generally stay open until 7 or even as late as 9. Because shop hours, particularly for the smaller shops, vary, it's a good idea to phone or check websites in advance. Stores that have late shopping—and not all do—are usually open until 7 or 8 pm on Thursday only. On Sunday, many shops open between 11 am and noon and close at 5 or 6 pm. Most stores are open on Sunday in December for the Christmas season.

WATCH YOUR LANGUAGE

Locals like to say that Brits and Americans are separated by a common language. Here are a few confusing terms to watch for when out and about in the shops:

Pants means underwear. Every other type of long-legged bottoms (except jeans and leggings) are called **trousers.** Also in the underwear category is the **vest** (undershirt in the United States); if you are looking for a vest, ask for a **waistcoat**.

Knickers are ladies' underwear. If you want pantyhose, ask for **tights**.

Jumper means a sweater—unless it's a cardigan, in which case it may be shortened to **cardie**. If you ask for a **sweater**, you may be offered a sweatshirt.

Men use **braces** to hold up their trousers; in England **suspenders** is another word for garters.

If you want some Adidas- or Nike-type athletic shoes, ask for **trainers**, not sneakers.

Don't ask for a pocketbook or a purse if you mean a **handbag**—the former will be incomprehensible, and the latter will produce a coin purse. If you ask for a fanny pack, it will produce a laugh—"fanny" means something altogether different in the United Kingdom; ask for a **bum-bag**.

Nightgowns are usually abbreviated to **nighties** and bathrobes may be **dressing gowns**.

A WORD ABOUT SERVICE

American standards of customer service are rare in London—you may find attentive customer service at old-school, traditional names and some independent stores, but salespeople elsewhere can seem abrupt or indifferent.

SHOPPING REVIEWS

ST. JAMES'S

ACCESSORIES

Fodor'sChoice ★ **Lock & Co. Hatters.** Need a silk top hat, a flat-weave Panama, or a traditional tweed flat cap? Or, for ladies, an occasion hat? James Lock of St. James's has been providing hats from this wood-paneled shop since 1676 for customers ranging from Admiral Lord Nelson, Oscar Wilde, and Frank Sinatra to, more recently, Robert Downey Jr., Guy Ritchie, and Kate Middleton, as well as trendsetting musicians and models. ⊠ 6 St. James's St., St. James's ☏ 020/7930–8874 ⊕ www.lockhatters.co.uk ⊗ Closed Sun. Ⓜ Green Park.

Fodor'sChoice ★ **Swaine Adeney Brigg.** Providing practical supplies for country pursuits since 1750, Swaine Adeney Brigg carries beautifully crafted umbrellas, walking sticks, and hip flasks, or ingenious combinations, such as the umbrella with a slim tipple-holding flask secreted inside the stem. The same level of quality and craftsmanship applies to the store's leather goods, which include attaché cases (you can buy the "Q Branch" model that James Bond carried in *From Russia with Love*) and wallets. You'll find scarves, caps, and the Herbert Johnson "Poet Hat," the iconic headgear (stocked since 1890) worn by Harrison Ford in every Indiana Jones film. ⊠ 7 Piccadilly Arcade, St. James's ☏ 020/7409–7277 ⊕ www.swaineadeneybrigg.com ⊗ Closed Sun., except by appointment Ⓜ Green Park.

ANTIQUES AND COLLECTIBLES

The Armoury of St. James's. Besides fine toy soldiers in lead or tin representing conflicts ranging from the Crusades through World War II with prices starting at £15 and going into four figures, the shop has regimental brooches and drums, historic orders and medals, royal memorabilia, and military antiques. ⊠ *17 Piccadilly Arcade, St. James's* ☎ *020/7493– 5082* ⊕ *www.armoury.co.uk* ⊗ *Closed Sun.* Ⓜ *Piccadilly Circus.*

BEAUTY

Floris. What did Queen Victoria, Mary Shelley, and Marilyn Monroe have in common? They all used products from Floris, one of the most beautiful shops in London, with gleaming glass-and-Spanish-mahogany showcases salvaged from the Great Exhibition of 1851. In addition to scents for both men and women (including the current queen), Floris has been making its own shaving products—plus combs, brushes, and fragrances—since 1730 (and is still owned by the same family), reflecting its origins as a barbershop. Other gift possibilities include goose-down powder puffs, a famous rose-scented mouthwash, and beautifully packaged soaps and bath essences. There's another branch in Belgravia. ⊠ *89 Jermyn St., St. James's* ☎ *0330/134–0180* ⊕ *www.florislondon. com* Ⓜ *Piccadilly Circus, Green Park.*

BOOKS

Fodor's Choice ★ **Hatchards.** This is the United Kingdom's oldest bookshop, open since 1797 and beloved by writers themselves—customers have included Oscar Wilde, Rudyard Kipling, and Lord Byron. Despite its wood-paneled, "gentleman's library" atmosphere and eclectic selection of books, Hatchards is owned by the large Waterstone's chain. Nevertheless, the shop still retains its period charm, aided by the staff's old-fashioned helpfulness and expertise. Look for the substantial number of books signed by notable contemporary authors on the well-stocked shelves. There's another branch in the St. Pancras International train station. ⊠ *187 Piccadilly, St. James's* ☎ *020/7439–9921* ⊕ *www.hatchards. co.uk* Ⓜ *Piccadilly Circus.*

CLOTHING

Dover Street Market. With its creative displays and eclectic, well-chosen mix of merchandise, this four-floor emporium is as much art installation as store. The merchandise and its configuration change every six months, so you never know what you will find, which is half the fun. The creation of Comme des Garçons' Rei Kawakubo, Dover Street Market showcases all of the label's collections for men and women alongside a changing roster of other ultrafashionable designers, including Gucci, Raf Simons, Balenciaga, Alaia, Loewe, Vetements, and Molly Goddard, all of whom have their own customized miniboutiques—plus sneaker and denim collaborations, eyeglass frames, and jewelry. An outpost of the Rose Bakery on the top floor makes for a good break. ⊠ *18–22 Haymarket, St. James's* ☎ *020/7518–0680* ⊕ *london.doverstreetmarket. com* Ⓜ *Piccadilly Circus.*

Turnbull & Asser. The Jermyn Street store sells luxurious jackets, cashmere sweaters, suits, ties, pajamas, ready-to-wear shirts, and accessories perfect for the billionaire who has everything. The brand is best known for its superb custom-made shirts—worn by Prince Charles and every

18

James Bond to appear in film, to name a few. These can be ordered at the nearby Bury Street or Davies Street branches, which are devoted to bespoke wear (Note: Bury and Davies are two separate stores). At least 15 separate measurements are taken, and the cloth, woven to the company's specifications, comes in 1,000 different patterns—the cottons feel as good as silk. The first order must be for a minimum of six shirts, which start at £195 each. ✉ *71–72 Jermyn St., St. James's* ☎ *020/7808–3000* ⊕ *www.turnbullandasser.co.uk* ⊘ *Closed Sun.* Ⓜ *Green Park.*

FOOD

Fodor'sChoice

★

Berry Bros. & Rudd. Nothing matches Berry Bros. & Rudd for rare offerings and a unique shopping experience. A family-run wine business since 1698 (Lord Byron was a customer), BBR stores more than 4,000 vintage bottles and casks in vaulted cellars that are more than 300 years old. The in-house wine school offers educational tasting sessions, while the dedicated spirits room also has an excellent selection of whiskeys, cognacs, rums, and more. The shop has a quirky charm, and the staff are extremely knowledgeable—and not snooty if you're on a budget. ✉ *63 Pall Mall, St. James's* ☎ *800/280–2440* ⊕ *www.bbr.com* ⊘ *Closed Sun.* Ⓜ *Green Park.*

Fortnum & Mason. Although F&M is jokingly known as "the Queen's grocer" and the impeccably mannered staff still wear traditional tailcoats, its celebrated food hall stocks gifts for all budgets, including irresistibly packaged luxury foods stamped with the gold "By Appointment" crest for under £5. Try the teas, preserves (including the unusual rose-petal jelly), condiments, or Gentleman's Relish (anchovy paste). The store's famous hampers are always a welcome gift. The gleaming food hall spans two floors and incorporates a sleek wine bar, with the rest of the store devoted to upscale housewares, men's and women's accessories and toiletries, a dedicated candle room, and a jewelry department featuring exclusive designs by breakthrough talent. If you start to flag, take a break in the tea salon, the Gallery café offering tastes of the food hall, the contemporary 45 Jermyn Street restaurant (the three-course set menu is good value), or an indulgent ice-cream parlor, where you can find decadent treats like a banana split or a less-traditional gin-and-cucumber float. There's another branch at St. Pancras International train station. ✉ *181 Piccadilly, St. James's* ☎ *020/7734–8040* ⊕ *www.fortnumandmason.com* Ⓜ *Green Park, Piccadilly Circus.*

Paxton & Whitfield. In business for more than 200 years, this venerable and aromatic London shop stocks hundreds of the world's greatest artisanal cheeses, particularly British and French varieties (a homesick General de Gaulle shopped here during World War II). The cheeses are laid on straw on refrigerated shelves, with tasting samples set out on a marble-top counter. You can pick up some ham, pâté, condiments, preserves, wine, or port, as well as cheese-related accessories like boards or knives. There's another branch in Chelsea. ✉ *93 Jermyn St., St. James's* ☎ *020/7930–0259* ⊕ *www.paxtonandwhitfield.co.uk* Ⓜ *Piccadilly Circus, Green Park.*

JEWELRY

Wartski. This family-run specialist in antique jewelry and precious objects boosted its fortunes when the founder's canny son-in-law snapped up confiscated treasures from the Bolshevik government after the Russian Revolution of 1917. As a result, this is the place to come if you're looking for a miniature carved Fabergé Easter Bunny, as well as a 1920s Cartier stickpin, Art Nouveau necklace by Lalique, or 17th-century gold signet ring. Even if you're not in the market to buy but are just interested in the history of jewelry, it's worth a visit. You can also order handmade wedding rings—Wartski created the engagement ring Prince William gave Kate Middleton. ✉ *60 St. James's St., St. James's* ☎ *0207/493–1141* ⊕ *www.wartski. com* ⊗ *Closed weekends* Ⓜ *Piccadilly.*

SHOES

Loake Shoemakers. Long established in England's Midlands and a provider of boots to the British armed forces in both world wars, this family-run firm specializes in classic handcrafted men's shoes. Whether you're after brogues, loafers, or deck shoes, the staff will take the time to ensure you have the right fit. In terms of quality and service, Loake represents real value for money, though they definitely aren't inexpensive. There's another branch on Bow Lane in The City. ✉ *39C Jermyn St., St. James's* ☎ *020/7734–8643* ⊕ *www.loake.co.uk* Ⓜ *Piccadilly.*

SPECIALTY STORES

Geo F. Trumper. If you don't have the time for an old-fashioned hot-towel shave at this "traditional gentlemen's barbers" established in 1875, pick up a razor, a shaving brush, or other mens' grooming accessory to take home for yourself or as a gift. The Extract of Limes Skin Food is a popular, zingy aftershave, and the Coconut Oil Hard Shaving Soap, which comes in a hand-turned wooden bowl, is a classic. There is also a store at 9 Curzon Street in Mayfair. ✉ *1 Duke of York St., St. James's* ☎ *020/7734–6553* ⊕ *www.trumpers. com* ⊗ *Closed Sun.* Ⓜ *Piccadilly Circus.*

MAYFAIR AND MARYLEBONE

MAYFAIR
ACCESSORIES

Mulberry. Staying true to its rural Somerset roots, this luxury goods company epitomizes *le style anglais,* a sophisticated take on the earth tones and practicality of English country style. Best known for highly desirable luxury handbags—such as the Lily, Chiltern, and Bayswater models—the company also produces gorgeous leather accessories, from wallets to luggage, as well as shoes and clothing for men and women. Aside from the New Bond Street flagship, there are branches in Knightsbridge, Covent Garden, Heathrow, and the Westfield centers, along with Mulberry concessions in most of the major upscale department stores. The small store on St. Christopher's Place in Marylebone stocks accessories only. ✉ *50 New Bond St., Mayfair* ☎ *020/7491–3900* ⊕ *www. mulberry.com* Ⓜ *Bond St.*

William & Son. William Asprey, scion of a jewelry dynasty, sells his carefully chosen, British-made luxury goods using a friendlier and less formal approach. You'll find all sorts of items here that you didn't know you needed, like Pininfarina brushed aluminum retractable pencils, green crocodile backgammon sets, or a silver champagne bottle stopper. The jewelry is tasteful and subtle rather than knock-your-eyes-out, and the store will also do custom work. ⊠ *34–36 Bruton St., Mayfair* ☎ *020/7493–8385* ⊕ *www.williamandson.com* ⊘ *Closed Sun.* Ⓜ *Bond St.*

ANTIQUES

Grays Antique Centre. There are approximately 200 dealers here, specializing in everything from Bakelite items to Mughal art. The majority focus on jewelry, ranging from contemporary to antique. Bargains are not out of the question, and proper pedigrees are guaranteed. Go on a weekday for the most choice; not all stalls are open on Saturday. Also try Grays at 1–7 Davies Mews around the corner: stalls there sell less expensive merchandise, including antique dolls at Glenda's and excellent vintage clothing at Vintage Modes. ⊠ *58 Davies St., Mayfair* ☎ *020/7629–7034* ⊕ *www.graysantiques.com* ⊘ *Closed Sun.* Ⓜ *Bond St.*

BOOKS AND STATIONERY

Fodor's Choice ★ **Heywood Hill.** Open since 1936, this is considered by some to be the best small bookstore in the English-speaking world—John Le Carré, who set a scene in *Tinker Tailor Soldier Spy* here, is a long-standing customer. Browse for a leather-bound volume on architecture, gardening, natural history, or topography—just some of the topics in which the antiquarian collection specializes. The contemporary selection emphasizes literature, history, biography, travel, architecture, and children's books, and the knowledgeable staff are happy to provide advice. During World War II, author Nancy Mitford helped keep the bookstore going. Today, the 12th Duke of Devonshire, a descendant of her brother-in-law, the 11th Duke, is the owner. ⊠ *10 Curzon St., Mayfair* ☎ *020/7629–0647* ⊕ *www.heywoodhill.com* ⊘ *Closed Sun.* Ⓜ *Green Park.*

Smythson of Bond Street. No hostess of any standing would consider having a leather-bound guest book made by anyone besides this elegant stationer, and the shop's social stationery and distinctive diaries with their pale-blue pages are the epitome of British good taste. These, along with other made-in-Britain leather goods including a small line of handbags, backpacks, and luggage tags, can be personalized. There are branches in Chelsea, Notting Hill, and The City, plus concessions in leading department stores. ⊠ *40 New Bond St., Mayfair* ☎ *020/3535–8009* ⊕ *www.smythson.com* Ⓜ *Bond St., Oxford Circus.*

Waterstone's. At this megabookshop (Europe's largest, with more than 8 miles of bookshelves) in a former art deco department store near Piccadilly Circus, browse for your latest purchase, attend one of the frequent meet-the-author events, or admire the view with a glass of wine at the 5th View Bar and Restaurant (open until 9); there's also a café in the basement. Waterstone's is the country's leading book chain, and it's pulled out all the stops to make its flagship as welcoming as a bookstore can be. There are several smaller branches throughout the city. ✉ *203–206 Piccadilly, Mayfair* ☎ *0207/851–2400* ⊕ *www.water- stones.com* Ⓜ *Piccadilly Circus.*

CLOTHING

Alexander McQueen. Since the legendary designer's untimely death in 2010, his right-hand woman, Sarah Burton, has been at the helm, receiving raves for continuing his tradition of theatrical, darkly roman- tic, and beautifully cut clothes incorporating corsetry, lace, embroidery, and hourglass silhouettes, all of which were exemplified in Burton's celebrated wedding dress for Kate Middleton. Can't afford a gala gown? Go home with a skull-print silk scarf. ✉ *4–5 Old Bond St., Mayfair* ☎ *020/7355–0088* ⊕ *www.alexandermcqueen.com* Ⓜ *Bond St.*

Belstaff. For years the purveyors of Britain's coolest motorcycle leath- ers, Belstaff has expanded into dresses, skirts, and handbags, as well as knitwear, boots, tops, and trousers for men, women, and children. Outerwear in general and leather jackets in particular remain a strength. All the items reflect the brand's functional yet unconventional heritage. Previous customers include Lawrence of Arabia, Amelia Earhart, and Che Guevara. There's another branch in Spitalfields. ✉ *135–137 New Bond St., Mayfair* ☎ *020/7495–5897* ⊕ *www.belstaff.co.uk* Ⓜ *Bond St.*

Browns. A trendsetting boutique since it opened in the 1970s, this shop occupying interconnecting town houses has been reinvigorated after a purchase by luxury e-tailer Farfetch.com. Browns focuses on well- established international luxury designers such as Vetements, Valen- tino, Marques Almeida, or Saint Laurent. The menswear, footwear, and accessories collections are equally well chosen. A new Shoreditch branch showcases new design talent, and if you're about to go down the aisle, check out the appointment-only bridal boutique at 12 Hinde Street in Marylebone. ✉ *23–27 S. Molton St., Mayfair* ☎ *020/7514– 0016* ⊕ *www.brownsfashion.com* Ⓜ *Bond St.*

Burberry. Known for its trademark tartan, this company has cultivated an edgy, high-fashion image in recent years, and new creative director and former Givenchy designer Ricardo Tisci is pushing the boundaries even more, bringing in a street-style influence. For those who prefer the traditional Burberry look, the raincoats are still a classic buy, along with plaid scarves in every color imaginable and handbags. If you're up for a trek, there's a huge factory outlet in Hackney on Chatham Place that has clothes and accessories for men, women, and children at half price or less. There are also branches in Knightsbridge, Covent Garden, and the Westfield shopping center in addition to this spectacular flagship store. ✉ *121 Regent St., Mayfair* ☎ *020/7806–8904* ⊕ *uk.burberry.com* Ⓜ *Piccadilly Circus.*

Fodor's Choice ★ **Fenwick.** A manageably sized department store, Fenwick is a welcome haven of affordability in a shopping area where stratospheric prices are the norm. The store is particularly strong on accessories (nota- bly lingerie, wraps, and hats), cosmetics, perfumes, and chic, wearable fashion by both big names and more niche designers such as Goat, J Brand, and Tory Burch. There are also three small spas (Chantecaille, La Prairie, and a Blink waxing room), various beauty services (including

18

a hair salon, nail bar, and Blink brow bar), and three restaurants plus a men's department in the basement. ✉ *163 New Bond St., Mayfair* ☎ *020/7629–9161* ⊕ *www.fenwick.co.uk* Ⓜ *Bond St.*

Isabel Marant London. The first London store from Marant, a favorite of French fashion editors, this airy skylit space is full of her signature slim-cut pants, slouchy knits, wedge sneakers, and rock-chick miniskirts, all exuding Left Bank boho cool. ✉ *29 Bruton St., Mayfair* ☎ *020/7499–7887* ⊕ *www.isabelmarant.com* ⊘ *Closed Sun.* Ⓜ *Bond St.*

Stella McCartney. It's not easy emerging from the shadow of a Beatle father, but Stella McCartney is a major force in fashion in her own right. Her signature jumpsuits and tuxedo pantsuits embody her design philosophy, combining minimalist tailoring with femininity and sophistication with ease of wear. Her love of functionality and clean lines has led to her branching off into lingerie, accessories, swimwear, and sportswear, designing a line for Adidas. A vegetarian like her parents, she refuses to use fur or leather, making her a favorite with similarly minded fashionistas. There's another boutique in South Kensington. ✉ *30 Bruton St., Mayfair* ☎ *020/7518–3100* ⊕ *www.stellamccartney.com* ⊘ *Closed Sun.* Ⓜ *Bond St.*

Victoria Beckham. Many were dubious when the former Spice Girl launched herself as a high-end designer, but her elegant yet wearable clothes soon made her a favorite with influencers and customers alike. This, her only stand-alone boutique, carries all the Beckham lines: the VVB diffusion line, the main collection, and accessories like bags, shoes, and eyewear, all displayed like artwork in the gallery-like space. ✉ *36 Dover St., Mayfair* ☎ *0207/042–0700* ⊕ *www.victoriabeckham.com* Ⓜ *Green Park, Piccadilly.*

Vivienne Westwood. From her beginnings as the most shocking and outré designer around, Westwood (now Dame Vivienne) has become a standard-bearer for high-style British couture. At the Chelsea boutique where she first sold the lavish corseted ball gowns, dandified nipped-waist jackets, and tartan-meets-punk daywear that formed the core of her signature look, you can still buy ready-to-wear—mainly items from the more casual Anglomania diffusion line and the exclusive Worlds End label, which draws from her archives. The small Davies Street boutique is devoted to couture (plus bridal), while the flagship Conduit Street store carries all of the above. There's also a men's collection at 18 Conduit Street. ✉ *44 Conduit St., Mayfair* ☎ *020/7439–1109* ⊕ *www.viviennewestwood.com* Ⓜ *Oxford Circus.*

DEPARTMENT STORES

Thomas Goode. This spacious luxury housewares shop has been at the same smart Mayfair address since 1845. The china, silver, crystal, and linen, whether from the store's own line or from luxury brands like Christofle and Puiforcat, are simply the best that money can buy, a legacy of its original customer base of international royals and heads of state. The store still holds two royal warrants, but anyone who can afford it can commission their own bespoke set of china. If such luxury is beyond you, visit anyway for the shop's small museum of plates, either antique or designed for royalty, including some created for Princess Diana's wedding. ⊠ *19 S. Audley St., Mayfair* ☎ *020/7499–2823* ⊕ *www.thomasgoode.co.uk* ☉ *Closed Sun.* Ⓜ *Green Park.*

FOOD

Charbonnel et Walker. Established in 1875, this master chocolatier's Mayfair shop specializes in traditional handmade chocolates (rose-petal creams and champagne truffles, for example) and has been creating these beautifully packaged, high-quality candies from long before most of today's fashionable brands appeared. Their drinking chocolate—coarsely grated fine chocolate in a tin—is worth carrying home in a suitcase. ⊠ *One The Royal Arcade, 28 Old Bond St., Mayfair* ☎ *020/7318–1075* ⊕ *www.charbonnel.co.uk* Ⓜ *Green Park.*

JEWELRY

Asprey. The company's "global flagship" store displays exquisite jewelry—as well as silver and leather goods, watches, china, and crystal—in a discreet, very British setting that oozes quality, expensive good taste, and hushed comfort. If you're in the market for an immaculate 1930s cigarette case, a silver cocktail shaker, a pair of pavé diamond and sapphire earrings, or a ladylike handbag, you won't likely be disappointed. And, for the really well-heeled, there's custom service available as well (Ringo Starr had a chess set made here). This store has occupied the premises since 1847, some 66 years after Asprey was established in 1781. ⊠ *167 New Bond St., Mayfair* ☎ *020/7493–6767* ⊕ *www.asprey.com* ☉ *Closed Sun.* Ⓜ *Green Park.*

Garrard. The oldest jewelry house in the world, Garrard has been in business since 1735. Between 1843 and 2007, the company was responsible for the upkeep of the Crown Jewels in the Tower of London and for creating several royal crowns (you can see some on display in the Tower). Today the focus is on precious gems in simple, classic settings, along with silver accessories. Although some collections are definitely contemporary (with items like minimalist hoop earrings or two-finger rings), many of the designs are traditional and impressive—which will be handy should you be in the market for an old-school diamond tiara. ⊠ *24 Albemarle St., Mayfair* ☎ *207/518–1070* ⊕ *www.garrard.com* ☉ *Closed Sun.* Ⓜ *Green Park.*

MEN'S CLOTHING

Alfred Dunhill. For more than 100 years, Dunhill has been synonymous with the most luxurious and sophisticated men's goods, including accessories, briefcases, and superbly tailored clothes. This Georgian mansion, their flagship, also features a barbershop, cellar bar, courtyard restaurant, and bespoke services, where you can order custom-fitted menswear or unique versions of the brand's celebrated leather goods. The smaller, original St. James's shop has been on Jermyn Street since 1906. ⊠ *Bourdon House, 2 Davies St., Mayfair* ☎ *020/3425–7300* ⊕ *www.dunhill.com* ☉ *Closed Sun.* Ⓜ *Bond St.*

Gieves and Hawkes. One of the grand men's tailoring houses of Savile Row, this company made its name outfitting British royals who served as officers in the armed forces. The company still supplies custom-made military uniforms, as well as beautifully tailored formal and civilian wear for clients who have included Winston Churchill, Ian Fleming,

18

and Michael Jackson. Prices for a bespoke suit start around £5,000 and made to measure at £1,150, but you can find ready-made versions from around £900 (separates from £200), while a new line of casualwear has several items under £200. Custom-made shoes are also available. ✉ *1 Savile Row, Mayfair* ☎ *020/7432–6403* ⊕ *www.gievesandhawkes.com* Ⓜ *Piccadilly Circus.*

Ozwald Boateng. The dapper menswear by Ozwald Boateng (pronounced "Bwa-teng") combines contemporary funky style with traditional Savile Row quality. His made-to-measure suits have been worn by the dandyish likes of Jamie Foxx, Mick Jagger, and Laurence Fishburne, who appreciate the sharp cuts, luxurious fabrics, and occasionally vibrant colors (even the more conservative choices have jacket linings in bright silk). ✉ *30 Savile Row, Mayfair* ☎ *020/7437–2030* ⊕ *www.ozwaldboateng.co.uk* ☉ *Closed Sun.* Ⓜ *Piccadilly Circus.*

SHOES

Nicholas Kirkwood. Kirkwood is one of Britain's most fashionable shoe designers, and this is his only retail boutique. You won't be able to hike in his imaginative, elegant, sky-high stilettos (be warned: prices are similarly high), but you will be able to make quite an entrance. There are also more wearable styles that are equally flattering and gorgeous. ✉ *5 Mount St., Mayfair* ☎ *020/7290–1404* ⊕ *www.nicholaskirkwood.com* ☉ *Closed Sun.* Ⓜ *Green Park.*

Rupert Sanderson. Designed in London and made in Italy, Sanderson's elegant shoes have been a huge hit in fashion circles with their lavish ornamentation on heels and flats alike. Red-carpet-ready high heels— worn by celebs including Claire Danes, Nicole Kidman, and Sandra Bullock—come in gorgeous colors and prints; peep toes are signature elements. The high prices reflect the impeccable craftsmanship. ✉ *19 Bruton Pl., Mayfair* ☎ *0207/491–2260* ⊕ *www.rupertsanderson.com* ☉ *Closed Sun.* Ⓜ *Bond St., Green Park.*

Sophia Webster. Gorgeous, fanciful shoes embellished with jeweled flowers, sequins, butterflies, and trademark wings at the heel fill Webster's first stand-alone boutique. This stylists' favorite is best known for her open-toed stilettos, but there are plenty of flat sandals, mid-height heels, platforms, and even clogs, as well as a sneaker collaboration with Puma. ✉ *Mount Street Mews, 124 Mount St., Mayfair* ☎ *0203/150–2960* ⊕ *www.sophiawebster.co.uk* ☉ *Closed Sun.* Ⓜ *Bond St.*

MARYLEBONE

ANTIQUES

Alfie's Antique Market. This four-story, bohemian-chic labyrinth is London's largest indoor antiques market, housing more than 75 dealers specializing in art, lighting, glassware, textiles, jewelry, furniture, and collectibles, with a particular strength in vintage clothing and 20th-century design. Come here to pick up vintage (1900–70) clothing, accessories, and luggage from Tin Tin Collectables, antique and vintage glassware and vases at Robinson Antiques, or a spectacular mid-20th-century Italian lighting fixture at Vincenzo Caffarella. The atmosphere may be funky, but the prices are not. There's also a rooftop café with free Wi-Fi if you need a coffee break. In addition to the market, this end of Church Street is lined with excellent antiques shops. ✉ *13–25 Church St., Marylebone* ☎ *020/7723–6066* ⊕ *www.alfiesantiques.com* ✆ *Closed Sun. and Mon.* Ⓜ *Marylebone.*

BEAUTY

Space.NK.apothecary. Aficionados of hard-to-find cult beauty products flock to this upscale chain that now has more than 20 locations throughout London. The minute you step inside, you're surrounded by dozens of luxurious and sought-after cosmetic and skin-care brands like Lipstick Queen, Chantecaille, Caudalie, By Terry, Perricone MD, and Nars, along with fragrances by the likes of Acqua di Parma and candles by Diptique. The helpful staff is happy to offer knowledgeable advice. The Notting Hill branch also offers spa treatments, while men have a branch of their own in Soho. ✉ *83A Marylebone High St., Marylebone* ☎ *020/7486–8791* ⊕ *uk.spacenk.com* Ⓜ *Baker St.*

BOOKS

Fodor's Choice ★ **Daunt Books.** An independent bookstore chain (there are additional branches in Belsize Park, Chelsea, Hampstead, Holland Park, and Cheapside), Daunt favors a thoughtful selection of contemporary and classic fiction and nonfiction. The striking Marylebone branch is an original Edwardian bookstore, where a dramatic room with a long oak-paneled gallery under lofty skylights houses the noted travel section, which includes not only guidebooks but also related literature and poetry. The Hampstead branch is strong on children's books. ✉ *83 Marylebone High St., Marylebone* ☎ *020/7224–2295* ⊕ *www.daunt-books.co.uk* Ⓜ *Baker St.*

CLOTHING

Matches Fashion. This carefully curated boutique carries fashion from a selection of 400 designers both rising and established, including Christopher Kane, Erdem, J.W. Anderson, Proenza Schouler, Vetements, McCartney, McQueen, Balenciaga, Balmain, Valentino, Saint Laurent, Marni, and Duro Olowu. There's also an equally stylish menswear department, plus jewelry, lingerie, footwear, and accessories. Other branches can be found in Notting Hill and southwest London. ✉ *87 Marylebone High St., Marylebone* ☎ *020/7487–5400* ⊕ *www.matches-fashion.com* Ⓜ *Regent's Park, Baker St.*

Reiss. With an in-house design team whose experience includes stints at Gucci and Calvin Klein and customers like Beyoncé and the Duchess of Cambridge, who wore a Reiss dress for her official engagement picture, this reliable chain brings luxury standards of tailoring and details to mass-market womens- and menswear. The sleek and contemporary style doesn't come cheap, but does offer value for money. There are branches in Knightsbridge, The City, Covent Garden, Chelsea, Hampstead, Islington, Soho, Kensington, and basically all over London. ✉ *10 Barrett St., Marylebone* ☎ *020/7486–6557* ⊕ *www.reiss.com* Ⓜ *Oxford St.*

DEPARTMENT STORES

Marks & Spencer. You'd be hard-pressed to find a Brit who doesn't have something in the closet from Marks & Spencer (or M&S, as it's popularly known). This major chain is famed for its classic dependable clothing for men, women, and children—affordable cashmere and lamb's wool

18

sweaters are particularly good buys—and occasionally scores a fashion hit. The food department at M&S is consistently good, especially for frozen food, and a great place to pick up a sandwich or premade salad on the go (look for M&S Simply Food stores all over town). The flagship branch at Marble Arch and the Pantheon location at 173 Oxford Street have extensive fashion departments. ✉ *458 Oxford St., Marylebone* ☎ *020/7935–7954* ⊕ *www.marksandspencer.com* Ⓜ *Marble Arch.*

Fodor's Choice
★
Selfridges. This giant bustling store (the second largest in the United Kingdom after Harrods) gives Harvey Nichols a run for its money as London's most fashionable department store. Packed to the rafters with clothes ranging from mid-price lines to the latest catwalk names, the store continues to break ground with its innovative retail schemes, especially the ground-floor Wonder Room (for extravagant jewelry and luxury watches), a dedicated Denim Studio, a Fragrance Bar where you can create custom perfume, an array of pop-ups ranging from spaces for designers such as Jil Sander to a healthy shot bar (if you need some colloidal silver to keep you going) or a collaboration with boutique boxing club BXR. The giant accessories hall has miniboutiques dedicated to top-end designers such as Chanel, Gucci, and Vuitton while the new Corner Shop offers U.K.-themed gifts and souvenirs at all price points. There are so many zones that merge into one another—from youth-oriented Miss Selfridge to audio equipment to the large, comprehensive cosmetics department—that you practically need a map. Don't miss the Shoe Galleries, the world's largest shoe department, which is filled with more than 5,000 pairs from 120 brands, displayed like works of art under spotlights. Take a break with a glass of wine at the rooftop restaurant or pick up some tea in the Food Hall as a gift. ✉ *400 Oxford St., Marylebone* ☎ *0800/123400* ⊕ *www.selfridges.com* Ⓜ *Bond St.*

JEWELRY
Kabiri. A carefully curated array of exciting contemporary jewelry by emerging and established designers from around the world is packed into this small shop. There is something to suit most budgets and tastes, though understated minimalism predominates. You can score an elegant, one-of-a-kind piece here for a very reasonable price. ✉ *94 Marylebone La., Marylebone* ☎ *020/7317–2150* ⊕ *www.kabiri.co.uk* Ⓜ *Baker St.*

SOHO AND COVENT GARDEN

SOHO
ACCESSORIES
Fodor's Choice
★
Peckham Rye. On the small cobblestone streets leading off Carnaby Street, among other little specialty shops, the family-run Peckham Rye sells heritage-style men's accessories: handmade silk and twill ties, bow ties, and scarves, all using traditional patterns drawn from the archives going back to 1799. Embodying the Ralph Lauren aesthetic even more than Ralph Lauren, the socks, striped shirts, and handkerchiefs attract modern-day dandies like Mark Ronson and David Beckham. Bespoke tailoring for men is also offered. ✉ *11 Newburgh St., Soho* ☎ *0207/734–5181* ⊕ *www.peckhamrye.com* Ⓜ *Oxford St.*

BOOKS

Fodor's Choice **Foyles.** Founded in 1903 by the Foyle brothers after they failed the Civil
★ Service exam, this family-owned bookstore is in a 1930s art deco build-
ing, once the home of the renowned art college Central Saint Martins.
One of London's best sources for textbooks and the United Kingdom's
largest retailer of foreign language books, with more than 200,000 titles
on its 4 miles of bookshelves, Foyles also stocks everything from popular
fiction to military history, sheet music, medical tomes, graphic novels,
and handsome, illustrated fine arts books. It also offers the store-within-
a-store Ray's Jazz (one of London's better outlets for music) and a cool
café. Foyles has branches in the Southbank Centre, the Westfield shopping center in Stratford, and Waterloo Station. ⊠ *107 Charing Cross Rd.,
Soho* ☎ *0207/437–5660* ⊕ *www.foyles.co.uk* Ⓜ *Tottenham Court Rd.*

CLOTHING

OTHER/Shop. Aimed at men and women in search of stylish cool, this
independent boutique stocks its own brand of entirely made-in-Eng-
land clothing, as well as accessories, housewares, books, and clothing
from other carefully selected, high-end cult brands such as Christopher Lemaire and Peter Jensen. The look is understated, slightly geeky,
and totally contemporary. ⊠ *3 Berwick St., Soho* ☎ *020/7734–6846*
⊕ *other-shop.com* Ⓜ *Oxford Circus.*

Wolsey. Specializing in men's knitwear since 1755, this long-established
company now sells rugged but stylish outerwear, sweaters, shirts, hats,
scarves, socks, T-shirts, sweatshirts, sleepwear, and underwear (the
undies of choice for polar explorers Roald Amundsen, Captain Robert
Scott, and Ernest Shackleton). The company also supplied woolen garments to British troops in 1914. It's not all heritage, though; Wolsey
makes hoodies as well, and its padded jackets and vests employ the
latest in thermalwear technology. The interior reflects this blend of the
traditional and the contemporary, with exposed brick walls, brushed
steel beams, and photographs of expeditions the brand has outfitted.
There's another branch in Covent Garden. ⊠ *83A Brewer St., Soho*
☎ *020/7434–4257* ⊕ *www.wolsey.com* Ⓜ *Piccadilly Circus.*

DEPARTMENT STORES

Fodor's Choice **Liberty.** The wonderful black-and-white mock-Tudor facade, created
★ from the timbers of two Royal Navy ships, reflects this store's origins
in the late-19th-century Arts and Crafts movement. Leading designers were recruited to create the classic art nouveau Liberty prints that
are still a centerpiece of the brand, gracing everything from cushions
and silk kimonos to embossed leather bags and photo albums. Inside,
Liberty is a labyrinth of nooks and crannies stuffed with thoughtfully
chosen merchandise, including niche beauty, perfume, footwear, and
housewares lines such as Soho Home, which features furniture and
textiles from the membership clubs. Clothes for both men and women
focus on high quality and high fashion, with labels like Roland Mouret
and Tomas Maier. The store regularly commissions new prints from
contemporary designers, and sells both these and its classic patterns
by the yard. If you're not so handy with a needle, an interior design
service will create soft furnishings for you. There's also a florist, a hair
salon, a traditional men's barber, branded beauty treatment rooms,

18

a brow bar, a piercing studio, and a foot spa. ✉ *Regent St., Soho* ☎ *020/7734–1234* ⊕ *www.liberty.co.uk* Ⓜ *Oxford Circus.*

FOOD

Fodor's Choice ★ **The Vintage House.** If whiskey is more to your taste than wine, visit the family-run Vintage House, which has the country's largest selection of single malts (more than 1,350), including many rare bottles and some exclusive to the shop. You'll also find more than 100 tequilas, plus rums, liqueurs, and Armagnacs, as well as Cuban cigars. The shop is open until 11 pm (10 pm on Sunday). ✉ *42 Old Compton St., Soho* ☎ *020/7437–2592* ⊕ *www.vintagehouse.london* Ⓜ *Leicester Sq.*

SHOES

Irregular Choice. If you want to blend in with the crowd, these shoes are not for you; but if you like footwear that is fun and flattering (not to mention reasonably priced), head for Irregular Choice. Styles tend toward Louis XIV–like court shoes ornamented with big ribbon ties or silk flowers, but there are also pumps in interesting patterns, glittery flats, and tropical-print platform sandals, as well as whimsical clutch bags and jewelry. Best of all, many have round toes and supportive heels, proving that comfortable doesn't have to be dull. ✉ *35 Carnaby St., Soho* ☎ *020/7494–4811* ⊕ *www.irregularchoice.com* Ⓜ *Oxford Circus.*

TOYS

FAMILY **Hamleys.** When British children visit London, this institution—the oldest toy store in the world—is at the top of their agenda. Its six floors hold the latest dolls, soft toys, video games, and technological devices, as well as old-fashioned pleasures like train sets, drum kits, and magic tricks, plus every must-have on the preteen shopping list (some parents may find the offerings to be overly commercialized, as they're heavy on movie and TV tie-ins). Hamleys is a madhouse at Christmastime, but the Santa's grotto is one of the best in town. There's a smaller branch in St. Pancras International train station and one near the Shard in south London. ✉ *188–196 Regent St., Soho* ☎ *0371/704–1977* ⊕ *www. hamleys.com* Ⓜ *Oxford Circus, Piccadilly Circus.*

COVENT GARDEN

BOOKS AND PRINTS

Grosvenor Prints. London's largest collection of 17th- to early-20th-century prints emphasizes views of the city and architecture as well as sporting and decorative motifs. The selection is eclectic, with prices ranging from £5 to the thousands. ✉ *19 Shelton St., Covent Garden* ☎ *020/7836–1979* ⊕ *www.grosvenorprints.com* ☉ *Closed Sun.* Ⓜ *Covent Garden, Leicester Sq.*

Fodor's Choice ★ **Stanfords.** When it comes to encyclopedic coverage, there is simply no better travel shop on the planet. At this location for more than 100 years, Stanfords is packed with a comprehensive selection of travel books and travel accessories, as well as ordinance surveys, cycle route maps, travel adaptors, globes, replicas of antique maps, mosquito nets, and more. Even the floor is decorated with giant maps. Whether you're planning a day trip to Surrey or an adventure to the South Pole, this should be your first stop. ✉ *12–14 Long Acre, Covent Garden* ☎ *020/7836–1321* ⊕ *www.stanfords.co.uk* Ⓜ *Covent Garden.*

CLOTHING

Jack Wills. The heritage and country sports-inspired styles here have a fresh, sexy edge. Crowds of lithe teens don't mind the pumping music while they browse the collection—trench coats, jeans, and dresses (LBDs, floral sundresses, rugby stripe jerseys) for the girls, and sweatshirts, athleisure jackets, chinos, and polo shirts for the boys. The store also carries backpacks, baseball hats, holdalls, branded water bottles, and other youthful lifestyle items. Other branches are in Soho and Battersea. ⊠ *136 Long Acre, Covent Garden* ☎ *020/7240–8946* ⊕ *www. jackwills.com* Ⓜ *Leicester Sq., Covent Garden.*

Paul Smith. British classics with an irreverent twist define Paul Smith's collections for women, men, and children. Beautifully tailored suits for men and women take hallmarks of traditional British style and turn them on their heads with humor and color, combining exceptional fabrics with flamboyant linings or unusual detailing. Gift ideas abound—wallets, scarves, phone cases, and distinctive belts and socks—all in Smith's signature rainbow stripes. There are several branches throughout London, in Notting Hill, Soho, Marylebone, Southwark, and Canary Wharf, plus a Mayfair shop that includes vintage furniture. ⊠ *40–44 Floral St., Covent Garden* ☎ *020/7379–7133* ⊕ *www. paulsmith.co.uk* Ⓜ *Covent Garden.*

Tabio. This Japanese-owned specialty store reflects the country's noted enthusiasm for socks and is the place to find them, as well as leg warmers, tights, and stockings, all in a wide assortment of weights. Styles range from functional to fanciful and patterns from simple and elegant to lively and attention-getting. There's another branch on King's Road in Chelsea. ⊠ *66 Neal St., Covent Garden* ☎ *020/7836–3713* ⊕ *www. tabio.com* Ⓜ *Covent Garden.*

HOUSEHOLD GOODS

Cath Kidston. Lovers of chintz and colorful patterns adore Cath Kidston's bright feminine signature look. Textiles bearing ginghams, polka dots, and lots of big blooming roses appear on everything in sight, from ceramics and bed linens to fine china, stationery, and doggie beds. There are clothing and nightwear lines for women and children, along with handbags, totes, knapsacks, and cosmetic bags. Branches can be found throughout the city, including in Marylebone, Chelsea, Notting Hill, St. Pancras International train station, and a flagship store on Piccadilly. ⊠ *28–32 Shelton St., Covent Garden* ☎ *020/7240–8324* ⊕ *www. cathkidston.co.uk* Ⓜ *Covent Garden.*

MARKETS

Covent Garden Market. This popular destination includes three separate market areas: the Apple Market, the East Colonnade Market, and the Jubilee Market. In the covered area originally designed by Inigo Jones and known as the Apple Market, 40 stalls sell handcrafted jewelry, prints, clothes (such as hand-painted dancewear), ceramics, and crafts Tuesday through Sunday, while Mondays are given over to antiques, curios, and collectables. The East Colonnade Market has stalls with mostly handmade specialty items that include handmade soaps and jewelry, as well as housewares, accessories, and magic tricks. The Jubilee Market, in Jubilee Hall toward Southampton Street, tends toward

18

the more pedestrian (kitschy T-shirts, unremarkable household goods, and the like) Tuesday through Friday, but has vintage collectibles and antiques on Monday and worthwhile handmade goods on weekends. Largely aimed at the tourist trade in the past, Covent Garden Market continues its ascent, introducing a more sophisticated image (and correspondingly high prices) with the opening of upscale restaurants and chains in the surrounding arcades, including the world's largest Apple Store and a Disney store; beauty outlets for Chanel, Bobbi Brown, and Dior; and boutiques for brands like Tumi, Mulberry and N. Peal. ■TIP→ Don't miss the magicians, musicians, and escape artists who perform in the open-air piazza; the performances are free (though contributions are welcome). ⊠ *The Piazza, off Wellington St., Covent Garden* ⊕ *www.coventgarden.london* Ⓜ *Covent Garden.*

SHOES

The Shop at Bluebird. The brainchild of the couple behind popular womenswear brand Jigsaw, this 15,000-square-foot space over three floors brings together men's and women's fashion from of-the-moment designers like Alexander Wang, Shrimps, and Peter Pilotto, as well as numerous hip denim lines like Acne Studios and Citizens of Humanity. There's also furniture, beauty products, art, homewares, and designer tech accessories—all chosen for style and originality—and an expansive restaurant on the second floor. It's worth visiting for the displays alone, which change regularly. There are other branches in Chelsea, St. James's, and on Duke Street in Mayfair. ⊠ *Carriage Hall, 29 Floral St., Covent Garden* ⊕ *www.theshopatbluebird.com* Ⓜ *Covent Garden.*

Fodor's Choice
★
United Nude. Cocreated by famed architect Rem Koolhaas (who also designed this Covent Garden flagship store) and Galahad Clark (of the Clarks shoes dynasty), this brand sells distinctive, futuristic designs that use up-to-the-minute techniques such as carbon-fiber heels and injection-molded soles. The shoes' edginess doesn't stop them from being flattering, affordable, and surprisingly comfortable. ⊠ *13 Floral St., Covent Garden* ☎ *0207/240–7106* ⊕ *www.unitednude.com* Ⓜ *Covent Garden.*

TOYS

FAMILY
Fodor's Choice
★
Benjamin Pollock's Toyshop. This landmark shop still carries on the tradition of its founder, who sold miniature theater stages made from richly detailed paper from the late 19th century until his death in 1937. Among his admirers was Robert Louis Stevenson, who wrote, "If you love art, folly, or the bright eyes of children, speed to Pollock's." Today the antique model theaters are expensive, but there are plenty of magical reproductions for less than £10. There's also an extensive selection of new but nostalgic puppets, marionettes, teddy bears, spinning tops, jack-in-the-boxes, and similar traditional children's toys from the days before batteries were required (or toys were even run on them). ⊠ *44 The Market Bldg., Covent Garden* ☎ *020/7379–7866* ⊕ *www.pollocks-coventgarden.co.uk* Ⓜ *Covent Garden.*

The Tintin Shop. Before there was Harry Potter, there was Tintin. Created by the Belgian cartoonist Hergé, the story of the fictional boy detective and his intrepid dog Snowy has been a cult favorite for generations. At this namesake shop devotees can find Tintin-related books, posters,

T-shirts, metal and resin figurines, die-cast model airplane, alarm clocks, and more. ✉ *34 Floral St., Covent Garden* ☎ *020/7836–1131* ⊕ *thet-intinshop.uk.com* Ⓜ *Covent Garden.*

BLOOMSBURY, HOLBORN, ISLINGTON, AND FITZROVIA

BLOOMSBURY

ACCESSORIES

Fodor's Choice ★ **James Smith & Sons Ltd.** This has to be the world's ultimate umbrella shop (it is definitely Europe's oldest), and a must for anyone interested in real Victorian London. The family-owned shop has been in this location on a corner of New Oxford Street since 1857 and sells every kind of umbrella, parasol, cane, and walking stick imaginable (including some containing a small flask or a corkscrew, or that fold out into a seat). The interior is unchanged since the 19th century; you will feel as if you have stepped back in time. Umbrellas range from about £40 for a folding umbrella to more than £265 for a classic man's umbrella with a carved animal-head handle and thousands for bespoke items. If the umbrella prices are too steep, there are smaller accessories like a horn shoehorn or letter opener that make perfect gifts. ✉ *Hazelwood House, 53 New Oxford St., Bloomsbury* ☎ *020/7836–4731* ⊕ *www.james-smith.co.uk* ⊙ *Closed Sun.* Ⓜ *Tottenham Court Rd., Holborn.*

BOOKS

Gay's the Word. Open since 1979, this is London's leading gay and lesbian bookshop. Thousands of titles, from literature and thoughtful nonfiction to erotica and prodiversity children's books, fill the shelves. The shop is a well loved fixture on the scene (it features prominently in the 2014 movie *Pride*) and often hosts discussion groups, readings, and other events. ✉ *66 Marchmont St., Bloomsbury* ☎ *020/7278–7654* ⊕ *www.gaystheword.co.uk* Ⓜ *Russell Sq.*

Fodor's Choice ★ **Maggs Bros. Ltd.** How could any book lover resist a shop with such a Dickensian name? Resembling the library of a bibliophilic gentleman more than a commercial enterprise, Maggs has been selling rare antiquarian books and manuscripts since 1853 and is one of the world's oldest and largest such dealers (it also deals in autographs). The staff—with specialists in early British and early European works, travel, and Japanese photography—are expert enough to advise important collectors, but are friendly and helpful to all interested visitors. Maggs also has a tradition of carrying works on subversion, extremism, punk, the occult, and more. There are occasional themed exhibitions featuring manuscripts and rare editions, and there's an annex shop on Curzon Street in Mayfair. ✉ *48 Bedford Sq., Bloomsbury* ☎ *020/7493–7160* ⊕ *www.maggs.com* ⊙ *Closed weekends* Ⓜ *Goodge St., Tottenham Court Rd.*

Fodor's Choice ★ **Persephone Books.** A must for all lovers of fiction and nonfiction by women writers, Persephone is a gem of a bookshop specializing in its own reprints of mostly neglected 20th-century works from predominately female authors. Exquisitely decorated endpapers make these books perfect gifts for your bibliophile friends. ✉ *59 Lamb's Conduit St., Bloomsbury* ☎ *020/7242–9292* ⊕ *www.persephonebooks.co.uk* ⊙ *Closed Sun.* Ⓜ *Russell Sq., Holborn.*

18

SPECIALTY STORES

Blade Rubber. This unique shop near the British Museum specializes in rubber stamps, with everything from businesslike "Paid" stamps to *Alice in Wonderland* characters, Egyptian gods, VW Beetles, flying saucers, and more. Get a custom-made personal stamp—a great gift for a young person—or bring back stamps of British icons like a double-decker bus, the Tower of London, or a bust of Shakespeare as souvenirs. It also carries scrapbooking materials and offers scrapbooking classes on Saturdays. ⊠ *12 Bury Pl., Bloomsbury* ☎ *020/7831–4123* ⊕ *www. bladerubberstamps.co.uk* Ⓜ *Holborn.*

HOLBORN

ANTIQUES

London Silver Vaults. Originally built in 1876 as Britain's first safe deposit building, with basement strong rooms for storing household valuables like jewelry, silver, and documents, this extraordinary underground space has been converted to more than 30 small units housing silver (plus a few jewelry) dealers, the majority of which are family businesses. Products range from 16th-century items to contemporary pieces (with everything in between), and from the spectacularly over-the-top costing thousands to smaller items—like teaspoons, candlesticks, or a set of Victorian cake forks—at £25. ⊠ *53–64 Chancery La., Holborn* ☎ *020/7242–3844* ⊕ *www.silvervaultslondon.com* ◷ *Closed Sun.* Ⓜ *Chancery La.*

ISLINGTON

HOUSEHOLD

Fodor's Choice ★ **TwentyTwentyOne.** Do not overlook this furniture, lighting, and accessories store if you love modernist design. This shop carries a huge selection of 20th-century classics, including pieces from Noguchi, Nouvel, Aalto, Prouvé, Saarinen, and the husband-and-wife team Robin and Lucienne Day, in the form of both originals and licensed reissues. Also among the offerings are contemporary pieces from modern masters like Tom Dixon, Thomas Heatherwick, and Marc Newson. The kids' line is particularly cool, with items like a classic elephant sculpture/toy from another married design team, Charles and Ray Eames. Small accessories like tote bags and cushions will easily fit into your luggage. ⊠ *274–275 Upper St., Islington* ☎ *020/7288–1996* ⊕ *www.twentytwentyone.com* Ⓜ *Highbury & Islington.*

FITZROVIA

CLOTHING

Fodor's Choice ★ **So Tiny London.** This small store has loads of imaginative gifts for babies and young children, such as distinctive onesies and T-shirts emblazoned with Union Jacks, "Darth Vader Is My Father," "Baby Gaga," and logos of rock bands like Pink Floyd, Motörhead, and the Rolling Stones. You'll also find pretty dresses with an English Rose print, dragon costumes for dress-up, Jellycat plush toys (favorites of royal babies William, Charlotte. and Louis), and child-friendly joke items like rubber chickens. ⊠ *64 Great Titchfield St., Fitzrovia* ☎ *020/7636–3501* ⊕ *www.sotinylondon.com* Ⓜ *Oxford Circus.*

Topshop. A hot spot for straight-from-the-runway affordable fashion, Topshop is destination shopping for teenagers and fashion editors alike. Clothes, shoes, and accessories are geared to the youthful end of the market, although there are also plenty of wearable items here for women who are young at heart and girlish of figure—so long as they can tolerate the loud music and busy dressing rooms. The store also features collections designed by a rotating roster of high-end designers and its own premium designer line called Topshop Unique. The amount of stock at this 90,000-square-foot flagship store is vast, but a clear layout helps make it navigable. Keep an eye out for pop-up extras like free minimakeovers, a blow-dry bar, and a hair salon, plus brow and nail bars. Topman brings the same fast-fashion approach to clothing for men. If the crowds become too much, head to one of the smaller Topshops in Knightsbridge, Marble Arch, The City, or Holborn. ⊠ *36–38 Great Castle St., Fitzrovia* ☎ *0207/927–7644* ⊕ *www.topshop.com* Ⓜ *Oxford Circus.*

EAST LONDON

ACCESSORIES

Fodor'sChoice
★
Bernstock Speirs. Here since 1982, Paul Bernstock and Thelma Speirs have put a quirky, fashionable spin on traditional hats for men and women, with street-smart trilbies, whimsical bunny-ear baseball caps, and knitted beanies that feature unusual colors and detailing (like veils, for instance). ⊠ *234 Brick La., Spitalfields* ☎ *020/7739–7385* ⊕ *www.bernstockspeirs.com* Ⓜ *Overground: Shoreditch High St.*

Deciem. One of the few brick-and-mortar outlets for beauty editors' favorite products by Deciem and its cult brands—The Ordinary (quality skin-care products at very reasonable prices thanks to stripped-down packaging and low margins) and its premium (though still affordable) range, Niod, which stands for "Non-Invasive Options In Dermal Science," epitomizing the brand's function-not-frills approach. In addition, the store stocks the umbrella company's food and health supplements as well as its hair-care, hand and body care, and men's grooming products. Other branches are in Covent Garden and the Boxpark on nearby Bethnal Green Road. ⊠ *Old Spitalfields Market, 18 Lamb St., Shoreditch* ☎ *020/3884–1959* ⊕ *www.deciem.com* Ⓜ *Shoreditch High St.*

CLOTHING

Absolute Vintage. This is a warehouse packed with a wide range of hand-picked items from the 1930s through the 1980s, but the specialty here is shoes and bags. The shop claims to have the largest collection of vintage shoes in the United Kingdom—more than 1,000 pairs—and, best of all, prices are reasonable. ⊠ *15 Hanbury St., Spitalfields* ☎ *020/7274–3883* ⊕ *www.absolutevintage.co.uk* Ⓜ *Overground: Shoreditch High St.*

Beyond Retro. The more than 10,000 vintage items for men and women here—from cowboy boots to bowling shirts to prom dresses—include the largest collection of American retro in the United Kingdom. There's another outpost in Dalston and one in Soho. ⊠ *110–112 Cheshire St., Spitalfields* ☎ *020/7297–9001* ⊕ *www.beyondretro.com* Ⓜ *Whitechapel. Overground: Shoreditch High St.*

18

Fodor's Choice
★

Hostem. Drawing style-conscious customers from nearby tech start-ups, Hostem is for the man who wants to be well dressed without looking like he's trying too hard, with a mixture of casual luxury, streetwear, and fashion-forward edge from tastemaker favorites including John Alexander Skelton, Casey Casey, and Geoffrey B. Small. The womenswear area offers pieces by designers like Prada and Amy Revier. There's also a bespoke service for clothing and exquisite men's shoes by cobbler Sebastain Tarek. It's achingly hip (clothes hang from a wooden "monolithic site specific sculpture"), but in superb taste. The store also operates a three-bedroom guesthouse (a converted Georgian town house in Whitechapel), where you can buy the crockery, bed linens, glassware, and more at the end of your stay. ⊠ *28 Old Nichol St., Shoreditch* ☎ *020/7739–9733* ⊕ *www. hostem.co.uk* Ⓜ *Overground: Shoreditch High St.*

Rokit. Magazine and music stylists love these two premises along Brick Lane that carry everything from handbags and ball gowns to jeans, military garb, and Western wear. The ever-changing stock spans the 1930s to the 1990s. There are also branches in Camden and Covent Garden. ⊠ *101 and 107 Brick La., Spitalfields* ☎ *020/7375–3864* ⊕ *www.rokit. co.uk* Ⓜ *Overground: Shoredith High St.*

Fodor's Choice
★

Sunspel. This British firm has been making fine men's underwear since the mid-19th century and it's still its specialty, along with luxury basics such as knitwear, outerwear, polo shirts, and swimwear. Prince Charles is a real-life customer and James Bond, a cinematic one (he wore their shorts in *Thunderball* and polo shirt in *Quantum of Solace*). The spy's creator, Ian Fleming, was another client and in fact has a new collection named after him. Sunspel also carries elegant, minimalist T-shirts, sweaters, and sweats for women. There are other branches in Marylebone, Notting Hill, St. James's, and Soho. ⊠ *7 Redchurch St., Shoreditch* ☎ *020/7739–9729* ⊕ *www.sunspel.com* Ⓜ *Overground: Shoreditch High St.*

FOOD

Fodor's Choice
★

Cundall & Garcia. All of the traditional or retro foodstuffs here—such as jars of locally produced honey, relish, or even "Mother's Ruin" gin—are British-made and make excellent and portable presents. Also available in this re-creation of a village shop are stylish gift baskets and old-fashioned picnic hampers, as well as freshly made take-out sandwiches (like honey roast ham with cheddar and apple and pear chutney), salads, homemade cakes, and hot daily specials. ⊠ *42 Brushfield St., Spitalfields* ☎ *020/7247–2487* ⊕ *www.agoldshop.com* ☉ *Closed Sun.* Ⓜ *Overground: Shoreditch High St.*

HOUSEHOLD GOODS

Fodor's Choice
★

Labour & Wait. Although mundane items like colanders and clothespins may not sound like ideal souvenirs, this shop (something of a hipster heaven selling both new and vintage items) will make you reconsider. The owners are on a mission to revive retro, functional British household goods, such as enamel kitchenware, genuine feather dusters, bread bins, bottle brushes, and traditional Welsh blankets. ⊠ *85 Redchurch St., Shoreditch* ☎ *020/7729–6253* ⊕ *www.labourandwait.co.uk* ☉ *Closed Mon.* Ⓜ *Overground: Shoreditch High St.*

MARKETS

Brick Lane. The noisy center of the Bangladeshi community is a hubbub of buying and selling on Sunday. Stalls have food, hardware, household and electrical goods, bric-a-brac, secondhand clothes, spices, and traditional saris. Some of the CDs and DVDs are pirated, and the bargain iron may not have a plug, so check carefully. Shoppers nevertheless flock to the market to enjoy the buzz, sample curries and Bangladeshi sweets, or indulge in salt beef on a bagel at Beigel Bake—London's 24-hour bagel bakery, a survivor of the neighborhood's Jewish past. Brick Lane's activity spills over into nearby Petticoat Lane Market, where there are similar goods but less atmosphere. ⊠ *Shoreditch* ⊕ *www.visitbricklane.org* ⊙ *Market closed Mon.–Sat.* Ⓜ *Aldgate E. Overground: Shoreditch High St.*

Fodor's Choice ★ **Broadway Market.** This parade of shops in hipster-centric Hackney (north of Regent's Canal) is worth visiting for the specialty bookshops, independent boutiques, organic cafés, neighborhood restaurants, and even a traditional (but now rare) pie-and-mash shop. But wait for Saturday (9–5), when it really comes into its own with a farmers' market and more than 100 street-food and produce stalls rivaling those of south London's famed Borough Market. Artisanal breads, cheeses, pastries, organic meats, waffles, fruit and vegetables, seafood, and international food offerings: this is foodie heaven. There are also stalls selling vintage clothes, crafts, jewelry, and more. ⊠ *Broadway Market, Hackney* ☏ *0787/246–3409* ⊕ *www.broadwaymarket.co.uk* ⊙ *Market closed. Mon.–Sat.* Ⓜ *London Fields.*

Fodor's Choice ★ **Columbia Road Flower Market.** London's premier flower market is about as pretty and photogenic as they come, with more than 50 stalls selling flowers, shrubs, bulbs, and trees—everything from bedding plants to 10-foot banana trees—as well as garden tools, pots, and accessories at competitive prices. The stallholders' patter is part of the fun. It's on Sunday only, and it's all over by 2 pm. Columbia Road itself is lined with 60 interesting independent shops purveying art, fashion, furnishings, and the local cafés are superb. ⊠ *Columbia Rd., Hoxton* ⊕ *www.columbiaroad. info* ⊙ *Market closed Mon.–Sat.* Ⓜ *Old St. Overground: Hoxton.*

Old Spitalfields Market. Once the East End's wholesale fruit and vegetable market and now restored to its original architectural splendor, this fine example of a Victorian market hall is at the center of the area's gentrified revival. The original building is largely occupied by shops (mostly upscale brands like Rag & Bone, Lululemon, and Superga, but some independents like trendy homeware-and-fashion purveyor The Mercantile), with traders' stalls in the courtyard. A modern shopping precinct under a Norman Foster–designed glass canopy adjoins the old building and holds approximately 70 traders' stalls. You may have to wade through a certain number of stalls selling cheap imports and tacky T-shirts to find the good stuff, which includes vintage and new clothing, handmade rugs and jewelry, hand-carved toy trains, vintage maps, unique baby clothes, rare vinyl, and cakes. Thursday is particularly good for antiques; Friday for a biweekly record fair; while weekends offer a little of everything. The new The Kitchens, 10 central dining venues showcasing small, independent chefs and restaurants, provide fresh takes on Nordic, Mexican, Japanese, and other world cuisines.

There are also indie street food stalls and some superior chain outlets. ⊠ *16 Horner Sq., Brushfield St., Spitalfields* ☎ *020/7375–2963* ⊕ *www. oldspitalfieldsmarket.com* ☉ *Stalls closed Mon.–Wed.* Ⓜ *Liverpool St. Overground: Shoreditch High St.*

MUSIC

Rough Trade East. Although many London record stores are struggling, this veteran indie-music specialist in the Old Truman Brewery seems to have gotten the formula right. The spacious surroundings are as much a hangout as a shop, complete with a stage for live gigs and a café. There's another branch on Talbot Road in Notting Hill. ⊠ *Dray Walk, Old Truman Brewery, 91 Brick La., Spitalfields* ☎ *020/7392–7788* ⊕ *www. roughtrade.com* Ⓜ *Liverpool St. Overground: Shoreditch High St.*

SOUTH OF THE THAMES

ART

Oxo Tower Wharf. The artisans creating fashion, jewelry, home accessories, textiles, prints and photographs, furniture, and other design items have to pass rigorous selection procedures to set up in these prime riverside studios, where they make, display, and sell their work. The Oxo Tower Restaurant & Brasserie on the top floor is expensive, but with its fantastic view of London, it's worth popping up for a drink. There's also a public terrace where you can take in the view. ⊠ *Oxo Tower Wharf, Bargehouse St., South Bank* ☎ *020/7021–1686 24-hr info* ⊕ *www.coinstreet.org* ☉ *Closed Mon.* Ⓜ *Waterloo.*

MARKETS

Bermondsey Square Antiques Market. The early bird catches the worm at this Friday market, so come before dawn (flashlight recommended) to bag a bargain at London's largest antiques market. Dealers also arrive before dawn to snap up the best curios and silver, paintings, objets d'art, and furniture. The early start grew out of a loophole in the law (dating from when the market began on the site in 1885) that said stolen goods bought during the hours of darkness could not be prosecuted as the origin of the goods could not be determined. While stolen goods are no longer welcome here, the market has expanded to some 200 stalls, including food, clothing, and crafts. It finishes at 2 pm. ⊠ *Long La. and Bermondsey Sq., Bermondsey* ⊕ *www.bermondseysquare.net* ☉ *Closed Sat.–Thurs.* Ⓜ *London Bridge.*

Fodor's Choice **Borough Market.** There's been a market in Borough since Roman times.
★ This latest incarnation, spread under the arches and railroad tracks leading to London Bridge Station, is where some of the city's best artisanal food producers set up stalls. Fresh coffees, gorgeous cheeses, chocolates, and baked goods complement the organically farmed meats, fresh fish, condiments, fruits, and vegetables.

Don't make any other lunch plans for the day; this is where celebrity chef Jamie Oliver's scallop man cooks them up fresh at Shell Seekers, and The Ginger Pig's rare-breed sausages sizzle on grills, while for the sweets lover there are chocolates, preserves, and Whirld's artisanal confectionery, as well as 18 restaurants and cafés, most above average. The Market Hall hosts workshops, tastings, and demonstrations, and also acts as a greenhouse. On Monday and Tuesday only stalls for hot food and produce are open.

On weekends, a separate, highly regarded market specializing in produce and street food operates on nearby Maltby Street. It was originally established by eight breakaway Borough Market traders. Stalls include African Volcano, purveyors of Mozambique-style hot sauces and marinades, and Raclette Brothers' superb melted cheese. ✉ *8 Southwark St., Borough* ☎ *020/7402–1002* ⊕ *www.boroughmarket.org.uk* ⊘ *Closed Sun.* Ⓜ *London Bridge.*

KENSINGTON, CHELSEA, KNIGHTSBRIDGE, AND BELGRAVIA

KENSINGTON
HOUSEHOLD GOODS

The Conran Shop. This is the brainchild of Sir Terence Conran, who has been a major influence on British taste since he opened Habitat in the 1960s. Although he is no longer associated with Habitat, his Conran Shops remain bastions of similarly clean, unfussy modernist design. Housewares from furniture to lighting, stemware, and textiles—both handmade and mass-produced, by famous names and emerging designers—are housed in a building that is a modernist landmark in its own right. Both the flagship store and the branch on Marylebone High Street are bursting with great gift ideas. ✉ *Michelin House, 81 Fulham Rd., South Kensington* ☎ *020/7589–7401* ⊕ *www.conran-shop.co.uk* Ⓜ *South Kensington.*

Mint. Owner Lina Kanafani has scoured the globe to curate an eclectic mix of conceptual statement furniture, art, ceramics, glassware, and home accessories. Mint also showcases avant-garde works by an international selection of up-and-coming designers and sells plenty of limited edition and one off pieces. If you don't want to ship a couch home, consider a miniature flower vase or a handmade ceramic pitcher. ✉ *2 North Terr., at Alexander Sq., South Kensington* ☎ *020/7225–2228* ⊕ *www.mintshop.co.uk* ⊘ *Closed Sun.* Ⓜ *South Kensington.*

Skandium. Scandinavia is having a moment in Britain. Skandium brings together many of the region's top designers of furniture, lighting, rugs, and housewares in two shops. The "Skandium Townhouse" showcases furniture from giants of Scandinavian Modernism like Artek, Fritz Hansen, and Georg Jensen, as well as non-Scandinavian modernists such as Knoll, in re-created domestic settings. Across the street, Skandium sells similarly Scandinavian soft furnishings, lighting, and accessories. Clean lines and stripped-down, unfussy elegance abound (although the Moomins make an appearance on ceramics). There's another branch in Marylebone. ✉ *35 Thurloe Pl., South Kensington* ☎ *0203/876–2744* ⊕ *www.skandium.com* Ⓜ *South Kensington.*

JEWELRY

Butler & Wilson. Specialists in bold costume jewelry and affordable glamour, Butler & Wilson attracts fans including the Duchess of Cambridge. It's added semiprecious stones to its foundation diamanté, colored rhinestone, and crystal collections. Flamboyant skull brooches or dainty floral earrings make perfect gifts. ✉ *189 Fulham*

18

Rd., South Kensington ☏ *020/7352–3045* ⊕ *www.butlerandwilson. co.uk* ⊘ *Closed Sun.* Ⓜ *South Kensington.*

CHELSEA

BOOKS

John Sandoe (Books) Ltd. This atmospheric warren that crams some 25,000 titles into an 18th-century building off King's Road is the antithesis of a soulless chain bookstore, so it's no surprise it has attracted equally idiosyncratic customers like Tom Stoppard and Keith Richards. Staff members are wonderfully knowledgeable (don't try to figure out how the stock is organized without their help), and there are a lot of them per customer—if a book isn't in stock, they will try to find it for you, even if it is out of print. ✉ *10 Blacklands Terr., Chelsea* ☏ *020/7589–9473* ⊕ *www.johnsandoe.com* Ⓜ *Sloane Sq.*

CLOTHING

Brora. The knitwear is cozy, but the style is cool in this contemporary Scottish cashmere emporium for men, women, and kids. There are dressed-up camisoles, sweaters and cardigans, and adorable baby ensembles, as well as noncashmere items such as picnic blankets and scarves. Other branches are in Marylebone, and Covent Garden; plus there's a clearance store farther down King's Road. ✉ *6–8 Symons St., Chelsea* ☏ *020/7730–2665* ⊕ *www.brora.co.uk* Ⓜ *Sloane Sq.*

Hackett. If Ralph Lauren isn't preppy enough for you, try Hackett, with branches in St. James's and Canary Wharf. Originally a posh thrift shop recycling cricket flannels, hunting pinks, Oxford brogues, and other staples of a British gentleman's wardrobe, Hackett now creates its own line and has become a genuine—and very good—men's outfitter. The look is traditional and classic best buys include polo shirts, corduroys, and striped scarves. There's also a boys' line for the junior man-about-town. ✉ *137–138 Sloane St., Chelsea* ☏ *020/7730–3331* ⊕ *www.hackett.com* Ⓜ *Sloane Sq.*

Jigsaw. The quality of fabrics and detailing belie the reasonable prices here, where clothes are classic yet trendy and elegant without being dull—and where cuts are kind to the womanly figure. The style is epitomized by the Duchess of Cambridge, who, as Kate Middleton before her marriage, was a buyer for the company. Although there are numerous branches across London, no two stores are the same. Preteens have their own line, Jigsaw Junior. ✉ *The Chapel, 6 Duke of York Sq., Chelsea* ☏ *020/730–4404* ⊕ *www.jigsaw-online.com* Ⓜ *Sloane Sq.*

DEPARTMENT STORES

Fodor's Choice ★ **Peter Jones.** This tasteful department store has been a beloved local institution since it opened in 1937, and the poet John Betjeman remarked that come the end of the world he would like to be in the haberdashery department of Peter Jones, "because nothing bad could ever happen there." It's the traditional default wedding-list option of Kensington & Chelsea brides, thanks to its outstanding selection of bed and bath linens (many provided by John Lewis, the store's parent company), flatware, ceramics, and glassware, with offerings at all price points. There's also an extensive and eclectic beauty department, as well as kitchenware and appliances, tech stuff, a florist, clothing, shoes, and accessories for the whole family, and pretty much everything else you can think of, along with a restaurant and a Clarins spa. ⊠ *Sloane Sq., Chelsea* ☎ *020/7730–3434* ⊕ *www.johnlewis.com/our-shops/peter-jones* Ⓜ *Sloane Sq.*

FOOD

L'Artisan du Chocolat. Praised by top chefs Gordon Ramsay and Heston Blumenthal, L'Artisan raises chocolate to an art form. "Couture" chocolates are infused with fruits, nuts, and spices (including such exotic flavorings as Szechuan pepper and tobacco). This is one of the few chocolate shops in the world that makes liquid salted caramels. There are other branches in Notting Hill and Kensington. ⊠ *89 Lower Sloane St., Chelsea* ☎ *0845/270–6996* ⊕ *www.artisanduchocolat.co.uk* Ⓜ *Sloane Sq.*

HOUSEHOLD GOODS

Designers Guild. Tricia Guild's exuberantly patterned fabrics, wallpapers, paints, furniture, and bed linens have decorated design-conscious British homes for several decades, and her soft-furnishings book has taught many budget-conscious do-it-yourselfers how to reupholster a sofa or make lined draperies. The shop also stocks contemporary furniture, wallpapers, and home accessories by other designers like Christian Lacroix. There's another branch in Marylebone. ⊠ *267–277 King's Rd., Chelsea* ☎ *020/351–5775* ⊕ *www.designersguild.com* ☾ *Closed Sun.* Ⓜ *Sloane Sq.*

SHOES

Fodor's Choice ★ **Manolo Blahnik.** Blink and you'll miss the discreet sign that marks fashionista footwear central. Blahnik, the man who single-handedly managed to revive the sexy stiletto, has been trading out of this small shop on a Chelsea side street since 1973. It's a must for shoe lovers with generous budgets. If you decide to wear your new Manolos, hop on Bus No. 11 or 22 or grab a cab—the nearest Tube station is about a 20-minute totter away. ⊠ *49–51 Old Church St., Chelsea* ☎ *020/7352–8622* ⊕ *www.manoloblahnik.com* ☾ *Closed Sun.* Ⓜ *Sloane Sq., South Kensington.*

SPECIALTY STORES

Green & Stone Art Materials. This fabulous cave of artists' materials, papers, art books, easels, and mannequins is one of the longest-established shops on King's Road. It began life in 1927 as part of the Chenil Gallery, run by a distinguished group that included the artist Augustus John and the playwright George Bernard Shaw. At the current location since 1934, the shop also has a framing service, antique paint boxes, and craft supplies. Francis Bacon and David Hockney have been among its clients. ⊠ *259 King's Rd., Chelsea* ☎ *020/7352–0837* ⊕ *www.greenandstone.com* Ⓜ *Sloane Sq.*

KNIGHTSBRIDGE

CLOTHING

Egg. Tucked away in a residential mews, this spartan shop in a former Victorian dairy is the brainchild of Maureen Doherty, once Issey Miyake's assistant. More than half the minimalist, unstructured styles for men and women—in natural luxury fabrics such as silk, cashmere,

18

and antique cotton—are handmade. Garments may be casually hung on hooks or folded on wooden tables, but the price tags are anything but unassuming. The clientele includes the likes of Donna Karan and British PM Theresa May. One-of-a-kind ceramics and jewelry are also on display. ⊠ *36 Kinnerton St., Knightsbridge* ☎ *020/7235–9315* ⊕ *www. eggtrading.com* ⊘ *Closed Sun.* Ⓜ *Knightsbridge.*

FAMILY   **Rachel Riley.** Specializing in traditional English style for boys and girls, Riley's luxurious, vintage-inspired collection includes classics like duffel coats and hand-smocked floral dresses. Mothers who love the Riley look (including the Duchess of Cambridge, who has put her royal offspring in Riley clothes) can pick up coordinating outfits for themselves here or at the Marylebone High Street location. ⊠ *14 Pont St., Knightsbridge* ☎ *020/7259–5969* ⊕ *www.rachelriley.co.uk* ⊘ *Closed Sun.* Ⓜ *Knightsbridge.*

Rigby & Peller. Many of London's most affluent women find their luxury lingerie (plus swimwear) here because the quality is excellent and the service impeccably knowledgeable—and perhaps because it's the Queen's favored underwear supplier and has provided maternity wear to the Duchess of Cambridge. Despite the upscale clientele, it's much friendlier than you might expect. Brands include Primadonna and Aubade as well as R&P's own line, and if the right fit eludes you, there's a made-to-measure service that starts at around £300. There are also branches in Mayfair, Chelsea, St. John's Wood, and The City. ⊠ *2 Hans Rd., Knightsbridge* ☎ *020/7225–4760* ⊕ *www.rigbyandpeller. com* Ⓜ *Knightsbridge.*

DEPARTMENT STORES

Harrods. With an encyclopedic assortment of luxury brands, this Knightsbridge institution, currently owned by the Qatar Investment Authority, has more than 300 departments and 25 eating and drinking options, all spread over 1 million square feet on a 4½-acre site. You can even get your eyes tested or buy a foreign villa. Now populated more by window-shopping tourists and superrich visitors from abroad than by the bling-averse natives, Harrods is best approached as the world's largest, most upscale and expensive mall. Focus on the spectacular food halls, the huge ground-floor perfumery and jewelry departments, the excellent Urban Retreat spa, and Shoe Heaven, Europe's biggest shoe department. The Superbrands area houses haute couture from 12 top international designers such as Dior, Fendi, Prada, Valentino, and Chanel, while the children's department has a mini-me version for the toddler who wouldn't be seen in anything less than the likes of Burberry, Baby Dior, Chloé for Kids, and Monclerr. Be prepared to brave the crowds, especially on weekends. ⊠ *87–135 Brompton Rd., Knightsbridge* ☎ *020/7730–1234* ⊕ *www.harrods.com* Ⓜ *Knightsbridge.*

Harvey Nichols. While visiting tourists flock to Harrods, local fashionistas shop at Harvey Nichols, aka "Harvey Nicks." The womenswear and accessories departments are outstanding, featuring top designers like Tom Ford, Elie Saab, Yeezy, Lanvin, Reem Acra, and just about every fashionable name you can think of. The furniture and housewares are equally gorgeous (and pricey), although they become somewhat more affordable during the biannual sales in January and July. The Fifth Floor bar is the place to see and be seen, but if you're in search of food, the same floor also has an all-day Modern European café, a branch of Burger & Lobster, the carnivore-friendly Zelman Meats, or sushi-to-go from Yo! Sushi. To keep you looking as box-fresh as your purchases, the Beauty Lounge features a rotating menu of treatments from brands such as Elemis, La Mer, and Dermalogia, plus makeovers, LED facials, IV vitamin infusions, and blow-dry, nail, and brow bars. ⊠ *109–125 Knightsbridge, Knightsbridge* ☎ *020/7235–5000* ⊕ *www. harveynichols.com* Ⓜ *Knightsbridge.*

BELGRAVIA
ACCESSORIES

Anya Hindmarch. Exquisite leather bags and personalized, printed canvas totes are what made Hindmarch famous, and this store sells her complete collection of bags, several with a whimsical motif. You can also order a custom piece like the "Be A Bag," a wash bag imprinted with your chosen photo. There are branches around the corner on Pont Street in Knightsbridge, Bond Street in Mayfair, and in Notting Hill. ⊠ *157-158 Sloane St., Belgravia* ☎ *0207/730–0961* ⊕ *www.anya-hindmarch.com* Ⓜ *Sloane Square.*

Fodor's Choice ★ **Philip Treacy.** Magnificent hats by Treacy are annual showstoppers on Ladies Day at the Royal Ascot races and regularly grace the glossy magazines' party and catwalk pages. Part Mad Hatter, part Cecil Beaton, Treacy's creations always guarantee a grand entrance and are favorites with both Hollywood and actual royalty. In addition to the extravagant, haute couture hats handmade in the atelier, less flamboyant ready-to-wear hats are also for sale, as are some bags. ⊠ *69 Elizabeth St., Belgravia* ☎ *020/7730–3992* ⊕ *www.philiptreacy. co.uk* ⊙ *Closed Sun.* Ⓜ *Sloane Sq.*

SPECIALTY STORES

Mungo & Maud. If you don't want to leave London without buying something for your pet, Mungo & Maud have something for your furry friend. Pick up a well-designed coat, leash, harness, bowl, toy, or comfortable bed that will make your dog the snazziest pooch in town (some collars are hand-stitched), or select from baskets, suede collars, and blankets for your cat. Even owners get a nod with luxurious merino throws (soon to be covered in pet hair), pet-themed jewelry, and leather poop pouches. ⊠ *79 Elizabeth St., Belgravia* ☎ *020/7022–1207* ⊕ *www. mungoandmaud.com* ⊙ *Closed Sun.* Ⓜ *Sloane Sq.*

NOTTING HILL

BOOKS

Fodor's Choice ★ **Books for Cooks.** It may seem odd to describe a bookshop as delicious-smelling, but on several days you can't but notice the aromas wafting out of the tiny café in the back of the shop—where the resident chef cooks a three-course set lunch for only £7, served from noon to 1 pm Tuesday through Friday. The dishes are drawn from recipes in the 8,000 cookbooks on the shelves. Just about every world cuisine is represented, along with a complete lineup of works by celebrity chefs. Before you

18

come to London, visit the shop's website to sign up for a specialized cooking workshop in the upstairs demonstration kitchen. ✉ *4 Blenheim Crescent, Notting Hill* ☎ *020/7221–1992* ⊕ *www.booksforcooks.com* ⊘ *Closed Sun. and Mon.* Ⓜ *Notting Hill Gate, Ladbroke Grove.*

CLOTHING

Aimé. French-Cambodian sisters Val and Vanda Heng-Vong launched this shop to showcase the best of French clothing and designer housewares. Expect to find cult French labels like Isabel Marant, Forte Forte, and Michel Vivien, along with housewares and a well-chosen collection of ceramics. Petit Aimé, next door, sells children's clothing. There's also a Shoreditch branch. ✉ *32 Ledbury Rd., Notting Hill* ☎ *020/7221–7070* ⊕ *www.aimelondon.com* ⊘ *Closed Sun.* Ⓜ *Notting Hill Gate.*

The Cross. One of the first "lifestyle boutiques" and still one of the best, this west London favorite carries luxury casual fashion by in-the-know favorites like Vanessa Bruno, Velvet, and Chinti & Parker, plus accessories, jewelry, housewares, and kids' clothes. The emphasis is on feminine and quirky boho chic. ✉ *141 Portland Rd., Notting Hill* ☎ *020/7727–6760* ⊕ *www.thecrossshop.co.uk* ⊘ *Closed Sun.* Ⓜ *Holland Park.*

FAMILY   **Marie Chantal.** If you love beautiful, tasteful, and somewhat formal clothing for babies and children, head to this boutique created by Princess Marie-Chantal of Greece. As you'd imagine, the look is elegant and the prices are high. Materials used include silk, linen, and Liberty prints (plus less fancy T-shirts). ✉ *61 Ledbury Rd., Notting Hill* ☎ *0207/243–0220* ⊕ *www.mariechantal.co.uk* ⊘ *Closed Sun.* Ⓜ *Notting Hill Gate.*

Raey. This affordable in-house offshoot line of high-end designer destination ⊕ *matchesfashion.com* has quickly become a fashion editors' favorite thanks to Raey's minimalist, wearable styles for men and women that use luxurious fabrics and superb cuts far above their price points (cotton jersey T-shirts start at £95 going up to shearling jackets for £1,200). This is the brand's first stand-alone store. Matches Fashion itself has boutiques next door and farther down the road. ✉ *83 Ledbury Rd., Notting Hill* ☎ *020/7221–1120* ⊕ *www.matchesfashion.com* Ⓜ *Notting Hill Gate.*

Rellik. Now in the modernist landmark known as the Trellick Tower and favored by the likes of Kate Moss, Rellik began as a stall in the Portobello Market. Vintage hunters looking to splurge can find a selection of YSL, Dior, Pierre Cardin, and Ossie Clark as well as items from lesser-known designers. ✉ *Trellick Tower, 8 Golborne Rd., Notting Hill* ☎ *020/8962–0089* ⊕ *www.relliklondon.co.uk* ⊘ *Closed Sun. and Mon.* Ⓜ *Westbourne Park.*

MARKETS

Portobello Market. *See full listing in Chapter 10: Notting Hill and Bayswater.*

MUSIC

Music & Video Exchange. This store is a music collector's treasure trove, with a constantly changing stock refreshed by customers selling and exchanging as well as buying. The ground floor focuses on rock, pop, indie, and punk, both mainstream and obscure, in a variety of formats ranging from vinyl to CD, cassette, and even minidisk. Don't miss the classical music in the basement and the soul, jazz, house, techno, reggae, and more upstairs. Like movies? There's a wide variety of Blu-ray and DVD box sets, as well as bargain classic and cult films. Keep an eye out for rarities—including first pressings and one-offs—in all departments. Similar exchanges for comics (No. 32) and books (No. 30) are on nearby Pembridge Road (also a destination for vintage clothing for men [No. 34] and women [No. 20], plus more clothing, accessories, and retro homewares [No. 28]). Note: Stock depends on what customers bring in to exchange, so you'll surely find many more DVDs with European (PAL) formatting than the North American–friendly NTSC format, but the store does get the latter occasionally. ✉ 38 Notting Hill Gate, Notting Hill ☎ 020/7243–8573 ⊕ www.mgeshops.com Ⓜ Notting Hill Gate.

SHOES
Emma Hope. The signature look of the footwear here is elegant and feminine, with pointed toes and kitten heels, often ornamented with bows, lace, crystals, or exquisite embroidery (such craftsmanship doesn't come cheap, unfortunately). Ballet flats and sneakers in velvet or animal prints provide glamour without sacrificing comfort. Small but perfectly formed handbags, as well as shoes and accessories for men, are stocked both here and in the Sloane Square branch. ✉ 207 Westbourne Grove, Notting Hill ☎ 020/7313–7490 ⊕ www.emmahope.com Ⓜ Notting Hill Gate.

REGENT'S PARK AND HAMPSTEAD

GIFTS
Susan Wainwright. If you're looking for an alternative to the cheesy and the mass-produced, this eclectic shop packs loads of distinctive, stylish, affordable gifts into a small space. The assortment includes handsome gloves and fake-fur accessories, handmade silver jewelry, tweed travel blankets, cashmere shawls, leather handbags, comfortable yet attractive robes and pajamas, natural-fiber baby and children's clothes and accessories, retro toys, sophisticated stationery, artisanal creams and lotions, and flasks and leather goods for him. Best of all, prices are reasonable. ✉ 31 South End Rd., Hampstead ☎ 020/7431–4337 Ⓜ Overground: Hampstead Heath.

HOUSEHOLD GOODS
Graham & Green. Combining style with practicality and a whimsical twist, this delightful interiors shop carries a broad but carefully curated selection of faux-fur throws, elegant lamps and lampshades, embroidered cushions, sheepskin rugs, agate or Venetian glass doorknobs, folding deck chairs (as found in the Royal Parks), shabby-chic sofas, ceramics and cutlery, dinosaur string lights, and more. There are branches in Notting Hill and Bayswater. ✉ 164 Regent's Park Rd., Primrose Hill ☎ 020/7586–2960 ⊕ www.grahamandgreen.co.uk Ⓜ Chalk Farm.

18

MARKETS

The Camden Markets. Begun in the early 1970s, when weekend stalls sold the output of nearby craft workshops, Camden Lock Market later expanded to four markets: Camden, Camden Lock, The Stables, and the Canal Market, all grouped around two locks on the Regent's Canal. Though much of the merchandise is targeted at young street-fashion aficionados as well as aging hippies, anyone with a taste for alternative culture—Goths are particularly well catered for—will also find plenty that appeals. This shopping experience is best suited to those who don't mind large crowds and a boisterous atmosphere (i.e., teenagers), especially on weekends. For many years, the markets have hosted more than 1,000 stalls offering a wide-ranging array of merchandise—vintage and new clothes, antiques and junk, rare vinyl, vintage board games, ceramics, Indian bedspreads, fetishwear, obscure band memorabilia, and toys.

The outdoor Camden Market on Camden High Street mainly sells cheap jeans, secondhand clothes, and tacky pop-culture paraphernalia; Camden Lock Market is the place to go for crafts; and The Stables Market, which has expanded into the so-called Catacombs (Victorian brick arches), has more than 700 shops and stalls and is where you go for furniture. The Canal Market has just been redeveloped and is now called Hawley Wharf, a mixed-use retail and residential development. All four markets are earmarked for redevelopment, so their focus is likely to change—if a scrappy, bohemian atmosphere appeals, enjoy it while you can. ⊠ *Camden High St. to Chalk Farm Rd., Camden Town* ⊕ *www.camdenmarket.com* Ⓜ *Camden Town, Chalk Farm.*

SHOES

Spice. Touring London requires a lot of walking, so if your feet are crying out for mercy, stop in at this long-established boutique that specializes in spiffy but comfortable shoes, sandals, and boots for men and women from brands like Coccinelle, Arche, and ChieMihara, as well as from its own Spice line. ⊠ *162 Regent's Park Rd., Primrose Hill* ☎ *020/7722–2478* ⊕ *www.spiceshu.co.uk* Ⓜ *Chalk Farm.*

SIDE TRIPS FROM LONDON

Updated by
Jack Jewers,
Sally Coffey,
and Ellin Stein

Londoners are undeniably lucky. Few urban populations enjoy such glorious—and easily accessible—options for day-tripping. Even if you have only one day to spare, head out of the city. A train ride past hills dotted with sheep, a stroll through a medieval town, or a visit to one of England's great castles could make you feel as though you've added another week to your vacation.

Not only is England extremely compact, but its train and bus networks, although somewhat inefficient and expensive compared with their European counterparts, are extensive and easily booked (though pricing structures can be confusing), making "a brilliant day out" an easy thing to accomplish.

Although you can do the Warner Bros. Harry Potter Studio Tour in a day, many of the towns near London would make for a frenzied day trip. And in summer, heavy crowds make it difficult to sightsee in a relaxed manner, so consider staying for a day or two instead. You'd then have time to explore a different England—one with quiet country pubs, tree-lined lanes, and neat fields.

PLANNING

WHAT IT COSTS			
$	$$	$$$	$$$$
Restaurants	Under £14	£14–£23	£24–£31	Over £31

Prices in the reviews are the average cost of a main course at dinner or, if dinner is not served, at lunch. Note: If a restaurant offers only prix-fixe (set-price) meals, it has been given the price category that reflects the full prix-fixe price.

TO GET TO ...	TAKE THE TRAIN FROM ...	TAKE THE BUS FROM ...
Cambridge	King's Cross (45–90 minutes, every 10 or 20 minutes); Liverpool St. (80 minutes, every 30 minutes)	Victoria Coach (about 3 hours, every 60–90 minutes)
Oxford	Paddington (55–110 minutes, every 3–20 minutes)	Victoria Coach (100 minutes, every half hour) or Oxford Tube, Buckingham Palace Rd. (100 minutes, every 12–20 minutes)
Stonehenge	Waterloo to Salisbury (90 minutes, every hour)	Victoria Coach to Amesbury (2 hours, about 3 times daily)
Stratford-upon-Avon	Marylebone (2–2½ hours, every 2 hours), or Euston (1½ hours, every 20 or 40 minutes or hourly)	Victoria Coach (3 hours 25 minutes, about 3 times daily)
Warner Bros. Harry Potter Studio Tour	Euston Station (20 minutes) to Watford, then shuttle bus to attraction	Watford (15 minutes, every 20 minutes), after taking London train from Euston.
Windsor	Paddington (25–50 minutes, every 5–30 minutes) or Waterloo (1 hour 5 minutes, every half hour)	Green Line Coach, Victoria (1 hour 5 minutes, hourly)

GETTING AROUND

Normally the towns near London are best reached by train. Bus travel costs less, but can take twice as long. Wherever you're going, plan ahead: check the latest timetables before you set off, and try to get an early start.

STATION TIPS

You can reach any of London's main-line train stations by Tube. London's bus stations can be confusing for the uninitiated, so here's a quick breakdown:

Green Line Coach Station is on Bulleid Way, in front of the Colonnades Shopping Centre on Buckingham Palace Road; it's the departure point for most Green Line and Megabus services.

Victoria Bus Station is where many of the local London bus services arrive and depart, and is directly outside the main exits of the train and Tube stations.

Victoria Coach Station is on Buckingham Palace Road: it's a five-minute walk from Victoria Tube station. This is where to go for coach departures; arrivals are at a different location, a short walk from here.

19

Side Trips
from London

CAMBRIDGE

60 miles northeast of London.

With the spires of its university buildings framed by towering trees and expansive meadows, its medieval streets and passages enhanced by gardens and riverbanks, the city of Cambridge is among the loveliest in England. The city predates the Roman occupation of Britain, but there's confusion over exactly how the university was founded. The most widely accepted story is that it was established in 1209 by a pair of scholars from Oxford, who left their university in protest over the wrongful execution of a colleague for murder.

This university town may be beautiful, but it's no museum. Even when the students are on vacation, there's a cultural and intellectual buzz here. Well-preserved medieval buildings sit cheek-by-jowl with the latest in modern architecture (for example, the William Gates building, which houses Cambridge University's computer laboratory) in this growing city—dominated culturally and architecturally by its famous university, whose students make up around one fifth of the city's 109,000 inhabitants, and beautified by parks, gardens, and the quietly flowing River Cam. One quintessential Cambridge pursuit is punting on the Cam (one occupant propelling the narrow, square-end, flat-bottom boat with a long pole), followed by a stroll along the Backs, the left bank of the river fringed by St. John's, Trinity, Clare, King's, and Queens' colleges, and by Trinity Hall.

VISITING THE COLLEGES

College visits are certainly a highlight of a Cambridge tour, but remember that the colleges are private residences and workplaces, even when school isn't in session. Each is an independent entity within the university; some are closed to the public, but at others you can see the chapels, dining rooms (called halls), and sometimes the libraries, too. Some colleges charge a fee for the privilege of nosing around. All are closed during exams (usually mid-April–late June), and the opening hours often vary. Additionally, all are subject to closure at short notice (especially King's); check the websites in advance. For details about visiting specific colleges not listed here, contact Cambridge University.

TOURS

City Sightseeing. This company operates open-top bus tours of Cambridge, including the Backs, colleges, and Botanic Gardens. Tours can be joined at marked bus stops in the city. Ask the tourist office about additional tours. ⊠ *Silver, Street East* ☏ *01789/299123* ⊕ *www.city-sightseeing.com* ✉ *From £18.50.*

Visit Cambridge. Walking tours are led by official Blue or Green Badge guides. The 1½- or 2-hour tours leave from the tourist information center at Peas Hill. Hours vary according to the tour, with the earliest leaving at 11 am and the latest at 1 or 2 pm. ⊠ *The Guildhall, Peas Hill* ☏ *01223/791501* ⊕ *www.visitcambridge.org/official-tours* ✉ *From £15.*

ESSENTIALS

Visitor Information Cambridge Visitor Information Centre. ⊠ *The Guildhall, Peas Hill* ☏ *01223/791500* ⊕ *www.visitcambridge.org.*

19

EXPLORING

Emmanuel College. The master hand of architect Sir Christopher Wren (1632–1723) is evident throughout much of Cambridge, particularly at Emmanuel, built on the site of a Dominican friary, where he designed the chapel and colonnade. A stained-glass window in the chapel has a likeness of John Harvard, founder of Harvard University, who studied here. The college, founded in 1584, was an early center of Puritan learning; a number of the Pilgrims were Emmanuel alumni, and they remembered their alma mater in naming Cambridge, Massachusetts. ⊠ *St. Andrew's St.* ☏ *01223/334200* ⊕ *www.emma.cam.ac.uk* ✉ *Free* ⊙ *Closed during exam periods.*

Fodor's Choice
★

Fitzwilliam Museum. In a Classical Revival building renowned for its grand Corinthian portico, "The Fitz," founded by the 7th Viscount Fitzwilliam of Merrion in 1816, has one of Britain's most outstanding collections of art and antiquities. Highlights include two large Titians, an extensive collection of French impressionist paintings, and many works by Matisse and Picasso. The opulent interior displays these treasures to marvelous effect, from Egyptian pieces like inch-high figurines and painted coffins to sculptures from the Chinese Han dynasty of the 3rd century BC. Other collections of note here include a fine collection of flower paintings, an assortment of medieval illuminated manuscripts, and a fascinating room full of armor and muskets. ⊠ *Trumpington St.* ☎ *01223/332900* ⊕ *www.fitzmuseum.cam.ac.uk* ⊠ *Free* ☉ *Closed Mon. except bank holidays.*

King's College. Founded in 1441 by Henry VI, King's College has a magnificent late-15th-century chapel that is its most famous landmark. Other notable architecture includes the neo-Gothic Porters' Lodge, facing King's Parade, which

was a comparatively recent addition in the 1830s, and the classical Gibbs building. ■TIP➔ Head down to the river, from where the panorama of college and chapel is one of the university's most photographed views. Past students of King's College include the novelist E.M. Forster, the economist John Maynard Keynes, and the World War I poet Rupert Brooke. ⊠ *King's Parade* ☎ *01223/331100* ⊕ *www.kings.cam. ac.uk* ⊠ *£9, includes chapel.*

Fodor's Choice
★ **King's College Chapel.** Based on Sainte-Chapelle, the 13th-century royal chapel in Paris, this house of worship is perhaps the most glorious flowering of Perpendicular Gothic in Britain. Henry VI, the king after whom the college is named, oversaw the work. From the outside, the most prominent features are the massive flying buttresses and the finger-like spires that line the length of the building. Inside, the most obvious impression is of great space—the chapel was once described as "the noblest barn in Europe"—and of light flooding in from its huge windows. The brilliantly colored bosses (carved panels at the intersections of the roof ribs) are particularly intense, although hard to see without binoculars. An exhibition in the chantries, or side chapels, explains more about the chapel's construction. Behind the altar is *The Adoration of the Magi*, an enormous painting by Peter Paul Rubens. ■TIP➔ The chapel, unlike the rest of King's College, stays open during exam periods. Every Christmas Eve, a festival of carols is sung by the chapel's famous choir. It's broadcast on national television and considered a quintessential part of the traditional English Christmas. To compete for the small number of tickets available, join the line at the college's main entrance early—doors open at 7 am. ⊠ *King's Parade* ☎ *01223/331212* ⊕ *www.kings.cam.ac.uk* ⊠ *£9, includes college and grounds* ☉ *Sometimes closed for events; check ahead to confirm.*

Fodor's Choice
★ **Polar Museum.** Beautifully designed, this museum at Cambridge University's Scott Polar Research Institute chronicles the history of polar exploration. There's a particular emphasis on the British expeditions of the 20th century, including the ill-fated attempt by Robert Falcon

Scott to be the first to reach the South Pole in 1912. Norwegian explorer Roald Amundsen reached the pole first; Scott and his men perished on the return journey, but their story became legendary. There are also collections devoted to the science of modern polar exploration; the indigenous people of northern Canada, Greenland, and Alaska; and frequently changing art installations. ⊠ *Scott Polar Research Institute, Lensfield Rd.* ☎ *01223/336540* ⊕ *www.spri.cam.ac.uk/museum* ⊠ *Free* ⊙ *Closed Sun. and Mon. except bank holidays.*

Queens' College. One of the most eye-catching colleges, with a secluded "cloister court" look, Queens' is named after Margaret, wife of Henry VI, and Elizabeth, wife of Edward IV. Founded in 1448 and completed in the 1540s, the college is tucked away on Queens' Lane, next to the wide lawns that lead down from King's College to the Backs. The college's most iconic piece of architecture is the wooden lattice Mathematical Bridge, first built in 1749. The original version is said to have been built without any fastenings, though the current bridge (reconstructed in 1902) is securely bolted. ⊠ *Queens' La.* ☎ *01223/335511* ⊕ *www.quns.cam.ac.uk* ⊠ *£3* ⊙ *Closed weekends Jan. and Feb. and during exam periods, certain wks Apr.–July; call to confirm.*

Trinity College. Founded in 1546 by Henry VIII, Trinity replaced a 14th-century educational foundation and is the largest college in either Cambridge or Oxford, with nearly 1,000 undergraduates. In the 17th-century great court, with its massive gatehouse, is **Great Tom,** a giant clock that strikes each hour with high and low notes. The college's true masterpiece is Sir Christopher Wren's **library,** colonnaded and seemingly constructed with as much light as stone. Among the things you can see here is A. A. Milne's handwritten manuscript of *The House at Pooh Corner.* Trinity alumni include Sir Isaac Newton, William Thackeray, Lord Byron, Lord Tennyson, and 31 Nobel Prize winners. ⊠ *St. John's St.* ☎ *01223/338400* ⊕ *www.trin.cam.ac.uk* ⊠ *£3* ⊙ *College and chapel closed exam period and event days; Wren library closed Sun.*

19

WHERE TO EAT

$$ | SEAFOOD | ✗ **Loch Fyne.** Part of a Scottish chain that harvests its own oysters, this airy, casual place across from the Fitzwilliam Museum is deservedly popular. The seafood is fresh and well prepared, served in a traditional setting with a modern ambience. **Known for:** Bradan Rost smoked salmon; Scottish oysters; great Scotch whisky menu. ⑤ *Average main: £17* ⊠ *37 Trumpington St.* ☎ *01223/362433* ⊕ *www.lochfyne-seafoodandgrill.co.uk.*

$$$$ | FRENCH | Fodor's Choice | ★ | ✗ **Midsummer House.** Beside the River Cam on the edge of Midsummer Common, this gray-brick 19th-century villa holds a two–Michelin star restaurant set in a comfortable conservatory. Fixed-price menus for lunch and dinner (with five to eight courses) present innovative French and Mediterranean-influenced dishes that often include apples from the trees in the garden. **Known for:** great river views; beautiful historic setting; special-occasion dining. ⑤ *Average main: £145* ⊠ *Midsummer Common* ☎ *01223/369299* ⊕ *www.midsummerhouse.co.uk* ⊙ *Closed Sun. and Mon. No lunch Tues.*

$$ ✕ **River Bar Steakhouse & Grill.** Across the river from Magdalene College,
MODERN BRITISH   this popular waterfront bar and grill serves delicious steak burgers and
pies, plus specialties such as lobster mac and cheese, and salmon steak
with molasses and spices. There's an extensive evening cocktail menu
as well. **Known for:** classic British mains; rooftop terrace dining; huge
cocktail menu. ⑤ *Average main: £20* ⊠ *Quayside, Thompsons La., off
Bridge St.* ☎ *01223/307030* ⊕ *www.riverbarsteakhouse.com.*

OXFORD

55 miles northwest of London.

With arguably the most famous university in the world, Oxford has
been a center of learning since 1167, with only the Sorbonne preced-
ing it. It doesn't take more than a day or two to explore its winding
medieval streets, photograph its ivy-covered stone buildings and ancient
churches and libraries, and even take a punt down one of its placid
waterways. The town center is compact and walkable, and at its heart
is Oxford University. Alumni of this prestigious institution include 48
Nobel Prize winners, 26 British prime ministers (including David Cam-
eron), and 28 foreign presidents (including Bill Clinton), along with
poets, authors, and artists such as Percy Bysshe Shelley, Oscar Wilde,
and W. H. Auden.

Oxford is northwest of London, at the junction of the rivers Thames
and Cherwell. The city is more interesting and more cosmopolitan than
Cambridge, and although it's also bigger, its suburbs aren't remotely
interesting to visitors. The interest is all at the center, where the old
town curls around the grand stone buildings, great restaurants, and
historic pubs. Victorian writer Matthew Arnold described Oxford's
"dreaming spires," a phrase that has become famous. Students rush
past on the way to exams, clad with antiquarian style in their requisite
mortar caps, flowing dark gowns, stiff collars, and crisp white bow ties.

■ **TIP →** Watch your back when crossing roads, as bikes are everywhere.

VISITING THE COLLEGES

You can explore the town's major sights in a day, but it takes more
than a day to spend an hour in each of the key museums and absorb
the college scene. Some colleges are open only in the afternoons dur-
ing university terms. When undergraduates are in residence, access is
often restricted to the chapels, dining rooms, and libraries, and you're
requested to refrain from picnicking in the quadrangles. All are closed
certain days during exams, usually mid-April–late June.

TOURS

City Sightseeing. This company runs hop-on, hop-off bus tours with
20 stops around Oxford. Your ticket, purchased from the driver, is
good for 24 hours. ☎ *01865/790522* ⊕ *www.citysightseeingoxford.
com* ⊠ *From £15.*

Oxford Visitor Information Centre. You can find information here on the
many guided walks of the city. The best way of gaining access to the
collegiate buildings is to take the two-hour university and city tour,
which leaves the Tourist Information Centre at 10:45 am and 1 and

Radcliffe Camera, an unmissable circular library at Oxford University

2 pm daily from March through October. You can book in advance online. ✉ *15–16 Broad St.* ☎ *01865/686430* ⊕ *www.experienceox-fordshire.org* 🎟 *From £14.*

EXPLORING

Fodor'sChoice
★

Ashmolean Museum. What might be Britain's greatest museum outside London is also the oldest museum in the United Kingdom that's always been open to the public. "The Ash," as locals call is, displays its rich and varied collections from the Neolithic to the present day over five stunning floors. Innovative and spacious galleries explore connections between priceless Greek, Roman, and Indian artifacts, as well as Egyptian and Chinese objects, all of which are among the best in the country. In the superb art collection, don't miss drawings by Raphael, the shell-encrusted mantle of Powhatan (father of Pocahontas), the lantern belonging to Guy Fawkes, and the Alfred Jewel, set in gold, which dates to the reign of King Alfred the Great (ruled 871–899). ✉ *Beaumont St.* ☎ *01865/278000* ⊕ *www.ashmolean.org* 🎟 *Free* ⊗ *Closed Mon. except bank holidays.*

The Bodleian Library and Radcliffe Camera. A vast library, the domed Radcliffe Camera is Oxford's most spectacular building, built in 1737–49 by James Gibbs in Italian baroque style. It's usually surrounded by tourists with cameras trained at its golden-stone walls. The Camera contains part of the Bodleian Library's enormous collection, begun in 1602 and one of six "copyright libraries" in the United Kingdom. Like the Library of Congress in the United States, this means it must by law contain a copy of every book printed in Great Britain. In addition, the Bodleian is a vast repository for priceless historical documents—including a Gutenberg Bible and a Shakespeare First Folio. The collection continues to grow by more than 5,000 items a week. Tours reveal the magnificent Duke Humfrey's Library, which was the original chained library, completed in 1488 (the ancient tomes are dusted once a decade) as well as the spots used to create Hogwarts in the Harry Potter films. Arrive early to secure tickets for the three to six daily tours. The standard tours can be prebooked, as can the extended tours on Wednesday and Saturday; otherwise, tours are first-come, first-served. Audio tours don't require reservations. ⊠ *Broad St.* ☎ *01865/287400* ⊕ *www.bodleian.ox.ac.uk* ⌑ *From £6* ⊘ *Sometimes closed for events; call to confirm.*

Christ Church. Built in 1546, the college of Christ Church is referred to by its members as "The House." This is the site of Oxford's largest quadrangle, Tom Quad, named after the huge bell (6¼ tons) that hangs in the Sir Christopher Wren–designed gate tower and rings 101 times at 9:05 every evening in honor of the original number of Christ Church scholars. The vaulted, 800-year-old chapel in one corner has been Oxford's cathedral since the time of Henry VIII. The college's medieval dining hall contains portraits of many famous alumni, including 13 of Britain's prime ministers, but you'll recognize it from its recurring role in the Harry Potter movies (although they didn't actually film here, the room was painstakingly re-created in a film studio). ∎ TIP→ **Plan carefully, as the dining hall is often closed between noon and 2 during term time.** Lewis Carroll, author of *Alice in Wonderland,* was a teacher of mathematics here for many years; a shop opposite the meadows on St. Aldate's sells Alice paraphernalia. ⊠ *St. Aldate's* ☎ *01865/276492* ⊕ *www.chch.ox.ac.uk* ⌑ *£8 (£10 in July and Aug.)* ⊘ *Sometimes closed for events; check website to confirm.*

Fodor'sChoice
★

Magdalen College. Founded in 1458, with a handsome main quadrangle and a supremely monastic air, Magdalen (pronounced *maud*-lin) is one of the most impressive of Oxford's colleges and attracts its most artistic students. Alumni include such diverse people as P. G. Wodehouse, Oscar Wilde, and John Betjeman. The school's large, square tower is a famous local landmark. ∎ TIP→ **To enhance your visit, take a stroll around the Deer Park and along Addison's Walk; then have tea in the Old Kitchen, which overlooks the river.** ⊠ *High St.* ☎ *01865/276000* ⊕ *www.magd.ox.ac.uk* ⌑ *£6* ⊘ *Closed mornings Oct.–June.*

FAMILY

Oxford University Museum of Natural History. This highly decorative Victorian Gothic creation of cast iron and glass, more a cathedral than a museum, is worth a visit for its architecture alone. Among the eclectic collections of entomology, geology, mineralogy, and zoology are the towering skeleton of a *Tyrannosaurus rex* and casts of a dodo's foot and head. There's plenty for children to explore and touch. ⊠ *Parks Rd.* ☎ *01865/272950* ⊕ *www.oum.ox.ac.uk* ⌑ *Free.*

FAMILY
Fodor'sChoice
★

Pitt Rivers Museum. More than half a million intriguing archaeological and anthropological items from around the globe, based on the collection bequeathed by Lieutenant-General Augustus Henry Lane Fox Pitt Rivers in 1884, are crammed into a multitude of glass cases and drawers. In an eccentric touch that's surprisingly thought-provoking, labels are handwritten, and items are organized thematically rather than geographically—a novel way to gain perspective. Give yourself plenty of time to wander through the displays of shrunken heads, Hawaiian feather cloaks, and fearsome masks. ⊠ *S. Parks Rd.* ☎ *01865/270927* ⊕ *www.prm.ox.ac.uk* 🖾 *Free (donations welcome).*

St. John's College. One of Oxford's most attractive campuses, St. John's has seven quiet quadrangles surrounded by elaborately carved buildings. You enter the first through a low wooden door. This college dates to 1555, when Sir Thomas White, a merchant, founded it. His heart is buried in the chapel (it's a tradition for students to curse as they walk over it). The Canterbury Quad represented the first example of Italian Renaissance architecture in Oxford, and the Front Quad includes the buildings of the old St. Bernard's Monastery. ⊠ *St. Giles* ☎ *01865/277300* ⊕ *www.sjc.ox.ac.uk* 🖾 *Free.*

University Church of St. Mary the Virgin. Seven hundred years' worth of funeral monuments crowd this galleried and spacious church, including the alter-step tombstone of Amy Robsart, the wife of Robert Dudley, who was Elizabeth I's favorite suitor. One pillar marks the site where Thomas Cranmer, author of the *Anglican Book of Common Prayer,* was brought to trial for heresy by Queen Mary I (Cranmer had been a key player in the Protestant reforms). He was later burned at the stake nearby on Broad Street. The top of the 14th-century tower has a panoramic view of the city's skyline—it's worth the 127 steps. The Vaults and Garden Café, part of the church accessible from Radcliffe Square, serves breakfasts and cream teas as well as good lunches. ⊠ *High St.* ☎ *01865/279111* ⊕ *www. university-church.ox.ac.uk* 🖾 *Church free, tower £4.*

University of Oxford Botanic Garden. Founded in 1621 as a healing garden, this is the oldest of its kind in the British Isles. Set on the river, the diverse garden displays 6,000 species ranging from lilies to citrus trees. There is a spacious walled garden, six luxuriant glass houses, including insectivorous and lily houses, and interesting medicinal, rock, and bog gardens to explore. Picnics are allowed, but you must bring your own food and drinks, as there's nowhere to buy them inside. ⊠ *Rose La.* ☎ *01865/286690* ⊕ *www.botanic-garden.ox.ac.uk* 🖾 *£5.*

WHERE TO EAT

$$
FRENCH
✕ **Brasserie Blanc.** Raymond Blanc's sophisticated brasserie in the Jericho neighborhood is the more affordable chain restaurant cousin of Le Manoir aux Quat'Saisons in Great Milton. The changing menu always lists a good selection of steaks and innovative adaptations of bourgeois French fare, sometimes with Mediterranean or Asian influences. **Known for:** French classics like bouillabaisse; affordable prix-fixe lunch menu; good wine selection. ⑤ *Average main: £17* ⊠ *71–72 Walton St.* ☎ *01865/510999* ⊕ *www.brasserieblanc.com.*

$$
MODERN BRITISH
✕ **Gee's.** With its glass-and-steel framework, this former florist's shop just north of the town center makes a charming conservatory dining room, full of plants and twinkling with lights in the evening. The menu concentrates on the best of Oxfordshire produce. **Known for:** sophisticated British dishes with local produce; prune-and-sherry ice cream

for dessert; affordable lunch and early dinner menus. $⑤ Average main: £16 ⊠ 61 Banbury Rd.* ☎ *01865/553540 ⊕ www.gees-restaurant.co.uk.*

$$ ✕ **Jamie's Italian.** One of chef Jamie Oliver's missions is to re-create the
ITALIAN   best rustic Italian fare all over the country, and it's no different at this
big and buzzing eatery. There's a diverse range of starters, pastas, and
mains like truffle tagliatelle with Parmesan and crab spaghetti with
fennel, capers, and garlic. **Known for:** star chef Jamie Oliver's Italian
hot spot; young and lively crowds; famed crab spaghetti. $⑤ *Average
main: £14 ⊠ 24–26 George St.* ☎ *01865/838383 ⊕ www.jamieoliver.
com/restaurants.*

STONEHENGE

85 miles southwest of London.

Almost five millennia after their construction, these stone circles on
the Salisbury Plain continue to pose fascinating questions. How were
the giant stones, some weighing as much as 45 tons, brought here,
possibly from as far away as Wales? What was the site used for?
Why were the stones aligned with the midsummer sunrise and the
midwinter sunset? But Stonehenge is more than just the megaliths; the
surrounding landscape is dotted with ancient earthworks, remains of
Neolithic settlements, and processional pathways, creating a complex
of ceremonial structures that testifies to the sophisticated belief system
of these early Britons.

GETTING HERE AND AROUND

From London, you need to first take a train to Salisbury. Stonehenge
Tour buses leave from Salisbury's train and bus stations every half hour
from 9:30 to 2:30, and then hourly from 3 to 5, from early June to
August; hourly from 10 to 4 from April to early June and September
through October; and 10 to 2 in November through March. Tickets
cost £15 or £29 (includes Stonehenge and a visit to Old Sarum). Other
options are a taxi or a custom tour. Drivers can find the monument near
the junction of A303 with A344.

EXPLORING

FAMILY   **Stonehenge.** Mysterious and ancient, Stonehenge has baffled archaeolo-
Fodor's Choice gists, not to mention the general public, for centuries. One of England's
★   most visited monuments (attracting over a million visitors a year) and
a UNESCO World Heritage Site, the circle of giant stones standing
starkly against the wide sweep of Salisbury Plain still has the capacity
to fascinate and move those who view it. Unattractive visitor facilities
have been removed to better establish the stones in their original con-
text of grass fields, other nearby monuments, and original processional
approach, the Avenue. Although general visitors can no longer enter
the stone circle itself (except by special arrangement; call for further
information), you can roam free over the surrounding landscape with
its Neolithic earthworks, some of which predate the stones. To best
experience the awe and mystery of Stonehenge, visit the circle in the
early morning or in the evening, when the crowds have dispersed.

Stonehenge was begun as early as 3000 BC with the construction of a circular earthwork enclosure. The nearby Cursus, long rectangular earthwork banks, were also created around this time. The stone circle itself was completed in stages, beginning around 2500 BC with the inner circle of bluestones, and continued to be changed and in use until around 1600 BC. The early inner circle was later surrounded by an outer circle of 30 sarsen stones, huge sandstone blocks weighing up to 25 tons, which are believed to have originated from the Marlborough Down. Within these two circles was a horseshoe-shape group of sarsen trilithons (two large vertical stones supporting a third stone laid horizontally across it) and within that another horseshoe-shape grouping of bluestones. The sarsens used in the trilithons averaged 45 tons. Many of the huge stones were brought here from great distances before the invention of the wheel, and it's not certain what ancient form of transportation was used to move them. Every time a reconstruction of the journey has been attempted, it has failed. The labor involved in quarrying, transporting, and carving these stones is astonishing, all the more so when you realize that it was accomplished about the same time as the construction of Egypt's major pyramids.

Stonehenge (the name derives from the Saxon term for "hanging stones") has been excavated several times over the centuries, but the primary reason for its erection remains unknown. It's fairly certain that it was a religious site, and that worship here involved the cycles of the sun; the alignment of the stones on the axis of the midsummer sunrise and midwinter sunset makes this clear. Viewed from the center of the stone circle, the sun rises adjacent to the Heel Stone at midsummer and sets between the stones of the tallest trilithon at midwinter. The Druids certainly had nothing to do with the construction: the monument had already been in existence for nearly 2,000 years by the time they appeared. Some historians have maintained that Stonehenge was a kind of Neolithic computer, with a sophisticated astronomical purpose—an observatory of sorts—though evidence from excavations in the early 20th century shows that it had once been used as a burial ground. Another possibility is that this Neolithic village was home to those who performed the religious rites at Stonehenge, where people gathered from far and wide to feast and worship.

19

Without direct access to the stones, it is not possible to closely examine their prehistoric carvings, some of which show axes and daggers, so bring a pair of binoculars to help make out the details on the monoliths. To fully engage your imagination, or to get that magical photo, it's worth exploring all aspects of the site, both near and far. An informative visitor center is located 1½ miles away (access to the stone circle is via a frequent shuttle), with parking, audio guide rental, a café, loads of branded merchandise, and an exhibition of prehistoric objects found at the site. There's also a dramatic display using time-lapse photography that puts you (virtually) in the center of the circle as the seasons change. Next to the visitor center are some re-created Neolithic huts that show how the people who built and used Stonehenge might have lived. Visits are by timed admission slots only. ✉ *Amesbury* ✛ *Junction of A360 and Airman's Corner* ☏ *0370/333–1181, 0370/333–0605 for stone circle access* ⊕ *www.english-heritage.org.uk* ✆ *£19.30 (walk-up); £16.50 (advance).*

WHERE TO EAT

$$ ✗ **Charter 1227.** Casual and friendly but still upscale, this second-floor
BRITISH restaurant overlooking Market Place offers seasonal menus blending
traditional British and European elements. Dishes prepared by the
owner-chef include roast duck breast with artichokes and a plum and
blackberry sauce, or panfried John Dory with a brioche-crumb coating
in a dill-and-lime sauce. **Known for:** prix-fixe lunches and early-bird
dinners; friendly service; no cocktail menu. Ⓢ *Average main: £19* ✉ *6/7
Ox Row, Market Pl., Salisbury* ☎ *01722/333118* ⊕ *www.charter1227.
co.uk* ☾ *Closed Sun. and Mon.*

STRATFORD-UPON-AVON

104 miles north of London.

Stratford-upon-Avon has become adept at accommodating the hordes
of people who stream in for a glimpse of William Shakespeare's world.
Filled with distinctive, Tudor half-timber buildings, this is certainly a
handsome town, and the Royal Shakespeare Theatre is a don't-miss
for those who want to see Shakespeare performed in England. But the
town can feel, at times, like a literary amusement park, so if you're not
a fan of the Bard, you may want to explore elsewhere.

TOURS AND TICKETS

Fodor'sChoice   **City Sightseeing.** These double-decker tour buses offer two options: a
★   hop-on, hop-off bus tour that allows you to create your own itinerary
around 11 landmarks in and around the town, and a six-hour marathon
that takes in all five of the Shakespeare family homes. ☎ *01789/299123*
⊕ *www.city-sightseeing.com/en/100/stratford-upon-avon* 🎫 *From £14.*

Fodor'sChoice   **Shakespeare Birthplace Trust.** The main places of Shakespearean inter-
★   est (Anne Hathaway's Cottage, Hall's Croft, Mary Arden's House,
Shakespeare's New Place, and Shakespeare's Birthplace) are run by
the Shakespeare Birthplace Trust, an independent charity that aims to
preserve and promote the properties. By far the most economical way
to visit the properties is to get a Full Story ticket (£20.25), which gives
unlimited access to all five houses for a year. ☎ *01789/204016* ⊕ *www.
shakespeare.org.uk.*

Stratford Town Walk. This walking tour runs every day of the year, even on
Christmas Day. There are also ghost-themed walks on Saturday nights
(booking in advance is essential). The meeting point is by the yellow
sign outside the Royal Shakespeare Company, opposite the junction
with Sheep Street. ☎ *01789/292478* ⊕ *www.stratfordtownwalk.co.uk*
🎫 *From £6.*

ESSENTIALS

Visitor Information Stratford-upon-Avon Tourist Information Centre.
✉ *Bridgefoot* ☎ *01789/264293* ⊕ *www.visitstratforduponavon.co.uk.*

EXPLORING

Hall's Croft. One of the finest surviving Jacobean (early-17th-century) town houses in England, this impressive residence (one of the best preserved of the Shakespeare family homes) has a delightful walled garden and was once the home of Shakespeare's eldest daughter, Susanna, and her husband, Dr. John Hall. John Hall was a wealthy physician who, by prescribing an herbal cure for scurvy, was well ahead of his time. One room is furnished as a medical dispensary of the period, and throughout the building are fine examples of heavy oak Jacobean furniture, including a child's high chair and some 17th-century portraits. The café serves light lunches and afternoon teas. ⊠ *Old Town* ☎ *01789/338533* ⊕ *www.shakespeare.org.uk* ◻ *£7.65; Full Story ticket £20.25 includes Anne Hathaway's Cottage and Gardens, Shakespeare's Birthplace, Shakespeare's New Place, and Mary Arden's Farm.*

Holy Trinity Church. This 13th-century church on the banks of the River Avon is the final resting place of William Shakespeare. He was buried here not because he was a famed poet but because he was a lay rector of Stratford, owning a portion of the township tithes. On the north wall of the sanctuary, over the altar steps, is the famous marble bust created by Gerard Jansen in 1623 and thought to be a true likeness of Shakespeare. The bust offers a more human, even humorous, perspective when viewed from the side. Also in the chancel are the graves of Shakespeare's wife, Anne; his daughter, Susanna; his son-in-law, John Hall; and his granddaughter's first husband, Thomas Nash. Also here is the christening font in which Shakespeare was baptized. ⊠ *Old Town* ☎ *01789/266316* ⊕ *www.stratford-upon-avon.org* ◻ *£3 donation requested.*

Fodor's Choice ★ **Royal Shakespeare Company.** One of the finest repertory troupes in the world and long the backbone of England's theatrical life, the Royal Shakespeare Company (RSC) performs plays year-round in Stratford and at venues across Britain. The stunning Royal Shakespeare Theatre, home of the RSC, has a thrust stage based on the original Globe Theater in London. The Swan Theatre, part of the theater complex and also built in the style of Shakespeare's Globe, stages plays by Shakespeare and his contemporaries such as Christopher Marlowe and Ben Jonson, and contemporary works are staged at The Other Place nearby. Prices start from £5 for rehearsals and previews. ■TIP➜ **Seats book up fast, but day-of-performance and returned tickets are sometimes available.** ⊠ *Waterside* ☎ *01789/403493* ⊕ *www.rsc.org.uk* ◻ *From £10.*

Fodor's Choice ★ **Shakespeare's Birthplace.** A half-timber house typical of its time, the playwright's birthplace is a much-visited shrine that has been altered and restored since Shakespeare lived here. Passing through the modern visitor center, you are immersed in the world of Shakespeare through a state-of-the-art exhibition that includes evocative audio and visuals from contemporary stagings of his plays. The house itself is across the garden from the visitor center. Colorful wall decorations and furnishings reflect comfortable, middle-class Elizabethan domestic life; you can view his father's workshop and you can see the very room where Shakespeare was born. Mark Twain and Charles Dickens were both pilgrims here, and

19

Stratford-upon-Avon honors Shakespeare's birthday with an annual procession.

you can see the signatures of Thomas Carlyle and Walter Scott scratched into the windowpanes. In the garden, actors present excerpts from his plays. There's also a café and bookshop on the grounds. ✉ *Henley St.* ☎ *01789/204016* ⊕ *www.shakespeare.org.uk* ✉ *£15.75; Full Story ticket £20.25, includes Anne Hathaway's Cottage and Gardens, Hall's Croft, Shakespeare's New Place, and Mary Arden's Farm.*

Fodor's Choice **Shakespeare's New Place.** This is the spot where Shakespeare lived for the
★ last 19 years of his life and where he wrote many of his plays, including *The Tempest*. Though the actual 15th-century building he inhabited was torn down in the 18th century, the site was imaginatively reinterpreted in 2016 as an outdoor space where the footprint of the original house can be traced. Each of his 38 plays is represented by a pennant in the Golden Garden, and his sonnets are engraved into the stone paving. Highlights include a mulberry tree that some believe was given to Shakespeare by King James I and a restored Elizabethan knot garden. A permanent exhibition inside the neighboring Nash's House tells the story of the New House and Shakespeare's family life within it; there's also a roof terrace, which provides views of the gardens. Nash's House was once home to Thomas Nash, the husband of Shakespeare's grand-daughter Elizabeth Hall. ✉ *22 Chapel St.* ☎ *01789/338536* ⊕ *www. shakespeare.org.uk* ✉ *£11.25; Full Story ticket £20.25, includes Anne Hathaway's Cottage and Gardens, Shakespeare's Birthplace, Hall's Croft, and Mary Arden's Farm.*

AROUND STRATFORD

Two additional stops on the Shakespeare trail are just outside Stratford; also nearby is spectacular Warwick Castle.

Fodor's Choice
★

Anne Hathaway's Cottage. The most picturesque of the Shakespeare Birthplace Trust properties, this thatched cottage on the western outskirts of Stratford is the family home of the woman Shakespeare married in 1582. The "cottage," actually a substantial Tudor farmhouse with latticed windows, is astonishingly beautiful. Inside it is surprisingly cozy with lots of period furniture, including the settle where Shakespeare reputedly conducted his courtship, and a rare carved Elizabethan bed. The cottage garden is planted in lush Edwardian style with herbs and flowers. Wildflowers are currently being grown in the adjacent orchard (a nod to what was grown in the garden in the Hathaways' time), and the neighboring arboretum has trees, shrubs, and roses mentioned in Shakespeare's works. ■TIP➔ **The best way to get here is on foot, especially in late spring when the apple trees are in blossom.** The signed path runs from Evesham Place (an extension of Grove Road) opposite Chestnut Walk. Pick up a leaflet with a map from the tourist office; the walk takes 25–30 minutes. ⊠ *Cottage La.* 🕾 *01789/338532* ⊕ *www. shakespeare.org.uk* 🖾 *£11.25; Full Story ticket £20.25, includes entry to Hall's Croft, Mary Arden's Farm, Shakespeare's New Place, and Shakespeare's Birthplace.*

FAMILY
Fodor's Choice
★

Mary Arden's Farm. This charming working farm was the childhood home of Shakespeare's mother, Mary Arden, and offers great insight into the farming methods employed in Tudor England. The rural heritage attraction, just 3 miles outside Stratford, is great for kids, who can try their hand at basket weaving and gardening, listen as the farmers explain their work in the fields, watch the cooks prepare food in the Tudor farmhouse kitchen, or play in the amazing timber-framed adventure playground. There are also daily falconry and archery displays and opportunities to meet the farm animals, as well as a good café. ⊠ *Station Rd., Wilmcote* 🕾 *01789/338535* ⊕ *www.shakespeare.org. uk* 🖾 *£14; Full Story ticket £20.25, includes Anne Hathaway's Cottage and Gardens, Hall's Croft, Shakespeare's New Place, and Shakespeare's Birthplace* ☉ *Closed Nov.–mid-Mar.*

19

FAMILY
Fodor's Choice
★

Warwick Castle. The vast bulk of this medieval castle rests on a cliff overlooking the Avon River and is considered "the fairest monument of ancient and chivalrous splendor which yet remains uninjured by time," to use the words of Sir Walter Scott. Today the company that runs the Madame Tussauds wax museums owns the castle, and it has become more theme park than authentic heritage site, but it is still a lot of fun. Warwick's two soaring towers, bristling with battlements, can be seen for miles: the 147-foot-high Caesar's Tower, built in 1356, and the 128-foot-high Guy's Tower, built in 1380. Warwick Castle's monumental walls enclose an impressive armory of medieval weapons, as well as state rooms with historic furnishings and paintings. Other exhibits explore the castle's history through the ages, display the sights and sounds of a great medieval household as it prepares for an important battle, and tell the story of a princess's fairy-tale wedding.

Be prepared both to play your part and be spooked in the gruesome dungeon experience (50 minutes and not recommended for under-10s) as you travel through scenes of torture, poisonings, and death sentences. Elsewhere, a working trebuchet (a kind of catapult), falconry displays, and rat-throwing (stuffed, not live) games add to the atmosphere. Below the castle, strutting peacocks patrol the 60 acres of grounds elegantly landscaped by Capability Brown in the 18th century. ■TIP→ Arrive early to beat the crowds. If you book online, you save 30% on ticket prices. Lavish medieval banquets take place throughout the year, and plenty of food stalls serve lunch. For the ultimate castle experience, you can "glamp" (glamorously camp) in a medieval tent, stay in a wooden lodge in the Knight's Village, or spend the night in your own luxury suite in the 14th-century Caesar's Tower. ⊠ *Castle La. off Mill St., Warwick* ☎ *01926/495421* ⊕ *www.warwick-castle.com* ⓈCastle £13, castle and dungeon £16.*

WHERE TO EAT

$
BRITISH
Fodor'sChoice
★

✕The Black Swan/The Dirty Duck. The only pub in Britain to be licensed under two names (the more informal one came courtesy of American GIs who were stationed here during World War II), this is one of Stratford's most celebrated and consistently rated pubs, attracting actors since the 18th-century days of thespian David Garrick. Along with your pint of bitter, you can choose from the extensive menu of baked potatoes, steaks, burgers, and grills; there are also good-value light bites. **Known for:** classic English pub atmosphere; reservations-only for dinner; veranda overlooking the river. Ⓢ *Average main: £12* ⊠ *Waterside* ☎ *01789/297312* ⊕ *www.oldenglishinns. co.uk/our-locations/the-dirty-duck-stratford-upon-avon.*

$$
MODERN BRITISH

✕Opposition. Hearty, warming meals are offered at this informal, family-style restaurant in a 16th-century building on the main dining street near the theaters. The English and international dishes—chicken roasted with banana in lime butter and served with curry sauce and basmati rice, for instance—win praise from the locals. **Known for:** historical ambience; plenty of vegetarian and healthy options; summertime crowds. Ⓢ *Average main: £16* ⊠ *13 Sheep St.* ☎ *01789/269980* ⊕ *www. theoppo.co.uk* ⊗ *Closed Sun.*

WARNER BROS. HARRY POTTER STUDIO TOUR

20 miles northwest of London.

Popular and family-friendly, the Warner Bros. Harry Potter Studio Tour has sets and props from the successful films, and plenty of engaging interactive diversions for all ages. The train and a special shuttle bus from Watford get you here.

EXPLORING

FAMILY
Fodor'sChoice
★

Warner Bros. Harry Potter Studio Tour. Attention all Muggles: this spectacular attraction just outside Watford immerses you in the magical world of Harry Potter for hours. From the Great Hall of Hogwarts—faithfully re-created, down to the finest detail—to magical props beautifully displayed in the vast studio space, each section of this attraction showcases the real sets, props, and special effects used in the eight movies. Visitors enter the Great Hall, a fitting stage for costumes from each Hogwarts house. You can admire the intricacies of the huge Hogwarts Castle model, ride a broomstick, try butterbeer, explore the Forbidden Forest, and gaze through the shop windows of Diagon Alley. The Hogwarts Express section—at a faithfully reproduced Platform 9¾—allows you to walk through a carriage of the actual steam train and see what it's like to ride with Harry and the gang. Tickets, pegged to a 30-minute arrival time slot, must be prebooked online. The studio tour is a 20-minute drive from St. Albans. You can also get here by taking a 20-minute train ride from London's Euston Station to Watford Junction (then a 15-minute shuttle-bus ride). Via car from London, use M1 and M25—parking is free. ⊠ *Studio Tour Dr., Leavesden Green* ☎ *0345/084–0900* ⊕ *www. wbstudiotour.co.uk* 🎟 *£41.*

> ### DID YOU KNOW?
>
> The Queen uses Windsor often—it's said she likes it much more than Buckingham Palace—spending most weekends here, often joined by family and friends. You know she's in when the Royal Standard is flown above the Round Tower but not in when you see the Union Jack.

WINDSOR CASTLE

19

21 miles west of London.

The tall turrets of Windsor Castle, one of the homes of the Royal Family, can be seen for miles around. The grand stone building is the star attraction in this quiet town with some remaining medieval elements—although Eton College, England's most famous public school, is also just a lovely walk away across the Thames.

ESSENTIALS

Visitor Information Royal Windsor Information Centre. ⊠ *Old Booking Hall, Windsor Royal Station, Thames St.* ☎ *01753/743900, 01753/743907 for accommodations* ⊕ *www.windsor.gov.uk.*

EXPLORING

Fodor'sChoice
★

Eton College. Signs warn drivers of "Boys Crossing" as you approach the splendid Tudor-style buildings of Eton College, the distinguished boarding school for boys ages 13–18 founded in 1440 by King Henry VI. It's all terrifically photogenic—during the college semester students still dress in pinstripe trousers, swallowtail coats, and stiff collars. Rivaling St. George's at Windsor in terms of size, the Gothic **Chapel** contains superb 15th-century grisaille wall paintings juxtaposed with modern stained glass by John Piper. Beyond the cloisters are the school's playing fields where, according to the Duke of Wellington, the Battle of Waterloo was really won, since so many of his officers had learned discipline and strategy during their school days. The most recent of the country's many prime ministers to have been educated here is David Cameron, who held the office from 2010 to 2016. The **Museum of Eton Life** has displays on the school's history and vignettes of school life. The school gives public tours on Friday afternoons from early May through early September, bookable online. ✉ *Brewhouse Yard, Eton* ☎ *01753/370100* ⊕ *www.etoncollege.com* 💷 *£10* ⊘ *Closed mid-Sept.–early May.*

Fodor's Choice
★

Windsor Castle. From William the Conqueror to Queen Victoria, the kings and queens of England added towers and wings to this brooding, imposing castle that is visible for miles, the largest inhabited castle in the world and the only royal residence in continuous use by the British Royal Family since the Middle Ages. Despite the multiplicity of hands involved in its design, the palace manages to have a unity of style and character. The most impressive view of Windsor Castle is from the A332 road, coming into town from the south. Admission includes an audio guide and, if you wish, a guided tour of the castle precincts. Entrance lines can be long in season, and you're likely to spend at least half a day here, so come early.

As you enter the castle, **Henry VIII's gateway** leads uphill into the wide castle precincts, where you're free to wander. Across from the entrance is the exquisite **St. George's Chapel** (closed Sunday). Here lie 10 of the kings of England, including Henry VI, Charles I, and Henry VIII (Jane Seymour is the only one of his six wives buried here). One of the noblest buildings in England, the chapel was built in the Perpendicular style popular in the 15th and 16th centuries, with elegant stained-glass windows; a high, vaulted ceiling; and intricately carved choir stalls. The colorful heraldic banners of the Knights of the Garter—the oldest British Order of Chivalry, founded by Edward III in 1348—hang in the choir. The ceremony in which the knights are installed as members of the order has been held here with much pageantry for more than five centuries. The elaborate **Albert Memorial Chapel** was created by Queen Victoria in memory of her husband.

The **North Terrace** provides especially good views across the Thames to Eton College, perhaps the most famous of Britain's exclusive public schools (confusingly, "public schools" in Britain are highly traditional, top-tier private schools). From the terrace, you enter the **State Apartments,** which are open to the public most days. On display to the left of the entrance to the State Apartments in Windsor Castle, **Queen Mary's Dolls' House** is a perfect miniature Georgian palace-within-a-palace, created in 1923. Electric lights glow, the doors all have tiny keys, and a miniature library holds Lilliputian-size books written especially for the young queen by famous authors of the 1920s. Five cars, including a Daimler and Rolls-Royce, stand at the ready. In the adjacent corridor are exquisite French couturier–designed costumes made for the two Jumeau dolls presented to the Princesses Elizabeth and Margaret by France in 1938.

Although a fire in 1992 gutted some of the State Apartments, hardly any works of art were lost. Phenomenal repair work brought to new life the **Grand Reception Room,** the **Green and Crimson Drawing Rooms,** and the **State and Octagonal Dining Rooms.** A green oak hammer-beam (a short horizontal beam that projects from the tops of walls for support) roof looms magnificently over the 600-year-old **St. George's Hall,** where the Queen gives state banquets. The State Apartments contain priceless furniture, including a magnificent Louis XVI bed and Gobelin tapestries; carvings by Grinling Gibbons; and paintings by Canaletto, Rubens, Van Dyck, Holbein, Dürer, and Bruegel. The tour's high points are the **Throne Room** and the **Waterloo Chamber,** where Sir Thomas Lawrence's portraits of Napoléon's victorious foes line the walls. You can also see arms and armor—look for Henry VIII's ample suit. A visit October to March also includes the Semi-State rooms, the private apartments of George IV, resplendent with gilded ceilings.

To see the castle come magnificently alive, check out the Changing the Guard, which takes place daily at 11 am April to July, and on alternate days at the same time August to March. Confirm the exact schedule before traveling to Windsor. Note that the State rooms (and sometimes the entire castle) are closed during official state occasions; dates of these closures are listed on the website or you can call ahead to check. ✉ *Castle Hill* ☎ *0303/123–7304 for tickets* ⊕ *www.royalcollection.org.uk* 🎫 *£22 for Precincts, State Apartments, Gallery, St. George's Chapel, and Queen Mary's Dolls' House; £12.10 when State Apartments are closed.*

Fodor'sChoice
★

Windsor Great Park. The remains of an ancient royal hunting forest, this park stretches for some 5,000 acres south of Windsor Castle. Much of it is open to the public and can be explored by car or on foot. Its chief attractions are clustered around the southeastern section, known (or at least marketed) as the **Royal Landscape.** These include **Virginia Water,** a 2-mile-long lake that forms the park's main geographical focal point. More than anything, however, the Royal Landscape is defined by its two beautiful gardens. **Valley Gardens,** located on the north shore of Virginia Water, is particularly vibrant in April and May, when the dazzling multicolored azaleas are in full bloom. If you're feeling fit, the romantic **Long Walk** is one of England's most photographed footpaths—the 3-mile-long route, designed by Charles II, starts in the Great Park and leads all the way to Windsor Castle.

Divided from the Great Park by the busy A308 highway, the smaller **Windsor Home Park,** on the eastern side of Windsor Castle, is the private property of the Royal Family. It contains **Frogmore House,** a lavish royal residence. Completed in 1684, Frogmore was bought by George III as a gift for his wife, Queen Charlotte. The sprawling white mansion later became a beloved retreat of Queen Victoria. Today it's mainly used for official functions, but you can visit by guided tour (£10) on a handful of days in June; see ⊕ *www.royalcollection.org.uk,* or call 0303/123–7321 for more information. ✉ *Entrances on A329, A332, B383, and Wick La.* ☎ *01753/860222* ⊕ *www.windsorgreatpark.co.uk* 🎫 *Free; Savill Garden £12 (free Jan. and Feb.).*

19

WHERE TO EAT

$$$$
MODERN BRITISH
Fodor's Choice
★

✕ **Fat Duck.** One of the top restaurants in the country, and ranked by many food writers among the best in the world, this extraordinary place packs in fans of hypercreative, hyperexpensive cuisine, who enjoy it for the theater as much as for the food. Culinary alchemist Heston Blumenthal is famed for the so-called molecular gastronomy he creates in his laboratory-like kitchen and his name has become synonymous with weird and funky taste combinations. **Known for:** creative and immersive dining experience; strict booking process and long waiting list for reservations; famed strange dishes like bacon-and-egg ice cream. ⑤ *Average main: £300* ✉ *High St., Bray* ☎ *01628/580333* ⊕ *www.thefatduck.co.uk* ⊘ *Closed Sun. and Mon.*

$$
BRITISH

✕ **Two Brewers.** Locals congregate in a pair of low-ceiling rooms at this tiny 17th-century establishment by the gates of Windsor Great Park. Those under 18 aren't allowed inside the pub (although they can be served at a few outdoor tables), but adults will find a suitable collection of wine, espresso, and local beer, plus an excellent menu with dishes like roasted cod with butter sauce and samphire, or steak frites with brandy and peppercorn. **Known for:** classic, adults-only British pub; traditional lunchtime roast on Sundays; historic setting. ⑤ *Average main: £16* ✉ *34 Park St.* ☎ *01753/855426* ⊕ *www.twobrewerswindsor.co.uk.*

UNDERSTANDING
LONDON

LONDON AT-A-GLANCE

ENGLISH VOCABULARY

LONDON AT-A-GLANCE

Fast Facts

Type of government: Representative democracy. In 1999 the Greater London Authority Act reestablished a single local governing body for the Greater London area, consisting of an elected mayor and the 25-member London Assembly. Elections, first held in 2000, take place every four years.

Population: Greater London 8.788 million

Population density: 3,900 people per square mile

Median age: 38.4

Language: English. More than 300 languages are spoken in London. All city government documents are translated into Arabic, Bengali, Chinese, Greek, Gujurati, Hindi, Punjabi, Turkish, Urdu, and Vietnamese.

Ethnic and racial groups: White British 70%, White Irish 3%, Other White 9%, Indian 6%, Bangladeshi 2%, Pakistani 2%, other Asian 2%, Black African 6%, Black Caribbean 5%, Chinese 1%, Other 3%.

Religion: Christian 58%, nonaffiliated 15%, Muslim 8%, Hindu 4%, Jewish 2%, Sikh 1%, other religion 1%, Buddhist 0.8%.

When a man is tired of London, he is tired of life; for there is in London all that life can afford.

—Samuel Johnson

Geography and Environment

Latitude: 51° N (same as Calgary, Canada; Kiev, Ukraine; Prague, Czech Republic)

Longitude: 0° (same as Accra, Ghana). A brass line in the ground in Greenwich marks the prime meridian (0° longitude).

Elevation: 49 feet

Land area: City, 67 square miles; metro area, 625 square miles

Terrain: River plain, rolling hills, and parkland

Natural hazards: Drought in warmer summers, minor localized flooding of the Thames caused by surge tides from the North Atlantic

Environmental issues: The city has been improving its air quality, but up to 1,600 people die each year from health problems related to London's polluted air. Only half of London's rivers and canals received passing grades for water quality from 1999 through 2001. More than £12 million ($22 million) is spent annually to ensure the city's food safety.

I'm leaving because the weather is too good. I hate London when it's not raining.

—Groucho Marx

ENGLISH VOCABULARY

You and a Londoner may speak the same language, but some phrases definitely get lost in translation once they cross the Atlantic.

BRITISH ENGLISH	ENGLISH

BASIC TERMS AND EVERYDAY ITEMS

bill	check
flat	apartment
holiday	vacation
lift	elevator
nappy	diaper
note	bill (currency)
plaster	Band-Aid
queue	line
row	argument
rubbish	trash
tin	can
toilet/loo/WC	bathroom

CLOTHING

braces	suspenders
bum bag	fanny pack
dressing gown	robe
jumper	sweater
pants/knickers	underpants/briefs
rucksack	backpack
suspender	garter
tights	pantyhose
trainers	sneakers
trousers	pants
vest	undershirt
waistcoat	vest

TRANSPORTATION

bonnet	hood
boot	trunk
coach	bus (long-distance)
pavement	sidewalk

BRITISH ENGLISH	ENGLISH
petrol	gas
pram	baby carriage
puncture	flat
windscreen	windshield

FOOD

aubergine	eggplant
banger	sausage
biscuit	cookie
chips	fries
courgette	zucchini
crisps	potato chips
jam	jelly
main course (or main)	entrée
pudding	dessert
rocket	arugula
starter	appetizer
sweet	candy
tea	early dinner

SLANG

all right	hi there
cheers	thank you
chuffed	pleased
fit	attractive
geezer	dude
guv'nor, gaffer	boss
hard	tough
mate	buddy
sound	good
Ta	thank you

TRAVEL SMART
LONDON

GETTING HERE AND AROUND

Central London and its surrounding districts are divided into 32 boroughs (33, counting the City of London). More useful for finding your way around, however, are the subdivisions of London into postal districts. The first one or two letters give the location: N means north, NW means northwest, and so on. Don't expect the numbering to be logical, however. You won't, for example, find W2 next to W3. The general rule is that the lower numbers, such as W1 or SW1, are closest to Buckingham Palace, but it is not consistent—SE17 is closer to the city center than E4, for example.

▌AIR TRAVEL

Flying time to London is about 6½ hours from New York, 7½ hours from Chicago, 11 hours from San Francisco, and 21½ hours from Sydney.

For flights out of London, the general rule is that you should be at the airport at least one hour before your scheduled departure time for domestic flights and two hours before international flights for off-peak travel.

Airline Security Issues Transportation Security Administration. ☎ 866/289-9673 ⊕ www.tsa.gov.

AIRPORTS

Most international flights to London arrive at either Heathrow Airport (LHR), 15 miles west of London, or at Gatwick Airport (LGW), 27 miles south of the capital. Most flights from the United States go to Heathrow, which is divided into five terminals, with Terminals 3–5 handling transatlantic flights. Gatwick is London's second gateway. It has grown from a European airport into an airport that also serves dozens of U.S. destinations. A third airport, Stansted (STN), is 35 miles northeast of the city; it handles European and domestic traffic. Three smaller airports, Luton (LTN), 30 miles

north of town, Southend (SEN), 40 miles to the east, and business-oriented London City (in east London E16) mainly handle flights to Europe.

Airport Information Gatwick Airport. ☎ 0344/892-0322 ⊕ www.gatwickairport. com. **Heathrow Airport.** ☎ 0844/335-1801 ⊕ www.heathrow.com. **London City Airport.** ☎ 020/7646-0088 ⊕ www.londoncityairport. com. **Luton Airport.** ☎ 01582/405100 ⊕ www. london-luton.co.uk. **Southend Airport.** ☎ 01702/538500 ⊕ www.southendairport.com. **Stansted Airport.** ☎ 0808/169-7031 ⊕ www. stanstedairport.com.

GROUND TRANSPORTATION

London has excellent if pricey bus and train connections between its airports and central London. If you're arriving at Heathrow, you can pick up a map and fare schedule at the Transport for London (TfL) Information Centre, in the Underground station serving Terminals 2–3. Train service can be quick, but the downside (for trains from all airports) is that you must get yourself and your luggage to the train via a series of escalators and connecting trams. Airport link buses (generally National Express airport buses) may ease the luggage factor and drop you off closer to central hotels, but they're subject to London traffic, which can be horrendous and make the trip drag on for hours. Taxis can be more convenient than buses, but beware that prices can go through the roof. Airport Travel Line has additional transfer information and takes advance booking for transfers between airports and into London.

Heathrow by Bus: National Express buses take one hour to reach the city center (Victoria) and cost from £5 one-way and £10 round-trip (book online for best prices). The National Express Hotel Hoppa service runs from all airports to 25 hotels near the airport (from £4.50). SkyShuttle offers a shared minibus service between Heathrow and any London hotel. The

FROM HEATHROW TO CENTRAL LONDON		
TRAVEL MODE	TIME	COST
Taxi	1 hour-plus	£48–90 (depending on traffic)
Heathrow Express Train	15 minutes	From £22 (£37 round-trip), £32 for first class
Underground	50 minutes	£6 one-way (less with Oyster card)
National Express Bus	1 hour	From £5 one-way

N9 night bus runs to Aldwych every 20 minutes midnight–5 am; it takes just over an hour and costs £2 (you need to pay with an Oyster card or a contactless debit/credit card). Please note: the N9 doesn't stop at Terminal 4; take Bus Nos. 490 or 482 to Terminal 5 and catch it there.

Heathrow by Tube and Train: The cheap, direct route into London is via the Piccadilly Line of the Underground (London's extensive subway system, or "Tube"). Trains normally run every four to eight minutes from all terminals from early morning until just before midnight. The 50-minute trip into central London costs £6 one-way and connects with other central Tube lines. The Heathrow Express train is comfortable and convenient, if costly, speeding into London's Paddington Station in 15 minutes. Standard one-way tickets cost £22 (£37 round-trip) and £32 for first class. Tickets are more expensive to buy on board, so book ahead (online is the cheapest option; at a counter/kiosk, less so). There's daily service 5:10 am (6:10 am on Sunday)–11:25 pm, with departures usually every 15 minutes. The Heathrow Connect service leaves from Paddington Station and makes five local stops before arriving at Terminals 2-3, 4, and 5. It takes 25 minutes, only a little more time than the Express, although trains are less frequent (two an hour in peak times). One-way tickets are £11.

Heathrow by Taxi: Taking a taxi from the airport into the city is an expensive and time-consuming option. The city's congestion charge (£11.50) may be added to the bill if your hotel is in the charging zone; you run the risk of getting stuck in traffic; and if you take a taxi from the stand, the price will be even more expensive (whereas a minicab booked ahead is a set price). The trip can take more than an hour and can cost in the region of £70, depending on time of day.

Gatwick by Bus: An hourly bus service runs from Gatwick's north and south terminals to London's Victoria Station, with stops at Hooley, Coulsdon, Mitcham, Streatham, Stockwell, and Pimlico. The journey takes upward of 90 minutes (depending on time of day) and costs from £5 one-way. The easyBus service runs to west London (Earl's Court) or Waterloo from as little as £2 if booked in advance; the later the ticket is booked online, the higher the price (up to £11 on board).

Gatwick by Train: The fast, nonstop Gatwick Express leaves for Victoria Station every 15 minutes 5:50 am–11:20 pm. The 30-minute trip costs from £18 one-way, and £32 round-trip (cheapest tickets are available online). The Thameslink Great Northern rail company runs nonexpress services that are cheaper; Thameslink trains run regularly throughout the day to St. Pancras International, London Bridge, and Blackfriars stations; departures are every 15 minutes (hourly during the night), and the journey takes 45–55 minutes. Tickets are from £11 one-way to St. Pancras International.

Stansted by Bus: Hourly service on National Express Airport bus A6 (24 hours a day) to Victoria Coach Station costs from £5 one-way, £10 round-trip, and takes about 1 hour 45 minutes (again, the cheapest tickets are only available online and in advance). Stops include Golders Green, Finchley Road, St. John's Wood, Baker Street, Marble Arch, and Hyde Park Corner. The easyBus service to Victoria via Baker Street costs from £2 one-way, but book early and online for best prices.

Stansted by Train: The Stansted Express to Liverpool Street Station (with a stop at Tottenham Hale) runs daily every 15 minutes, 5:30 am–12:30 am. If booked online, the 50-minute trip costs from £7 one-way and £14 round-trip; tickets cost more when purchased on board or nearer travel time.

Luton by Bus and Train: An airport shuttle runs from Luton Airport to the nearby Luton Airport Parkway Station, from which you can take a train or bus into London (this shuttle is free if you have bought a rail ticket in advance; otherwise it's £2 one-way). From there, the Thameslink Great Northern train service runs to St. Pancras, Farringdon, Blackfriars, and London Bridge. The journey takes about 30 minutes. Trains leave every 10 minutes or so during the day, and hourly during the night. Single tickets cost from £11 one-way, if booked in advance. The Green Line 757 bus service from Luton to Victoria Station runs three times an hour, takes about 90 minutes, and costs from £11 one-way, if booked in advance.

TRANSFERS BETWEEN AIRPORTS
Allow at least two to three hours for an interairport transfer. The cheapest option—but most complicated—is public transportation: from Gatwick to Stansted, for instance, you can catch the nonexpress commuter train from Gatwick to Victoria Station, take the Tube to Liverpool Street Station, then catch the train to Stansted from there. To get from Heathrow to Gatwick by public transportation, take the Tube to King's Cross, then change to the Victoria Line, get to Victoria Station, and then take the commuter train to Gatwick.

The National Express airport bus is the most direct option. Between Gatwick and

Heathrow, buses pick up passengers every 15–20 minutes 5:35 am–midnight from both airports. The trip takes around 75 minutes, and the fare is from £12 one-way, but it's advisable to book tickets in advance. National Express buses between Stansted and Gatwick depart every 30–45 minutes and can take 3–4½ hours, depending on traffic. The adult one-way fare is from £15. Some airlines may offer shuttle services as well—check with your travel agent in advance of your journey.

Contacts easyBus. ⊕ www.easybus.co.uk. **Gatwick Express.** ☎ 0345/850–1530 ⊕ www.gatwickexpress.com. **Heathrow Express.** ☎ 0345/600–1515 ⊕ www.heathrowexpress.com. **National Express.** ☎ 0871/781–8181 ⊕ www.nationalexpress.com. **SkyShuttle.** ☎ 0845/481–0960 ⊕ www.skyshuttle.co.uk. **Stansted Express.** ☎ 0345/600–7245 ⊕ www.stanstedexpress.com. **Thameslink.** ☎ 0345/026–4700 ⊕ www.thameslinkrailway.com.

Transfer Information Airport Travel Line. ☎ 0871/200–2233 ⊕ www.travelline.co.uk.

FLIGHTS
British Airways is the national flagship carrier and offers mostly nonstop flights from more than 20 U.S. cities to Heathrow and Gatwick airports, along with flights to Manchester, Birmingham, and Glasgow. It also offers flights to New York from London City Airport near Docklands.

Airline Contacts American Airlines. ☎ 800/433–7300 in U.S., 0844/369–9899 in U.K., 020/7660–2300 in U.K. ⊕ www.aa.com. **British Airways.** ☎ 800/247–9297 in U.S., 0844/493–0787 in U.K. ⊕ www.britishairways.com. **Delta Airlines.** ☎ 800/241–4141 for international reservations, 020/7660–0767 in U.K. ⊕ www.delta.com. **United Airlines.** ☎ 800/864–8331 for international reservations, 0845/607–6760 in U.K., 020/7136–0582 in U.K. ⊕ www.united.com. **Virgin Atlantic.** ☎ 800/862–8621 in U.S., 0344/874–7747 in U.K. ⊕ www.virgin-atlantic.com.

▮ BIKE TRAVEL

Nicknamed "Boris bikes" after the former mayor and dedicated cyclist Boris Johnson, a 24-hour bike-rental program called Santander Cycles enables Londoners to pick up a bicycle at one of more than 750 docking stations and return it at another. The first 30 minutes are free, then it's £2 for every 30-minute period thereafter. There is also a £2-per-day access charge. You pay at the docking station, using credit or debit cards only (cash is not accepted)—simply follow the instructions on the touch screen and away you go.

▮ BUS TRAVEL

ARRIVING AND DEPARTING

National Express is the biggest British long-distance bus operator and the nearest equivalent to Greyhound. It's not as fast as traveling by train, but it's comfortable (with bathrooms on board). Services depart mainly from Victoria Coach Station, a well-signposted short walk behind the Victoria mainline train station. The departures point is on the corner of Buckingham Palace Road; this is also the main information point. The arrivals point is opposite, at Elizabeth Bridge. National Express buses travel to all large and mid-size cities in southern England and the midlands. Scotland and the north are not as well served. The station is extremely busy around holidays and weekends. Arrive at least 30 minutes before departure so you can find the correct exit gate. Smoking is not permitted on board.

Another bus company, Megabus, offers cross-country fares for as little as £1 per person. The company's single- and double-decker buses serve an extensive array of cities across Great Britain with a cheerful budget attitude. In London, buses for all destinations depart from the Green Line bus stand at Victoria Station. Megabus does not accommodate wheelchairs, and the company strictly limits luggage

to one piece per person checked, and one piece of hand luggage.

Green Line serves the counties surrounding London, as well as airports. Bus stops (there's no central bus station) are on Buckingham Palace Road, between the Victoria train station and Victoria Coach Station.

Tickets on many long-distance routes are cheaper if purchased in advance, and traveling midweek costs less than over weekends and at holiday periods.

GETTING AROUND LONDON

Private, as opposed to municipal, buses are known as coaches. Although London is famous for its double-decker buses, the old beloved rattletrap Routemasters, with the jump-on, jump-off back platforms, now only serve a single "heritage" route (No. 15)—from Trafalgar Square down Fleet Street and on to St. Paul's Cathedral and the Tower of London. That said, modernized Routemaster buses have taken to the streets on other routes.

Bus stops are clearly indicated; signs at bus stops feature a red TfL symbol on a plain white background. You must flag the bus down at some stops. Each numbered route is listed on the main stop, and buses have a large number on the front with their end destination. Not all buses run the full route at all times; check with the driver to be sure. You can pick up a free bus guide at a TfL Travel Information Centre (at Euston, Liverpool Street, Piccadilly Circus, King's Cross, and Victoria Tube stations; and at Heathrow Airport).

Buses are a good way of seeing the town, particularly if you plan to hop on and off to cover many sights, but don't take a bus if you're in a hurry, as traffic can really slow them down. To get off, press the red "Stop" buttons mounted on poles near the doors. You will usually see a "Bus Stopping" sign light up. Expect to get sardined during rush hour, 8–9:30 am and 4:30–6:30 pm.

Night buses, denoted by an "N" before their route numbers, run midnight–5 am on a more restricted route than day buses. However, some night-bus routes should be approached with caution, and the top deck avoided (the danger is that muggings are most likely to occur there, since it's farthest from both the exit doors and the driver). All night buses run by request stop, so flag them down if you're waiting, or push the button if you want to alight.

All London buses are now cash-free, which means you must buy your ticket *before* you board the bus. There are a number of ways to do this. One-day paper bus passes are available at underground and rail stations as well as London Transport Visitor Centres and cost £5. An easier, and cheaper, option is to pay by prepaid Oyster card or "contactless" bank card. Visitor Oyster cards must be purchased before you arrive; they cost £5 (plus postage), but a day's bus travel is capped at £4.50. Normal Oyster cards (also £5) are available from ticket desks at all major airports or at any Tube station and are transferable if you have money left over. Contactless cards are the future of London travel: you touch a compatible debit or credit card on a bus or Tube-station's reader, and the fare is automatically debited from your bank account.

One alternative is to buy a one- or seven-day Travelcard, which is good for both Tube and bus travel. Travelcards can be bought at Tube stations, rail stations, and travel information centers. However, note that seven-day Travelcards bought in London *must be loaded onto an Oyster card.* Although using a Travelcard may save you some money, it might be easier to just add additional money to your Oyster card as needed, since there are machines at all Tube stations and at lots of London newsagents. A seven-day paper Travelcard can only be purchased in advance, online. However you buy your ticket, just make sure you have one: traveling without a valid ticket makes you liable for a significant fine (£80). Buses are supposed to swing by most stops every five or six minutes, but in reality you often end up waiting a bit longer, although those in the city center are quite reliable.

Long-Distance Bus Contacts easyBus. ⊕ *www.easybus.co.uk.* **Green Line.** ☎ *0344/801–7261* ⊕ *www.greenline. co.uk.* **Megabus.** ☎ *0900/160–0900* ⊕ *www.megabus.com.* **National Express.** ☎ *0871/781–8181* ⊕ *www.nationalexpress. com.*

Bus Information Transport for London. ☎ *0343/222–1234* ⊕ *www.tfl.gov.uk.* **Victoria Coach Station.** ⊠ *164 Buckingham Palace Rd., Victoria* ☎ *0343/222–1234* Ⓜ *Victoria.*

▌CAR TRAVEL

The best advice on driving in London is this: don't. London's streets are a winding mass of chaos, made worse by one-way roads. Parking is also restrictive and expensive, and traffic is tediously slow at most times of the day; during rush hours (8–9:30 am and 4:30–6:30 pm) it often grinds to a standstill, particularly on Friday, when everyone wants to leave town. Avoid city-center shopping areas, including the roads feeding Oxford Street, Kensington, and Knightsbridge. Other main roads into the city center are also busy, such as King's Cross and Euston in the north. Watch out also for cyclists and motorcycle couriers, who weave between cars and pedestrians that seem to come out of nowhere, and you may get a heavy fine for straying into a bus lane during its operating hours—check the signs.

If you are staying in London for the duration of your trip, there's virtually no reason to rent a car, because the city and its suburbs are widely covered by public transportation. However, you may want a car for day trips to castles or stately homes out in the countryside. Consider renting your car in a medium-size town in the area where you'll be traveling, and then journeying there by train and picking up the car once you arrive. Rental rates are generally reasonable, and insurance costs are lower than in comparable U.S.

cities. Rates generally begin at £20 per day for a small economy car (such as a subcompact General Motors Vauxhall Corsa, or Renault Clio), usually with manual transmission. Air-conditioning and unlimited mileage generally come with the larger-size automatic cars.

In London your U.S. driver's license is acceptable (as long as you are over 23 years old, with no driving convictions). If you have a driver's license from a country other than the United States, it may not be recognized in the United Kingdom. An International Driver's Permit is a good idea no matter what; it's available from the American or Canadian Automobile Association (AAA and CAA, respectively) and, in the United Kingdom, from the Automobile Association (AA) or Royal Automobile Club (RAC). International permits are universally recognized, and having one may save you a problem with the local authorities.

Remember that Britain drives on the left, and the rest of Europe on the right. Therefore, if you cross the Channel into Britain in a right-side rental, you may want to leave it there and pick up a left-side rental.

CONGESTION CHARGE

Designed to reduce traffic through central London, a congestion charge has been instituted. Vehicles (with some exemptions) entering central London on weekdays 7 am–6 pm (excluding public holidays) have to pay £11.50 per day; it can be paid up to 90 days in advance, or on the day of travel, or on the following "charging day," when the fee goes up to £14. Day-, month-, and yearlong passes are available on the Congestion Charging page of the Transport for London website, at gas stations, parking lots (car parks), by mail, by phone, and by SMS text message. One day's payment is good for all access into the charging zone on that day. Traffic signs designate the entrance to congestion areas, and cameras read car license plates and send the information to a database. Drivers who don't pay the congestion charge by midnight of the next

charging day following the day of driving are penalized £160, which is reduced to £80 if paid within 14 days.

Information Congestion Charge Customer Service. ☎ 0343/222–2222 in U.K. only, ⊕ www.tfl.gov.uk/modes/driving/congestion-charge. **Transport for London.** ☎ 0343/222–1234 ⊕ www.tfl.gov.uk.

GASOLINE

Gasoline (petrol) is sold in liters and is expensive (at this writing about £1.20 per liter—around $5.40 per gallon). Unleaded petrol, denoted by green pump lines, is predominant. Premium and Super Premium are the two varieties, and most cars run on regular Premium. Supermarket pumps usually offer the best value. You won't find many service stations in the center of town; these are generally on main, multilane trunk roads away from the city center. Service is self-serve, except in small villages, where gas stations are likely to be closed on Sunday and late evening. Most stations accept major credit cards.

PARKING

During the day—and probably at all times—it's safest to believe that you can park nowhere except at a meter, in a pay-and-display bay, or in a garage; otherwise, you run the risk of an expensive ticket, plus possibly even more expensive clamping and towing fees (some boroughs are clamp-free). Restrictions are indicated by the "No Waiting" parking signpost on the sidewalk (these restrictions vary from street to street), and restricted areas include single yellow lines or double yellow lines, and Residents' Parking bays. Parking at a bus stop is prohibited, and parking in bus lanes is restricted. On Red Routes, indicated by red lines, you are not allowed to park or even stop. It's illegal to park on the sidewalk, across entrances, or on white zigzag lines approaching a pedestrian crossing.

Meters have an insatiable hunger in the inner city—20p may buy you just three minutes—and many will permit only a maximum two-hour stay. Coin meters (which take 10p, 20p, 50p, £1, and £2 coins) are being phased out. Some meters take payment by credit card, but increasingly meters in central London are pay-and-display machines that require payment by cell phone. You will need to set up an account to do this (⊕ *www. westminster.gov.uk*). Meter parking is free after 6:30 or 8:30 in the evening, on Sunday, and on holidays; always check the sign. In the evening, after restrictions end, meter bays are free. After meters are free, you also can park on single yellow lines—but not double yellow lines. In the daytime, take advantage of the many NCP parking lots in the center of town (from about £9 per hour, up to six hours).

Information NCP. ☎ *0345/050–7080* ⊕ *www. ncp.co.uk.*

ROADSIDE EMERGENCIES

If your car is stolen, you're in a car accident, or your car breaks down and there's nobody around to help you, contact the police by dialing 999 (or 911 from a cell phone with a U.S. SIM card).

The general procedure for a breakdown is the following: position the red hazard triangle (which should be in the trunk of the car) a few paces away from the rear of the car. Leave the hazard warning lights on. Along highways (motorways), emergency roadside telephone booths are positioned at intervals within walking distance. Contact the car-rental company or an auto club. The main auto clubs in the United Kingdom are the Automobile Association (AA) and the Royal Automobile Club (RAC). If you're a member of the American Automobile Association (AAA), check your membership details before you depart for Britain; under a reciprocal agreement, roadside assistance in the United Kingdom should cost you nothing. You can join and receive roadside assistance from the AA on the spot, but the charge is higher (around £95) than a simple membership fee.

Emergency Services American Automobile Association. ☎ *800/564–6222* ⊕ *www.aaa. com.* **Automobile Association.** ☎ *0800/085– 2721, 161/333–0004 from outside U.K., 0800/887766 for emergency roadside assistance from mobile phones* ⊕ *www.theaa.com.* **Royal Automobile Club.** ☎ *0333/200–0999 for emergency roadside assistance, 0330/159– 1111 for membership inquiries* ⊕ *www.rac. co.uk.*

RULES OF THE ROAD

London is a mass of narrow, one-way roads and narrow, two-way streets no bigger than the one-way roads. The speed limit is either 20 or 30 mph—unless you see the large 40 mph signs found only in the suburbs. Speed bumps are sprinkled about with abandon in case you forget. Speed is strictly controlled and cameras, mounted on occasional lampposts, photograph speeders for ticketing.

Medium-size circular intersections are often designed as "roundabouts" (marked by signs in which three curved arrows form a circle). On these, cars travel left in a circle and incoming cars must yield to those already on their way around from the right. Make sure you're in the correct lane when approaching a roundabout—this will make leaving the roundabout at your desired exit easier. Stay in the left lane if you wish to go left, the middle lane for going straight ahead, and the right-hand lane for turning right. Signal when about to leave the roundabout.

Jaywalking is not illegal in London and everybody does it, despite the fact that striped crossings with blinking yellow lights mounted on poles at either end—called "zebra crossings"—give pedestrians the right-of-way to cross. Cars should treat zebra crossings like stop signs if a pedestrian is waiting to cross or already starting to cross. It's illegal to pass another vehicle at a zebra crossing. At other crossings (including intersections) pedestrians must yield to traffic, but they do have the right-of-way over traffic turning left at controlled crossings.

Traffic lights sometimes have arrows directing left or right turns; try to catch a glimpse of the road markings in time, and don't get into the turn lane if you mean to go straight ahead. Turning on a red light is not permitted. Signs at the beginning and end of designated bus lanes give the time restrictions for use (usually during peak hours); if you're caught driving on bus lanes during restricted hours, you will be fined. By law, seat belts must be worn in the front and back seats. Drunk-driving laws are strictly enforced, and it's safest to avoid alcohol altogether if you'll be driving. The legal limit is 80 milligrams of alcohol per 100 milliliters of blood, which roughly translated means two units of alcohol—two small glasses of wine, one pint of beer, or one glass of whiskey.

■ DLR: DOCKLANDS LIGHT RAILWAY

For reaching destinations in east London, the quiet, driverless Docklands Light Railway (DLR) is a good alternative, with interesting views of the area.

The DLR connects with the Tube network at Bank and Tower Hill stations as well as at Canary Wharf. It goes to London City Airport, the Docklands financial district, and Greenwich, running 5:30 am–12:30 am Monday–Saturday, 7 am–11:30 pm Sunday. The DLR takes Oyster cards, contactless bank cards, and Travelcards, and fares are the same as those on the Tube.

Information Transport for London. ☎ *0343/222-1234* ⊕ *www.tfl.gov.uk.*

■ RIVER BUS

One legacy of the 2012 Olympics was a new push to develop river travel as part of London's overall public transportation system. The service, operated by Thames Clippers, stops at eight piers between London Eye/Waterloo and Greenwich, with peak-time extensions to Putney in the west and Woolwich Arsenal in the east. The Waterloo–Woolwich

commuter service runs 7:20 am–10:40 pm on weekdays, 9:30 am–11:45pm on weekends (peak-time frequency: every 20 minutes). Tickets are £9.60, with a one-third discount for Travelcard holders and a 20% discount for Oyster card holders. When there are events at the O2 (North Greenwich Arena), a half-hourly express service runs to and from Waterloo starting three hours before the event. Thames Clippers also operate the special Tate to Tate Boat, a 15-minute trip between Tate Modern and Tate Britain that costs £9.60. Boats run every 30 minutes, from 10 to 4 on weekdays and 9 to 7 on weekends. A River Roamer ticket (£19.50 per day) offers unlimited river travel after 9 am.

Contacts Thames Clippers. ⊕ *www.thames-clippers.com.*

■ TAXI

Universally known as "black cabs" (even though many of them now come in other colors), the traditional big black London taxicabs are as much a part of the city's streetscape as red double-decker buses, and for good reason: the unique, spacious taxis easily hold five people, plus luggage. To earn a taxi license, drivers must undergo intensive training on the history and geography of London. The course, and all that the drivers have learned in it, is known simply as "the Knowledge." There's almost nothing your taxi driver won't know about the city. Partly because of lobbying efforts by the black cab industry, companies such as Uber have yet to make significant inroads into the London market, although the battle is ongoing.

Hotels and main tourist areas have cabstands (just take the first in line), but you can also flag one down from the roadside. If the orange "For Hire" sign on the top is lighted, the taxi is available. Cab drivers sometimes cruise at night with their signs unlighted so that they can choose their passengers and avoid those they think might cause trouble. If you see an unlighted, passengerless cab, hail it: you might be lucky.

Fares start at £2.60 and charge by the minute—a journey of a mile (which might take 6–13 minutes) will cost £6–£9.40 (the fare goes up 10 pm–5 am—a system designed to persuade more taxi drivers to work at night). A surcharge of £2 is applied to a telephone booking. At Christmas and New Year, there is an additional surcharge of £4. You may, but do not have to, tip taxi drivers 10% of the tab. Usually passengers round up to the nearest pound.

Minicabs, which operate out of small, curbside offices throughout the city, are generally cheaper than black cabs, but they are less reliable and less trustworthy. These are usually unmarked passenger cars, and their drivers are often not native Londoners, and do not have to take or pass "the Knowledge" test. Still, Londoners use them in droves because they are plentiful and cheap. If you choose to use them, do not ever take an unlicensed cab: anyone who curb-crawls looking for customers is likely to be unlicensed. Unlicensed cabs have been associated with many crimes and can be dangerous. All cab companies with proper dispatch offices are likely to be licensed. Look for a small purple version of the Underground logo on the front or rear window with "private hire" written across it.

There are plenty of trustworthy and licensed minicab firms. For London-wide service try Lady's and Gent's MiniCabs, or Addison Lee, which uses comfortable minivans but requires that you know the full postal code for both your pickup location and your destination. When using a minicab, always ask the price in advance when you phone for the car, then verify with the driver before the journey begins.

Black Cabs Dial-a-Cab. ☎ *020/7253–5000 for cash bookings, 020/7251–0581 for inquiries* ⊕ *www.dialacab.co.uk.*

Minicabs Addison Lee. ☎ *020/7387–8888* ⊕ *www.addisonlee.com.* **Lady's and Gent's MiniCabs.** ☎ *020/8888–9999* ⊕ *www.ladysandgentsminicabs.com.*

▌ TRAIN TRAVEL

The National Rail Enquiries website is the clearinghouse for information on train times and fares as well as the main place for booking rail journeys around Britain—and the earlier the better. Tickets bought two to three weeks in advance can cost a quarter of the price of tickets bought on the day of travel. However, journeys within commuting distance of city centers are sold at unvarying set prices, and those can be purchased on the day you expect to make your journey without any financial penalty. You may also be able to purchase a PlusBus ticket, which adds unlimited bus travel at your destination. Note that, in busy city centers such as London, all travel costs more during morning rush hour. You can purchase tickets online, by phone, or at any train station in the United Kingdom. Check the website or call the National Rail Enquiries line to get details of the train company responsible for your journey and have them give you a breakdown of available ticket prices. Regardless of which train company is involved, many discount passes are available, such as the 16–25 Railcard (for which you must be under 26 and provide a passport-size photo), the Senior Railcard, and the Family & Friends Travelcard, which can be bought from most mainline stations. But if you intend to make several long-distance rail journeys, it can be a good idea to invest in a BritRail Pass, available to non-U.K. residents (which you must buy before you leave home).

You can get a BritRail Pass valid for London and the surrounding counties, for England, for Scotland, or for all of Britain. Discounts (usually 20%–25%) are offered if you're between 16 and 25, over 60, traveling as a family or a group, or accompanied by a British citizen. The pass includes discounts on the Heathrow Express and Eurostar. BritRail Passes come in two basic varieties. The Consecutive Pass allows travel on consecutive days, and the FlexiPass allows a number of travel days within a set period of time. The cost (in U.S. dollars) of a BritRail Consecutive Pass adult ticket for 8 days is $376 standard and $560 first-class; for 15 days, $560 and $825; and for 22 days, $699 and $1,048. The cost of a BritRail FlexiPass adult ticket for 4 days' travel within one month is $332 standard and $481 first-class; for 8 days' travel within one month, $476 and $708; and for 15 days' travel within *two* months, $715 and $1,057. Prices drop by about 20% for off-peak travel passes November–February.

Most long-distance trains have refreshment carriages, called buffet cars. Most trains these days also have "quiet cars," where the use of cell phones and music devices is banned. Smoking is forbidden in all railcars.

Generally speaking, rail travel in the United Kingdom is expensive and the ticketing system unnecessarily convoluted: for instance, a round-trip ticket to Bath from London can cost more than £150 per person at peak times, although for an off-peak ticket purchased far enough in advance, that price can drop to £20 or even less. It's best to avoid the frantic business commuter rush (before 9:30 am and 4:30–7 pm). Credit cards are accepted for train fares paid in person, by phone, and online.

Delays are not uncommon, but they're rarely long. You almost always have to go to the station to find out if there's going to be one (because delays tend to happen at the last minute). Luckily, most stations have coffee shops, restaurants, and pubs where you can cool your heels while you wait for the train to get rolling. National Rail Enquiries provides an up-to-date state-of-the-railroads schedule.

Most of the time, first-class train travel in England isn't particularly first class. Some train companies don't offer at-seat service, so you still have to get up and go to the buffet car for food or drinks. First class is generally booked by business travelers on expense accounts because crying babies and noisy families are quite rare in first class and quite common in standard class.

Short of flying, taking the Eurostar train through the Channel Tunnel is the fastest way to reach the continent: it's 2 hours 15 minutes from London's St. Pancras International Station to Paris's Gare du Nord. You can also go from St. Pancras to Midi Station in Brussels in around two hours, or to Amsterdam in 3 hours 40 minutes. If purchased in advance, round-trip tickets from London to Belgium, Holland, or France cost from as little as £59, especially if you travel in the very early or very late hours of the day. If you want to bring your car over to France (ask the rental company if this is permitted), you can use the Eurotunnel Shuttle, which takes 35 minutes from Folkestone to Calais, plus at least 30 minutes to check in. The Belgian border is just a short drive northeast of Calais.

Information BritRail Travel. ☎ 866/938–7245 in U.S. and Canada ⊕ www.britrail.com. **Eurostar.** ☎ 03432/186186 ⊕ www.eurostar.com. **National Rail Enquiries.** ☎ 0345/748–4950 ⊕ www.nationalrail.co.uk.

Channel Tunnel Car Transport Eurotunnel. ☎ 0844/335–3535 in U.K., +33/3–21–00–20–61 from outside Europe ⊕ www.eurotunnel.com.

∎ UNDERGROUND TRAVEL: THE TUBE

London's extensive Underground train system (the Tube) has color-coded routes, clear signage, and many connections. Trains run out into the suburbs, and all stations are marked with the London Underground circular symbol. (Do not be confused by similar-looking signs reading "subway," which is British for "pedestrian underpass.") Trains are all one class; smoking isn't allowed on board or in the stations. There is also an Overground network serving the farther reaches of Inner London.

Some lines have multiple branches (Central, District, Northern, Metropolitan, and Piccadilly), so be sure to note which branch is needed for your particular destination. Do this by noting the end destination on the lighted sign on the platform, which also tells you how long you'll have to wait until the train arrives. Compare that with the end destination of the branch you want. When the two match, that's your train.

London is divided into six concentric zones (ask at Underground ticket booths for a map and booklet, which give details of the ticket options), so be sure to buy a ticket for the correct zone or you may be liable for an on-the-spot fine of £80. Don't panic if you do forget to buy a ticket for the right zone: just tell a station attendant that you need to buy an "extension" to your ticket. Although you're meant to do that in advance, if you're an out-of-towner, they generally don't give you a hard time. You also can pay your fare using an Oyster card.

Oyster cards are "smart cards" that can be charged with a cash value and then used for discounted travel throughout the city. A Visitor Oyster card, which you must buy before arriving in the United Kingdom, costs £5. Normal Oyster cards also cost £5 and you can open an Oyster account online or pick up an Oyster card at any London Underground station, and then prepay any amount you wish for your expected travel while in the city. Each time you take the Tube or bus, you place the blue card on the yellow readers at the entrance and the amount of your fare is deducted.

Passengers using Oyster cards pay lower rates. For one-way Tube fares paid in cash, a flat £4.90 price per journey now applies across all central zones (1–2), whether you're traveling 1 stop or 12. However, the corresponding Oyster card fare is £2.40 off-peak, £2.90 peak. One-day Travelcards used to be a good value for the money, but now, costing from £12.70 per card, they're a much less attractive option. If you're planning several trips in one day, it's much cheaper to buy an Oyster card: because of the system's daily "cap," you can make as many journeys as you want in Zones 1–2 for just £6.80 (or, in Zones 1–3 for £8). If you're going to be in town for several days, a seven-day Travelcard gives you the same value as an Oyster card (£34 for Zones 1–2, £62 for Zones 1–6). Children aged 11–15 can travel at discounted rates on the Tube and travel free on buses and trams with an Oyster photocard (order at least four weeks before date of travel), while those under 11 travel free on all buses, and on the Tube if accompanied by an adult or with an Oyster photocard. Young people aged 16–18 and students over 18 get discounted Tube fares with an Oyster photocard. Oyster card Tube fares start at £2 and go up depending on the number of zones you're covering, the time of day, and whether you're traveling into Zone 1. Most fares have been frozen until 2020.

However, although Oyster cards sound like the way of the future, they will soon be a thing of the past. Moves are underway to gradually phase out Oyster cards and to encourage passengers to move to a system of direct payments using their bank debit or credit cards instead. In practice, this means swiping a "contactless" bank card instead of your Oyster card at ticket barriers. The cheaper fares available to Oyster card holders are the same as those who pay by contactless cards.

Tube trains now run for 24 hours a day on weekends on five major lines: Piccadilly, Victoria, Northern, Central, and Jubilee. On all other lines the usual timetable still applies, with trains running from just after 5 am Monday to Saturday, and with the last services leaving central London between midnight and 12:30 am. On Sunday, trains start an hour later and finish about an hour earlier. The frequency of trains depends on the route and the time of day, but normally you should not have to wait more than 10 minutes in central areas.

There are TfL Travel Information Centres at the following Tube stations and travel locations: Liverpool Street (Mon.–Sat. 8 am–6 pm, Sun. 9 am–6 pm); Piccadilly Circus (9:30 am–4 pm); King's Cross, Paddington, and Euston (Mon.–Sat. 8 am–6 pm, Sun. 8:30 am–6 pm); Victoria (8 am–6 pm); Gatwick Airport, North & South terminals (9:15 am–4 pm); and at Heathrow Airport, Terminals 2 and 3 and Underground stations (7:30 am–8:30 pm).

Important note: You need to have your ticket (Oyster card, Travelcard, or regular ticket) handy in order to exit the turnstiles of the Tube system, not just to enter them.

Information Transport for London.
☎ *0343/222 1234* ⊕ *www.tfl.gov.uk.*

▌ NAVIGATING LONDON

London is a confusing city to navigate, even for people who've visited it a few times. Its streets are arranged in medieval patterns that no longer make much sense, meaning that you can't always use logic to find your way around. A good map is essential, and public transportation can be a lifesaver: buses will take you magically from point A to point B, and the Tube is often the quickest way to reach your destination. Here are some basic tips to help you find your way around.

■ Although free tourist maps can be handy, they're usually quite basic and include only major streets. If you're going to be doing lots of wandering around, buy the pocket-size map book *London A–Z*, which is sold in bookstores and Tube and train stations throughout the city. Its detailed maps are invaluable.

■ To find your way, look for tall landmarks near where you are headed: the London Eye, for example, or the cross atop St. Paul's Cathedral—or the most obvious of all, Big Ben.

■ If you get properly lost, the best people to ask are the Londoners hustling by you, who know the area like nobody else. The worst people to ask are the people working in souvenir kiosks, and street vendors handing out the local *Evening Standard* newspaper; they're famously rude and unhelpful to lost tourists.

■ The tourist hubs of Soho, Covent Garden, Leicester Square, and Trafalgar Square are separated from one another by only a few blocks. Taking the Tube from one to another actually takes longer than walking.

■ On the other hand, when you're lost, the Tube is often the shortest distance between two points. Don't hesitate to use it.

ESSENTIALS

∎ BUSINESS SERVICES AND FACILITIES

There are several Color Company outlets and Mail Boxes Etc. locations in London to handle your photocopying, next-day mail, and packaging needs. Check their websites for more locations.

Contacts The Color Company (*FedEx Office*). ⊠ *1 Curzon St., Mayfair* ☏ *020/7717–4900* ⊕ *www.color.co.uk* Ⓜ *Green Park.* **Mail Boxes Etc.** ⊠ *19–21 Crawford St., Marylebone* ☏ *020/7224–2666* ⊕ *www.mailboxes-etc.co.uk* Ⓜ *Marylebone.*

∎ COMMUNICATIONS

INTERNET

If you're traveling with a laptop, carry a spare battery and adapter: new batteries and replacement adapters are expensive. If you do need to replace them, head to Tottenham Court Road (W1), which is lined with computer specialists. For Apple computers, there's the Apple Stores on Regent Street off Oxford Street, and in the Covent Garden Piazza. John Lewis department store and Selfridges, on Oxford Street (W1), also carry a limited range of computer supplies.

In London, free Wi-Fi is increasingly available in hotels, pubs, coffee shops—even certain branches of McDonald's—and broadband coverage is widespread; generally speaking, the pricier the hotel, the more likely you are to find Wi-Fi there, though it is not usually included in rates.

Contacts Cybercafes. ⊕ *www.cybercafes. com.*

PHONES

The good news is that you can now make a direct-dial telephone call from virtually any point on Earth. The bad news? You can't always do so cheaply. Calling from a hotel is almost always the most expensive option; hotels usually add huge surcharges to all calls, particularly international ones. Calling cards usually keep costs to a minimum, but only if you purchase them locally. And then there are cell phones, which are also likely to be cheaper than calling from your hotel.

The minimum charge from a public phone is upwards of 60p for a two-minute call. To make cheap calls it's a good idea to pick up an international phone card, available from newsstands, which can be used from residential, hotel, and public pay phones. With these, you can call the United States for as little as 5p per minute.

To dial from the United States or Canada, first dial 011, then Great Britain's country code, 44. Continue with the local area code, dropping the initial "0." The code for London is 020 (so from abroad you'd dial 20), followed by a 7 for numbers in central London, or an 8 for numbers in the Greater London area. Freephone (toll-free) numbers start with 0800 or 0808; low-cost national information numbers start with 0345, 0344, or 0343.

A word of warning: 0900 numbers are *not* toll-free numbers; in fact, numbers beginning with this prefix are "premium rate" numbers, and it costs extra to call them. The amount varies and is usually relatively small when dialed from within the country, but it can be excessive when dialed from outside the United Kingdom.

CALLING WITHIN BRITAIN

There are three types of phones: those that accept (1) only coins, (2) only British Telecom (BT) phone cards, or (3) BT phone cards and credit cards, although with the advent of cell phones, it's increasingly difficult to find any type of public phone, especially in London.

The coin-operated phones are of the push-button variety; the workings of coin-operated telephones vary, but there are usually instructions on each unit. Most take 10p, 20p, 50p, £1, and £2 coins. Insert the coins *before* dialing (the minimum charge is 60p). If you hear a repeated single tone after dialing, the line is busy; a continual tone means the number is unobtainable (or that you have not dialed the prefix—or not the correct prefix). The indicator panel shows you how much money is left; add more whenever you like. If there is no answer, replace the receiver and your money will be returned.

There are dozens of different directory-assistance providers—but beware, they have become increasingly expensive. For an automated service that is free from all U.K. landlines and cell phones, try 0800/118–3733. To find a number anywhere in Britain, you'll need to know the town and the street (or at least the neighborhood) of the person or organization for which you're requesting information. For the operator, dial 100.

You don't have to dial London's central area code (020) if you are calling inside London itself—just the eight-digit telephone number. However, you do need to use it if you're dialing a 0207 (Inner London) number from a 0208 (Outer London) number, and vice versa.

For long-distance calls within Britain, dial the area code (which begins with 01), followed by the number. The area-code prefix is used only when you are dialing from outside the destination. In provincial areas, the dialing codes for nearby towns are often posted in the booth.

CALLING OUTSIDE BRITAIN

For assistance with international calls, dial 155.

To make an international call from London, dial 00, followed by the country code and the local number.

The United States country code is 1.

Access Codes AT&T Direct. 0808/234–5071 in U.K. **MCI.** 0800/279–5088 in U.K., 800/888–8000 for U.S. and other areas. **Sprint International Access.** 0808/234–6616 in U.K.

CALLING CARDS

Public card phones operate either with cash or with special cards that you can buy from post offices or newsstands. Ideal for longer calls, they are composed of units of 10p, and come in values of £5, £10, and more. To use a card phone, lift the receiver, insert your card, and dial the number. An indicator panel shows the number of units used. At the end of your call, the card will be returned. Where credit cards are taken, slide the card through, as indicated.

CELL PHONES

If you have a multiband phone (Britain uses different frequencies from those used in the United States) and your service provider uses the world-standard GSM network (as do T-Mobile, AT&T, and Verizon), you can probably use your phone abroad. Roaming fees can be steep, however: 99¢ per minute is considered reasonable. And overseas you normally pay the toll charges for incoming calls. It's almost always cheaper to send a text message than to make a call, since text messages have a very low set fee (often less than 5¢).

If you just want to make local calls, consider buying a new SIM card (note that your provider may have to unlock your phone for you to use a different SIM card) and a prepaid service plan in London. You'll then have a local number and can make local calls at local rates. If your trip is extensive, you could also simply buy a new cell phone in your destination, as the initial cost will be offset over time.

■ TIP→ If you travel internationally frequently, save one of your old cell phones or buy a cheap one online; ask your cell phone company to unlock it for you, and take it with you as a travel phone, buying a new SIM card with pay-as-you-go service in each destination.

Any cell phone can be used in Britain if it's tri-band/GSM. Travelers should ask their cell phone company if their phone is tri-band and what network it uses, and make sure it is activated for international calling before leaving their home country.

You can rent a cell phone from most car-rental agencies in London. Some upscale hotels now provide loaner cell phones to their guests. Beware, however, of the per-minute rates charged, as these can be shockingly high.

Contacts Cellular Abroad. ☎ *800/287–5072 in U.S., 310/862-7100 international, 800/3623-3333 in U.K.* ⊕ *www.cellular-abroad.com.* **Mobal.** ☎ *888/888-9162 in U.S., 01543/426-999 in U.K.* ⊕ *www.mobal. com.* **Planet Fone.** ☎ *888/988-4777* ⊕ *www. planetfone.com.*

■ CUSTOMS AND DUTIES

You're always allowed to bring goods of a certain value back home without having to pay any duty or import tax. But there's a limit on the amount of tobacco and liquor you can bring back duty-free, and some countries have separate limits for perfumes; for exact figures, check with your customs department. The values of so-called "duty-free" goods are included in these amounts. When you shop abroad, save all your receipts, as customs inspectors may ask to see them as well as the items you purchased. If the total value of your goods is more than the duty-free limit, you'll have to pay a tax (most often a flat percentage) on the value of everything beyond that limit.

There are currently two levels of duty-free allowance for entering Britain: one for goods bought outside the European Union (EU) and the other for goods bought within the EU.

Of goods bought outside the EU you may import the following duty-free: 200 cigarettes or 100 cigarillos or 50 cigars or 250 grams of tobacco; 4 liters of still wine and 16 liters of beer and, in addition, either 1 liter of alcohol over 22% by volume (most spirits), or 2 liters of alcohol under 22% by volume (fortified or sparkling wine or liqueurs).

Of goods bought within the EU, you should not exceed the following (unless you can prove they are for personal use): 800 cigarettes, 400 cigarillos, 200 cigars, or 1 kilo of tobacco, plus 10 liters of spirits, 20 liters of fortified wine such as port or sherry, 90 liters of wine, or 110 liters of beer.

Pets (dogs and cats) can be brought into the United Kingdom from the United States without six months' quarantine, provided that the animal meets all the PETS (Pet Travel Scheme) requirements, including microchipping and vaccination. Other pets have to undergo a lengthy quarantine, and penalties for breaking this law are severe and strictly enforced.

Fresh meats, vegetables, plants, and dairy products may be imported from within the EU. Controlled drugs, switchblades (aka flick knives), obscene material, counterfeit or pirated goods, and self-defense sprays may not be brought into the United Kingdom; firearms (both real and imitation) and ammunition, as well as souvenirs made from endangered plants or animals, are barred except with relevant permits.

Information HM Revenue and Customs. ☎ *0300/200-3700* ⊕ *www.hmrc.gov.uk.* **U.S. Customs and Border Protection.** ⊕ *www. cbp.gov.*

■ ELECTRICITY

The electrical current in London is 220–240 volts (coming into line with the rest of Europe at 230 volts), 50 cycles alternating current (AC); wall outlets take three-pin plugs, and shaver sockets take two round, oversize prongs. For converters, adapters, and advice, stop in one of the many STA Travel shops around London or at Nomad Travel.

Consider making a small investment in a universal adapter, which has several types of plugs in one lightweight, compact unit. Most laptops and cell phone chargers are dual voltage (i.e., they operate equally well on 110 and 220 volts), and thus require only an adapter. These days the same is true of small appliances such as hair dryers. Always check labels and manufacturer instructions to be sure. Don't use 110-volt outlets marked "For Shavers Only" for high-wattage appliances such as hair dryers.

Contacts Nomad Travel. ✉ 11 S. Moulton St., Mayfair ☎ 0134/155–5061 ⊕ www. nomadtravel.co.uk. **Walkabout Travel Gear.** ⊕ www.walkabouttravelgear.com.

▌ EMERGENCIES

London is a relatively safe city, though crime does happen (more so than in New York City), especially in tourist meccas. If you need to report a theft or an attack, head to the nearest police station or dial 999 for police, fire, or ambulance; be prepared to give the telephone number you're calling from. If you have a cell phone with a U.S. SIM card, dial 911 instead. National Health Service hospitals give free round-the-clock treatment in Accident and Emergency sections, where waits can be up to four hours, depending on the severity of your ailment or injury. If you are admitted to a hospital for treatment, or referred to a hospital by a general practitioner, as a non-EU foreign visitor you will be expected to pay for any treatment you receive before you leave the country. Prescriptions are valid only if made out by doctors registered in the United Kingdom. All branches of Boots are dispensing pharmacies.

Dental Care Dental Emergency Care Service. ☎ 020/8748–9365 ⊕ www.24houremergencydentist.co.uk. **UCL Eastman Dental Hospital.** ✉ 256 Gray's Inn Rd., King's Cross ☎ 020/3456–7899 ⊕ www.uclh.nhs.uk Ⓜ Russell Sq., King's Cross St. Pancras.

Foreign Embassies U.S. Embassy. ✉ 33 Nine Elms La., Battersea ☎ 020/7499–9000 ⊕ uk. usembassy.gov Ⓜ Vauxhall.

General Emergency Contacts Ambulance, fire, police. ☎ 999 in U.K. only, 112 pan-European.

Hospitals and Clinics Charing Cross Hospital. ✉ Fulham Palace Rd., Fulham ☎ 020/3311–1234 ⊕ www.imperial.nhs. uk/charingcross Ⓜ Hammersmith. **Medical Express Clinic.** ✉ 117A Harley St., Marylebone ☎ 020/7499–1991 ⊕ www.medicalexpressclinic.co.uk Ⓜ Regent's Park. **Royal Free Hospital.** ✉ Pond St., Hampstead ☎ 020/7794–0500 ⊕ www.royalfree.nhs. uk Ⓜ Belsize Park. **St. Thomas's Hospital.** ✉ Westminster Bridge Rd., Lambeth ☎ 020/7188–7188 ⊕ www.guysandstthomas. nhs.uk Ⓜ Westminster. **University College Hospital.** ✉ 235 Euston Rd., Bloomsbury ☎ 020/3456–7890 ⊕ www.uclh.nhs.uk Ⓜ Euston Sq., Warren St.

Hotlines Samaritans. ☎ 116–123 Freephone ⊕ www.samaritans.org.

Pharmacies Boots. ✉ 44–46 Regent St., Piccadilly Circus ☎ 020/7734–6126 ⊕ www. boots.com Ⓜ Piccadilly Circus.

▌ HOLIDAYS

Standard holidays are New Year's Day, Good Friday, Easter Monday, May Day (first Monday in May), spring and summer bank holidays (last Monday in May and August, respectively), Christmas, and Boxing Day (December 26). On Christmas Eve and New Year's Eve, some shops, restaurants, and businesses close early. Some museums and tourist attractions may close for at least a week around Christmas, or operate on restricted hours—call to verify.

▌ MAIL

Stamps can be bought from post offices (generally open weekdays 9–5:30, Saturday 9–noon), from stamp machines outside post offices, and from some newsagents and newsstands. Mailboxes are known as post or letter boxes and are painted bright red; large tubular ones are set on the edge of sidewalks, whereas smaller boxes are set into post-office walls. Allow seven days for a letter to reach the United States. Check the Yellow Pages for a complete list of branches, though you cannot reach individual offices by phone.

Airmail letters up to 10 grams (0.35 ounce) to North America, Australia, and New Zealand cost £1.25. Letters under 9.4 inches by 6.4 inches within Britain are from 67p for first class, 58p for second class. Large letters (larger than 9.4 inches by 6.4 inches, smaller than 13.8 inches by 9.8 inches) cost from £1.01 first class, 79p second class within the United Kingdom, depending on weight. Airmail is assessed by weight alone.

If you're uncertain where you'll be staying, you can have mail sent to you at the London Main Post Office, c/o poste restante. The post office will hold international mail for one month.

Contact Post Office. ☎ 0345/722-3355 ⊕ www.postoffice.co.uk.

Main Branch London Main Post Office. ✉ 24–28 William IV St., Charing Cross ⊕ www. postoffice.co.uk Ⓜ Charing Cross.

SHIPPING PACKAGES

Most department stores and retail outlets can ship your goods home. You should check your insurance for coverage of possible damage. Private delivery companies such as DHL, FedEx, and Parcelforce offer two-day delivery service to the United States, but you'll pay a considerable amount for the privilege.

Express Services DHL. ☎ 0844/248-0844 ⊕ www.dhl.com. **FedEx.** ☎ 0345/600-0068 ⊕ www.fedex.com. **Parcelforce.** ☎ 0344/800-4466 ⊕ www.parcelforce.com.

▌ MONEY

London is one of the most expensive cities in the world: getting around is expensive, eating can be pricey, travel costs are steep, and hotels aren't cheap. However, for every yin there's a yang, and travelers do

get a break in other places: most museums are free, for example, and Oyster cards help cut the price of travel.

ATMS AND BANKS

Your own bank will probably charge a fee for using ATMs abroad; the foreign bank you use may also charge a fee. Nevertheless, you'll usually get a better rate of exchange at an ATM than you will at a currency-exchange office or even when changing money in a bank. And extracting funds as you need them is a safer option than carrying around a large amount of cash.

▌TIP→ PINs with more than four digits are not recognized at ATMs in many countries (including England). If yours has five or more, remember to change it before you leave.

Credit cards or debit cards (also known as check cards) will get you cash advances at ATMs, which are widely available in London. To make sure that your Cirrus or Plus card (to cite just two of the leading names) works in European ATMs, have your bank reset it to use a four-digit PIN before your departure.

CREDIT CARDS

▌TIP→ Remember to inform your credit-card company before you travel, especially if you're going abroad and don't travel internationally very often. Otherwise, the credit-card company might put a hold on your card owing to unusual activity—not a good thing halfway through your trip. Record all your credit-card numbers—as well as the phone numbers to call if your cards are lost or stolen—in a safe place, so you're prepared should something go wrong. MasterCard and Visa have general numbers you can call (collect if you're abroad) if your card is lost, but you're better off calling the number of your issuing bank, because MasterCard and Visa usually just transfer you to your bank; your bank's number is usually printed on your card.

If you plan to use your credit card for cash advances, you'll need to apply for a

PIN at least two weeks before your trip. Although it's usually cheaper (and safer) to use a credit card abroad for large purchases (so you can cancel payments or be reimbursed if there's a problem), note that some credit-card companies *and* the banks that issue them add substantial percentages to all foreign transactions, whether they're in a foreign currency or not. Check on these fees before leaving home, so there won't be any surprises when you get the bill.

■ TIP→ Before you charge something, ask the merchant whether he or she plans to do a dynamic currency conversion (DCC). In such a transaction the credit-card processor (the shop, restaurant or hotel, not Visa or MasterCard) converts the currency and charges you in dollars. In most cases, you'll pay the merchant a 3% fee for this service in addition to any credit-card company and issuing-bank foreign-transaction surcharges.

Dynamic currency conversion programs are becoming increasingly widespread. Merchants who participate in them are supposed to ask whether you want to be charged in dollars or the local currency, but they don't always do so. And even if they do offer you a choice, they may well avoid mentioning the additional surcharges. The good news is that you *do* have a choice. And if this practice really gets your goat, you can avoid it entirely thanks to American Express; with its cards, DCC simply isn't an option. Note, however, that not all vendors in London accept American Express cards, though its acceptance is on the rise.

Credit cards are accepted virtually everywhere in London.

Reporting Lost Cards American Express. ☎ 800/528-4800 in U.S., 0800/917-8047 in U.K. ⊕ www.americanexpress.com. **Diners Club.** ☎ 800/234-6377 in U.S., 0345/862-2935 in U.K. ⊕ www.dinersclub. com. **MasterCard** ☎ 800/627-8372 in U.S., 0800/964767 in U.K. ⊕ www.mastercard.com.

Visa. ☎ 800/847-2911 in U.S., 020/7795-5777 in U.K. ⊕ www.visa.com.

CURRENCY AND EXCHANGE

The unit of currency in Great Britain is the pound sterling (£), divided into 100 pence (p). Bills (called notes) come in denominations of £50, £20, £10, and £5; coins are for £2, £1 (100p), 50p, 20p, 10p, 5p, 2p, and 1p.

Even if a currency-exchange booth has a sign promising no commission, rest assured that there's some kind of huge hidden fee. And as for rates, you're almost always better off getting foreign currency at an ATM or exchanging money at a bank or post office.

■ TIP→ Banks never have every foreign currency on hand, and it may take as long as a week to order. So if you're planning to exchange funds before leaving home, don't wait until the last minute.

■ PACKING

London's weather is unpredictable. It can be cool, damp, and overcast, even in summer, but the odd summer day can be uncomfortably hot, as not many public venues, theaters, or the Tube are air-conditioned. In general, you'll need a heavy coat for winter and light clothes for summer, along with a lightweight coat or jacket. Always pack a small umbrella that you can easily carry around with you. Pack as you would for any American city: jackets and ties for expensive restaurants and nightspots, casual clothes elsewhere. Jeans are popular in London and are perfectly acceptable for sightseeing and informal dining. Sports jackets are popular with men. In five-star hotels, men can expect to be asked to wear a jacket and tie in the restaurant and bar, and women might feel out of place unless they're in nice clothes. Otherwise, for women, ordinary dress is acceptable just about everywhere.

▍PASSPORTS AND VISAS

U.S. citizens need only a valid passport to enter Great Britain for stays of up to six months. If you're within six months of your passport's expiration date, renew it before you leave—nearly expired passports are not strictly banned, but they make immigration officials anxious and may cause you problems.

PASSPORTS

It's always surprising how few Americans have passports—just under 40% at this writing. This number is expected to grow now that it is impossible to reenter the United States from trips to neighboring Canada or Mexico without one. Remember this: a passport verifies both your identity and nationality—a great reason to have one.

U.S. passports are valid for 10 years. You must apply in person if you're getting a passport for the first time; if your previous passport was lost, stolen, or damaged; or if your previous passport has expired and was issued more than 15 years ago or when you were under 16. All children under 18 must appear in person to apply for or renew a passport. Both parents must accompany any child under 14 (or send a notarized statement with their permission) and provide proof of their relationship to the child.

There are 24 regional passport offices, as well as 7,000 passport acceptance facilities in post offices, public libraries, and other governmental offices. If you're renewing a passport, you can do so by mail. Forms are available at passport acceptance facilities and online.

The cost to apply for a new passport is $140 for adults, $95 for children under 16; renewals are $140. There is an additional "execution fee" of $35. Allow six weeks for processing, both for first-time passports and renewals. For an expediting fee of $60 you can reduce this time to about two weeks. If your trip is less than two weeks away, you can get a passport even more rapidly by going to a passport

office with the necessary documentation. Private expediters can get things done in as little as 48 hours, but charge hefty fees for their services.

■TIP➔ Before your trip, make two copies of your passport's data page (one for someone at home and another for you to carry separately). Or scan the page and email it to someone at home and/or yourself.

VISAS

A visa is essentially formal permission to enter a country. Visas allow countries to keep track of you and other visitors—and generate revenue (from application fees). You *always* need a visa to enter a foreign country; however, many countries routinely issue tourist visas on arrival, particularly to U.S. citizens. When your passport is stamped or scanned in the immigration line, you're actually being issued a visa. Sometimes you have to stand in a separate line and pay a small fee to get your stamp before going through immigration, but you can still do this at the airport on arrival. Getting a visa isn't always that easy. Some countries require that you arrange for one in advance of your trip. There's usually—but not always—a fee involved, and said fee may be nominal ($10 or less) or substantial ($100 or more).

If you must apply for a visa in advance, you can usually do it in person or by mail. When you apply by mail, you send your passport to a designated consulate, where your passport will be examined and the visa issued. Expediters—usually the same ones who handle expedited passport applications—can do all the work of obtaining your visa for you; however, there's always an additional cost (often more than $50 per visa).

Most visas limit you to a single trip—basically during the actual dates of your planned vacation. Other visas allow you to visit as many times as you wish for a specific period of time. Remember that requirements change, sometimes at the drop of a hat, and the burden is on you to make sure that you have the appropriate visas. Otherwise, you'll be turned away at the airport or, worse, deported after you arrive in the country. No company or travel insurer gives refunds if your travel plans are disrupted because you didn't have the correct visa.

U.S. Passport Information U.S. Department of State. ☎ 877/487–2778 ⊕ travel.state.gov/passport.

U.S. Passport and Visa Expediters A. Briggs Passport & Visa Expeditors. ☎ 800/806–0581 ⊕ www.abriggs.com. **American Passport Express.** ☎ 800/455–5166 ⊕ www.americanpassport.com. **Travel Document Systems.** ☎ 800/874–5100, 202/638–3800 ⊕ www.traveldocs.com. **Travel the World Visas.** ☎ 866/886–8472 ⊕ www.world-visa.com.

∎ SAFETY

The rules for safety in London are the same as in New York City or any big metropolis. If you're carrying a considerable amount of cash and do not have a safe in your hotel room, it's a good idea to keep it in something like a money belt, but don't get cash out of it in public. Keep a small amount of cash for immediate purchases in your pocket or purse.

Beyond that, use common sense. In central London, nobody will raise an eyebrow at tourists studying maps on street corners, and don't hesitate to ask for directions. However, outside of the center, exercise general caution about the neighborhoods you walk in: if they don't look safe, take a cab. After midnight, outside of the center, take cabs rather than wait for a night bus. Although London has plenty of so-called minicabs—normal cars driven by self-employed drivers in a cab service—don't ever get into an unmarked car that pulls up offering you "cab service." Take a licensed minicab only from a cab office, or, preferably, a normal London "black cab," which you flag down on the street.

If you carry a purse (called a handbag by the Brits), keep a firm grip on it (or even disguise it in a local shopping bag). Store only enough money in your handbag to cover casual spending. Distribute the rest of your cash and any valuables among deep front pockets, inside jacket or vest pockets, and a concealed money pouch. Never leave your bag beside your chair or hanging from the back of your chair. Be careful with backpacks, as pickpockets can unzip them on the Tube, or even as you're traveling up an escalator.

Advisories U.S. Department of State. ⊕ travel.state.gov.

∎ TAXES

Departure taxes are divided into two bands. The Band A tax on a per-person economy fare for flights of under 2,000 miles is £13; Band B, for everything over, is £75. The fee is subject to government tax increases.

The British sales tax (V.A.T., value-added tax) is 20%. The tax is almost always included in quoted prices in shops, hotels, and restaurants.

Most travelers can get a V.A.T. refund (no minimum amount is required) by either the Retail Export or the more cumbersome Direct Export method. Many, but not all, large stores provide these services, but only if you request them; they will handle the paperwork. For the Retail Export method, you must ask the store for Form VAT 407 when making a purchase (you must have identification—passports are best). Some retailers will refund the amount on the spot, but others will use a refund company or the refund booth at the point when you leave the country. For the latter, have the form stamped like any customs form by U.K. customs officials when you leave the country, or, if you're visiting several European Union countries, when you leave the EU. After you're through passport control, take the form to a refund-service counter for an on-the-spot refund (which is usually the quickest and easiest option), or mail it to the address on the form (or the envelope with it) after you arrive home. You receive the total refund stated on the form (the retailer or refund company may deduct a handling fee), but the processing time can be long, especially if you request a credit-card adjustment. This may be preferable to a check, however, as U.S. banks will charge a fee for depositing a check in a foreign currency.

With the Direct Export method, the goods are shipped directly to your home. You must have a Form VAT 407 certified by customs, the police, or a notary public when you get home and then send it back to the store, which will refund your money. For inquiries, contact Her Majesty's Revenue & Customs office.

Global Blue (formerly, Global Refund) is a worldwide service with 270,000 affiliated stores and more than 200 Refund Offices. Its refund form, called a Tax Free Check, is the most common across the European continent. The service issues refunds in the form of cash, check, or credit-card adjustment.

V.A.T. Refunds Global Blue. ☎ 866/706–6090 in U.S., 800/32–111–111 in U.K. ⊕ www.globalblue.com. **Her Majesty's Revenue & Customs.** ☎ 0300/200–3701 within U.K., 292/050–1261 from outside U.K. ⊕ www.hmrc.gov.uk/vat.

∎ TIME

London is five hours ahead of New York City at most times of the year. In other words, when it's 3 pm in New York (or noon in Los Angeles), it's 8 pm in London. Note that Great Britain and most European countries also move their clocks ahead for the one-hour differential when daylight saving time goes into effect (although they make the changeover several weeks after the United States).

Time Zones Timeanddate.com. ⊕ www.timeanddate.com/worldclock.

∎ TIPPING

Tipping is done in Britain just as in the United States, but at a lower level. Tipping less than you would back home in restaurants—and not tipping at all in pubs—is not only accepted, but standard. Do not tip movie or theater ushers, elevator operators, or bar staff in pubs—although you can always offer to buy the latter a drink.

TIPPING GUIDELINES FOR LONDON	
Bartender	In cocktail bars, if you see a tip plate, it's fine to leave £1–£2. For table service, tip 10% of the cost of the bill. However, the gratuity is often included in the check at more expensive bars.
Bellhop	£1 per bag, depending on the level of the hotel.
Hotel Concierge	£5 or more, if a service is performed for you.
Hotel Doorman	£1 for hailing taxis or for carrying bags to check-in desk.
Hotel Maid	It's extremely rare for hotel maids to be tipped; £1–£2 would be generous.
Porter at Airport or Train Station	£1 per bag
Skycap at Airport	£1–£3 per bag
Taxi Driver	Optional 10%–12%, perhaps a little more for a short ride.
Tour Guide	Tipping optional; £1–£2 would be generous.
Waiter	10%–15%, with 15% being the norm at high-end restaurants; nothing additional if a service charge is added to the bill.
Other	Restroom attendants in expensive restaurants expect some small change (50p or so). Tip coat-check personnel £1 unless there is a fee (then nothing). Hairdressers and barbers get 10%–15%.

∎ TOURS

BIKE TOURS

Whether you join the Santander Cycles hire scheme or just, per usual, get one from a rental shop, remember that London is still a busy metropolis: unless you're familiar with riding in London traffic, the best way to see it on two wheels is probably to contact one of the excellent cycle-tour companies.

Santander Cycles. ☎ *0343/222–6666* ⊕ *www.tfl.gov.uk/modes/cycling/ santander-cycles.*

Tour Operators Cycle Tours of London. ☎ *07788/994430* ⊕ *www.biketoursoflondon. com.* **Fat Tire Bike Tours.** ☎ *07882/338779* ⊕ *www.fattirebiketours.com.* **London Bicycle Tour Company.** ☎ *020/7928–6838* ⊕ *www. londonbicycle.com.*

BOAT TOURS

Year-round, but more frequently April–October, boats cruise the Thames, offering a different view of the London skyline. Most leave from Westminster Pier, Charing Cross Pier, and Tower Pier. Downstream routes go to the Tower of London, Greenwich, and the Thames Barrier via Canary Wharf. Upstream destinations include Kew, Richmond, and Hampton Court (mainly in summer). Most of the launches seat between 100 and 250 passengers, have a public-address system, and provide a running commentary on passing points of interest. Some include musical entertainment. Depending on the destination, river trips may last from one to four hours.

Details on all other operators are available as a PDF from Transport for London's River Services page ⊕ *www.tfl.gov. uk.*

River Cruise Operators Bateaux London. ☎ *020/7695–1800* ⊕ *www.bateauxlondon. com.* **London Duck Tours.** ☎ *020/7928–3132* ⊕ *www.londonducktours.co.uk.* **Thames Cruises.** ☎ *020/7928–9009* ⊕ *www. thamescruises.com.* **Thames River Boats.** ☎ *020/7930–2062* ⊕ *www.wpsa.co.uk.*

Thames River Services. ☎ *020/7930–4097* ⊕ *www.thamesriverservices.co.uk.*

BUS, COACH, AND TAXI TOURS

Guided sightseeing tours from the top of double-decker buses, which are open-top in summer, are a good introduction to the city, as they cover all the main central sights. A number of companies run daily bus tours that depart (usually 8:30–9 am) from central points. In hop-on, hop-off fashion, you may board or alight at any of the numerous stops to view the sights and reboard on the next bus. Most companies offer this hop-on, hop-off feature, but others, such as Best Value, remain guided tours in traditional coach buses. Tickets can be bought from the driver and are good all day. Prices vary according to the type of tour. For that more personal touch, try out a guided tour in a taxi.

Bus Tour Operators Best Value Tours. ☎ *0870/803–1316* ⊕ *www.bestvaluetours. co.uk.* **Big Bus Tours.** ☎ *020/7808–6753* ⊕ *www.bigbustours.com.* **Black Taxi Tour of London.** ☎ *020/7935–9363* ⊕ *www.blacktaxi-tours.co.uk.* **Golden Tours.** ☎ *020/7630–2028 in U.K., 800/509–2507 in U.S.* ⊕ *www.golden-tours.co.uk.* **Original London Sightseeing Tour.** ☎ *020/8877–1722* ⊕ *www.theoriginal-tour.com.* **Premium Tours.** ☎ *020/7713–1311, 800/931–0141 in U.S.* ⊕ *www.premiumtours. co.uk.*

CANAL TOURS

The tranquil side of London can be found on narrow boats that cruise the city's two canals, the Grand Union and Regent's Canal; most vessels operate on the latter, which runs between Little Venice in the west (nearest Tube: Warwick Avenue on the Bakerloo Line) and Camden Lock (about 200 yards north of Camden Town Tube station). Fares start at about £15 for 1½-hour round-trip cruises.

Canal Tour Operators Jason's Trip. ⊕ *www. jasons.co.uk.* **London Waterbus Company.** ☎ *020/7482–2550* ⊕ *www.londonwaterbus. com.*

EXCURSIONS

Evan Evans, Green Line, and National Express all offer day excursions by bus to places within easy reach of London, such as Hampton Court, Oxford, Stratford-upon-Avon, and Bath.

Tour Operators Evan Evans. ☏ *020/7950–1777, 800/422–9022 in U.S.* ⊕ *www.evanevanstours.co.uk.*

WALKING TOURS

One of the best ways to get to know London is on foot, and there are many guided and themed walking tours available. For more options, pick up a copy of *Time Out* magazine and check the weekly listings for upcoming one-off tours.

Walking Tour Operators Blood and Tears Walk. ☏ *07905/746733* ⊕ *www.shockinglondon.com.* **Blue Badge.** ☏ *020/7403–1115* ⊕ *www.britainsbestguides.org.* **Context London.** ☏ *020/3514–1780, 800/691–6036 in U.S.* ⊕ *www.contexttravel.com/city/london.* **London Walks.** ☏ *020/7624–3978* ⊕ *www.walks.com.* **Richard Jones's London Walking Tours.** ☏ *020/8530–8443* ⊕ *www.londondiscoverytours.co.uk.* **Shakespeare City Walk.** ☏ *07905/746733* ⊕ *www.shakespeareguide.com.*

▌VISITOR INFORMATION

You can get good information at the Travel Information Centre near the Eurostar arrivals area at St. Pancras International train station and at Victoria and Liverpool Street stations. These are helpful if you're looking for brochures for London sights, or if something's gone horribly wrong with your hotel reservation—if, for example, you don't have one—as they have a useful reservations service. The Victoria Station center, opposite Platform 8, is open daily 8 am–6 pm; the King's Cross/St. Pancras center, the Euston Station center (opposite Platform 10), and the center at Paddington Station (opposite Platform 1) are open Monday–Saturday 8 am–6 pm and Sunday 8:30 am–6 pm. The center at Liverpool Street is open Monday–Saturday 8 am–6 pm and Sunday 9 am– 6pm, while the one at Piccadilly Circus Tube station is open daily 9:30 am–4 pm. The Travel Information Centre at Heathrow is open daily 7:30 am–8:30 pm, and at Gatwick Airport (North and South terminals) daily 9:15 am–4 pm. There are also London Tourist Information Centres in Greenwich and some other Outer London locations.

Official Websites: ⊕ *www.visitbritain.com* ⊕ *www.visitlondon.com*

Other Websites: ⊕ *www.londontown.com* ⊕ *www.standard.co.uk* ⊕ *www.bbc.co.uk*

Entertainment Information: ⊕ *www.timeout.com/london* ⊕ *www.officiallondontheatre.co.uk*

INDEX

PHOTO CREDITS

NOTES

NOTES

NOTES

NOTES

NOTES

NOTES

NOTES

NOTES

ABOUT OUR WRITERS

Jo Caird is a travel and arts journalist who writes on theater, visual arts, film, literature, and food and drink, as well as cycling and scuba diving. Her travel stories, city guides, and arts features appear regularly in the *Guardian*, the *Independent*, the *Sunday Telegraph*, the *Economist*, *Condé Nast Traveler*, and *World of Interiors*. Born and raised in London, Caird has an endless fascination for the city, and is delighted to write about it whenever the opportunity arises. For this edition, she updated the Westminster and St. James; Soho and Covent Garden; East London; Greenwich; Thames Upstream; and the Performing Arts chapters. Follow her on Twitter (⊕ *www.twitter.com/jocaird*) or visit her website (⊕ *www.jocaird.com*).

James O'Neill loves London and—as his work updating our chapters on Mayfair and Marylebone; Bloomsbury and Holborn; Notting Hill and Bayswater; and Travel Smart for this edition proves—loves rediscovering it, too. Although originally from Ireland, he's lived in London for almost 20 years—and still loves it just as much now as he did back then. He has written extensively for TV (BBC and Channel 4), the stage, and the page. He is currently finishing his debut novel, which is set in—where else?—London.

Having studied in London and never left—aside from a brief sojourn in Madrid—**Toby Orton** has experienced everything in the capital from Hackney to Notting Hill, Highgate to Peckham, and still finds it the most inspiring city in the world. He credits the bookshops, bars, galleries, clubs, and streets of London with making him the person he is today. He has written about travel, cycling, food, and drink

for a range of websites and publications. He updated the Where to Stay chapter this edition.

Ellin Stein has written for publications on both sides of the Atlantic, including the *New York Times*, the *Times* (London), the *Guardian*, the *Telegraph*, and *InStyle*, for whom she was European correspondent. Her book *That's Not Funny, That's Sick: The National Lampoon and the Comedy Insurgents Who Captured the Mainstream*, was published by W. W. Norton & Co. in 2013. Originally from Manhattan, she has lived in London for two decades. For this edition, she updated our chapters on The City; Kensington, Chelsea, Knightsbridge, and Belgravia; South of the Thames; Regent's Park and Hampstead; and Shopping.

London restaurant maven **Alex Wijeratna** is permanently blown away by the capital's rocket-fueled restaurant scene. From locavore heroes and street-food gourmet democrats, to global gastro-panjandrums, Alex tickles out the best joints that restaurant-mad London has to offer. Alex has also written for the *Times* (London), the *Guardian*, the *Independent*, the *Daily Mail*, the *Daily Express*, and the *Face*. For this edition, he updated the Where to Eat, Nightlife, and Experience London chapters.